KEEP GOING WITH LATIN

A Continuation of *Getting Started with Latin:
Beginning Latin For Homeschoolers and
Self-Taught Students of Any Age*

WILLIAM E. LINNEY

ARMFIELD ACADEMIC PRESS

Published by Armfield Academic Press

Chief editorial consultant: Michael D. Sweet

Editorial consultants: Katherine L. Bradshaw, Jenni Glaser, Marcello Lippiello, Andrew Morehouse, Benjamin R. Turnbull

Illustrations: Olivia Mizner, lessons 82, 84, 90. William Linney, lessons 38, 47, 58, 91, 110.

ISBN: 978-1-62611-008-3

CONTENTS

PREFACE

My first book, *Getting Started with Latin*, was a labor of love. I wrote it to help homeschooled and self-taught students learn beginning Latin at home, without a teacher. Since the publication of *Getting Started with Latin*, the response has been positive (except for that one nasty email I got a few years back). People seem to like the one-thing-at-a-time format of the book, which never leaves them lost and wondering what just happened like other books do. This is significant because homeschooled and self-taught students are a special group of people who need specialized materials—products that allow them to learn at home without access to a teacher who specializes in that particular subject.

Over the years, I have received many requests for a sequel to *Getting Started with Latin*. People have said to me, "Hey, I finished *Getting Started with Latin*, and it was the best Latin book ever. What do I do now?" I didn't have a good answer for them. At first, I thought I would never write a sequel because I couldn't figure out a way to continue introducing new grammar concepts in that same one-thing-at-a-time format. But after several years of learning how to speak Latin, I began to think that I could create a sequel that involved conversational Latin. I realized that if I did it that way, I could continue to present new grammatical information to you while at the same time equipping you to practice the language by speaking it. And that's the story of how this book became a reality.

Like its predecessor, *Keep Going with Latin* is designed to accomplish several educational goals. I have designed this book to...

- Be self-explanatory, self-paced, self-contained, and inexpensive
- Allow the student to make progress with or without a teacher
- Provide plenty of practice exercises after each new concept so that the student can master each idea before moving on to the next one
- Provide audio recordings for aural practice and supplementary instruction
- Avoid making Latin any more difficult than it actually is

Keep Going with Latin was created to meet the unique needs of homeschooled and self-taught students. It is self-contained, with no extra materials to purchase (such as pronunciation tapes, answer keys, or teacher's editions). It's also in a large format to make it easier to use, and non-consumable so it can be used with multiple children. The answer key is in the back of the book, and there are free pronunciation recordings and author's commentary recordings available for download. The website for this book is the same as it was for *Getting Started with Latin*.

www.GettingStartedWithLatin.com

In this book, new words and concepts are introduced in a gradual yet systematic fashion. Each lesson provides ten exercises for practicing the new material while reviewing material from previous lessons.

Keep Going with Latin makes Latin accessible to students of any age or educational background. Because this book moves so gradually, you probably will not say *This is too hard for me. I quit!* Instead, these bite-size lessons leave you encouraged and ready to continue. But when you do finish this book, don't let your Latin studies end there. Learning and using a foreign language is quite a thrill—so keep going, and above all, have fun with it!

William E. Linney

HOW TO USE THIS BOOK

This book is structured around one main teaching method: Teach one concept at a time and let the student master that concept before introducing the next one. With that in mind, read the tips listed below to help you use this book to the greatest advantage.

THE NEW WORD

Start each lesson by observing the new word for that particular lesson. All Latin words in this book are in **bold print** so they will be easy to recognize. The meaning of the new word is in *italics*. In some lessons you will learn a new concept and in others you will simply review material from previous lessons.

PRONUNCIATION

The best way to learn correct pronunciation is by listening and copying what you hear. Visit www.GettingStartedWithLatin.com to access the free pronunciation recordings. In these recordings, each new word and exercise is read aloud so you can not only read but also hear the exercises. You may listen to these recordings on your computer, smart phone, or other listening device. These free audio recordings will help you achieve proper pronunciation and provide you with lots of opportunities for aural translation practice.

If needed, there will be a written pronunciation tip at the beginning of the lesson. These tips are there to give you a general idea of how the word sounds and to help you avoid the most likely pronunciation errors. To further assist you in achieving proper pronunciation, there are two pronunciation charts at the end of the book.

Many of the homeschool parents I have met and worked with seem to be very concerned about Latin pronunciation. They are worried that they will somehow cause permanent damage to their child's intellect if they mispronounce Latin vowels or if they choose to emulate the wrong style of pronunciation. Please allow me to address this issue. Classical pronunciation is the style of pronunciation used in the Latin departments of most colleges and universities. Latin scholars use this type of pronunciation because it is supposed to reflect the way Latin was pronounced by the ancient Romans. Ecclesiastical (church) pronunciation, on the other hand, is the style of pronunciation used by the Roman Catholic Church. Roman Catholic students may want to employ this type of pronunciation because they may have the opportunity to use it in the recitation of prayers or in other religious activities.

Regardless of which pronunciation style you choose, please don't lose any sleep over it. You should, of course, do your best to pronounce the words correctly. But please remember that if you do mispronounce a word, you will not ruin your child's education. And, the Latin Police will not come to your home and arrest you.

GRAMMATICAL INFORMATION

If needed, a lesson may contain an explanation of how to use the new word introduced in that lesson. Charts and examples are used to give you a clear presentation of the grammar knowledge needed for that particular lesson.

The book's website has special audio commentary recordings which have been prepared by the author. These recordings cover each lesson in detail, so if you have any trouble understanding the material presented in a lesson, you will have plenty of help on hand.

SPEAKING LATIN

If I could recommend any one particular thing that could help you learn Latin better, faster, and more easily, it would be to speak the Latin language. Yes, you read that correctly—I said to speak Latin. This advice might sound unusual to you because unlike modern languages such as French, German, or Chinese, Latin is no longer spoken as a national language. And we can't travel back in time to talk to the ancient Romans, either. However, from an educational perspective, there are many benefits to speaking Latin.

If you only read Latin and translate it into English, your experience with Latin will be limited. When you translate Latin, here is the sequence of events: 1) You see a Latin word. 2) You try to think of the English equivalent of that word. 3) When the English equivalent pops into your head, it brings with it the meanings, thoughts, and feelings associated with it. The problem with this process is that it is mostly focused on English, not Latin. Sure, you start out with Latin, but everything ends up as English.

But when you *speak* Latin, your mind remains focused on Latin. Since you can't depend on English to express yourself verbally, you must keep the Latin words you know in the forefront of your mind, using them to formulate thoughts and to create meaningful sentences. And as you speak Latin more and more, you will begin to associate images, thoughts, and feelings with the Latin words themselves, not just with their English translations. This will help you to form a more direct, intimate connection with the Latin language.

So, as you go through this book, don't just read and translate the exercises—also incorporate speaking and listening into your daily study habits. There are several ways to do this. One way is to have conversations in Latin with another person such as a teacher, parent, family member, or fellow student. You can talk about the things that happen in the exercises, or you can role-play by acting out one of the dialogues in the exercises. If you don't have anybody to talk to, don't worry—you can still do something that I call *narration*. Narration is, as I imagine it, talking to yourself. You can read some exercises in Latin and then begin to talk about them in Latin, retelling or restating what happened. You can pretend to be one of the characters in the exercises and speak in the first person. You can talk to your dog or cat (they won't mind a bit). Another useful technique is to close your eyes and see the story in your mind's eye while you narrate what is happening in Latin. The goal here is somehow, some way, to get you saying something in Latin every day.

Above all, don't think of Latin as a museum exhibit that sits inside a glass display case—something that can only be looked at but never touched or handled. Instead, try to view Latin as something that you can pick up, touch, examine—even play with. Don't be afraid to make mistakes! Mistakes are an important part of the learning process. Roll up your sleeves and jump fully into the Latin language, and you will experience the language in a more fulfilling and satisfying way.

THE EXERCISES

Armed with the knowledge of the new word and how to use it, begin to translate the exercises. In a homeschool environment, it is probably best to have students write their answers in a notebook. Older students and adults may prefer to do the exercises mentally. Next, turn to the answer key in the back of the book to see if your translations are correct. By comparing the exercises and the answers, you will learn from your mistakes. Translating the exercises over and over (even memorizing them) will enhance learning and speed your progress. After you have translated the exercises and you know what they mean, listen to the audio recordings over and over for practice. The more you listen, the faster your progress will be.

These exercises are often humorous and silly. You'll meet greedy pirates, kings and queens who want bigger castles, a few misbehaving children, sailors with questionable social skills, and other silly characters. But even though these exercises are silly, they are intended to teach you some serious knowledge about the Latin language!

REPEATED LISTENING

After you have studied the exercises and you know what they mean, you are in a position to use an extremely effective language learning technique. This technique is when you hear or read understandable material in the foreign language that you are studying. If you are studying a foreign language, and you hear or read lots of material that you can't understand, it doesn't really do you any good. But if you hear or read something that is at your current level of learning, you are getting some good practice interpreting that language because the material is understandable.

Here's how this applies to you: once you have studied the exercises for a certain lesson, and you know what the exercises mean, you should listen to the audio recordings for that lesson over and over. Don't just listen once or twice—listen to them a hundred times, until everything you hear sounds natural to you. Listen in the car, while cleaning up, etc. This study method will help your brain to process, absorb, and get used to the language.

LATIN COMPOSITION

For an additional challenge, you can try to translate the answers in the answer key back into the original language using the knowledge you have gained from that lesson. This is a great learning tool because it requires you to think about the material from a completely different direction. Try it and see! Again, it is probably best to write these exercises in a notebook.

QUICK REVIEW

To help you review things you learned in the past, I will sometimes give you a box of text that looks like this:

> QUICK ✎ REVIEW
>
> In these boxes I will provide you with a quick review (as the title suggests) of something that you have already learned in a previous lesson. So pay attention!

DON'T PUT THE CART BEFORE THE HORSE

Do not skip ahead to a future lesson. Because each lesson builds directly on the preceding lessons, do the lessons in the order given. If you start to feel lost or confused, back up a few lessons and review. Or, take a break and come back to the material at a later time. Remember that review and repetition are essential when learning any language. One of the best things you can do to improve your understanding of this new language is to review the lessons repeatedly.

STAY FLEXIBLE

Everyone has a different learning style, so use this book in ways that fit your needs or the needs of your students. You can learn as a family, on your own, or in a homeschool environment. Be creative! You could even have one night of the week when the entire family is forbidden to speak English! Who knows? You may think of a way to use this book that no one else has thought of (putting it under the short leg of the kitchen table does not count).

TESTS AND QUIZZES

To give a student a test or quiz, simply back up to a previous lesson and have the student translate those exercises without looking at the answers. Then, the teacher or parent can grade the exercises using the answers in the back of the book. Another possibility would be to test the student's listening skills by having him or her translate the exercises directly from the audio recording for that lesson.

SCHEDULING

Some homeschool parents like a lot of structure in their teaching schedules, while others prefer a less structured learning environment. Depending on your personal preferences, you may either plan to cover a certain number of lessons in a certain period of time, or allow your students to determine their own pace. It's up to you.

HOW MUCH TIME PER DAY?

A few minutes a day with this book is better than longer, less frequent sessions. Thirty minutes a day is ideal for language study. Of course, this may vary with each student's age, ability, and interest level.

SELF-TAUGHT ADULTS

Adults who use this book will enjoy the freedom of learning whenever and wherever they please. High school and college students may use it to get a head start before taking a traditional class at their school, to satisfy curiosity, or to try something new. Busy adults may use it to study at lunchtime, break time, or while commuting to work (as long as someone else is driving the vehicle). The short lessons in this book will fit any schedule.

SURF THE NET!

Don't forget about the website that accompanies this book. Here's that web address again, in case you missed it:

www.GettingStartedWithLatin.com

It has free resources to aid you in your studies. Be sure to check it out!

LESSON ONE

WELCOME BACK!

If you are reading this right now, you probably know that this book is a continuation of my super-simple introduction to Latin called *Getting Started with Latin*. Therefore, right from the very start, the exercises in this book will make use of all the vocabulary and grammar from *Getting Started with Latin*. This book will still use the same one-thing-at-a-time method that you are used to, but at a slightly more advanced level.

And, like before, there are plenty of free audio recordings to help you learn. Visit www.GettingStartedWithLatin.com to access the free pronunciation recordings and author's commentary recordings. In these free audio recordings, each new word and exercise is read aloud so you can hear how everything sounds and practice listening skills. You may listen to these recordings on your computer, smart phone, tablet, or however you wish. For important information about how to make the best use of these recordings, see the section at the beginning of the book called How to Use This Book.

QUICK ✐ REVIEW

In English, when you use an apostrophe to show possession, you must make sure that the apostrophe is in the correct place. If a noun does not end with the letter *s*, put an apostrophe followed by the letter *s*, like this: *Catherine's book*. Sometimes a singular noun will end with the letter *s* just because that's the way it's spelled. Still, you treat it the same as if it did not end with an *s*—you add an apostrophe and an *s*, like this: *The class's favorite subject* or *James's cat*. If you want to show that something belongs to more than one person, and the plural noun ends with the letter *s*, put the apostrophe after the *s*, at the very end of the word, like this: *The sailors' boat*.

LESSON TWO

SPOKEN LATIN

The Latin language has a long, rich history with several periods of development. It was spoken by the ancient Romans for over 1000 years. After the fall of the Roman Empire, Latin slowly began to change into Italian, French, Spanish, and other European languages. After a while, these languages sounded nothing like Latin. But the Latin language was preserved because it continued to be used as a religious and academic language. In medieval Europe, Latin was used in universities for teaching and lecturing. In Paris, for example, there is a section of the city known as the Latin Quarter because the university students who lived there in the Middle Ages spoke Latin.

Up until the 20th century, Latin was the language of science. Famous scientists like Copernicus, Johannes Kepler, and Tycho Brahe all wrote works in Latin. And one of the most important scientific works ever, Sir Isaac Newton's *Philosophiae Naturalis Principia Mathematica*, was written in Latin. Even today, folks (like me) gather at workshops just to speak Latin. In fact, spoken Latin is making its way back into the classroom as an effective teaching and learning tool.

I'm telling you this so that you can begin to view Latin not only as a language that you read in books, but as a language that you can speak just like any other language. This isn't some new thing I just made up—people have been speaking Latin for thousands of years. So if anybody out there tells you that you can't or shouldn't speak Latin, don't believe them—that's just nonsense!

My earlier book, *Getting Started with Latin*, was designed for complete beginners. In that book, I needed to introduce you to basic, fundamental concepts of the Latin language. Now that you have gone through *Getting Started with Latin*, you have a basic understanding of the language and you are ready to learn more Latin—and we will do that in this book, but in a way that is also designed to get you speaking the language. As you go along, you will not only learn grammar, but also words, phrases, and idioms which you can use to carry on a simple conversation in Latin.

No matter what language you are learning, whether it's a modern language or an ancient one, it is essential to the learning process to try to speak and use the language instead of just memorizing grammar rules and word lists. By speaking the language, you will internalize it, getting the language into your heart and mind. And when you speak Latin, not only will you learn it more thoroughly, but you will have more fun, too. If you only learn to translate Latin, the Latin language lives on the printed page. But if you learn to speak Latin, the language lives inside of you—and that's exciting! So stick with me through this process and let's bring the Latin language to life!

(QUICK ✏ REVIEW)

In Latin, the letter *i* can be used two ways: as a vowel, and as a consonant. In the word **nāvigō**, the letter *i* is a vowel. But in the word **iam**, the *i* at the beginning of the word is being used as a consonant (that's called a *consonantal i*). When used as a consonant, the letter *i* makes a *yuh* sound. So, the word **iam** sounds something like *yahm*. In some textbooks, a consonantal *i* is written as a *j* to distinguish it from a regular *i*. Therefore, in some textbooks the word **iam** will look like **jam**. A famous example is the name Julius Caesar. The *j* at the beginning of the word *Julius* is really a *consonantal i*. So really, it should be spelled **Iūlius** (pronounced *YOO-lee-uhs*). In this book, I will use the letter *j* just for the sake of simplicity.

LESSON THREE

ROMAN NAMES

As you learn to speak Latin, you will find it both fun and educational to pick a Latin name for yourself. For this reason, over the next few lessons we will talk about how names work in Latin. And since we are talking about names, I thought it would be fun to give you a quick overview of ancient Roman names. Because of the way these names are structured, it's easier if we start out with aristocratic male names.

In ancient Roman culture, aristocratic Roman males usually had a name consisting of three parts: the **praenōmen**, the **nōmen**, and the **cognōmen**. As an example, let's observe the name of one of the most famous Romans in history—Julius Caesar (100–44 BC). But "Julius Caesar" wasn't his full name—like other aristocrats, he had three names. Here's his full name with each part conveniently labeled:

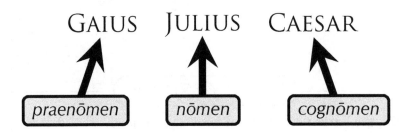

Let's talk about each part of this name, starting with the **praenōmen**. The word **praenōmen** consists of two parts. The first part of the word (the **prae-** part) means *before* and **nōmen** means *name*. So literally, the word **praenōmen** means *before-name*. A **praenōmen** was a Roman male's personal name, like today's Bob, Fred, and Kevin. Interestingly, there was a relatively small pool of personal names for aristocratic males—names which were recycled and reused over and over: names like **Gāius**, **Titus**, and **Marcus**. Sometimes, Roman males would be named according to the order in which they were born. The word **tertius** means *third*, so the third son might be named **Tertius**. Likewise, they might be named **Quīntus** *(fifth)*, **Sextus** *(sixth)*, or **Decimus** *(tenth)*.

The middle name is called the **nōmen**. As you just learned a moment ago, the word **nōmen** means *name*. The **nōmen** indicated the large clan or extended family to which that person belonged. The ancient Romans were very eager to maintain their family's reputation and honor, especially by remembering and celebrating the great deeds of their ancestors. A Roman family's clan name may have stretched back even for centuries. Julius Caesar's **nōmen**, or clan name, was **Jūlius** (pronounced *YOO-lee-uhs*).

Lastly, we have the **cognōmen**. The word **cognōmen** is just the word **nōmen** but with a prefix. The prefix **co-** can mean things like *with* or *together*. So, the **cognōmen** was the name that went along with someone's clan name. Ancient Roman clans could be large, with several different branches, and the **cognōmen** indicated what branch of the clan a person was part of. For Julius Caesar, the **cognōmen** showed that he was from the Caesar branch of the Julius clan. So, when you see the name **Gāius Jūlius Casear**, you could interpret that name to mean something like this: *Gaius, from the Caesar branch of the Julius clan.*

An aristocratic woman's name was usually the same as her family's **nōmen** (that is, the clan name) but in feminine form. Therefore a girl born into the **Jūlius** clan would be named **Jūlia**. A girl born into the **Tullius** clan would be called **Tullia**, and a girl born into the **Cornēlius** clan would be called **Cornēlia**. These feminine names are first declension nouns. After that, there could be her father's cognomen in the genitive case, indicating what branch of the family she is from. For example, if Marcus Licinius Crassus had a daughter, she could possibly have been called **Licinia Crassī**, meaning *Licinia of the Crassus branch*. Sometimes, daughters would be distinguished from one another by adding adjectives to their names such as **Major** *(older)* and **Minor** *(younger)*. Also they could be given birth order adjectives (feminine, of course) like **Secunda** *(second)* and **Tertia** *(third)*.

I hope you have enjoyed this brief overview of Roman names—but as you search out a name for yourself, here's something to keep in mind: *Latin* doesn't necessarily mean *Roman*. The Latin language was made famous by the ancient Romans, but it outlived them by many centuries—on into the Middle Ages, and later the Renaissance. Therefore, you could pick a Latin name from any period of Latin that suits your fancy.

QUICK ✎ REVIEW

The ablative of means can be used to show what object or instrument is used to accomplish a task. So, if you want to say *I am guarding the island with sword and shield*, you could say **Ego īnsulam gladiō et scūtō servō**. You can also use it to show what material you are making something with—so if you want to say *I am building a wall with wood*, you could say **Mūrum lignō aedificō**.

LESSON FOUR

CHOOSING A LATIN NAME

Now that you know a little about Roman names, it's time for you to pick your own Latin name so you can make up Latin sentences about yourself and have Latin conversations with other people. With that in mind, let's look at a few of the specific ways you can choose a Latin name for yourself.

LATINIZE YOUR EXISTING NAME

One way to find a Latin name for yourself is to find the Latin version of your name, if one exists. My name, for example, is William (people call me Bill) so I can use the Latin version of William which is **Gulielmus**. If your name is Peter, the Latin way to say that would be **Petrus**. If your name is Katherine, Catherine, Kathryn, Cathy, Katie, or Kate, you could call yourself **Catharīna**. Charles would be **Carolus**. If your name is Julie or Juliana, you could be **Jūlia**. Frank or Francis would be **Franciscus**. Helen is **Helena**. Robert is **Rōbertus**. Paul is **Paulus**. The Latin way to say James is **Jācōbus**. Louis could be **Lūdovīcus**. Emily comes from **Aemilia**. Tony or Anthony would be **Antōnius**. Christopher would be **Christophorus**. Terence, Terry, or Terrie could be **Terentius** (male) or **Terentia** (female). Joe or Joseph would be **Jōsēphus**.

Some of you may already have a Latin name right now! For example, if your name is Julia, Rex, Victoria, Victor, Amanda, Leo, or Claudia, your name is already Latin and you don't need to change anything!

TRANSLATE YOUR NAME'S MEANING

For some folks, their last name is a word that means something—for example, names like Baker, Miller, Fisher, or Cooper (barrel maker). If your last name means something, you could try to translate that particular word into Latin and use that as your Latin name. If your name doesn't mean anything in English, it could mean something in another language. For instance, the names Mueller and Metzger are German words that mean *miller* and *butcher*. The French names DuBois and Beaumont mean *from the woods* and *beautiful hill*. So, if your last name is a word that means something, it might (or might not) translate well into Latin as something like **Cūpārius/Cūpāria** *(barrel maker)*, **Molīnārius/Molīnāria** *(miller)*, or **Lanius/Lania** *(butcher)*.

6

Perhaps your last name is a color such as Brown, Green, or White. If so, you might be able to translate that color name into Latin and use that as your name. For example, if your last name is White, you could be **Albus** or **Alba**. Sound familiar, Harry Potter fans?

A NAME FROM A PHYSICAL CHARACTERISTIC

You could name yourself based on a physical characteristic. For example, the Latin adjective **calvus**, **calva**, **calvum** means *bald*—so if you are a bald guy you could name yourself **Calvus**. The adjective **rūfus**, **rūfa**, **rūfum** means *red*, so if you have red hair you could be **Rūfus** or **Rūfa**. The adjective **flāvus**, **flāva**, **flāvum** means things like *yellow*, *golden*, or *blonde*—so if you have blonde hair you could give yourself the related Roman name **Flāvius** or **Flāvia**.

A NAME FROM HISTORY

Is there a figure from history whom you admire? Someone such as Boudica, Cincinnatus, Cleopatra, or Marius? Just take that name for yourself—nobody is stopping you!

A NAME FROM MYTHOLOGY

Is there a name from Greek or Roman mythology that you like? You could be Diana, Romulus, Minerva, etc.

PICK A NAME YOU LIKE!

In this lesson I have tried to give you some ideas or places to start looking for a Latin name. For the sake of simplicity, you may want to pick a name from the first or second declensions since you already know those noun endings—but it's really up to you. Of course, if you pick a name from the third declension, or a name of Greek origin, you will have to learn different endings for that particular name. But honestly, the most important thing here is to pick a name that you like—so have fun with it!

QUICK ✏ REVIEW

The dative case is used to show the indirect object in a sentence. The indirect object is the party in the sentence who is benefiting or receiving. Examples: **Rēgīna Portiae pecūniam dat** (*The queen is giving money to Portia*). **Pūblius puerīs cibum cotīdiē dat** (*Publius gives food to the boys daily*).

7

LESSON FIVE

DECLINING NAMES

In Latin, a person's name is a noun just like any other noun, and it can have any of the various endings of its declension. For example, a name like **Claudia** is a feminine noun of the first declension while a name like **Rōbertus** is a masculine noun of the second declension. Therefore in this lesson, let's get accustomed to using a person's name in the various noun cases by going through some example sentences. This will also be a good chance for you to review the various endings of the first and second declensions. In each example, the names are underlined for clarity.

NOMINATIVE

- **<u>Claudia</u> ad oppidum ambulat.** *(Claudia is walking to the town.)*
- **<u>Rōbertus</u> agrum arat.** *(Robert is plowing the field.)*

GENITIVE

- **Casa <u>Claudiae</u> est magna.** *(Claudia's house is large.)*
- **Ad casam <u>Rōbertī</u> ambulō.** *(I am walking to Robert's house.)*

DATIVE

Note: In a Latin sentence, the indirect object often comes before the direct object.

- **<u>Claudiae</u> pecūniam damus.** *(We are giving money to Claudia.)*
- **Nauta <u>Rōbertō</u> fābulam narrat.** *(The sailor is telling a story to Robert.)*

ACCUSATIVE

- **Puellae <u>Claudiam</u> spectant.** *(The girls are watching Claudia.)*
- **Puerī <u>Rōbertum</u> spectant.** *(The boys are watching Robert.)*

8

ABLATIVE

- **Ad actam cum <u>Claudiā</u> ambulant.** *(They are walking to the seashore with Claudia.)*
- **Ad patriam cum <u>Rōbertō</u> nāvigāmus.** *(We are sailing to the homeland with Robert).*

Again, these names are from the first and second declensions. As I mentioned before, if you pick a name for yourself from the third declension, or a name of Greek origin, the endings will be different.

Translate these exercises, treating the names as you would any other noun.

EXERCISES

1. **Jūlia saepe ā silvā ad oppidum ambulat.**
2. **Marcus et Claudia magnam casam aedificant.**
3. **Paulus et Fausta in agrīs saepe labōrant.**
4. **Fīliī Christophorī oppidum servant.**
5. **Fīlia Flāviae multum argentum habet.**
6. **Quīntus Jōsēphō pecūniam saepe dat.**
7. **Cornēlium spectāmus.**
8. **Puerī in scaphā cum Rōmulō sunt.**
9. **Carolus gladium Claudiī habet.**
10. **Catharīna terram cum Helenā arat.**

Answers on page 254.

QUICK REVIEW

In English, the word *you* can be singular or plural—you can use it to address one person or more than one person. But that can be confusing at times, especially in a book like this one where you need to know specifically when things are singular or plural. So, to help you learn, in this book I will use the word *you* for singular *you* and the word *y'all* for plural *you* just as I did in *Getting Started with Latin*. Example: **Ad īnsulam nāvigātis** *(Y'all are sailing to the island).*

LESSON SIX

NEW WORD   **ubi**

MEANING   *where*

The word **ubi** means *where*. You can use **ubi** to ask a simple question, as seen in these examples:

- **Ubi sum?** *(Where am I?)*
- **Ubi es?** *(Where are you?)*
- **Ubi est scapha?** *(Where is the boat?)*
- **Ubi sunt puerī?** *(Where are the boys?)*

EXERCISES

1. **Ubi est agricola?**
2. **Ubi est Aurēlia?**
3. **Ubi sunt scūtum et gladius?**
4. **Jūlia et Pūblius in casā sunt, sed ubi est Claudius?**
5. **Puerī cum Jūliō ab oppidō ad silvam ambulant.**
6. **Rēgīna magnum mūrum circum oppidum aedificat.**
7. **Puellae saxa portant.**
8. **Fīlius Marcī Lucrētiam amat, sed Lucrētia Pūblium amat.**
9. **Sine lignō, scapham aedificāre nōn possumus.**
10. **Helena puellae cibum dat.**

Answers on page 254.

QUICK ✏ REVIEW

For every neuter noun, the nominative plural will always end in **-a.** So the nominative plural form of **scūtum** *(shield)* is **scūta.** Also, for every neuter noun, the accusative forms will be exactly the same as the nominative forms. Therefore the accusative singular of **scūtum** is **scūtum,** and the accusative plural is **scūta.**

LESSON SEVEN

THE VOCATIVE CASE

In *Getting Started with Latin*, I explained to you that there are five noun cases. But there is one additional case that I have not mentioned yet (don't get mad or anything). The reason I haven't mentioned it until now is because it is not usually shown in noun declension charts (in textbooks, at least). It's called the *vocative case*. A noun in the vocative case is what you use when you directly address someone. In each of these sentences, the underlined word is a vocative.

- Mom! Give me my lunch money!
- Officer! I didn't realize I was speeding.
- Fluffy! Get off the kitchen table!

In each of these sentences, someone is addressing someone directly—Mom, a police officer, and Fluffy the cat. In Latin, when we speak directly to someone or call out directly to someone in this manner, the person's name is in the vocative case.

The vocative case in Latin is easy to learn. Most of the time, whether singular or plural, the vocative case is exactly the same as the nominative case, so nothing changes, and there isn't anything to remember. Below, observe that each of the following nouns is the same in the vocative case as it is in the nominative case. Observe as I take nominative nouns and turn them into vocative nouns.

- **Jūlia ⟶ Jūlia!**
- **nauta ⟶ Nauta!**
- **puerī ⟶ Puerī!**

So, for the nouns shown above, the vocative is exactly the same as the nominative case. But there are a couple of situations in which the vocative form is different from the nominative form. This applies to masculine names from the second declension. For second declension names that end in **-us**, the ending changes to **-e** for the vocative, like this:

- **Marcus ⟶ Marce!**

- **Quīntus → Quīnte!**
- **Gulielmus → Gulielme!**

The *e* at the end of these words is a short *e*. So, if you call out to Marcus and say **Marce!**, it will sound something like *MARR-keh*, with a short second syllable, not *MARR-KAY*, with a long second syllable.

For second declension masculine names that end in **-ius**, the vocative will not end with the letter *e*. Instead, it will end with a long *i*, like this:

- **fīlius → Fīlī!**
- **Jūlius → Jūlī!**
- **Claudius → Claudī!**

These endings only affect singular nouns—in the plural, vocatives are always the same as the nominative case.

You will often see the interjection **ō** before a noun in the vocative case, like this:

- **Ō Jūlia!**
- **Ō puerī!**
- **Ō puella!**
- **Ō nautae!**

The interjection **ō** doesn't really translate to anything. It's similar to when we sometimes say *oh* in English, like this:

> <u>Oh</u> Fred, I'm so sorry to hear about your pet llama.

In this book, I will use **ō** with nouns in the vocative whenever possible to help you identify the vocative case more easily.

EXERCISES

1. **Ō Puer, ubi sunt agricolae?**
2. **Ō Tullia, ubi est Lūcius?**
3. **Ō fīlī, ubi est Aurēlia?**

4. **Ō Claudia, ubi est Lucrētia?**
5. **Ō Claudī, ubi est pecūnia Marcī?**
6. **Lāvīnia saepe circum īnsulam natat.**
7. **Rūfus et Helena pugnant!**
8. **Ō Marce, ubi est cibus nautārum?**
9. **Decimus saepe puellīs fābulam narrat.**
10. **Incolae īnsulae numquam rēgīnae pecūniam dant.**

Answers on page 254.

QUICK ✐ REVIEW

A complementary infinitive is an infinitive that works along with an-other verb. In *Getting Started with Latin,* you got lots of practice using complementary infinitives with the verb **possum**, like this: **Scapham aedificāre possum** *(I am able to build a boat).*

QUICK ✐ REVIEW

There are a few words from *Getting Started with Latin* that you may not remember either because they didn't get used very often, or be-cause they came near the end of the book. The verb **dēsīderō** means *I long for* or *I desire* (and can also mean to miss someone). **Maneō** means to *I stay* or *I remain*. **Incola** means *inhabitant*. **Quod** means *because*. **Dēleō** means *I destroy*. **Dōnum** means *gift*. **Pugnō** means *I fight*. **Superō** means *I conquer*. **Servō** means *I guard*. **Caelum** means *sky*. **Saxum** means *rock*. **Aurum** means *gold*. **Argentum** means *silver*. **Laetus, laeta, laetum** means *happy*.

13

LESSON EIGHT

NEW WORD   **cūr**

MEANING   *why*

With the word **cūr**, you can ask why someone is doing something, like this:

Cūr ad actam ambulās? *(Why are you walking to the seashore?)*

EXERCISES

1. **Ō Quīnte, cūr ad silvam ambulās?**
2. **Cūr circum īnsulam nāvigāmus? Nōn sumus nautae!**
3. **Ō Lāvīnia, cūr Diāna in oppidō est?**
4. **Ō puerī malī, cūr pugnātis?**
5. **Ō Tullia, ubi sunt gladiī virōrum?**
6. **Cūr agrōs arāmus? Nōn sumus agricolae!**
7. **Cūr fīliae Cornēliī ad magnam īnsulam cum nautīs nāvigant?**
8. **Ō nauta, cūr puerīs semper fābulās malās narrās?**
9. **Tiberius in silvā ambulāre nōn potest quod bestiās timet.**
10. **Flāvia casam saxīs lignōque aedificat.**

Answers on page 254.

QUICK ✏ REVIEW

When the preposition **in** takes the accusative case, it can mean *into*, like this: **In silvam ambulāmus** *(We are walking into the forest)*. But when **in** takes the ablative case, it can mean *in* or *on*, like these examples: **Sumus in silvā** *(We are in the forest)*. **Jūlia in īnsulā est** *(Julia is on the island)*.

LESSON NINE

EACH EXERCISE CAN BE A LITTLE CONVERSATION!

In *Getting Started with Latin*, the exercises were mainly just statements, usually consisting of one or two sentences at most. But in this book I would like to have longer, more conversational exercises—exercises in which people are talking to each other. This will give you more reading (and listening!) practice while at the same time helping you learn how to speak Latin.

To help make this happen, I will be using this diamond-shaped symbol to show you when a new person starts talking: ♦ Here's how an exercise might look with the diamond symbol separating two different speakers:

Ō Christophore, ubi est Fausta? ♦ In oppidō est.

So, when you read these little conversations, imagine two different people talking to each other. In the example above, the first person says **"Ō Christophore, ubi est Fausta?"** and the other person says **"In oppidō est."** In the audio recordings that accompany this book, there will be two different voices speaking so that you can more fully experience the conversational aspect of these exercises.

EXERCISES

1. **Ō Paula, ubi est Lucrētia? ♦ Lucrētia ad īnsulam cum Jūliā et Faustā natat.**
2. **Fīlia rēgīnae semper agricolīs pecūniam dat.**
3. **Virī īnsulae gladiīs et scūtīs pugnant. ♦ Oppidum dēlent!**
4. **Ubi est Portia? ♦ Portia magna saxa ab agrīs portat. ♦ Portia est valida!**
5. **Ō virī īnsulae! Cūr nautae īnsulam superant? ♦ Nautae īnsulam superant quod gladiōs nōn habēmus.**
6. **Scapham vidēre nōn possum. Ō puella, ubi est scapha Rōbertī?**
7. **Cūr Petrus terram nōn arat? ♦ Petrus nōn est agricola.**
8. **Cūr Fulvia laeta est? ♦ Multam pecūniam habet. ♦ Ubi est Fulvia? ♦ Pecūniam in casā numerat.**
9. **Cūr agrōs arāmus? Nōn sumus agricolae. ♦ Agricolae sumus!**
10. **Ego semper puerīs puellīsque cibum dō.**

Answers on page 254.

LESSON TEN

NEW WORD   **salvē**

MEANING   *hello*

PRONUNCIATION TIP: In classical pronunciation, **salvē** will sound something like *SALL-way*. In ecclesiastical pronunciation it will sound like *SALL-vay* (with a *v* sound).

Since you are learning how to speak Latin, you should probably learn how to say *hello*. There are two ways to say hello, depending on whether you are saying *hello* to one person or more than one person. If you are saying *hello* to just one person, say **salvē**, like this:

> **Salvē, Helena.** *(Hello, Helen.)*

To say hello to more than one person, you must add the ending **-te** to the end of **salvē**, and it becomes **salvēte**, like this:

> **Salvēte, puellae.** *(Hello, girls.)*

EXERCISES

1. **Salvēte, Tullia et Petre!** ♦ **Salvē, ō Cornēlia!**
2. **Salvē, ō Rōberte!** ♦ **Salvē, Claudia!**
3. **Salvēte, Jūlia et Jūlī!** ♦ **Salvē, ō Rūfe!**
4. **Salvē, Semprōnia! Ubi est Lāvīnia?** ♦ **In casā cum puellīs et puerīs est.**
5. **Salvē, nauta! Ad patriam sine cibō nāvigāre nōn potes.** ♦ **Cibum nōn habeō, sed pecūniam habeō.**
6. **Aurēlia est fēmina valida!** ♦ **Cūr Aurēlia fēmina valida est?** ♦ **Valida est quod cotīdiē aquam ad casam portat.**
7. **Ō Pūblī, ubi est rēgīna?** ♦ **In oppidō est. Puerīs puellīsque cibum dat.**
8. **Salvēte, nautae. Ubi est scapha?** ♦ **Nōn habēmus scapham.** ♦ **Cūr?** ♦ **Agricolae sumus.**
9. **Ō Marce, ubi est lūna?** ♦ **Lūna in caelō est!**
10. **In scaphā manēre nōn possum, sed natāre nōn possum!**

Answers on page 254.

LESSON ELEVEN

NEW WORD   **nesciō**

MEANING   *I don't know*

PRONUNCIATION TIP: In classical pronunciation **nesciō** sounds something like *NESS-key-oh,* but in ecclesiastical pronunciation it sounds more like *NESS-shee-oh.*

The Latin verb **sciō** means *I know.* It is related to the English word *science.* But the prefix **ne-** negates **sciō,** like this:

ne + sciō = nesciō

You can use **nesciō** to answer a question, like this:

- **Ubi est scapha?** *(Where is the boat?)* ♦ **Nesciō.** *(I don't know.)*
- **Ō Paule, ubi est Jūlia?** *(Paul, where is Julia?)* ♦ **Nesciō.** *(I don't know.)*

EXERCISES

1. **Ō Decime, ubi est Jūlia?** ♦ **Nesciō.**
2. **Ō Fausta, ubi est Jōsēphus?** ♦ **Nesciō, sed Tiberius in casā est.**
3. **Salvē, ō Rōberte! Ubi est lignum?** ♦ **Nesciō.**
4. **Ō Fulvia, ubi est gladius?** ♦ **In scaphā.**
5. **Nauta numquam sine cibō et pecūniā ad īnsulam nāvigat.**
6. **Cūr mūrum lignō aedificās?** ♦ **Lignum est validum.**
7. **Cūr ad patriam nāvigātis?** ♦ **Ad patriam nāvigāmus quod patriam dēsīderāmus.**
8. **Ō Semprōnia, ubi est Carolus?** ♦ **Carolus cum rēgīnā est. Carolus rēgīnae dōnum dat.**
9. **Īnsulam timēmus.** ♦ **Cūr?** ♦ **Īnsula multās bestiās habet!**
10. **Salvēte, ō Rūfe et Christophore. Cūr ad īnsulam natātis?** ♦ **Scapham nōn habēmus.**

Answers on page 255.

LESSON TWELVE

NEW WORD   **domī**

MEANING   *at home*

It's a long story, but the word **domī** is an adverb that means *at home.* This word is related to English words like *domestic* and *domesticated.* Here's an example of how to use **domī** in a sentence.

Pūblius est domī. *(Publius is at home.)*

EXERCISES

1. **Claudius domī est.**
2. **Ō Tiberī, ubi est Jūlius? ♦ Domī est.**
3. **Ō Jūlia, ubi es? ♦ Domī sum.**
4. **Ubi est Carolus? ♦ Nesciō, sed Portia in agrō est.**
5. **Ō Semprōnia, ubi est Cornēlia? ♦ Domī est.**
6. **Salvēte, ō Rōberte et Claudia. ♦ Salvē, ō Tullia!**
7. **Puellae saepe ab actā ad silvam ambulant.**
8. **Ō Aurēlia, cūr dōnum habētis? ♦ Saepe puellīs oppidī dōna damus.
   ♦ Ego numquam dōna dō quod pecūniam nōn habeō.**
9. **Ō Rōmule, cūr gladium Tiberiī habēs? ♦ Oppidum servō quod mūrum circum oppidum nōn habēmus.**
10. **Incolae oppidī mūrum saxīs aedificant.**

Answers on page 255.

QUICK ✏ REVIEW

When you put **est** first in a sentence, it can mean *there is,* as seen in this sentence: **Est puer in scaphā** *(There is a boy in the boat).* Likewise, when you put **sunt** first it can mean *there are:* **Sunt stellae in caelō** *(There are stars in the sky).*

LESSON 13

NEW WORD   **habitō / habitāre**

MEANING   *I live / to live*

Our new word for this lesson is a verb of the first conjugation. It is related to our English word *habitat*, which is a place where a person or animal lives.

You can use the verb **habitō** along with **ubi** to ask where someone lives, like this:

Ubi habitās? *(Where do you live?)*

Or use **habitō** with a preposition to tell where someone lives:

Quīntus et Decimus in silvā habitant. *(Quintus and Decimus live in the forest.)*

EXERCISES

1. **In oppidō nōn habitō. Ego in silvā habitō.** ♦ **Sunt bestiae magnae in silvā. Bestiās timeō!**
2. **Matthaeus in īnsulā habitat, sed patriam dēsīderat.** ♦ **Cūr?** ♦ **Patriam amat.**
3. **Ō Jōsēphe, ubi habitās?** ♦ **Ego in īnsulā habitō.**
4. **Numquam ad patriam nāvigāmus. Semper manēmus in īnsulā.**
5. **Gladiīs et scūtīs oppidum semper servāmus.** ♦ **Cūr?** ♦ **Oppidum amāmus quod in oppidō habitāmus.**
6. **Quīntus nōn est agricola, sed agrōs arat quod cibum nōn habet.** ♦ **Quīntus agricola est!**
7. **Pecūniam nōn habēmus.** ♦ **Pecūniam nōn habētis quod numquam labōrātis!**
8. **Fulvia nōn est laeta.** ♦ **Cūr?** ♦ **Magnum agrum arat.**
9. **Salvē, ō puella. Ubi est Helena?** ♦ **Nesciō.**
10. **Rūfus est puer malus!** ♦ **Cūr?** ♦ **Cum Quīntō semper pugnat!**

Answers on page 255.

LESSON 14

NEW WORD   **valē**

MEANING   *goodbye*

PRONUNCIATION TIP: In classical pronunciation this word sounds like *WAH-lay*, but in ecclesiastical pronunciation it sounds like *VAH-lay*.

Valē, our new word for this lesson, is similar to **salvē** because it has both a singular form and a plural form. **Valē** is for when you want to say goodbye to just one person, like this:

> **Valē, ō Jūlia.** *(Goodbye Julia.)*

Valēte is plural, for when you want to say goodbye to more than one person:

> **Valēte, Jūlia et Jācōbe.** *(Goodbye, Julia and James.)*

EXERCISES

1. **Valēte, ō agricolae!** ◆ **Nōn sumus agricolae. Nautae sumus.**
2. **Valēte, ō Portia et Semprōnia.** ◆ **Valē, ō Christophore.**
3. **Valē, ō Rōmule. Ad īnsulam nāvigō.** ◆ **Valē, ō Marce.**
4. **Salvēte, ō Fausta et Aurēlia.** ◆ **Salvē, ō Decime! Ubi est Paulus?** ◆ **Nesciō.**
5. **Ō puer, ubi habitās?** ◆ **Ego in casā prope actam habitō.**
6. **Ubi sunt Cornēlia et Pūblius?** ◆ **Domī sunt.**
7. **Ō Claudī, cūr gladium nōn habēs?** ◆ **Numquam gladium habeō, sed semper scūtum portō.**
8. **Ubi habitātis?** ◆ **Sumus incolae magnārum īnsulārum.**
9. **Ō virī patriae, cūr mūrum aedificātis?** ◆ **Mūrum aedificāmus quod patriam servāmus.**
10. **Numquam ad īnsulam natō.** ◆ **Cūr?** ◆ **Natāre nōn possum.**

Answers on page 255.

LESSON 15

NEW WORD   **hodiē**

MEANING   *today*

PRONUNCIATION TIP: The accent is on the first syllable, so it sounds something like *HOE-dee-ay*.

As I mentioned before, many Latin words are just combinations of two smaller words. **Hodiē**, our new word for this lesson, is probably a combination of the word **hōc** and the word **diē** (pronounced *DEE-aay*). **Hōc** means *this* and **diē** means *day*. It's a long story, but these words are in the ablative case because they express time, with the meaning *on this day*.

EXERCISES

1. **Salvē. Ubi est Titus?** ♦ **Titus hodiē domī nōn est.** ♦ **Cūr?** ♦ **Nesciō.** ♦ **Valē.**
2. **Cūr Petrus et Titus hodiē labōrant? Numquam agrōs arant.** ♦ **Nesciō.**
3. **Fulvia et Cornēlia hodiē in agrīs labōrant. Terram arant.**
4. **Nautae hodiē ad īnsulam nōn nāvigant.** ♦ **Cūr?** ♦ **In patriā manent.**
5. **Ō Aemilia, ubi est Rūfus hodiē?** ♦ **Domī est.** ♦ **Cūr domī est?** ♦ **In casā labōrat.**
6. **Puellae puerīque hodiē ab oppidō ad actam ambulant.** ♦ **Cūr?** ♦ **In oppidō habitant, sed actam dēsīderant.** ♦ **Ego hodiē ad actam ambulāre nōn possum.**
7. **Virī scūta habent, sed gladiōs nōn habent.** ♦ **Virīs gladiōs dare possumus.**
8. **Oppidum servāre nōn possumus.** ♦ **Cūr?** ♦ **Nōn est mūrus circum oppidum.** ♦ **Mūrum lignō et saxīs hodiē aedificāre possumus.**
9. **Fīlius Lucrētiae ad īnsulam natāre nōn potest.**
10. **Puellae ā scholā ad casam cotīdiē ambulant.**

Answers on page 255.

LESSON 16

ASKING QUESTIONS

In Latin, you can turn any statement into a question by adding a special ending to the first word of the sentence. Often, the word to which we add this special ending is the verb, which has been moved to the beginning of the sentence. Here's a simple sentence that we can work with, just for practice:

Nauta es.

That sentence means *You are a sailor.* Now observe as I move the verb to the beginning of the sentence and add the suffix **-ne** to it.

Esne nauta?

Now the sentence is a question which means *Are you a sailor?* By adding **-ne** to the end of the first word, I have converted that sentence into a question. Here's another sentence we can practice with:

Aurēlia est in silvā.

This sentence means *Aurelia is in the forest.* Now observe again as I move the verb to the front of the sentence and add the suffix **-ne** to it.

Estne Aurēlia in silvā?

Now the sentence is a question which means *Is Aurelia in the forest?* By adding **-ne** to the end of the first word, again, I have converted the sentence into a question.

The word you add **-ne** to doesn't have to be a verb—it can also be a pronoun. Observe this simple sentence:

Ego scapham aedificō. *(I am building a boat).*

The first word of the sentence is the pronoun **ego**. We can leave **ego** as the first word of the sentence and add the **-ne** suffix to it, like this:

Egone scapham aedificō? *(Am I building a boat?)*

So, be on the lookout for the **-ne** suffix attached to the first word of a sentence! If you see that, the sentence is a question!

EXERCISES

1. **Estne Aurēlia domī?** ♦ **Aurēlia hodiē ad actam ambulat. Aurēlia actam amat!**

2. **Ō nauta, narrāsne puerīs fābulam malam?** ♦ **Ego semper fābulās malās narrō!** ♦ **Cūr?** ♦ **Nauta sum!**

3. **Sumne nauta?** ♦ **Nesciō. Habēsne scapham?** ♦ **Habeō multās scaphās.** ♦ **Nāvigāsne?** ♦ **Cotīdiē ad patriam nāvigō.** ♦ **Nauta es!**

4. **Egone agricola sum?** ♦ **Nesciō. Habēsne agrōs?** ♦ **Agrōs habeō.** ♦ **Arāsne agrōs?** ♦ **Cotīdiē.** ♦ **Agricola es!**

5. **Salvē, ō Tullia. Ubi sunt fīliae Jōsēphī?** ♦ **In silvā cum Semprōniā et Cornēliā habitant.**

6. **Habēsne pecūniam?** ♦ **Pecūniam nōn habeō, sed argentum aurumque habeō.**

7. **Habēmusne cibum? Habēmusne aquam?** ♦ **Cibum et aquam habēmus.**

8. **Jūlius cum Rūfō pugnat!** ♦ **Cūr?** ♦ **Rūfus pecūniam Jūliī habet.** ♦ **Rūfus est puer malus!**

9. **Ō nauta, est aqua in scaphā!** ♦ **Ad īnsulam nāvigāre nōn possumus!** ♦ **Valē!**

10. **Ō Rōmule, ubi est cibus virōrum? Cibum non habent.** ♦ **Nesciō. Virīs cotīdiē cibum damus.** ♦ **Cūr?** ♦ **Incolae patriae cibum nōn habent.**

Answers on page 256.

QUICK ✐ REVIEW

Most first declension nouns are feminine, but there are a few of them that are masculine: **poēta**, **agricola**, **incola**, and **nauta**. So, if you put an adjective along with one of these nouns, it needs to be masculine, like in these examples: **nauta validus**, **multī agricolae**, **poētās malōs**.

LESSON 17

PRONOUNS

You already have some experience working with pronouns, but over the next few lessons we are going to learn more about how pronouns work in Latin. So, with that in mind, let's review what you already know before we move forward.

A pronoun is a word that can take the place of a noun. Pronouns are words like *he, she, it, I, we, you*, and *they*. Pronouns are used differently in Latin than they are in English. In English, for example, you must include a pronoun along with a verb. Observe this sentence:

I walk.

In English, the pronoun is totally separate from the verb. The word *I* shows who is doing the action, and the word *walk* shows the kind of activity that is happening. So, in English, it takes two words to express the thought *I walk*. But in Latin, look at what we can do:

Ambulō.

In Latin, we can say *I walk* with just one word, while in English it requires two words. The word **ambulō** shows not only who is doing the action, but also what kind of action is happening—all in one word.

But there is more to the story. Latin also has pronouns just like English does. Observe this sentence:

Ego ambulō.

Ego is a pronoun that means *I*. So in Latin, we have pronouns just like English does. But the difference here is that Latin pronouns are optional. You can use them if you want, or leave them out if you want.

At this point, you might be wondering—if a Latin verb already tells you who is doing the action, why do we need pronouns in Latin? To answer this question, let's take a moment to think about pronouns in general, and how they are useful to writers and speakers.

24

WHAT DO PRONOUNS DO, EXACTLY?

In both written and spoken language, pronouns can be useful in several ways. Let's examine some of the ways pronouns can help people express themselves.

Perhaps the most common way that pronouns are helpful is when we have already used a certain noun, and we don't want to repeat that same noun again. Observe this example:

> Susanne is wearing a blue dress. <u>Susanne</u> bought it last week.

Instead of repeating the word *Susanne* in the second sentence, we can replace it with a pronoun, like this:

> Susanne is wearing a blue dress. <u>She</u> bought it last week.

In this way, pronouns can help us avoid repeating the names of the things or people we are talking about.

Another way that a pronoun can be helpful is when you want to make a sentence more clear. Compare these two sentences and see if you notice anything in particular.

- While walking to work, thinking about Latin, I stopped for coffee.
- I, while walking to work, thinking about Latin, stopped for coffee.

Which of those two sentences was easier to understand? Probably the second one, because the pronoun *I* is at the beginning of the sentence. Because the pronoun *I* is at the beginning, it is clear right from the start who is doing the action in the sentence. But in the first sentence, because the pronoun is delayed until the end, it isn't clear at first who is doing the action—you have to wait a little to find out who is doing the walking and thinking (and coffee drinking). Therefore, I would argue that in the second sentence, putting the pronoun first makes the meaning of the sentence more clear to the reader or listener.

Here's another way pronouns can clarify the meaning of a sentence. Compare these two sentences and see if you notice anything.

- Broccoli tastes terrible.
- To me, broccoli tastes terrible.

In the first sentence, someone is making a universal statement about broccoli—the statement is not limited in any way. But in the second sentence, the speaker uses the pronoun *me* to limit the statement. The speaker is saying that while others might enjoy the taste of broccoli, to his or her taste buds, it tastes terrible. So again, a pronoun helps to clarify the sentence, enabling the speaker to express himself or herself more precisely.

Here's one last example—compare these sentences and see if anything comes to mind.

- Mistakes were made.
- I made mistakes.

In the first sentence, the speaker has arranged the words in such a way that there is no pronoun needed. The verb is a passive verb, so the sentence has a certain impersonal kind of sound to it. If you say "Mistakes were made," you can acknowledge that someone made a mistake without revealing exactly who it was that made the mistake (I've seen politicians say this kind of thing on TV and in the newspaper). But in the second sentence, the speaker uses the pronoun *I* to show specifically who made the mistakes, taking personal responsibility for them. So again, a pronoun adds clarity, emphasis, and expressiveness to the sentence.

The point here is that pronouns can be useful in any language. As far as Latin is concerned, you already know one Latin pronoun, **ego**, and you'll learn a few more useful pronouns as you go through the rest of this book.

QUICK REVIEW

The preposition **ā, ab** *(from)* has two spellings. Generally speaking, if the next word starts with a vowel, it is spelled **ab**, as in **ab oppidō** *(from the town)*. But if the next word starts with a consonant, it is spelled **ā**, as in **ā silvā** *(from the forest)*. This preposition takes the ablative case.

LESSON 18

NEW WORD   **tū**

MEANING   *you*

In the last lesson, we talked about pronouns and how they can help to make a sentence more clear and expressive. In this lesson, it's time to learn a new pronoun: the word **tū** which means *you*. In English, the word *you* can be singular or plural, but the Latin pronoun **tū** is singular, for when you are talking to only one person. There is a separate pronoun for when you want to say plural *you*, but you don't need to know that word yet.

Like **ego**, you can either include or leave out the word **tū**. Observe these sentences:

- **Ambulās.** *(You walk.)*
- **Tū ambulās.** *(You walk.)*

Both sentences mean the same thing: *You walk.* Again, you aren't required to use **tū** along with a second person singular verb, but you may find places where using the pronoun **tū** makes your sentence more clear or emphasizes the subject more, especially if you are speaking Latin with other people.

Also, when you want to ask a question, you can start out the sentence with the pronoun **tū** and add the **-ne** suffix to it, like this:

     Tūne ambulās? *(Are you walking?)*

EXERCISES

1. **Habitās in oppidō.**
2. **Tū habitās in oppidō.**
3. **Habitāsne in oppidō?**
4. **Tūne in oppidō habitās?**
5. **Ō fīlī, ego cotīdiē agrōs arō, sed tū semper in casā manēs.** ◆ **Ego hodiē labōrāre nōn possum. Valē.**

6. **Ō Aemilia, cūr ad īnsulam natās?** ♦ **Scapham nōn habeō!** ♦ **Ego scapham habeō sed aquam timeō.**

7. **Ad scholam nōn ambulāmus. Domī hodiē manēmus.** ♦ **Puerī malī estis!**

8. **Virī validī agrōs arant, et saxa ab agrīs portant.**

9. **Rēgīna semper fīliābus Faustae pecūniam et cibum dat.** ♦ **Cūr?** ♦ **Rēgīna est fēmina bona.** ♦ **Ubi fīliae Faustae habitant?** ♦ **In silvā habitant.**

10. **Salvē, ō Tullia. Habēsne scapham?** ♦ **Salvē. Multās scaphās habeō.** ♦ **Cūr multās scaphās habēs? Tūne ad īnsulās saepe nāvigās?** ♦ **Cotīdiē ad īnsulās nāvigō.**

Answers on page 256.

QUICK ✏ REVIEW

When you add the suffix **-que** to a noun, it's like putting the word *and* before that noun. Examples: **Puerī puellaeque natant** *(The boys and girls are swimming)*. **Aurum argentumque habēmus** *(We have gold and silver)*.

LESSON 19

NEW WORD   **equus, equī**

MEANING   *horse*

OK, pardner—it's time to saddle up and ride a new noun! The word **equus** is related to several English words. The word *equine* means *related to horses,* and the word *equestrian* means *related to the art of riding horses.* **Equus** is a masculine noun of the second declension.

While we are learning about horses, let's also learn the word **stabulum**, which means *stable* (the enclosure where a horse stands). That's a neuter noun of the second declension. Here's a practice sentence just for...um...practice.

Equus est in stabulō. *(The horse is in the stable.)*

EXERCISES

1. **Equus in stabulō nōn est. Ubi est equus?** ♦ **Nesciō. Sumne agricola?**

2. **Salvē, ō agricola. Cūr habēs multōs equōs?** ♦ **Nōn sum agricola. Nauta sum. Scaphās habeō.**

3. **Salvē, ō Jūlia! Ubi est Lucrētia?** ♦ **Nesciō, sed Cornēlius cum equīs in stabulō est.** ♦ **Valē.**

4. **Ō Rōberte, ubi est scapha hodiē?** ♦ **Scapham ad aquam portāmus.** ♦ **Cūr scapham portātis?** ♦ **Hodiē ad īnsulās cum gladiīs et scūtīs nāvigāmus.** ♦ **Nōn potestis pugnāre cum virīs īnsulārum!**

5. **Equus in agrō nōn est. Ubi est equus?** ♦ **Equus hodiē agricolam ad oppidum portat.**

6. **Ubi est lūna? Ubi sunt stēllae?** ♦ **In caelō sunt!**

7. **Estne mūrus circum oppidum?** ♦ **Rēgīnā mūrum saxīs aedificat.**

8. **Fīliae rēgīnae nōn sunt laetae.** ♦ **Cūr?** ♦ **Cornēlia puellīs hodiē fābulam nōn narrat.**

9. **Virī validī et fēminae validae oppidum servant, sed oppidum nōn habet mūrum. Sine mūrō, oppidum servāre nōn possunt.** ♦ **Habentne gladiōs?** ♦ **Scūta habent, sed gladiōs nōn habent.**

10. **Ō Lucrētia, tū rēgīnae argentum aurumque dare nōn potes!** ♦ **Cūr rēgīnae dōnum dare nōn possum?** ♦ **Agricolae sumus! Aurum nōn habēmus! Argentum nōn habēmus!**

Answers on page 256.

LESSON 20

YES AND NO

In Latin, we don't have words that translate exactly to *yes* and *no*. Instead, there are several ways to respond to a "yes or no" question. Let's examine a few common ways to respond to questions in Latin. Here's a simple question we can practice with:

Estne Jūlia in scaphā? *(Is Julia in the boat?)*

One way to answer a "yes or no" question is to repeat back the verb of the question. We do this in English sometimes—for example, if somebody says to me in English *Is Julia in the boat?* I might respond by saying *She is.* And you can do the same thing in Latin. Observe this miniature conversation:

Estne Jūlia in scaphā? *(Is Julia in the boat?)* ♦ **Est.** *(She is.)*

The word **est** can mean *he is, she is*, or *it is*. But when you respond to the question about Julia by saying **est**, everyone knows that you intend it to mean *She is* because of the context—since someone just now asked you about Julia, it's obvious that you are referring to her. If, on the other hand, Julia is not in the boat, you can respond like this:

Estne Jūlia in scaphā? *(Is Julia in the boat?)* ♦ **Nōn est.** *(She is not.)*

Again, because of the context, the person you are talking to will know that your answer means *She is not*, because it is clear that you are referring to Julia.

So, repeating back the verb is one way to answer a question. But we do have other ways to answer questions in Latin. For example, the word **ita** means something like *yes* or *it is so* (it is often used this way in Roman plays). Here's an example of how you can use it:

Estne Jūlia in scaphā? *(Is Julia in the boat?)* ♦ **Ita.** *(Yes.)*

Another way to answer a question in the affirmative is with the word **certē**, which means *certainly*. In classical pronunciation, **certē** sounds something like *KERR-*

30

tay, and in ecclesiastical pronunciation it sounds something like *CHAIR-teh*. Also there is the word **minimē** (pronounce *MINN-neh-may*). **Minimē** means *Not at all!*

- **Estne Jūlia in scaphā?** *(Is Julia in the boat?)* ◆ **Certē!** *(Certainly!)*
- **Estne Jūlia in scaphā?** *(Is Julia in the boat?)* ◆ **Minimē!** *(Not at all!)*

Here's a quick review: you can answer a "yes or no" question by repeating back the verb, or by using words such as **ita**, **certē**, and **minimē**. And let's not forget **nesciō**, which is always useful.

EXERCISES

1. **Tūne pecūniam habēs?** ◆ **Certē!**
2. **Estne schola in oppidō?** ◆ **Est.**
3. **Sumusne in scaphā?** ◆ **Sumus.** ◆ **Cūr? Nōn sum nauta, et aquam timeō.** ◆ **Ad patriam hodiē nāvigāmus.**
4. **Vidēsne tū equum?** ◆ **Minimē.** ◆ **Ubi est equus? Estne equus in stabulō?** ◆ **Nesciō.**
5. **Ō Quīnte, habēsne tū equum?** ◆ **Minimē. Ego equum nōn habeō, scapham nōn habeō, pecūniam nōn habeō, et cibum nōn habeō!**
6. **Salvē, ō Semprōnia. Ubi est casa Rōbertī? Habitatne Rōbertus in oppidō?** ◆ **Ita, Rōbertus in oppidō habitat. Casa Rōbertī est prope scholam.** ◆ **Valē.**
7. **Ō puellae, potestisne natāre?** ◆ **Certē. Cotīdiē natāmus. Circum īnsulam natāre possumus!** ◆ **Puellae validae estis!** ◆ **Ita. Validae sumus quod cotīdiē natāmus.**
8. **Estne Lucrētia hodiē domī?** ◆ **Est. Lucrētia hodiē prope casam labōrat.** ◆ **Cūr?** ◆ **Lucrētia hodiē scapham aedificat.**
9. **Ō Jōsēphe, habēsne scapham?** ◆ **Ita. Magnam scapham habeō.** ◆ **Ubi est scapha?** ◆ **Fīliī Rōmulī hodiē scapham habent. Scapha fīliōs Rōmulī ad īnsulam portat.**
10. **Ō Cornēlia, esne laeta?** ◆ **Nōn sum laeta!** ◆ **Cūr laeta nōn es, ō Cornēlia?** ◆ **Ego Pūblium amō, sed Pūblius amat Aurēliam.** ◆ **Amatne Pūblius Aurēliam?** ◆ **Ita. Aurēliam amat.** ◆ **Tūne Pūblium amās?** ◆ **Certē.** ◆ **Cūr Pūblium amās? Pūblius est poēta, et pecūniam nōn habet.**

Answers on page 256.

31

LESSON 21

NEW WORD   **cūrō / cūrāre**

MEANING   *I take care of / to take care of*

Cūrō is a verb of the first conjugation. It's related to English words like *curator* and *cure*. You can use **cūrō** with a direct object in the accusative case, like this:

     Ego equōs cūrō. *(I am taking care of the horses.)*

EXERCISES

1. **Nautae malī numquam scaphās cūrant!**
2. **Helena et Tiberius semper equōs cūrant.**
3. **Ō Rōberte, potesne tū hodiē puerōs et puellās cūrāre?** ♦ **Certē. Multōs fīliōs et multās fīliās habeō.**
4. **Decimus et Rūfus sunt puerī malī.** ♦ **Cūr puerī malī sunt?** ♦ **Puerī sunt malī quod equōs nōn cūrant!** ♦ **Ubi sunt equī?** ♦ **In stabulō.** ♦ **Cibum equīs dare possumus.**
5. **Ō Decime, habitāsne in silvā?** ♦ **Minimē. Ego prope actam in casā habitō.** ♦ **Cūr prope actam habitās?** ♦ **Actam amō. Multās scaphās habeō.**
6. **Ubi est Claudius hodiē? Labōratne in agrīs?** ♦ **Minimē, Claudius hodiē labōrāre nōn potest.** ♦ **Cūr?** ♦ **Nesciō.** ♦ **Valē.**
7. **Salvēte, ō Semprōnia et Rōmule. Habētisne equōs?** ♦ **Ita. Equōs validōs habēmus quod agricolae sumus.**
8. **Ō agricola, cūr Jōsēphō equum dās?** ♦ **Jōsēphō equum dō quod Jōsēphus est agricola, sed equum nōn habet.**
9. **Ubi puerī habitant?** ♦ **Puerī in oppidō habitant.** ♦ **Habitāsne tū in oppidō?** ♦ **Minimē, ego in silvā habitō.**
10. **Cūr puerī prope scaphās sunt?** ♦ **Nautae hodiē fābulās narrant.** ♦ **Ō nautae malī, cūr semper puerīs fābulās malās narrātis?**

Answers on page 257.

LESSON 22

NEW WORD   **bonus, bona, bonum**

MEANING   *good*

This lesson is a bonus lesson—and I mean that literally because our new word for this lesson is **bonus**, **bona**, **bonum**. This is a first and second declension adjective, and in case you were wondering, yes, it is the source of our English word *bonus*.

EXERCISES

1. **Matthaeus est agricola bonus quod semper agrōs cūrat.**
2. **Claudia est puella bona.** ♦ **Cūr puella bona est?** ♦ **Puella est bona quod cotīdiē in agrō labōrat et equōs in stabulō cūrat.** ♦ **Claudia est puella bona et valida!**
3. **Paulus et Rōmulus sunt fīliī bonī.** ♦ **Cūr fīliī bonī sunt?** ♦ **Numquam pugnant, et semper in agrīs labōrant.** ♦ **Puerī sunt bonī!** ♦ **Ita. Sed Lūcius est fīlius malus quod numquam equōs cūrat.** ♦ **Portatne Lūcius lignum ā silvā?** ♦ **Minimē.**
4. **Rēgīna patriae est bona quod semper patriam servat, et saepe virīs fēminīsque patriae cibum dat.**
5. **Ō agricolae, sumus puellae bonae et puerī bonī quod semper equōs cūrāmus.** ♦ **Habēmusne equōs?** ♦ **Nōn estis agricolae bonī.**
6. **Rūfus et Claudia puellās puerōsque cūrant.**
7. **Ō Tertī, ubi sunt fēminae hodiē?** ♦ **Nesciō. Nōn sunt domī.** ♦ **Estne Gulielmus domī?** ♦ **Minimē.** ♦ **Estne Rūfus domī?** ♦ **Est. In casā hodiē labōrat.** ♦ **Valē.**
8. **Puellae puerīque cotīdiē ad scholam ambulant. Puellae bonae et puerī bonī sunt.**
9. **Fīlia rēgīnae est puella bona.** ♦ **Cūr puella bona est?** ♦ **Saepe puellīs oppidī cibum dat.**
10. **In casā malā habitāmus.** ♦ **Cūr casa est mala?** ♦ **Casa est mala quod in silvā prope bestiās est!** ♦ **Suntne bestiae in silvā?** ♦ **Certē! Sunt multae bestiae in silvā!** ♦ **In casā malā habitāmus.**

Answers on page 257.

LESSON 23

NEW WORD   **porcus, porcī**

MEANING   *pig*

Our new word for this lesson is a real "boar." **Porcus** is a masculine noun of the second declension. And, as you might have guessed, it's the original source of our English word *pork*.

EXERCISES

1. **Salvē, ō Semprōnia. Esne tū agricola?**   ◆   **Ita. Multōs porcōs equōsque habeō.**

2. **Ō Petre, cūr porcum habēs? Tūne es agricola?**   ◆   **Minimē. Ego porcum ad agricolam portō.**   ◆   **Cūr?**   ◆   **Agricola multōs porcōs habet.**

3. **Ego īnsulam timeō.**   ◆   **Cūr īnsulam timēs?**   ◆   **Sunt magnī porcī in īnsulā.**   ◆   **Tūne porcōs timēs?**   ◆   **Magnōs porcōs timeō.**

4. **Salvēte, ō porcī. Habētisne cibum?**   ◆   **Minimē, cibum nōn habēmus!**

5. **Ego multam pecūniam habeō, sed tū pecūniam nōn habēs.**   ◆   **Cūr pecūniam habēs?**   ◆   **Pecūniam habeō quod semper labōrō in agrīs!**

6. **Ubi est Rūfus? Labōratne in stabulīs?**   ◆   **Minimē. Rūfus ad actam ambulat. Nōn est domī.**

7. **Ō Aemilia, potesne scaphās vidēre?**   ◆   **Minimē. Scaphās vidēre nōn possum quod lūna nōn est in caelō.**

8. **Ō Christophore, cūr tū agricola es?**   ◆   **Agricola sum quod terram amō. Laetus sum quod cotīdiē porcōs equōsque cūrō.**   ◆   **Tūne agricola bonus es?**   ◆   **Certē, agricola bonus sum.**   ◆   **Valē.**

9. **Helena in silvā ambulat.**

10. **Helena in silvam ambulat.**

Answers on page 257.

LESSON 24

NEW WORD   **absum**

MEANING   *I am absent*

The word **absum** is a combination of two words. It's really just the word **sum**, but with the preposition **ab** prefixed to it.

     ab + sum = absum

As you already know, **ab** means *from,* and **sum** means *I am.* So literally, **absum** means to be "from" somewhere, in the sense of being away or being absent from there. In fact, this word is the source of our English word *absent.*

Any form of **sum** can have the **ab-** prefix. Here are the six present tense forms of **absum**.

	SINGULAR	PLURAL
FIRST PERSON	**absum**	**absumus**
SECOND PERSON	**abes**	**abestis**
THIRD PERSON	**abest**	**absunt**

So, **absum** means *I am absent,* **abes** means *you are absent,* and so on, and so forth. Here are a few example sentences to help you get started working with **absum**.

- **Abes.** *(You are absent.)*
- **Jācōbus abest.** *(James is absent.)*
- **Ubi est Lāvīnia? Abestne?** *(Where is Lavinia? Is she absent?)*
- **Ubi estis? Abestis.** *(Where are y'all? Y'all are absent.)*
- **Puellae absunt.** *(The girls are absent.)*

35

OK, you get the idea. Now try these exercises.

EXERCISES

1. **Christophorus abest. Ubi est Christophorus? ♦ Nesciō.**
2. **Ubi est Petrus? ♦ Abest. ♦ Ubi Petrus habitat? ♦ Nesciō.**
3. **Ubi est Aemilia ? ♦ Nesciō. ♦ Estne Rūfus domī? ♦ Ita.**
4. **Estne Aurēlia domī? ♦ Mimimē, Aurēlia abest. ♦ Ubi est Aurēlia? ♦ In oppidō est.**
5. **Puellae absunt. Ubi sunt puellae? ♦ Puellae hodiē ad silvam ambulant. ♦ Cūr ad silvam ambulant? ♦ Silvam amant!**
6. **Ubi est Sempronia? ♦ Equōs in stabulīs curat. ♦ Sempronia est fēmina bona.**
7. **Esne tū Claudia? ♦ Claudia sum. ♦ Salvē, ō Claudia!**
8. **Puerī malī equōs nōn curant! ♦ Cūr? Ubi sunt puerī? ♦ Absunt. ♦ Nōn sunt agricolae bonī.**
9. **Ō puellae, cūr cotīdiē ad actam ambulātis? ♦ Actam amāmus! ♦ Hodiē ad actam ambulāre nōn potestis quod agricolae sumus et multōs porcōs habēmus. Habentne porcī cibum hodiē?**
10. **Salvē, ō Carole. ♦ Salvēte, ō Helena et Petre. Cūr domī nōn estis? ♦ In oppidō hodiē sumus quod cibum nōn habēmus. ♦ Habētisne pecūniam? ♦ Ita. ♦ Valēte!**

Answers on page 257.

(QUICK ✐ REVIEW)

In a Latin sentence, the indirect object is in the dative case. Many years ago, I asked my Latin professor to explain to me the basic idea of the dative case, and he told me this, which I think is worth memorizing: "The indirect object is the party in the sentence who is benefiting or receiving."

LESSON 25

NEW WORD   **pīrāta, pīrātae**

MEANING   *pirate*

Our new noun for this lesson is similar to the nouns **poēta**, **agricola**, **incola**, and **nauta**, because it looks feminine but is really a masculine noun of the first declension. And, as you might guess, it's where we get our English word *pirate*.

EXERCISES

1. **Pīrātae malī ad patriam nāvigant! ♦ Habēmusne gladiōs? ♦ Ita. ♦ Habēmusne scūta? ♦ Ita, scūta habēmus. ♦ Cum pīrātīs pugnāre possumus!**

2. **Ō nauta, esne pīrāta? ♦ Minimē. Nauta bonus sum. ♦ Cūr multum aurum habēs? ♦ Nōn habeō multum aurum. ♦ Cūr multum argentum habēs? ♦ Nesciō. ♦ Tū pīrāta es!**

3. **Ō Rōmule, cūr īnsulam timēs? ♦ Timeō īnsulam quod multī pīrātae in īnsulā habitant. Virī malī sunt! Ego ad īnsulam numquam nāvigō. ♦ Tū ad īnsulam numquam nāvigās quod scapham nōn habēs.**

4. **Pīrātīs pecūniam numquam damus. ♦ Cūr? ♦ Pecūniam nōn habēmus.**

5. **Ō agricola, equī absunt. Ubi sunt equī? ♦ Nōn habeō equōs. Habeō porcōs.**

6. **Cūr Semprōnia hodiē abest? ♦ Nesciō. ♦ Ubi est Semprōnia? ♦ Domī est.**

7. **Tūne equum habēs, ō Cornēlī? ♦ Ita, habeō multōs equōs. ♦ Ego magnum porcum habeō.**

8. **Salvē, ō pīrāta. ♦ Salvē. Habēsne tū pecūniam? Habēsne aurum? Habēsne argentum? ♦ Minimē! Valē!**

9. **Tertius est fīlius bonus. ♦ Cūr? ♦ Fīlius bonus est quod numquam cum puerīs malīs pugnat, et cotīdiē porcōs cūrat. ♦ Tertius est puer bonus!**

10. **Pīrātae aurum argentumque habent.**

Answers on page 258.

37

LESSON 26

NEW WORD   **aegrōtō / aegrōtāre**

MEANING   *I am sick / to be sick*

Aegrōtō is a verb of the first conjugation.

At British universities, an *aegrotat* is a note from a doctor saying that a student is too sick to attend class or take an exam. It's called an *aegrotat* because in Latin, **aegrōtat** is the third person singular form of our new verb for this lesson. It means *he, she,* or *it is sick.*

	SINGULAR	PLURAL
FIRST PERSON	**aegrōtō**	**aegrōtāmus**
SECOND PERSON	**aegrōtās**	**aegrōtātis**
THIRD PERSON	**aegrōtat**	**aegrōtant**

EXERCISES

1. **Tiberius hodiē in agrō labōrāre nōn potest quod aegrōtat.**
2. **Salvē, Aemilia. Cūr tū abes? Aegrōtāsne hodiē? ♦ Minimē. Ad scholam ambulō.**
3. **Ō puer, cūr tū ad scholam nōn ambulās? ♦ Nōn sum puer malus. Hodiē aegrōtō.**
4. **Ō agricola, porcōs hodiē cūrāre nōn possumus. ♦ Cūr? ♦ Aegrōtāmus. ♦ Fortasse domī hodiē manēre potestis. Ego porcīs cibum dare possum.**
5. **Ō Marce, cūr tū equōs numerās? ♦ Multōs equōs in stabulīs habēmus.**
6. **Fīlia Quīntī Rūfum amat. ♦ Cūr amat Rūfum? ♦ Rūfus est vir bonus. Semper agrōs cūrat, et puerīs numquam fābulās malās narrat, et saepe patriam servat. ♦ Rūfus est agricola bonus et vir bonus!**

7. Suntne domī puellae? ♦ Minimē. Absunt. Puellae ab actā ad silvam ambulant. ♦ Cūr? ♦ Silvam amant.

8. Ego magnum porcum videō. ♦ Ubi est magnus porcus? ♦ In agrō. ♦ Habēmusne porcōs? ♦ Minimē, equōs habēmus. ♦ Cūr porcus in agrō est? ♦ Nesciō.

9. Cūr virī īnsulae cum virīs oppidī pugnant? ♦ Nesciō, sed oppidum dēlent! ♦ Habēsne scūtum? Habēsne gladium? ♦ Minimē. ♦ Sine gladiīs et scūtīs pugnāre nōn possumus! ♦ Valē.

10. Salvē, ō Portia. Ubi Jūlia habitat? Habitatne Jūlia in silvā cum bestiīs? ♦ Ita, Jūlia in silvā habitat.

Answers on page 258.

QUICK ✏ REVIEW

Generally speaking, the accusative case is associated with motion going toward something, but the ablative case is associated with motion going away from something—that is, separation. That's why prepositions like **ad** take the accusative case and prepositions like **ā**, **ab** take the ablative case.

LESSON 27

NEW WORD   **nunc**

MEANING   *now*

Nunc is an adverb that means *now*. Use it like you would use the word *now* in English.

EXERCISES

1. **Tūne nunc in oppidō habitās?** ♦ **Minimē, in silvā habitō.** ♦ **Cūr tū in silvā habitās?** ♦ **Silvam amō.** ♦ **In silvā habitāre nōn possum quod bestiās timeō.**

2. **Salvēte, ō Jācōbe et Lucrētia. Ubi est Tullia nunc?** ♦ **Tullia abest.** ♦ **Aegrōtatne Tullia?** ♦ **Tullia nunc abest quod puerōs puellāsque cūrat.**

3. **Sumne domī?** ♦ **Minimē, tū in scaphā es! Nāvigāmus nunc ad patriam.** ♦ **Ad patriam nāvigāre nōn possum. Ego aegrōtō!**

4. **Decimus vir validus est.** ♦ **Cūr?** ♦ **Vir validus est quod cotīdiē lignum, aquam, et saxa portat.** ♦ **Cūr Decimus lignum portat?** ♦ **Nunc mūrum lignō aedificat.**

5. **Ō Carole, cūr multam pecūniam nunc habēs?** ♦ **Pecūniam habeō quod cotīdiē in agrīs labōrō et porcōs cūrō. Nunc pecūniam numerō.**

6. **Labōrantne fīliae Quīntī in agrīs?** ♦ **Ita, nunc terram arant.** ♦ **Habentne equī cibum in stabulīs?** ♦ **Minimē, sed ego equōs et porcōs cūrāre hodiē possum.**

7. **Ō Rūfe, amāsne Faustam?** ♦ **Ita. Faustam amō. Et Claudiam amō.**

8. **In scaphā tū magna saxa portāre nōn potes!** ♦ **Sed scapha est magna!**

9. **Cūr Rōmulus mūrum hodiē aedificat?** ♦ **Oppidum nōn habet mūrum. Sine mūrō oppidum servāre nōn possumus.** ♦ **Cūr Rōmulus mūrum circum oppidum aedificat? Rōmulus in oppidō nōn habitat.** ♦ **Nesciō.**

10. **Cūr tū nunc aegrōtās?** ♦ **In scaphā sumus!** ♦ **Tū pīrāta es! Tū aegrōtāre nōn potes!** ♦ **Sed aegrōtō.** ♦ **Tū nōn es pīrāta bonus.**

Answers on page 258.

LESSON 28

NEW WORD   **fortasse**

MEANING   *perhaps*

PRONUNCIATION TIP: The emphasis or stress is on the second syllable, so it sounds something like *for-TAH-seh*.

Our new word for this lesson is related to other Latin words like **fōrtūna** which means *fortune* and **fōrs** which means *chance*.

Here's an example sentence with the word **fortasse**:

Ubi sunt equī? *(Where are the horses?)* ♦ **Nesciō. Fortasse in agrō sunt.** *(I don't know. Perhaps they are in the field.)*

EXERCISES

1. **Paulus abest. Ubi est Paulus nunc?** ♦ **Nesciō. Fortasse domī manet quod aegrōtat.**
2. **Salvē. Lucrētia et Semprōnia absunt. Ubi sunt nunc?** ♦ **Nesciō, sed fortasse in oppidō sunt.** ♦ **Valē.**
3. **Agricola validus saxa ab agrīs portat.** ♦ **Cūr?** ♦ **Sunt multa saxa in agrō. Agricola agrum cum multīs saxīs arāre nōn potest.**
4. **Gulielmus abest. Ubi nunc est Gulielmus?** ♦ **Fortasse in silvā est.** ♦ **Gulielmus nōn est in silvā. Gulielmus numquam in silvā ambulat quod bestiās timet.**
5. **Ubi sumus? Ubi est scapha? Sumusne in īnsulā?** ♦ **Fortasse. Terram videō, et aqua est circum terram. Sumusne in īnsulā?** ♦ **Tū nōn es nauta bonus.**
6. **Fīlius Rōbertī abest et agrum nōn arat. Ubi nunc est fīlius Rōbertī?** ♦ **Nesciō.** ♦ **Fīlius Rōbertī est puer malus!**
7. **Equus nōn est validus. Puerum ab oppidō ad silvam portāre nōn potest.** ♦ **Fortasse puer ad silvam ambulāre potest.** ♦ **Puer ad silvam sine cibō et aquā ambulāre nōn potest.** ♦ **Fortasse porcus puerum portāre potest?** ♦ **Porcus puerum portāre nōn potest!**

41

8. **Cornēlia et Portia hodiē in oppidum dōna portant. Cūr ad oppidum dōna portant?** ♦ **Rēgīna hodiē in oppidō adest. Saepe Cornēlia et Portia rēgīnae dōna dant quod rēgīnam amant.**

9. **Christophorus semper patriam gladiō et scūtō servat.**

10. **Habentne porcī cibum hodiē?** ♦ **Habēmusne porcōs?** ♦ **Certē! Multōs porcōs habēmus! Tū agricola malus es!**

Answers on page 259.

QUICK ✏ REVIEW

If you take the genitive singular form of a noun and remove the ending, you are left with the *genitive stem*. For example, the genitive singular form of **ager** is **agrī**. If you remove the ending from **agrī**, you are left with **agr-**, which is the genitive stem. Not all textbooks refer to this stem as the genitive stem. Some call it the *stem*, others call it the *theme*, while others call it the *base*. But it doesn't really matter what you call it—all those names are referring to the same thing. In this book, for maximum clarity, I will call it the genitive stem just as I did in *Getting Started with Latin*.

LESSON 29

NEW WORD   **aeger, aegra, aegrum**

MEANING   *sick*

PRONUNCIATION TIP: In classical pronunciation, **aeger** will sound like *EYE-gerr*, but in ecclesiastical pronunciation it will sound something like *EH-jerr*, with a soft *g* sound.

This new adjective probably looks familiar to you because you already know a word related to it: the verb **aegrōtō**. It's a first and second declension adjective, but this particular one is special because the masculine form ends in **-er** instead of **-us**, as you might expect. This means that in the masculine gender, the declension pattern of this adjective will be the same kind as the noun **ager** *(field)*. So, the genitive singular of **aeger** will be **aegrī**. (By the way, **aeger** and **ager** look very similar, so don't get them confused).

To get you started, here are some examples with this new adjective in the different genders.

- **vir aeger** *(sick man)*
- **fēmina aegra** *(sick woman)*
- **oppidum aegrum** *(sick town)*

So, it's no big deal. The only thing to remember here is that the masculine forms have the same kind of declension pattern as **ager**. That's all there is to it. Everything else is the same as all the other first and second declension adjectives you know.

Now that you know the adjective **aeger, aegra, aegrum**, you know two ways to say *I am sick* in Latin. Observe:

- **Aegrōtō.** *(I am sick.)*
- **Aeger/aegra sum.** *(I am sick.)*

If you continue to study Latin, you will find that just as in English, there can be several ways to say the same thing. Learning to say the same thing in different ways is a normal part of learning any new language.

EXERCISES

1. **Ubi est Jūlia? Cūr Jūlia abest hodiē?** ♦ **Jūlia est aegra hodiē.**
2. **Estne Tiberius nunc domī? Aegrōtatne?** ♦ **Ita. Hodiē Tiberius est aeger.**
3. **Ō Pūblī, ubi est equus? In stabulō nōn est.** ♦ **Nesciō. Nunc porcōs cūrō.**
4. **Vidēre nōn possum.** ♦ **Tū vidēre nōn potes quod lūna nōn est in caelō.** ♦ **Cūr sumus in silvā? Bestiās silvārum timeō!** ♦ **Ego bestiās nōn timeō quod gladium habeō.**
5. **Ō Carole, ubi est Cornēlia hodiē? Aegrōtatne?** ♦ **Minimē. Numquam Cornēlia aegrōtat. Domī est, sed nōn est aegra.**
6. **Ō Tullia, potesne hodiē labōrāre?** ♦ **Ita, nōn aegrōtō. Agrōs cūrāre possum et porcīs cibum dare possum.**
7. **Salvēte ō agricolae! Habētisne equum?** ♦ **Nōn sumus agricolae. Poētae sumus.** ♦ **Fortasse fābulam bonam habētis?** ♦ **Certē, multās fābulās bonās habēmus. Poētae bonī sumus!**
8. **Habetne rēgīna multam pecūniam?** ♦ **Ita, rēgīna multam pecūniam habet.** ♦ **Habetne rēgīna aurum?** ♦ **Certē. Rēgīna multum aurum et multum argentum habet.**
9. **Poēta fīliābus Semprōniae nunc fābulam bonam narrat.** ♦ **Fīliae Semprōniae fābulās amant.**
10. **Ō Lāvīnia, cūr domī cum Claudiā es?** ♦ **Claudiam hodiē cūrō quod aegrōtat.** ♦ **Tū fēmina bona es!**

Answers on page 259.

QUICK ✏ REVIEW

A conjugation is a pattern of verb forms. In Latin, there are four conjugations, and each verb belongs to one of those conjugations. So far, you have worked with the first conjugation and second conjugation. For verbs of the first conjugation, the infinitive ends in **-āre** and the letter *a* comes before the personal ending. Examples: **nāvigat, ambulāmus, spectās.** For verbs of the second conjugation, the infinitive ends in **-ēre** and the letter *e* comes before the personal ending. Examples: **vidēs, habēmus, manent.**

LESSON 30

NEW WORD   **adsum**

MEANING   *I am present*

Our new word for this lesson is the opposite of **absum**. Instead of meaning *I am absent*, it means *I am present*.

Like **absum**, the word **adsum** is also a combination of two words: **ad** and **sum**.

> **ad** + **sum** = **adsum**

The preposition **ad** means *to*, but it can also mean several other things like *at, near, against*, etc. So literally, **adsum** has the idea of being "at" someplace, in the sense of being present there. Translate it into English as *I am present*.

Any form of **sum** can have the **ad-** prefix. Here are the six present tense forms of **adsum**:

	SINGULAR	PLURAL
FIRST PERSON	**adsum**	**adsumus**
SECOND PERSON	**ades**	**adestis**
THIRD PERSON	**adest**	**adsunt**

So, **adsum** means *I am present*, **ades** means *you are present*, and so on, and so forth. Here are a few example sentences to help you start working with **adsum**.

- **Rēgīna adest.** *(The queen is present.)*
- **Tertius et Claudia adsunt**. *(Tertius and Claudia are present.)*
- **Ubi est Helena? Adestne?** *(Where is Helen? Is she present?)*

- **Nautae adsunt.** *(The sailors are present.)*

EXERCISES

1. **Ubi est Gulielmus?** ♦ **Adsum!**
2. **Salvēte, ō puerī. Cūr Tiberius abest?** ♦ **Nesciō. Fortasse hodiē aegrōtat.** ♦ **Tiberius hodiē nōn est aeger. Domī est, sed nōn est aeger.**
3. **Puellae adsunt, sed puerī absunt. Ubi sunt puerī? Suntne puerī aegrī?** ♦ **Ita. Puerī domī sunt quod aegrōtant.**
4. **Salvēte, ō puerī! Ō Jūlī, adestne Matthaeus?** ♦ **Minimē, Matthaeus abest.** ♦ **Ubi est Matthaeus?** ♦ **Nesciō. Fortasse Matthaeus nunc cum agricolīs in agrīs labōrat.** ♦ **Matthaeus numquam in agrīs labōrat.**
5. **Quīntus abest. Ubi est Quīntus?** ♦ **Fortasse mūrum oppidī servat.** ♦ **Habēmusne mūrum?** ♦ **Ita. Magnum mūrum circum oppidum habēmus.**
6. **Egone in casā hodiē manēre possum?** ♦ **Certē, tū in casā manēre potes.**
7. **Ō Jācōbe, cūr porcī cibum nōn habent?** ♦ **Agricolae malī porcōs nōn cūrant.** ♦ **Ō agricolae malī, cūr porcīs cibum nōn datis?**
8. **Salvē, ō Rōmule. Cūr Claudius abest? Aegrōtatne?** ♦ **Ita, hodiē Claudius est aeger. Domī Claudium cūrō.** ♦ **Tū vir bonus es. Valē.**
9. **Ō Jōsēphe, cūr es laetus hodiē?** ♦ **Ego Lucrētiam amō!** ♦ **Cūr tū Lucrētiam amās?** ♦ **Lucrētia est fēmina bona. Semper laeta est, et semper puerīs puellīsque oppidī cibum dat.** ♦ **Lucrētia est fēmina bona!** ♦ **Ita, Lucrētiam amō quod fēmina bona est.**
10. **Salvē, ō Tullia. Cūr tū scaphās spectās?** ♦ **Scaphās cotīdiē spectō quod scaphās amō.** ♦ **Pīrātās videō!**

Answers on page 259.

QUICK ✏ REVIEW

Whenever I introduce a new noun to you, I will give you both the nominative singular and genitive singular forms. Whenever you learn a new Latin noun, you must memorize both of those forms—not just the nominative singular!

LESSON 31

NEW WORD   **valeō / valēre**

MEANING   *I am well / to be well*

Our new word for this lesson is a verb of the second conjugation. It can mean things like *I am well* or *I am strong*. It's related to the adjective **validus, valida, validum** which means *strong*. It is also related to the word **valē**, because when you say **valē** you are literally saying to someone, *Be well!* Also, this word is related to English words like *valent, valency, value,* and *valor*.

	Singular	Plural
First Person	**valeō**	**valēmus**
Second Person	**valēs**	**valētis**
Third Person	**valet**	**valent**

Infinitive	**valēre**

Valeō is the opposite of **aegrōtō**, because it means things like *I am well, I am strong,* or *I am healthy*. Here's an example sentence with **valeō**:

Lūcius nōn aegrōtat. Hodiē valet. (*Lucius is not sick. Today he is well.*)

EXERCISES

1. **Ō Catharīna, tūne aegra hodiē es?** ♦ **Minimē, valeō!**
2. **Agricola hodiē equōs cūrāre nōn potest.** ♦ **Agricola est aeger, sed valēmus. Fortasse equōs cūrāre possumus.**

3. Puerōs cūrō quod aegrī sunt. Estne Claudia aegra hodiē? ◆ Minimē, Claudia valet. In casā nunc labōrat.

4. Ad scholam hodiē ambulāre nōn possumus. Aegrōtāmus! ◆ Ō puellae malae! Nōn aegrōtātis, sed valētis. Domī hodiē manēre nōn potestis. ◆ Fortasse ad actam ambulāre possumus.

5. Puellae puerīque absunt nunc. Ubi sunt? Aegrōtantne puerī et puellae? ◆ Nesciō, sed Cornēlia et Matthaeus adsunt.

6. Ō Portia, ego Christophorum amō. ◆ Amāsne tū Christophorum? ◆ Ita. Puer bonus est. ◆ Ego Christophorum amō. ◆ Tūne Christophorum amās? ◆ Ita. ◆ Christophorum amāmus, sed Christophorus Helenam amat.

7. Scapham tū aedificāre nōn potes, ō Pūblī. ◆ Cūr? ◆ Tū lignum nōn habēs. ◆ Sed prope silvam sumus. Fortasse lignum ā silvā portāre possumus. ◆ Fortasse, sed magnae bestiae in silvā habitant. ◆ Fortasse bestiae hodiē absunt.

8. Ō Aemilia, habitāsne prope actam? ◆ Minimē, in oppidō habitō. ◆ Tūne casam habēs? ◆ Ita, habeō casam prope mūrum oppidī.

9. Adestne Rōmulus? ◆ Minimē. Rōmulus in silvam cum Rūfō ambulat.

10. Ubi est fīlius Paulī? ◆ Fīlius Paulī porcōs nunc cūrat, et equīs cibum dat.

Answers on page 260.

QUICK ✏ REVIEW

In Latin, adjectives generally come after the noun they modify: **Equum validum habeō** *(I have a strong horse)*. But adjectives of size or quantity generally come before the noun they modify: **Multam pecūniam habeō** *(I have much money)*.

LESSON 32

NEW WORD **discipulus / discipula**

MEANING *male student / female student*

Our new words for this lesson are related to the English words *discipline* and *disciple*. For a female student, use the word **discipula**, a feminine noun of the first declension. For a male student, use the word **discipulus**, which is a masculine noun of the second declension. If there is a group of students comprised of both males and females, use the masculine plural form, **discipulī**.

EXERCISES

1. **Salvē, ō Rōmule. Ubi sunt discipulī?** ◆ **Discipulī in scholā sunt, sed Carolus nōn est in scholā. Carolus abest.** ◆ **Cūr Carolus abest?** ◆ **Carolus aeger est. Domī est.**

2. **Discipulī absunt.** ◆ **Fortasse ad actam ambulant. Discipulī actam amant!** ◆ **Discipulī malī sunt!**

3. **Discipulī adsunt, sed cibum nōn habent. Cūr cibum nōn habent?** ◆ **Nesciō, sed nunc discipulīs cibum damus.**

4. **Discipulī absunt. Ubi sunt?** ◆ **Nesciō. Fortasse discipulī domī sunt.**

5. **Claudia abest. Ubi est Claudia?** ◆ **Ad silvam cum discipulīs ambulat.**

6. **Ō Tullia, cūr Claudius nunc in silvam ambulat?** ◆ **Lignum ē silvā ad oppidum portat.** ◆ **Cūr lignum portat?** ◆ **Incolae oppidī mūrum lignō circum oppidum aedificant.** ◆ **Cūr mūrum aedificant?** ◆ **Sunt multī pīrātae prope oppidum.**

7. **Ō Aurēlia, esne discipula?** ◆ **Ita, discipula sum. Ego ad scholam cotīdiē ambulō.**

8. **Salvē, ō Tite. Valēsne hodiē?** ◆ **Ita, ego valeō hodiē, sed fīlia Marcī aegrōtat.** ◆ **Cūr aegrōtat fīlia Marcī?** ◆ **Nesciō, sed hodiē domī est.** ◆ **Valē, ō Tite.** ◆ **Valē.**

9. **Ubi est porcus?** ◆ **Habēmusne porcum?** ◆ **Ita. Porcum habēmus, sed nunc abest. Ubi est porcus?** ◆ **Nesciō.** ◆ **Tū agricola malus es.**

10. **Salvēte, ō discipulae. Ego hodiē adsum, sed Tiberius abest.** ◆ **Cūr Tiberius abest? Valetne Tiberius?** ◆ **Minimē. Tiberius aegrōtat.** ◆ **Estne Tiberius domī?** ◆ **Ita, domī est. Fīliī fīliaeque Tiberiī cūrant Tiberium.**

Answers on page 260.

49

LESSON 33

NEW WORD   **magister / magistra**

MEANING   *male teacher / female teacher*

PRONUNCIATION TIP: The accent is on the middle syllable, so in classical pronuncation, **magister** sounds like *mah-GIST-stair* and in ecclesiastical pronunciation it sounds like *mah-JEE-stair*.

Our new words for this lesson are related to the English word *master*. In fact, *master* is what the word **magister** means, in the sense of *schoolmaster*. So that's why we translate it into English as *teacher*. It's also related to English words like *magistrate* and *magistracy*.

A **magister** would be a male teacher. That's a masculine noun of the second declension. It has the same declension pattern as **ager**, so the genitive singular form would be **magistrī**. **Magistra** is a feminine noun of the first declension. If there is a group of teachers comprised of both males and females, use the masculine plural form, **magistrī**.

Remember that the genitive stem can be found by taking the genitive singular form of a noun and removing the ending. For the noun **magister**, the genitive singular form is **magistrī**. So if we remove the ending, that leaves **magistr-**. That's the genitive stem for this particular noun. You can use the genitive stem as a base to which you can add the various endings for that particular declension.

Here's a chart for **magister** so you can observe once again how the genitive stem functions. The nominative singular and genitive singular forms are circled.

	SINGULAR	PLURAL
NOMINATIVE (SUBJ./PRED. NOM.)	magister	**magistrī**
GENITIVE (POSSESSION)	magistrī	**magistrōrum**
DATIVE (IND. OBJECT)	**magistrō**	**magistrīs**
ACCUSATIVE (DIRECT OBJECT)	**magistrum**	**magistrōs**
ABLATIVE (MANY USES)	**magistrō**	**magistrīs**

50

The genitive stem is a *very* important concept in Latin, so remember it! You'll need it again in the near future!

EXERCISES

1. **Portia et Cornēlia nunc magistrae sunt. ♦ Cūr magistrae sunt? ♦ Discipulās amant. Scholam amant. ♦ Magistrae bonae sunt!**
2. **Estne Claudius magister? ♦ Minimē, Claudius est discipulus.**
3. **Ō Semprōnia, tūne discipula es? ♦ Minimē. Magistra nunc sum, sed scholam nōn habeō. ♦ Fortasse virī fēminaeque oppidī scholam aedificāre possunt. ♦ Fortasse. Magistra bona sum!**
4. **Adestne Petrus? ♦ Adsum! Salvē, ō magistra! ♦ Salvē, ō discipule!**
5. **Ō virī oppidī, cūr cotīdiē lignum ā silvā portātis? ♦ Scholam aedificāmus. ♦ Cūr? ♦ Magister multōs disicpulōs habet, sed scholam nōn habet. ♦ Virī bonī estis!**
6. **Ō equī, valētisne hodiē? Habētisne cibum? ♦ Valēmus, et cibum habēmus.**
7. **Ō Rūfe, cūr tū numquam ad īnsulam nāvigās? ♦ Saepe ad īnsulam nāvigō. ♦ Tūne scapham habēs? ♦ Minimē. Nāvigō in scaphā Rōbertī. Rōbertus est nauta bonus. Ad īnsulam hodiē cum Rōbertō nāvigō.**
8. **Cornēlia in silvam ambulat. Bestiās nōn timet.**
9. **Ō Marce, potesne natāre? ♦ Ita, natāre possum, sed numquam natō quod pīrātās timeō.**
10. **Magistra saepe discipulīs fābulās narrat.**

Answers on page 260.

QUICK ✏ REVIEW

The verb **dō** means *I give*. It is a verb of the first conjugation, but it is irregular because in several places it has a short *a* where you would expect a long *a*. For example, the infinitive is not **dāre**, but **dare**. Likewise, the first person plural is not **dāmus**, but **damus**. And the second person plural is not **dātis**, but **datis**.

LESSON 34

NEW WORD   **doceō / docēre**

MEANING   *I teach / to teach*

Doceō is a verb of the second conjugation. The infinitive is **docēre**.

Our new word for this lesson is related to English words like *doctor*, *doctrine*, and *docent* (someone who guides you around a museum).

Remember that in the second conjugation the letter *e* comes before the personal ending, and the infinitve ends in **-ēre**. Notice the long mark (called a *macron*) over the *e* in the **-ēre** ending.

Here's a chart so you can review the characteristics of the second conjugation while learning the different forms of **doceō**.

	SINGULAR	PLURAL
FIRST PERSON	**doceō**	**docēmus**
SECOND PERSON	**docēs**	**docētis**
THIRD PERSON	**docet**	**docent**

INFINITIVE	**docēre**

EXERCISES

1. **Magister sum. Cotīdiē discipulōs doceō.**
2. **Esne magister?** ♦ **Minimē, discipulōs nōn doceō.**

52

3. **Sumusne magistrī? Docēmusne discipulōs?** ♦ **Ita, cotīdiē discipulōs docēmus. Magistrī sumus.** ♦ **Possumusne hodiē domī manēre?**

4. **Schola multōs discipulōs habet, sed magistrās nōn habet.** ♦ **Cūr?** ♦ **Schola pecūniam nōn habet.** ♦ **Fortasse ego discipulōs docēre possum.**

5. **Ō Cornēlia, ubi est magistra? Magistra abest.** ♦ **Nesciō. Fortasse ad actam nunc ambulat.** ♦ **Magistra est mala! Fortasse tū hodiē discipulās docēre potes.**

6. **Discipulae bonae ad scholam cotīdiē ambulant, sed discipulae malae semper absunt.**

7. **Videō Rūfum, Cornēliam, et Jōsēphum...sed ubi est Titus?** ♦ **Nesciō. Abestne Titus?** ♦ **Ita. Fortasse Titus domī aegrōtat.** ♦ **Minimē, Titus nōn est aeger. Discipulus malus est, sed nōn est aeger.**

8. **Ō Lāvīnia, amāsne Rōmulum?** ♦ **Minimē, ego Quīntum amō.** ♦ **Quīntus est vir bonus, sed magister est, et pecūniam nōn habet.** ♦ **Fortasse, sed magnam casam cum equīs stabulīsque habet.**

9. **In oppidō habitō. Habitātisne in silvā?** ♦ **Minimē! Prope bestiās habitāre nōn possumus.**

10. **Tūne nāvigās ad patriam?** ♦ **Ita. Hodiē ad patriam nāvigō.** ♦ **Cūr ad patriam nāvigās?** ♦ **Nāvigō quod natāre nōn possum.**

Answers on page 261.

QUICK ✐ REVIEW

By now you know well the fact that Latin word order is much more flexible than English word order. There are however, a few general patterns of Latin word order that are worth knowing. Generally speaking, the subject will come first, then the indirect object, then the direct object, and then the verb. Of course, other words will be in there somewhere too, but that's just a general outline!

LESSON 35

NEW WORD   **parvus, parva, parvum**

MEANING   *small*

Our new word for this lesson is a first and second declension adjective.

EXERCISES

1. **Schola est parva, sed multōs discipulōs habēmus. ♦ Fortasse rēgīna magnam scholam aedificāre potest. ♦ Fortasse. Rēgīna multam pecūniam habet, sed pecūniam nōn habēmus.**

2. **Ego bestiās īnsulae nōn timeō. ♦ Cūr? ♦ Bestiae īnsulae sunt parvae. Ego parvās bestiās nōn timeō. ♦ Timēsne magnās bestiās? ♦ Ita. Ego numquam in silvā ambulō quod magnae bestiae in silvā habitant.**

3. **Cornēlius est magister. In parvā scholā docet. ♦ Cūr schola Cornēliī est parva? ♦ Cornēlius multōs disciplulōs nōn habet.**

4. **Jūlia est fēmina bona. ♦ Cūr? ♦ Semper equōs in stabulīs cūrat. Cotīdiē equīs cibum aquamque dat.**

5. **Ō Aemilia, cūr abes? Discipulae hodiē adsunt, sed tū abes. ♦ Hodiē domī maneō. Laeta sum domī. ♦ Tū domī manēre nōn potes! ♦ Cūr domī manēre nōn possum? ♦ Domī manēre nōn potes quod tū magistra es! Discipulās docēs!**

6. **Ubi est Catharīna hodiē? ♦ Adsum! ♦ Salvē, ō Catharīna! ♦ Salvē, ō magistra.**

7. **Ō Cornēlia et Helena, puellae bonae estis. ♦ Cūr? ♦ Puellae bonae estis quod numquam pugnātis cum puerīs, semper porcōs cūrātis, cotīdiē ad scholam ambulātis, et discipulae bonae estis.**

8. **Valēte, ō incolae oppidī. Ad patriam nunc ambulāmus.**

9. **Tū equus bonus es. ♦ Nōn sum equus. Sum porcus! ♦ Tūne porcus es? ♦ Tū agricola malus es.**

10. **Incolae oppidī mūrum saxīs aedificant. ♦ Cūr? ♦ Pīrātās timent. Pīrātae saepe ab īnsulīs ad oppidum nāvigant.**

Answers on page 261.

LESSON 36

HOW TO SAY "THIS" IN LATIN

In Latin, the word for *this* can have many different forms depending on case, number, and gender. Let's take it slowly and start by learning the nominative singular form of each gender.

The masculine form is the word **hic**. In classical pronunciation, **hic** is pronounced *hick*, and in ecclesiastical pronunciation it is pronounced something like *heek*. You can use **hic** with masculine nouns, like in these examples:

- **hic vir** *(this man)*
- **hic equus** *(this horse)*
- **hic nauta** *(this sailor)*

The feminine form is the word **haec**. In classical pronunciation, **haec** is pronounced *hike*, and in ecclesiastical pronunciation it is pronounced something like *heck*. You can use **haec** with feminine nouns, like in these examples:

- **haec fēmina** *(this woman)*
- **haec casa** *(this house)*
- **haec rēgīna** *(this queen)*

The neuter form is the word **hoc**. In both classical and ecclesiastical pronunciation, **hoc** sounds like *hoke*, but with the jaw more open. You can use **hoc** with neuter nouns, like in these examples:

- **hoc oppidum** *(this town)*
- **hoc scūtum** *(this shield)*
- **hoc dōnum** *(this gift)*

So, just for practice, repeat these three words in order: **hic, haec, hoc.**

Again, these forms are the nominative singular form of each of the three genders. If we took these nominative forms and put them in a chart, it would look like this:

55

	MASCULINE	FEMININE	NEUTER
NOMINATIVE (SUBJ./PRED. NOM.)	hic	haec	hoc
GENITIVE (POSSESSION)			
DATIVE (IND. OBJECT)			
ACCUSATIVE (DIRECT OBJECT)			
ABLATIVE (MANY USES)			

Since these forms are nominative singular, we will only practice using them in places where they are accompanying a nominative singular noun. We will not study the genitive, dative, accusative, or ablative forms in this book.

EXERCISES

1. **Hic equus est magnus.**
2. **Haec fēmina est fīlia Tiberiī.**
3. **Hoc oppidum est parvum, sed multōs incolās habet.**
4. **Hic puer est malus! ♦ Cūr? ♦ Numquam equōs cūrat, et semper pugnat cum puellīs!**
5. **Haec scapha est parva, sed valida. ♦ Ita, sed tū saxa in scaphā portāre nōn potes.**
6. **Hoc lignum est validum.**
7. **Haec schola parva est, sed multōs discipulōs habet. ♦ Sed discipulī malī sunt.**
8. **Hic vir scaphās spectat. ♦ Cūr scaphās spectat? ♦ Fortasse nauta est. ♦ Hic vir nauta nōn est! Pīrāta est!**
9. **Haec magistra multōs discipulōs docet.**
10. **Ō magistra, habeō fābulam bonam. Fortasse discipulīs fābulam narrāre possum. ♦ Minime, Rūfe. Tū semper discipulīs fābulās malās narrās. Fābulam malam narrāre nōn potes. ♦ Fābulās malās saepe narrō, ō magistra, sed haec fābula est bona.**

Answers on page 261.

LESSON 37

NEW WORD   **bibliothēca, bibliothēcae**

MEANING   *library*

Bibliothēca is a feminine noun of the first declension.

As long as we are talking about libraries, let's learn the word for *librarian*. The word for a female librarian is the first declension noun **bibliothēcāria**. For a male librarian, the word is the second declension noun **bibliothēcārius**. These words are probably the longest Latin words you know, weighing in at seven syllables each!

We English speakers often use the preposition *at* to say where someone is. We say things like *at school, at the library, at the store,* etc. When the ancient Romans wanted to say that kind of thing, they used the preposition **in**, like this:

     Quīntus est in bibliothēcā. *(Quintus is at the library.)*

Of course, the Latin preposition **in** can also mean *inside*, so the sentence **Quīntus est in bibliothēcā** could also be saying that Quintus is inside the library, as opposed to being outside of the library. So, when you translate this kind of exercise, think about the context of the sentence and try to translate it in the way that sounds the most natural in English.

EXERCISES

1. **Ō Petre, estne bibliothēca in oppidō? ♦ Ita, est parva bibliothēca in oppidō. Prope scholam est. ♦ Bibliothēcās amō! Fortasse ad bibliothēcam ambulāre possumus.**

2. **Ō Semprōnia, tūne es bibliothēcāria? ♦ Ita, bibliothēcāria sum. In bibliothēcā labōrō.**

3. **Ō Jācōbe, cūr Rūfus ad bibliothēcam nunc ambulat? Et cūr dōnum portat? ♦ Aurēlia est bibliothēcāria in bibliothēcā. Rūfus Aurēliam amat.**

4. **Ō Fulvia, haec scapha est magna. ♦ Minimē, haec scapha parva est. ♦ Haec scapha multōs nautās portāre potest!**

57

5. Ō Tullia, ubi habitat hic puer? ♦ Hic puer in oppidō habitat.

6. Discipulī ā scholā ad bibliothēcam ambulant.

7. Adestne Marcus? Valetne hodiē? ♦ Minimē, Marcus abest. ♦ Ubi est Marcus? ♦ Nesciō. Fortasse domī est. ♦ Fortasse aeger est.

8. Virī bonī īnsulam servant, sed scūta nōn habent. ♦ Habentne virī gladiōs? ♦ Ita, gladiōs habent. ♦ Ubi sunt virī? ♦ Virī nunc in scaphīs sunt. Circum īnsulam nunc nāvigant.

9. Hic magister malus numquam discipulōs docet. ♦ Cūr? ♦ Nesciō. Semper abest. ♦ Fortasse discipulōs docēre possumus. ♦ Minimē! Nōn sumus magistrī!

10. Ō Petre, cūr in scaphā sumus? ♦ Īnsulam servāmus. ♦ Cūr īnsulam servāmus? ♦ Īnsulam servāmus quod multī pīrātae ad īnsulam cum gladiīs nunc nāvigant. ♦ Habēmusne gladiōs? ♦ Gladiōs nōn habēmus. ♦ Fortasse ego domī manēre possum, et tū īnsulam servāre potes.

Answers on page 261.

QUICK ✎ REVIEW

When a certain noun has a masculine form and a feminine form (like **discipulus** and **discipula**) use masculine plural forms to refer to a group made up of both males and females.

LESSON 38

THE THEATER

At first, the ancient Romans didn't have permanent theaters. Instead, they would build a temporary wooden theater when they needed one and then tear it down afterward. Plays would be performed in these temporary theaters at annual religious festivals. The first permanent theater in Rome was built by a powerful Roman general named Pompey the Great (that's **Pompēius Magnus** in Latin). Pompey's huge theater complex, which was finished in 55 BC, included not only a theater, but also gardens, and even a place for the Roman Senate to meet. In fact, it was in this very meeting place (called a **cūria**) where Julius Caesar was assassinated a little over ten years later.

The basic design of the Roman theater, like many elements of Roman culture, was borrowed from the Greeks. The typical Greek theater was carved into a hillside and had a semicircular shape. Here's a simple diagram I made so you can see its major features as if looking down from above.

A TYPICAL GREEK THEATER

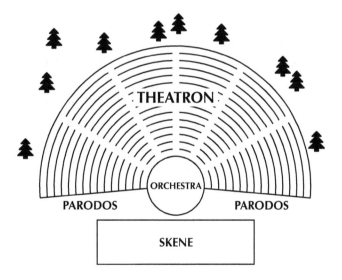

The Greek theater changed over time, but here are a few major features to know about: the *theatron* was the seating area. This Greek word is related to a Greek verb that means *to see*. It's the source of the Latin word **theātrum** and our English word *theater*. The *orchestra* was a circular area where the play was performed.

59

The *skene* (pronounced *skay-NAY*) was the backdrop of the play. The *parodos* was a side passage leading to the orchestra area.

Hundreds of years later, when the Romans started to build permanent theaters, they made several changes. Instead of being carved into a hillside like Greek theaters, Roman theaters were generally freestanding structures. Also, the **orchēstra** was no longer a complete circle because the stage (called the **pulpitum**) came right up to the seating area, giving the **orchēstra** a semicircular shape. The **cavea** was the seating area. The **scaenae frōns** was the stage's backdrop, usually with three doors from which actors could enter or exit.

A TYPICAL ROMAN THEATER

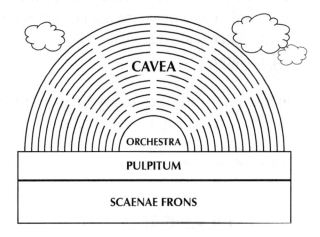

So, as far as Latin goes, you'll want to know the Latin noun **theātrum** (pronounced *tay-AAH-trum*). It's a neuter noun of the second declension.

In the last lesson, I mentioned that the Romans used the preposition **in** as we English speakers often use the preposition *at*. So when the Romans said **in theātrō**, it meant basically what we mean today when we say *at the theater*. It could also mean *inside the theater*. Again, try to translate these phrases in the way that sounds the most natural in English.

EXERCISES

1. **Hoc theātrum magnum est!**
2. **Ō Aurēlia, ubi nunc est Claudia?** ♦ **Claudia in theātrō est.** ♦ **Claudia theātrum amat!**
3. **Ō Rūfe, ubi est theātrum?** ♦ **Nōn habēmus theātrum in patriā.** ♦ **Fortasse rēgīna theātrum aedificāre potest.** ♦ **Fortasse, sed incolae patriae multam pecūniam nōn habent.**

60

4. Ō magistra, ubi discipulī sunt hodiē? ♦ Multī discipulī sunt domī hodiē quod aegrōtant, sed tū ades quod valēs. ♦ Ita, valeō, sed fortasse hodiē domī manēre possum. Valē, ō magistra.

5. Hic porcus est magnus! Cūr porcus est magnus? ♦ Agricola porcō cotīdiē multum cibum dat.

6. Ubi est Pūblius? ♦ In stabulō est. Equum cūrat. ♦ Cūr Pūblius equum cūrat? Pūblius nōn est agricola.

7. Ō Helena, tūne es magistra? ♦ Ita, ego discipulōs cotīdiē doceō.

8. Estne Quīntus magister? ♦ Minimē. Quīntus est discipulus malus! ♦ Num Quīntus discipulus malus est? ♦ Ita, discipulus malus est. Cotīdiē abest, et saepe domī manet.

9. In silvam puellae puerīque ambulant.

10. Parva est haec bibliothēca. Ubi est bibliothēcāria? ♦ Nesciō.

Answers on page 262.

QUICK ✎ REVIEW

The adjective **magnus**, **magna**, **magnum** can mean *large* or *great*. When you see this adjective with an inanimate object such as a boat, it probably means *large*: **magna scapha** *(large boat)*. But if you see this adjective describing a person, it probably means *great* in the sense of important, influential, or powerful: **magna rēgīna** *(a great queen)*.

LESSON 39

NEW WORD   **liber, librī**

MEANING   *book*

Our new word for this lesson is related to the English word *library*. It's a masculine noun of the second declension, with the same declension pattern as the noun **ager** and **magister**.

In ancient times, the word **liber** really referred to a scroll. The book, as we know it today, was invented later, and it was called a **cōdex**. But **liber** means a book in the sense of a long written document, so it's OK if we translate it as *book*.

EXERCISES

1. **Hic liber est malus! ♦ Cūr? ♦ Fābulam malam habet.**
2. **Cūr ambulātis ad bibliothēcam? ♦ Librōs ad bibliothēcam portāmus. Librōs bonōs amāmus.**
3. **Haec bibliothēca parva est, sed multōs librōs habet. ♦ Haec bibliothēca est parva, sed bona.**
4. **Cūr magistra discipulīs librōs hodiē dat? ♦ Sine librīs, magistra discipulōs docēre nōn potest.**
5. **Magister fīliābus rēgīnae fābulam narrat. ♦ Cūr? ♦ Puellae fābulās amant.**
6. **Tūne equōs hodiē cūrās? ♦ Ita. Ego agricola sum, et equōs cotīdiē cūrō.**
7. **Ō Fausta, cūr semper in bibliothēcā ades? Amāsne librōs? ♦ Minimē. Marcum amō. Marcus est bibliothēcārius.**
8. **Habetne Semprōnia equum? ♦ Minimē, sed scapham habet. ♦ Cūr? ♦ Semprōnia saepe ad patriam nāvigat. ♦ Cūr ad patriam nāvigat? ♦ Fīlia Semprōniae in patriā habitat.**
9. **Ubi est poēta hodiē? ♦ Poēta est in theātrō. Hodiē puellīs et puerīs fābulās narrat. ♦ Puellae puerīque fābulās amant!**
10. **Ō bibliothēcārī, habēsne tū librum bonum? ♦ Tū in bibliothēcā es. Haec bibliothēca multōs librōs habet. ♦ Fortasse hic liber est bonus.**

Answers on page 262.

LESSON 40

NEW WORD   **novus, nova, novum**

MEANING   *new*

Our new word for this lesson is…well, literally a "new" word. It's a first and second declension adjective which is related to English words like *novel* and *novelty*. This adjective is unusual because it often comes *before* the noun it modifies, like this:

Novum equum habeō. *(I have a new horse.)*

EXERCISES

1. **Novum librum habeō. ♦ Novōs librōs amō. ♦ Cūr? ♦ Bibliothēcāria sum.**
2. **Hoc oppidum novam bibliothēcam habet. ♦ Ubi est nova bibliothēca? ♦ Prope scholam est.**
3. **Ō fēmina, estne bibliothēca in oppidō? ♦ Ita, et ego nova bibliothēcāria sum! Habēmus multōs librōs. Ego librōs cotīdiē cūrō.**
4. **Ō fīlī, cūr Jācōbus abest? ♦ Nesciō. Fortasse Jācōbus in agrō est. Saepe in agrīs labōrat. ♦ Jācōbus hodiē nōn labōrat! In theātrō nunc est!**
5. **Ubi est Jōsēphus? ♦ Oppidum gladiō scūtōque servat. ♦ Cūr? ♦ Mūrum nōn habēmus circum oppidum. ♦ Fortasse novum mūrum aedificāre potestis. ♦ Multa saxa habēmus. ♦ Fortasse saxīs mūrum aedificāre potestis.**
6. **Cūr Decimus ad īnsulam cum puerīs et puellīs nōn natat? Timetne aquam? ♦ Ita, Decimus aquam timet.**
7. **Sumusne in scaphā? ♦ Sumus. ♦ Cūr? ♦ Hodiē ad patriam nāvigāmus. ♦ Aegrōtō. Hodiē nāvigāre nōn possum.**
8. **Ō Cornēlia, tūne porcum habēs? ♦ Ita. Ego multōs porcōs habeō.**
9. **Egone agricola sum? ♦ Nesciō. Arāsne tū agrōs? ♦ Ita. ♦ Cūrāsne equōs? ♦ Cotīdiē. ♦ Tū agricola es.**
10. **Discipulōs docēre nōn possumus. ♦ Cūr? ♦ Haec schola librōs nōn habet. ♦ Prope bibliothēcam sumus. Fortasse tū et discipulī ad bibliothēcam ambulāre potestis. Bibliothēca multōs librōs habet.**

Answers on page 262.

LESSON 41

NEW WORD   **properō / properāre**

MEANING   *I hurry / to hurry*

The verb **properō** is a verb of the first conjugation. Notice that **properāre**, the infinitive, ends in -**āre**.

EXERCISES

1. **Ō Carole, cūr properās nunc ad scholam? ◆ Magister sum. Discipulās cotīdiē doceō. ◆ Sed aeger es hodiē. Tū domī hodiē manēre potes. ◆ Nōn sum aeger! Ego hodiē valeō! Valē!**
2. **Ō fīlī, cūr properās? ◆ Ad scholam properō quod bonus discipulus sum. Valē!**
3. **Ō nauta, cūr ad īnsulam properāmus? ◆ Multī pīrātae ad īnsulam nunc nāvigant. ◆ Fortasse ab īnsulā nāvigāre possumus. ◆ Timēsne pīrātās?**
4. **Sumne magistra? ◆ Nesciō. Tūne discipulōs cotīdiē docēs? ◆ Ita. ◆ Magistra es.**
5. **Ō fēminae, cūr ad scholam properātis? ◆ Magistrae sumus. ◆ Valēte, ō magistrae.**
6. **Ubi est Rūfus? ◆ Nesciō. Rūfus abest. ◆ Cūr Rūfus abest? ◆ Nesciō. Fortasse Rūfus domī est. ◆ Fortasse Rūfus in theātrō est. ◆ Hoc oppidum theātrum nōn habet.**
7. **Labōrāsne tū in novā bibliothēcā? ◆ Ita. Cotīdiē librōs cūrō quod bibliothēcāria sum. ◆ Ubi est nova bibliothēca? ◆ In oppidō, prope casam Rōmulī.**
8. **Puellae puerīque ad actam properant. ◆ Cūr? ◆ Actam amant!**
9. **Ō magistra, tūne novōs librōs habēs? ◆ Haec schola novōs librōs nōn habet. Sine novīs librīs, discipulōs docēre nōn possumus.**
10. **Ō Decime, ego nunc novum porcum habeō. ◆ Estne magnus porcus? ◆ Ita, hic porcus est magnus. Ego porcō multum cibum cotīdiē dō.**

Answers on page 263.

LESSON 42

NEW WORD   **ē, ex**

MEANING   *out of*

Our new word for this lesson is a preposition that takes the ablative case. It's related to English words like *exit, export,* and *exclamation.* This preposition is similar to a preposition you already know: the preposition **ā, ab** because it can be spelled two ways depending on what comes after it. If the next word starts with a consonant, it will be spelled **ē**. But if the next word starts with a vowel, it will be spelled **ex**. Here are a couple of practice sentences to get you started working with this useful preposition.

- **Ambulō ē casā.** *(I am walking out of the house.)*
- **Ambulō ex oppidō.** *(I am walking out of the town.)*

You can also use this preposition to show that you are using a certain material to build or make something. For example, if you use rock as source material to build a house, you can say this:

    Casam ē saxō aedificō. *(I am building a house out of rock.)*

In that example, the speaker not saying that the rocks themselves are being stacked up to make the house, but that rock is the material from which the house is being built. Therefore, the house is being built "out of" rock.

If someone is using the rocks themselves to build something, say, by stacking up the rocks on top of each other, you can express that kind of thought in Latin by using the ablative of means without a preposition, like this:

    Mūrum saxīs aedificō. *(I am building a wall with rocks.)*

In that example, the speaker is not saying that rock is a source material for building, but that the rocks themselves are being used to build the wall. Therefore, the word **saxīs** is an ablative of means, and you don't need to use a preposition.

EXERCISES

1. **Agricolae ex oppidō ad agrōs properant.** ◆ **Cūr?** ◆ **Hodiē agrōs arant.** ◆ **Fortasse in agrīs hodiē labōrāre possumus.** ◆ **Minimē. Agricolae nōn sumus!**

2. **Aemilia ē scholā in bibliothēcam properat.** ◆ **Cūr?** ◆ **Aemilia est bibliothēcāria. Cotīdiē in bibliothēcā labōrat. Librōs cūrat, et semper puellīs puerīsque fābulās narrat.** ◆ **Aemilia bibliothēcāria bona est!**

3. **Agricolae lignum ē silvā portant.** ◆ **Cūr lignum portant?** ◆ **Hodiē parvam casam ē lignō aedificant.** ◆ **Cūr casam aedificant?** ◆ **Carolus casam nōn habet. Carolus in silvā habitat, sed nunc in casā habitāre potest.**

4. **In bibliothēcā habitō.** ◆ **Minimē, tū in bibliothēcā nōn habitās.** ◆ **Sed semper in bibliothēcā adsum.** ◆ **Tū bibliothēcārius es! Tū in bibliothēcā labōrās, sed in bibliothēcā nōn habitās!**

5. **Claudius ē novā bibliothēcā cum multīs librīs properat. Librōs amat!** ◆ **Ita, Claudius est discipulus bonus.**

6. **Ō Flāvia, esne magistra?** ◆ **Certē. Cotīdiē discipulās doceō.**

7. **Hoc oppidum nunc est magnum.** ◆ **Ita, magnum est. Hoc oppidum habet magnam scholam, novam bibliothēcam, et magnum mūrum.** ◆ **Multī virī et multae fēminae nunc in oppidō habitant.** ◆ **Novum theātrum ē lignō nunc aedificant.**

8. **Salvēte, ō porcī!** ◆ **Salvē, ō agricola.** ◆ **Valētisne hodiē?** ◆ **Ita. Valēmus hodiē.** ◆ **Habētisne cibum?** ◆ **Ita. Cibum habēmus, et hic cibus est bonus. Tū es agricola bonus.**

9. **Ō Rōberte, aegrōtantne Aemilia et Christophorus hodiē? Absunt hodiē.** ◆ **Minimē, valent.** ◆ **Cūr absunt?** ◆ **Nesciō. Fortasse domī sunt.**

10. **Virī fēminaeque novum oppidum aedificant.** ◆ **Cūr?** ◆ **Hoc oppidum est parvum, et multōs fīliōs et fīliās habent.** ◆ **Ubi est novum oppidum?** ◆ **Prope silvam est.**

Answers on page 263.

LESSON 43

NEW WORD **macellum, macellī**

MEANING *market*

In ancient Rome, a **macellum** was a sort of storefront or stall where you could buy meat, fish, or fresh vegetables. Let's translate **macellum** into English as *market*. It's a neuter noun of the second declension.

EXERCISES

1. **Hoc macellum est malum! ♦ Cūr? ♦ Malum est quod cibum bonum nōn habet.**
2. **Ō Rōmule, cūr ad macellum properās? ♦ Cibum nōn habeō. ♦ Cūr cibum nōn habēs, ō Rōmule? ♦ Multōs fīliōs et multās fīliās habeō.**
3. **Salvē, ō Semprōnia! Cūr ad bibliothēcam properās? ♦ Ego librōs bonōs amō.**
4. **Cibum nōn habēmus. ♦ Hoc oppidum multa macella habet, sed pecūniam nōn habēmus. ♦ Pecūniam nōn habēmus, sed porcum habēmus. Fortasse… ♦ Minimē!**
5. **Ubi est magistra? Et cūr haec fēmina adest? ♦ Magistra abest quod aegrōtat. Haec fēmina hodiē est magistra.**
6. **Egone adsum? ♦ Ita, ades. ♦ Ubi sum? ♦ Domī es. Aeger es.**
7. **Rēgīna sum. ♦ Ō Lucrētia, rēgīna nōn es. Bibliothēcāria es. ♦ Sum rēgīna librōrum. Semper librōs cūrō et servō. ♦ Tū nōn es rēgīna! Bibliothēcāria es! ♦ Sum rēgīna bibliothēcae.**
8. **Ō Quīnte, amāsne Aurēliam? ♦ Minimē, ego Claudiam amō. ♦ Claudia Tiberium amat. ♦ Cūr Claudia Tiberium amat? ♦ Tiberius multam pecūniam habet, et magnam casam habet. ♦ Ego multōs porcōs habeō.**
9. **Ō fīlia, ubi est novus liber? Liber abest. ♦ Nesciō. Fortasse Marcus novum librum ad bibliothēcam nunc portat.**
10. **In bibliothēcam puer properat. ♦ Nunc ē bibliothēcā cum multīs librīs properat.**

Answers on page 263.

LESSON 44

NEW WORD   **obsōnō / obsōnāre**

MEANING   *I grocery shop / to grocery shop*

Our new word for this lesson is a verb of the first conjugation. It basically means to go out and buy food or provisions. Let's translate it into English as *to grocery shop*.

	SINGULAR	PLURAL
FIRST PERSON	**obsōnō**	**obsōnāmus**
SECOND PERSON	**obsōnās**	**obsōnātis**
THIRD PERSON	**obsōnat**	**obsōnant**

INFINITIVE	**obsōnāre**

EXERCISES

1. **Numquam cibum in casā habēmus. ♦ Cūr? ♦ Numquam obsōnāmus! ♦ Fortasse hodiē obsōnāre possumus. ♦ Pecūniam nōn habēmus!**
2. **Ō Tullia, ubi nunc est Carolus? ♦ Carolus nunc obsōnat quod cibum nōn habēmus.**
3. **Obsōnāre nōn possum quod hoc macellum est parvum et malum.**
4. **Salvē, ō Pūblī. Ubi nunc labōrās? ♦ In macellō labōrō. ♦ Ubi est macellum? ♦ In oppidō, prope casam Helenae.**
5. **Nautae ab īnsulā cum multō argentō et multō aurō nāvigant. ♦ Fortasse pīrātae sunt! ♦ Minimē, nautae bonī sunt.**

6. Hoc oppidum theātrum nōn habet. ♦ Fortasse novum theātrum ē lignō aedificāre possumus. Prope silvam habitāmus, et multum lignum habēmus. ♦ Lignum ē silvā ad oppidum portāre possumus.

7. Ō Tullia, tū fīlia bona es, et puella bona es. ♦ Egone puella bona sum? ♦ Ita. Numquam cum puerīs pugnās, et discipula bona es. Semper equōs cūrās et porcīs cotīdiē cibum dās.

8. Ō Jācōbe, cūr ad macellum ambulāmus? ♦ Obsōnāmus.

9. Estne haec fēmina bibliothēcāria? ♦ Ita. Bibliothēcāria est. In novā bibliothēcā labōrat. Cotīdiē librōs cūrat et librōs numerat.

10. Cūr virī puerīque ex oppidō properant? ♦ Ad scaphās properant. ♦ Cūr ad scaphās nunc properant? ♦ Pīrātae malī ex īnsulīs ad patriam nāvigant. Virī puerīque scaphīs patriam servant. ♦ Agricolae sunt! Nāvigāre nōn possunt! ♦ Agricolae sunt, sed nāvigāre possunt. Agricolae et nautae sunt.

Answers on page 264.

QUICK 🖉 REVIEW

You already know that the preposition **in** can have different meanings. When **in** takes the accusative case, it can mean *into*, and when it takes the ablative case it can mean *in* (inside something) or *on* (on top of something). But during the remainder of this book, you will find that the preposition **in** can also be translated into English with the word *at*. In English, we use the word *at* a lot—we use expressions like *at school, at the theater, at the library,* etc. If you want to say that kind of thing in Latin, you can use **in** plus the ablative to say it.

LESSON 45

NEW WORD   īrātus, īrāta, īrātum

MEANING   *angry*

Our new word for this lesson is a first and second declension adjective. It is related to English words like *irate* (very angry) and *irascible* (easily angered).

EXERCISES

1. **Ō Rōberte, cūr Paulus est īrātus?** ◆ **Paulus est īrātus quod pecūniam nōn habet.** ◆ **Paulus numquam labōrat.**

2. **Ō Cornēlia, cūr Semprōnia est īrāta?** ◆ **Semprōnia est īrāta quod haec bibliothēca est parva et librōs bonōs nōn habet.** ◆ **Fortasse ad theātrum ambulāre possumus.**

3. **Cūr hic agricola īrātus est?** ◆ **Novus equus abest.** ◆ **Ubi est equus? Estne equus in stabulō?** ◆ **Minimē. Equus in stabulō nōn est.**

4. **Aurēliam videō. Ē bibliothēcā cum multīs librīs properat.** ◆ **Aurēlia semper multōs librōs ē bibliothēcā portat. Librōs amat!**

5. **Haec puella est Tullia.** ◆ **Estne fīlia Marcī?** ◆ **Ita, Tullia est fīlia Marcī.** ◆ **Estne discipula?** ◆ **Ita. Tullia est discipula bona. Numquam domī manet, sed cotīdiē ad scholam properat.**

6. **Ubi est Rūfus?** ◆ **Rūfus ad macellum properat. In oppidō obsōnat quod cibum nōn habēmus.**

7. **Hic bibliothēcārius est īrātus!** ◆ **Cūr?** ◆ **Īrātus est quod discipulī malī librōs dēlent in bibliothēcā!** ◆ **Discipulī bonī numquam librōs dēlent.**

8. **Tūne īrāta es?** ◆ **Minimē. Laeta sum.** ◆ **Cūr?** ◆ **Laeta sum quod hodiē novum librum habeō.**

9. **Ō fīlia, cūr mūrum circum oppidum aedificāmus?** ◆ **Prope silvam habitāmus. Sunt multae bestiae in silvā.** ◆ **Ubi est lignum?**

10. **Salvē, ō Helena. Ego novus magister sum.** ◆ **Salvē.** ◆ **Habēmusne discipulōs bonōs?** ◆ **Haec schola est schola puellārum. Puerōs nōn habēmus, sed multae puellae adsunt.** ◆ **Suntne puellae discipulae bonae? Discipulās malās docēre nōn possum.** ◆ **Ita. Semper adsunt, et numquam pugnant.**

Answers on page 264.

LESSON 46

NEW WORD   **quoque**

MEANING   *also, too*

PRONUNCIATION TIP: The accent is on the first syllable, so **quoque** sounds something like *KWO-kweh*.

The word **quoque** is like our English words *also* and *too*. Use **quoque** with nouns, like in these examples:

- **Ego discipulus sum. Tū quoque es discipulus.** *(I am a student. You also are a student.)*

EXERCISES

1. **Aemilia in agrīs labōrat. Lāvīnia quoque in agrīs labōrat.** ♦ **Cūr?** ♦ **Sunt multa saxa in agrīs. Lāvīnia et Aemilia saxa ex agrō portant.**

2. **Lūna nunc in caelō est, et stellae quoque adsunt.** ♦ **Fortasse stēllās numerāre possumus!** ♦ **Minimē, stēllās numerāre nōn possumus.**

3. **Tū novum librum habēs! Cūr habēs novum librum?** ♦ **Magistra sum, et multōs discipulōs doceō.** ♦ **Tūne habēs scholam?** ♦ **Minimē, scholam nōn habeō. In bibliothēcā discipulōs doceō.**

4. **Saepe ad novam bibliothēcam ambulō.** ♦ **Ego quoque. Librōs amō.** ♦ **Ad bibliothēcam saepe ambulō quod Jūliam amō. Jūlia est bibliothēcāria. In bibliothēcā labōrat.**

5. **Salvē, ō Cornēlia. Valēsne hodiē?** ♦ **Ita, valeō.** ♦ **Cūr properās ad oppidum?** ♦ **Obsōnō. Ad macellum nunc properō quod in casā cibum nōn habēmus, sed multōs fīliōs et multās fīliās habēmus.**

6. **Hoc oppidum est parvum, sed haec bibliothēca magna est.**

7. **Hoc oppidum mūrum nōn habet.** ♦ **Cūr, ō Lucrētia?** ♦ **Lignum nōn habēmus.** ♦ **Fortasse ē silvā lignum portāre possumus.** ♦ **Fortasse, sed nōn sum valida.** ♦ **Minimē! Tū valida es! Tū lignum ē silvā portāre potes, et ego quoque lignum portāre possum.**

8. **Hic vir est Christophorus. Christophorus est bibliothēcārius.**

9. **Īrātus sum.** ♦ **Ego quoque!** ♦ **Cūr īrāta es?** ♦ **Īrāta sum quod hoc oppidum theātrum nōn habet. Cūr tū īrātus es?** ♦ **Ego īrātus sum quod hoc oppidum nōn habet bibliothēcam.**

10. **Ō fīlī, cūr porcus in casā est?** ♦ **Tūne īrātus es?** ♦ **Ita! Īrātus sum! Cūr porcus in casā est?** ♦ **Porcus aegrōtat. In casā porcum cūrō.**

Answers on page 264.

71

LESSON 47

NEW WORD   **thermopōlium, thermopōliī**

MEANING   *cafe*

In ancient Rome, a **thermopōlium** was an establishment somewhat like a cafe or fast-food restaurant where you could walk in and buy a hot meal. The word **thermopōlium** is borrowed from ancient Greek. The first part of the word (the **thermo-** part) means *hot*. It's the same root word that is found at the beginning of the word *thermometer*. The second part of the word (the **-pōlium** part) refers to a place where you sell something. It's related to the Greek verb that means *to sell*. So literally, the word **thermopolium** means *a place where you sell something hot*. In this case, food!

In a **thermopōlium** there would be a counter with food containers, sort of like a buffet. Here's a graphic I made to show you what the counter looked like (the wavy lines are supposed to be heat rising from the food).

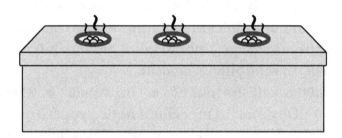

Thermopōlium is a neuter noun of the second declension.

EXERCISES

1. **Ubi est thermopōlium? ♦ Thermopōlium est prope casam Rōbertī.**
2. **Hoc oppidum nōn habet thermopōlium. ♦ Cūr? ♦ Parvum oppidum est.**
3. **Ubi sumus? In oppidō? In silvā? ♦ In scaphā sumus! ♦ Cūr in scaphā sumus? ♦ In scaphā sumus quod pīrātae sumus! ♦ Sumne pīrāta? Ego pīrātās timeō! ♦ Tū pīrāta malus es.**

4. Cibum domī nōn habēmus. Fortasse ad macellum ambulāre possumus. Obsōnāre possumus. ◆ Pecūniam habēmus. Fortasse ad thermopōlium ambulāre possumus. Thermopōlium Claudiae cibum bonum habet!

5. Tertius īrātus est. ◆ Cūr? ◆ Cibum nōn habet. Pecūniam nōn habet. ◆ Fortasse Tertiō pecūniam dare possumus. ◆ Minimē!

6. Cūr īrātus es? ◆ Īrātus sum quod sumus in bibliothēcā, sed bibliothēcārium nōn videō. Ubi est bibliothēcārius? Ubi sunt novī librī? ◆ Nesciō. ◆ Haec bibliothēca est mala.

7. Ō Fausta, estne Jūlia magistra? Docetne discipulōs? ◆ Minimē. Jūlia est bibliothēcāria. Librōs cotīdiē cūrat et servat.

8. Equī sunt īrātī! ◆ Cūr? ◆ Cibum in stabulīs nōn habent. ◆ Rūfus equōs nōn cūrat! ◆ Fortasse Rūfus aegrōtat. ◆ Minimē! Rūfus in theātrō est!

9. Ō Rōmule, cūr properās ad oppidum? ◆ Ad theātrum properō. Ego theātrum amō. ◆ Ego quoque theātrum amō. Fortasse ego quoque ad theātrum ambulāre possum. ◆ Ita, tū quoque potes.

10. Puellae ex oppidō properant. ◆ Cūr? ◆ Nesciō. Fortasse ad actam properant.

Answers on page 265.

QUICK ✎ REVIEW

You would expect the dative plural and ablative plural forms of **fīlia** to be **fīliīs**. But the dative and ablative plural forms of **fīlia** can be **fīliābus** so you can tell them apart from the dative plural and ablative plural forms of **fīlius**.

LESSON 48

NEW WORD   **fessus, fessa, fessum**

MEANING   *tired*

Our new word for this lesson is a first and second declension adjective.

EXERCISES

1. **Fessus sum.** ◆ **Cūr?** ◆ **Magister sum. Discipulōs doceō.** ◆ **Ego quoque fessa sum.**
2. **Ego hodiē obsōnāre nōn possum.** ◆ **Cūr? Tūne fessa es?** ◆ **Ita. Fessa sum. Domī maneō.**
3. **Hoc oppidum est parvum.** ◆ **Hoc oppidum nōn habet macellum.** ◆ **Hoc oppidum nōn habet thermopōlium bonum.** ◆ **Cūr adsumus?** ◆ **Magnam bibliothēcam cum multīs librīs habet.**
4. **Ego hodiē obsōnāre nōn possum.** ◆ **Cūr? Cibum nōn habēmus domī.** ◆ **Obsōnāre nōn possum quod fessa sum. Hodiē domī maneō.**
5. **Ō Helena, habēsne fīliōs?** ◆ **Ita. Semper fessa sum quod multōs fīliōs fīliāsque habeō.**
6. **Salvēte, ō discipulī.** ◆ **Valē, ō magister.** ◆ **Cūr ē scholā properātīs?**
7. **Hic agricola multōs porcōs habet, sed equōs nōn habet.** ◆ **Cūr?** ◆ **Stabulum nōn habet.**
8. **Salvē, ō Aurēlia. Valēsne hodiē? Esne tū fessa?** ◆ **Minimē, valeō hodiē. Nōn sum fessa.**
9. **Hic puer est fīlius Tulliae.**
10. **Hic equus Jūliam ad oppidum portāre nōn potest.** ◆ **Cūr?** ◆ **Fessus est.** ◆ **Fortasse Jūlia ad oppidum ambulāre potest.** ◆ **Jūlia quoque fessa est.**

Answers on page 265.

LESSON 49

QUESTIONS THAT EXPECT A CERTAIN ANSWER

Sometimes, a question is just a question—we ask about something, not really expecting any particular answer. Observe this question:

> Will you let Jimmy borrow the car?

In that example, the speaker isn't expecting any certain answer—he or she simply wants to know whether or not Jimmy will be allowed to borrow the car.

Other times, when we ask a question, you can tell by the way the question is worded that we are expecting a certain answer. In the example below, what kind of answer do you think the speaker wants to receive?

> You are going to let Jimmy borrow the car, right?

It seems that the person asking that question wants the answer to be *yes*. Now, read this next example and see if you can tell what kind of answer the speaker wants.

> You aren't going to let Jimmy borrow the car, are you?

The person asking this question definitely wants the answer to be *no*.

So, in English, we can ask questions with different wordings, depending on what answer we want or expect. You can ask a question that expects no particular answer, a question that expects the answer to be *yes* or a question that expects the answer to be *no*. And in Latin, we can ask questions in these same ways—and that's what we will learn how to do over the next couple of lessons.

LESSON 50

QUESTIONS EXPECTING A "YES" ANSWER

A while ago, I taught you how to use the **-ne** ending to turn a sentence into a question, like this:

Estne Rūfus in agrō? *(Is Rufus in the field?)*

That kind of question is formed by adding **-ne** to the first word of the sentence. But here is the new thing I want to teach you in this lesson: you can also add that same **-ne** suffix to the word **nōn**, like this:

nōn + ne = nōnne

The idea here is that with the **-ne** ending, the word **nōn** now expresses the idea of *not*, but in a "questiony" kind of way. So the word **nōnne** translates to English as something like *Is it not…?* or *Isn't it true that…?* When a person is asking a question and starts out the question with the word **nōnne**, it means that the person asking the question wants or expects the answer to the question to be *yes*.

Let's go through some examples so you can practice working with **nōnne**. Here's an example in the first person: imagine a man who is contemplating his career choices…

Nōnne agricola sum?

This man is asking whether or not he is a farmer. But he starts out the question with **nōnne**, so it means that he expects the answer to be *yes*. Therefore we could translate this question into English a couple of different ways:

- I'm a farmer, right?
- Am I not a farmer?

The first translation was more informal, reflecting modern speech. The second translation sounded more formal, or perhaps old-fashioned—but it was more literal, because it set up the word *not* in a "questiony" kind of way, which is really

76

what the word **nōnne** communicates. Here's another example, this time in the second person.

Nōnne ad silvam ambulās?

Here, someone is asking someone else whether or not that person is walking to the forest. But since the question starts out with **nōnne**, you can tell that the speaker expects or wants the answer to be *yes*. We can translate this kind of sentence into English a couple of different ways:

- You are walking to the forest, right?
- Are you not walking to the forest?
- Aren't you walking to the forest?
- You are walking to the forest, aren't you?

The first translation was more informal and colloquial, while the second one was more formal or old-fashioned. The third one was the same as the second one, but with the words *are* and *not* contracted into *aren't*. The fourth one was the same as the third one, but with the "aren't you" part of the sentence moved to the end. Let's look at one last example, this time in the third person.

Nōnne equus est in agrō?

In this example, somebody is asking whether or not the horse is in the field. But since he or she is starting out the question with **nōnne**, you can tell that the person asking the question wants or expects the answer to be *yes*. And again, you can translate this question into English several ways:

- The horse is in the field, right?
- Is not the horse in the field?
- Isn't the horse in the field?
- The horse is in the field, isn't it?

Well, you get the idea. In the grand scheme of things, it doesn't really matter which way you translate it into English—the important thing here is that you understand the *feeling* of the question, and the viewpoint or expectations of the person asking the question. In the answer key, I will translate the exercises as simply as possible, using stock phrases like these:

77

- Right?
- Aren't you?
- Isn't she?
- Aren't they?

When you see these phrases in the answer key, they will help you understand how to translate **nōnne** into English.

EXERCISES

1. **Salvē, ō Petre! Nōnne cibum habēs?** ♦ **Ita. Cibum habeō.**
2. **Nōnne haec bibliothēca multōs librōs habet?** ♦ **Ita. Haec bibliothēca est magna, et multōs librōs habet.**
3. **Nōnne est thermopōlium in oppidō?** ♦ **Ita. Est thermopōlium bonum in oppidō prope casam Semprōniae.**
4. **Nōnne discipula es?** ♦ **Ita, ego discipula sum. Et tū?** ♦ **Ego quoque sum discipulus.**
5. **Nōnne equōs cotīdiē cūrās?** ♦ **Certē, equōs semper cūrō. Equīs cotīdiē cibum dō.**
6. **Nōnne agricolae sunt fessī?** ♦ **Ita. Agricolae sunt fessī quod hodiē terram arant.**
7. **Nōnne nautae adsunt?** ♦ **Minimē. Absunt.**
8. **Salvē. Sumusne prope bibliothēcam?** ♦ **Ita. Tū bibliothēcam vidēre potes.** ♦ **Ita, nunc ego bibliothēcam vidēre possum.**
9. **Obsōnantne nunc Decimus et Tullia?** ♦ **Ita, ad macellum nunc properant.**
10. **Salvēte, ō equī. Nōnne cibum habētis?** ♦ **Minimē! Porcī cibum habent, sed cibum nōn habēmus!** ♦ **Nōnne aquam habētis?** ♦ **Minimē!** ♦ **Agricola malus sum.**

Answers on page 265.

LESSON 51

QUESTIONS EXPECTING A "NO" ANSWER

In the last lesson, I showed you how to create a Latin question in which the speaker expects or wants the answer to be *yes*. In this lesson, you will learn how to create the very opposite—a question in which the speaker expects or wants the answer to be *no*. To make this kind of question, you will need to know a new Latin word: the word **num**.

The word **num** functions just like **nōnne**. Put it at the beginning of a question, and it expresses that the speaker wants or expects the answer to be *no*. Just for practice, let's go through some examples just as we did with **nōnne**. Here's another sentence about the farmer who is reflecting on his career choices…

Num agricola sum?

In this example, someone is asking whether or not he is a farmer. But he starts out the question with **num**, so it means that he expects the answer to be *no*. In English, we usually make this kind of statement by adding a question to the end of the sentence, like this:

I'm not a farmer, am I?

There aren't as many ways to translate this kind of question into English as there were with **nōnne**. The main method we will use to translate this kind of question into English is tagging the question on at the very end of the sentence. Here's another example, but this time in the second person:

Num agricola es?

We can translate this question into English like this:

- You aren't a farmer, are you?
- You're not a farmer, are you?

The only difference between those two translations was where the contraction is—between *are* and *not*, or between *you* are *are*. But they both share the *are you?* question tagged on at the end.

EXERCISES

1. **Num pīrāta es?**
2. **Nōnne pīrāta es?**
3. **Num fessa es? ♦ Fessa sum et īrāta! ♦ Cūr fessa es? Cūr īrāta es? ♦ Īrāta sum quod equum nōn habēmus. Cūr ad oppidum ambulāmus? ♦ Ego quoque fessus sum. Ad oppidum ambulāmus quod macellum est in oppidō. Cibum nōn habēmus. ♦ Obsōnāre hodiē nōn possum. ♦ Cūr? Cibum nōn habēmus! ♦ Fessa sum!**
4. **Nōnne pīrāta es? ♦ Ita, pīrāta sum. ♦ Ego aurum nōn habeō!**
5. **Num magistra es? ♦ Minimē. Nōn sum magistra. Bibliothēcāria sum. ♦ Nōnne labōrās in bibliothēcā? ♦ Ita, in magnā bibliothēcā labōrō. Cotīdiē librōs cūrō et servō.**
6. **Num Tertius in silvā habitat? ♦ Minimē, Tertius in silvā nōn habitat. Tertius in magnā casā in oppidō habitat.**
7. **Num hic equus cibum habet? ♦ Minimē. Equus cibum nōn habet. ♦ Cūr? ♦ Equus cibum nōn habet quod Marcus est puer malus! Marcus numquam equōs cūrat!**
8. **Num rēgīna ad īnsulam nāvigat? ♦ Minimē. Rēgīna semper in patriā manet. Numquam ad īnsulam nāvigat. ♦ Cūr rēgīna numquam ad īnsulam nāvigat? ♦ Pīrātae malī in īnsulā habitant!**
9. **Num Flāvia Rōbertum amat? ♦ Minimē, Flāvia Decimum amat. ♦ Cūr? ♦ Decimus est vir bonus. Magnam casam habet, et pecūniam quoque habet.**
10. **Obsōnatne Quīntus? ♦ Ita, Quīntus obsōnat quod cibum in casā nōn habēmus.**

Answers on page 265.

LESSON 52

NEW WORD   **inter**

MEANING   *between, among*

PRONUNCIATION TIP: The accent is on the first syllable, so it sounds something like *INN-terr.*

Our new word for this lesson is found in many English words such as *intercontinental, internet, interstate, intervention, intercede, intermediate, intermittent, interlocking,* and *interjection...*the list goes on and on.

Inter is a preposition that takes the accusative case. You can use it with two nouns to mean *between*, like this:

> **Macellum est inter bibliothēcam et thermopōlium.**   *(The market is between the library and the cafe.)*

Notice that in that sentence, both the word **bibliothēcam** and **thermopōlium** are in the accusative case because they are both objects of the preposition **inter**.

Or, you can use it with a plural noun to mean *among*, like this:

> **Sunt multī pīrātae inter insulās.**   *(There are many pirates among the islands.*

EXERCISES

1. **Ubi est casa Lucrētiae?**   ♦   **Casa Lucrētiae est inter actam et silvam.**   ♦   **Num casa Lucrētiae est prope actam?**   ♦   **Minimē. Lucrētia prope silvam habitat.**
2. **Ō puella, ubi est bibliothēca?**   ♦   **Bibliothēca est inter scholam et macellum.**   ♦   **Nōnne bibliothēca librōs bonōs habet?**   ♦   **Certē, bibliothēca habet multōs librōs bonōs.**   ♦   **Librōs amō. Ad bibliothēcam nunc ambulō.**

3. Sunt multae scaphae inter patriam et īnsulam. ♦ Num pīrātae sunt? ♦ Minimē, nōn sunt pīrātae.

4. Ō Lucrētia, cūr properās ad thermopōlium Quīntī? ♦ Thermopōlium Quīntī bonum cibum habet!

5. Num īrātus es?

6. Nōnne īrātus es? ♦ Ita. Īrātus sum quod fessus sum. Cotīdiē ad macellum properō quod multās fīliās et multōs fīliōs habēmus. Cotīdiē obsōnō.

7. Num aegrōtās, ō Marce? ♦ Minimē, ego hodiē valeō.

8. Haec īnsula est mala. ♦ Cūr haec īnsula est mala? ♦ Est īnsula pīrātārum! Multī pīrātae in īnsulā habitant. ♦ Ego pīrātās timeō! ♦ Ego quoque pīrātās timeō. Fortasse nunc ad patriam nāvigāre possumus. ♦ Ita. Sunt multī pīrātae inter īnsulās!

9. Nōnne est bibliothēca in oppidō? ♦ Ita, hoc oppidum habet novam bibliothēcam, sed bibliothēca est parva. ♦ Habetne oppidum theātrum? ♦ Minimē. Incolae oppidī librōs amant, sed theātra nōn amant.

10. Aurēlia adest, Semprōnia adest, Tullia adest. ♦ Claudia abest. ♦ Ubi est Claudia? Num aegrōtat Claudia? ♦ Nesciō. Fortasse Claudia domī est.

Answers on page 266.

LESSON 53

NEW WORD   **popīna, popīnae**

MEANING   *restaurant*

PRONUNCIATION TIP: The accent is on the second syllable, so it sounds something like *po-PEE-nah*.

In ancient Roman times, a **popīna** was similar to a **thermopōlium**, but perhaps more of a tavern, where people would sit and eat. Therefore we will translate it as *restaurant*. **Popīna** is a feminine noun of the first declension.

EXERCISES

1. **Nōnne haec popīna cibum malum habet?** ♦ **Ita. Hic cibus est malus.** ♦ **Fortasse equīs cibum dare possumus.** ♦ **Fortasse porcīs cibum dare possumus.**

2. **Ō Cornēlia, habetne hoc oppidum popīnam bonam?** ♦ **Certē. Est popīna bona prope casam Rōbertī. Inter mūrum oppidī et bibliothēcam est.**

3. **Tū in popīnā hodiē labōrāre nōn potes quod aeger es.** ♦ **Nōn aegrōtō! Valeō hodiē!** ♦ **Minimē, tū aegrōtās. Hodiē tū domī manēre potes.**

4. **Ō fīlī, ubi est schola?** ♦ **Nesciō.** ♦ **Nōnne discipulus es?** ♦ **Ita, discipulus sum.** ♦ **Tū discipulus malus es.**

5. **Cūr Lucrētia cotīdiē ad bibliothēcam ambulat?** ♦ **Lucrētia librōs amat, et bibliothēcārium quoque amat.** ♦ **Ego quoque librōs bonōs amō.**

6. **Rūfus ē novā popīnā cum cibō bonō properat!**

7. **Num aegrōtat nova magistra?** ♦ **Minimē, magistra valet et hodiē adest. Discipulī quoque adsunt.**

8. **Ō fīliae, cūr properāmus nunc ad macellum?** ♦ **Obsōnāmus quod cibum nōn habēmus.** ♦ **Fortasse ad popīnam ambulāre possumus. Popīna Quīntī cibum bonum habet.** ♦ **Minimē! Pīrātae et virī malī semper in popīnā Quīntī adsunt, et saepe fābulās malās narrant.** ♦ **Sed...cibum bonum habet.**

9. **Ex oppidō nunc ambulāmus.** ♦ **Cūr?** ♦ **In magnam silvam ambulāmus.** ♦ **Num bestiās timētis?** ♦ **Minimē, bestiās silvae nōn timēmus quod gladiōs scūtaque habēmus.**

10. **Ō poēta, fortasse tū puerīs puellīsque fābulam bonam narrāre potes.** ♦ **Ego numquam fābulās malās narrō!**

Answers on page 266.

LESSON 54

NEW WORD   **cēnō / cēnāre**

MEANING   *I have dinner / to have dinner*

Cēnō is a verb of the first conjugation. Here's an example sentence:

In popīnā cēnō. *(I am having dinner in/at the restaurant).*

EXERCISES

1. **Cūr numquam in popīnā cēnāmus, ō Christophore?** ♦ **Pecūniam numquam habēmus!** ♦ **Fortasse domī cēnāre possumus.**

2. **Nōnne in thermopōliō cēnāre possumus?** ♦ **Fortasse, sed virī malī saepe in thermopōliō adsunt.** ♦ **Adsuntne pīrātae?** ♦ **Ita. Pīrātae adsunt, et semper fābulās malās in thermopōliō narrant.**

3. **Ō magister, ubi hodiē est Gulielmus?** ♦ **Gulielmus domī est quod aegrōtat.** ♦ **Gulielmus nōn est aeger. Abest quod puer malus est et discipulus malus quoque est!**

4. **Salvē, ō Catharīna.** ♦ **Salvē, ō Pūblī.** ♦ **Nōnne valēs hodiē?** ♦ **Ita, valeō. Ad bibliothēcam ambulō.** ♦ **Cūr ad bibliothēcam ambulās? Num bibliothēcāria es?** ♦ **Ita, sum bibliothēcāria. Ego cotīdiē in bibliothēcā labōrō. Librōs servō et cūrō.**

5. **Ō Carole, cūr tū habēs magnam casam?** ♦ **Multōs fīliōs et multās fīliās habeō!** ♦ **Nōnne fessus es?** ♦ **Ita, semper fessus sum.**

6. **Ō fīlia, cūr domī nōn es? Nōnne aegra es?** ♦ **Minimē, nōn aegrōtō. Valeō. Ad actam nunc ambulō cum fīliābus Cornēliī. Esne īrātus?** ♦ **Minimē, nōn sum īrātus. Valē, ō fīlia.**

7. **Ubi sumus? Num in scaphā sumus?** ♦ **Minimē, ē popīnā ambulāmus.** ♦ **Aegrōtō.**

8. **Nōnne magistra es?** ♦ **Ita, sum magistra. Cotīdiē discipulōs doceō. Ego bibliothēcāria quoque sum.** ♦ **Labōrāsne in novā bibliothēcā?** ♦ **Ita, librōs cotīdiē cūrō.** ♦ **Ubi est nova bibliothēca?** ♦ **Nova bibliothēca est prope mūrum oppidī, inter scholam et casam Rōmulī.**

9. **Ō Rōberte, Tiberium amō.** ♦ **Num Tiberium amās? Tiberius pīrāta est!** ♦ **Tiberius nōn est pīrāta!** ♦ **Tiberius est pīrāta. Cūr Tiberius**

multum aurum argentumque habet?   ♦   Nesciō. Fortasse multam pecūniam habet.   ♦   Et cūr magnam scapham habet?   ♦   Nesciō. Fortasse scaphās aedificat. Fortasse nauta est.   ♦   Minimē! Tiberius est pīrāta malus!

10. **Ō Paule, cūr scapham ē lignō aedificās?**   ♦   **Scapham ē saxō aedificāre nōn possum.**

Answers on page 266.

LESSON 55

NEW WORD   **dē**

MEANING   *about*

Our new word for this lesson is a preposition that takes the ablative case. **Dē** can mean several different things depending on the context, such as *from* or *down from*. But another common meaning of **dē** is *about*, in the sense of telling you what subject a book or story is about. Here are a couple of examples of what I mean:

- **Hic liber est dē equīs.** *(This book is about horses.)*
- **Nauta puellīs fābulam dē pīrātīs narrat.** *(The sailor is telling a story about pirates to the girls.)*

Many works of Latin literature have the word **dē** in the title. For example, the first declension noun **amīcitia** means *friendship*, and when the great roman orator Marcus Tullius Cicero wrote a treatise about friendship, he called it **Dē Amīcitiā** *(About Friendship)*. In that title, **amīcitiā** is the object of the proposition **dē**, so it is in the ablative case.

EXERCISES

1. **Discipulōs dē porcīs hodiē doceō.**
2. **Ō bibliothēcāria, hic liber nōn est dē scaphīs. ♦ Nōn sum bibliothēcāria. Tū in thermopōliō es.**
3. **Marcus fābulam dē fēminīs validīs patriae narrat.**
4. **Nunc cēnāre nōn possumus quod cibum in casā nōn habēmus. ♦ Est popīna in oppidō. ♦ Ego pecūniam habeō. Fortasse in popīnā cēnāre possumus. Num pecūniam habēs? ♦ Minimē. Sed tū pecūniam habēs.**
5. **Nōnne īrāta es? ♦ Minimē. Laeta sum. ♦ Cūr laeta es? ♦ Laeta sum quod Jācōbus abest. ♦ Jācōbus est puer malus!**
6. **Ō Rōmule, habēsne equōs? ♦ Ita, multōs equōs habeō. Porcōs quoque habeō.**
7. **Hoc macellum est magnum! ♦ Ita. Multum cibum habet.**
8. **Ō Claudia, ubi est novum thermopōlium? ♦ Novum thermopōlium est in oppidō, inter magnum macellum et theātrum. ♦ Nōnne theātrum est parvum? ♦ Ita, theātrum est parvum.**
9. **Jūlius nunc obsōnāre nōn potest quod aegrōtat. ♦ Num aeger est Jūlius? ♦ Ita, aeger est. ♦ Cibum in casā nōn habeō. Fortasse tū obsōnāre potes. ♦ Pīrāta sum. Ego numquam obsōnō.**
10. **Cūr numquam natāmus? ♦ Multī pīrātae inter īnsulās sunt. ♦ Fortasse, sed hodiē pīrātās nōn videō. Nunc natāre possumus!**

Answers on page 267.

LESSON 56

NEW WORD **interdum**

MEANING *sometimes*

PRONUNCIATION TIP: The accent is on the second syllable, so it sounds something like *in-TER-dumm*.

Here's an example sentence with **interdum**:

Interdum in silvā ambulō. *(Sometimes I walk in the forest.)*

EXERCISES

1. **Interdum in popīnā cēnāmus.**
2. **In silvā ambulāre nōn possum.** ♦ **Cūr?** ♦ **Bestiās silvae timeō. Fortasse circum silvam ambulāre possumus.** ♦ **Fessus sum. Circum silvam ambulāre nōn possum.**
3. **Interdum dē theātrō doceō.**
4. **Haec bibliothēca est magna!** ♦ **Ita, haec bibliothēca multōs librōs habet. Biblothēcārius sum. Librōs cūrō.** ♦ **Cūr tū bibliothēcārius es?** ♦ **Librōs bonōs amō.**
5. **Ō Tiberī, esne tū agricola?** ♦ **Ita.** ♦ **Cūrāsne porcōs?** ♦ **Interdum porcōs cūrō, et equōs interdum cūrō.**
6. **Bestiae ē silvā properant!** ♦ **Bestiās timeō! Valē!**
7. **Ubi est Claudia hodiē? Num aegrōtat?** ♦ **Adest. Claudia nōn aegrōtat, sed Tertius et Decimus domī sunt quod aegrī sunt.**
8. **Pīrātae ex oppidō cum multō argentō properant.** ♦ **Sunt multī pīrātae inter oppida.**
9. **Novam bibliothēcam in oppidō habēmus!** ♦ **Fortasse nova bibliothēca novōs librōs habet.** ♦ **Fortasse. Ubi est nova bibliothēca?** ♦ **Nesciō. Nova est.**
10. **Ō Helena, cūr tū numquam in macellō obsōnās?** ♦ **In macellō interdum obsōnō, sed saepe in thermopōliīs cēnō quod prope macellum nōn habitō.**

Answers on page 267.

LESSON 57

NEW WORD   **argentāria, argentāriae**

MEANING   *bank*

Our new word for this lesson is related to a word you already know: **argentum**, which means *silver*. **Argentāria** is a feminine noun of the first declension.

EXERCISES

1. **Haec argentāria est parva, sed multam pecūniam habet! ♦ Et multum argentum quoque habet! ♦ Fortasse aurum quoque habet!**
2. **Ō Rūfe, cūr nunc ad argentāriam properās? ♦ Pecūniam nōn habeō. ♦ Cūr pecūniam nōn habēs? ♦ Magister sum. ♦ Fortasse rēgīna magistrīs pecūniam dare potest. Rēgīna multam pecūniam habet.**
3. **Ō Claudia, ubi est argentāria? ♦ Argentāria est in oppidō, inter bibliothēcam et thermopōlium Marcī.**
4. **Ubi sunt nautae? ♦ In popīnā cēnant. Fābulās malās narrant. ♦ Cūr semper fābulās malās narrant? ♦ Nautae semper fābulās malās narrant.**
5. **Ō Frederīce, nōnne saepe tū ad actam ambulās? ♦ Ita. Interdum ad actam ambulō. Interdum in silvā ambulō.**
6. **Pīrātae novam argentāriam aedificant in oppidō. ♦ Cūr argentāriam aedificant? ♦ Multam pecūniam habent, et aurum quoque habent. Scaphae pīrātārum cum multō aurō nāvigāre nōn possunt.**
7. **Ō Carole, cūr hodiē nōn obsōnās? ♦ Ō Cornēlia, hodiē obsōnāre nōn possum. Hodiē aegrōtō. Fessus sum. Fortasse tū hodiē obsōnāre potes. ♦ Tū nōn aegrōtās! ♦ Num īrāta es? ♦ Īrāta sum quod aeger nōn es!**
8. **Salvēte, ō puellae et puerī. ♦ Cūr ades? Num nova magistra es? ♦ Ita, sum nova magistra.**
9. **Hoc oppidum est parvum. Bibliothēcam nōn habēmus. Popīnās bonās nōn habēmus. Argentāriam nōn habēmus! ♦ Nōnne macellum habētis? ♦ Minimē!**
10. **Ō Aemilia, habēsne novum librum? ♦ Ita. Hic liber est dē theātrīs.**

Answers on page 267.

LESSON 58

ROMAN RELIGION

The ancient Greeks and Romans were polytheists. They believed in many different gods and goddesses, and built many temples for them. In the city of Rome, there was a special area in the middle of the city called the **forum** where the Romans conducted business, gave speeches, decided court cases, and even held gladiatorial games. In and around the Roman forum there were many different temples dedicated to various gods and goddesses.

Below, I have prepared a diagram of a Roman temple for you. In Greco-Roman architecture, each feature of a building has a specific name or term associated with it. In the diagram, I have labeled the most important parts of the temple so you can begin to familiarize yourself with the various architectural terms.

A TYPICAL
ROMAN TEMPLE

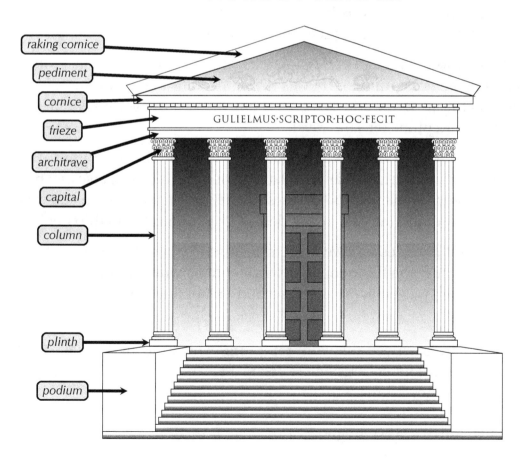

Many of the gods and goddesses in Roman mythology were borrowed from or identified with Greek gods and goddesses, but the Romans had different names for them. For example, the chief god of the Greek pantheon was named Zeus, but in Roman mythology his name was **Juppiter**. And in Greek mythology, Zeus's wife was named Hera, but to the Romans she was **Jūnō**.

The Romans also had different names for the various humans in their mythological stories. For example, in the famous Greek poem by Homer called *The Odyssey*, a Greek named Odysseus spent ten years trying to sail home—but to the Romans, his name was **Ulixēs** or **Ulyssēs**. And the Greek Heracles, famous for his twelve labors, was called **Hercules** by the Romans.

Greek myth has had a huge influence on literature and culture, so as you study Latin, don't "myth" your chance to learn the stories and characters of Greek mythology. In the meantime, just to improve your Latin skills, I would like to introduce to you the names of a few Roman gods and goddesses. Some gods and goddesses have names from the third declension (which you don't know yet), but the ones I'm giving you here have names from the first and second declensions.

Minerva was the Roman goddess of wisdom, identified with the Greek goddess Athena. She was born fully grown (and fully armed) from the head of her father, Jupiter (Zeus to the Greeks).

Neptune was the Roman god of the seas, and also of horses. His proper Latin name is **Neptūnus**. He was identified with the Greek god Poseidon. In the ancient world, sea travel could be very dangerous, so sailors prayed to Neptune for safe travel.

Vulcan was the blacksmith of the gods and was also the god of fire. His proper Latin name is **Vulcānus** (related to our English word *volcano*) but to the Greeks his name was Hephaestus. He walked with a limp and was married to Venus, the Roman goddess of love (Aphrodite to the Greeks).

Diāna was the goddess of several seemingly unrelated things such as childbirth, hunting, and the moon. She was identified with the Greek goddess Artemis, and was often pictured as a hunter, holding a bow and arrow.

Also, I would like to teach you the word **templum**, which means *temple*. It's a neuter noun of the second declension. Here are a few practice sentences to get you going with these new words:

- **Templum Minervae est magnum.** *(The temple of Minerva is large.)*

90

- **Nautae sunt in templō Neptūnī.** *(The sailors are in the temple of Neptune.)*
- **Sunt multa templa in patriā.** *(There are many temples in the homeland.)*
- **Templum Diānae prope bibliothēcam est.** *(The temple of Diana is near the library.)*

EXERCISES

1. **Nōnne templa sunt in oppidō?** ♦ **Ita, est templum in oppidō. Templum Diānae est.** ♦ **Estne templum Diānae magnum?** ♦ **Minimē, templum est parvum.**
2. **Ubi est popīna?** ♦ **In oppidō, prope templum Vulcānī.**
3. **Ō Quīnte, cūr nautae in templō Neptūnī sunt?** ♦ **Nautae interdum dōna ad templum portant.** ♦ **Cūr nautae dōna ad templum Neptūnī portant?** ♦ **Nautae hodiē ad īnsulās nāvigant. Sunt multī pīrātae inter īnsulās.**
4. **Cūr hoc parvum templum in silvā est?** ♦ **Nesciō. Fortasse templum Diānae est.** ♦ **Nōn sunt multa templa in silvā.**
5. **Sunt multī virī et multae fēminae in templō hodiē.** ♦ **Cūr?** ♦ **Nesciō.** ♦ **Estne templum Minervae?** ♦ **Ita, hoc templum est templum Minervae.** ♦ **Nunc ē templō ambulant.**
6. **Ō fīlī, ubi est templum Vulcānī?** ♦ **Nesciō. Fortasse templum Vulcānī est prope argentāriam.**
7. **Hoc templum est magnum!** ♦ **Ita, est templum Minervae!**
8. **Num argentāria est parva?** ♦ **Minimē, haec argentāria est magna quod multum argentum habet.** ♦ **Argentum videō.** ♦ **Ego aurum quoque videō.**
9. **Ō Aurēlia, ubi cēnāmus hodiē?** ♦ **Fessa sum. Fortasse in novā popīnā cēnāre possumus.** ♦ **Ubi est haec nova popīna?** ♦ **Nova popīna est prope templum Neptūnī, inter macellum et argentāriam.**
10. **Nōnne Lucrētia ad macellum nunc ambulat?** ♦ **Ita, Lucrētia nunc obsōnat. Ad macellum et ad bibliothēcam quoque ambulat.** ♦ **Habetne Lucrētia librum?** ♦ **Ita, librum dē equīs habet, sed hodiē Lucrētia librum ad bibliothēcam portat.**

Answers on page 268.

LESSON 59

NEW WORD   **ante / post**

MEANING   *before, in front of / after, behind*

These prepositions can refer to both time and space. For example, **ante** can mean *before* as in *before lunch*, or it can means *in front of*, as in *in front of the house*. Likewise, **post** can mean *after* as in *after lunch*, or *behind*, as in *behind the chair*.

These new prepositions may look familiar to you because they are part of several common expressions. For example, **ante bellum** means *before the war*, meaning before the American Civil War. Therefore, if you find an old house from before the American Civil War, you could call it an **ante bellum** house. Likewise, a **post mortem** (literally *after death*) is an autopsy, and a **postscriptum** (abbreviated P. S.) is something you write after the main body of a letter.

In this book, just so you can practice using them, I will use **ante** and **post** to refer to space, meaning in front of or behind physical objects. Here are two example sentences to get you going:

- **Ante templum Minervae sumus.** *(We are in front of the temple of Minerva.)*
- **Thermopōlium est post bibliothēcam.** *(The cafe is behind the library.)*

EXERCISES

1. **Sumus ante thermopōlium. Ubi es?** ♦ **Post thermopōlium sum.**
2. **Discipulī sunt ante scholam, sed ubi est Pūblius? Pūblius et Claudia absunt.** ♦ **Nesciō. Fortasse in bibliothēcā sunt. Pūblius et Claudia librōs amant.** ♦ **Nōnne bibliothēca est post scholam?** ♦ **Ita, bibliothēca post scholam est.**
3. **Ō Cornēlia, cūr nautae ante templum Neptūnī sunt?** ♦ **Nesciō. Fortasse ad templum dōna portant.**
4. **Equus Marcī est ante popīnam. Fortasse Marcus in popīnā est.** ♦ **Ita, Marcus in popīnā nunc cēnat.**

5. **Incolae oppidī magnum templum aedificant. ♦ Num ē lignō templum aedificant? ♦ Minimē, ex aurō templum aedificant! ♦ Incolae oppidī multum aurum habent!**

6. **Ō fīlī, ubi est equus? Nōn est in stabulō. Equus abest. ♦ Fortasse equus est post casam. ♦ Minimē, ō fīlī. Equus nōn est post casam. ♦ Fortasse equus pecūniam ad argentāriam portat. ♦ Minimē! Equī pecūniam nōn habent! ♦ Fortasse equus in templō Neptūnī est. ♦ Nunc īrāta sum!**

7. **Cūr magistrī sunt fessī? ♦ Magistrī sunt fessī hodiē quod discipulī sunt malī.**

8. **Portia interdum in bibliothēcam sine librīs ambulat, et ē bibliothēcā cum multīs librīs properat. Portia librōs amat! ♦ Portia est discipula bona. Nunc Portia librum dē rēgīnīs patriae habet.**

9. **Num hic discipulus aegrōtat? ♦ Minimē, hic discipulus valet. In scholā manēre potest.**

10. **Nautae cibum nōn habent. Fortasse tū et ego cibum ad nautās portāre possumus. ♦ Ita, sed cibum nōn habēmus! ♦ Fortasse ad macellum nunc ambulāre possumus.**

Answers on page 268.

LESSON 60

NEW WORD   **per**

MEANING   *through*

PRONUNCIATION TIP: **Per** sounds something like *pair*, not like *purr*.

Our new word for this lesson is a preposition that takes the accusative case. Here's a practice sentence:

Ambulō per silvam. *(I am walking through the forest.)*

EXERCISES

1. Cūr per oppidum ambulāmus? Num ad novam bibliothēcam ambulāmus? ♦ Ita, nunc ad novam bibliothēcam ambulāmus. ♦ Cūr? ♦ Helena est bibliothēcāria. ♦ Nōnne tū Helenam amās? ♦ Fortasse.

2. Ō puerī, cūr ambulātis per silvam? Haec silva multās bestiās habet! ♦ Bestiās nōn timēmus! ♦ Sed bestiae silvae sunt magnae! Fortasse circum silvam ambulāre potestis.

3. Ō Jūlia, cūr per agrōs properās? ♦ Ad scholam properō. ♦ Tū discipula bona es! Valē!

4. Haec fēmina est pīrāta! ♦ Minimē, haec fēmina nōn est pīrāta. ♦ Cūr librum dē pīrātīs habet? ♦ Librum dē pīrātīs habet quod bibliothēcāria est. Haec fēmina nōn est pīrāta.

5. Per scholam ambulō, sed discipulās nōn videō. Ubi sunt discipulae? Num discipulae hodiē aegrōtant? ♦ Minimē. Discipulae in bibliothēcā sunt.

6. Ō Tullia, cūr bibliothēcāria es? ♦ Bibliothēcāria sum quod librōs amō. ♦ Ego quoque librōs amō. Hodiē novum librum habeō. ♦ Estne liber bonus? ♦ Ita, hic liber est bonus.

7. Hic equus aquam nōn habet. Cūr? ♦ Rūfus est puer malus. Numquam equum cūrat. ♦ Ubi nunc est Rūfus? ♦ Nesciō.

8. Ō Quīnte, cūr magnōs librōs hodiē portās? Num ad bibliothēcam ambulās? ♦ Minimē, ad scholam nunc ambulō. Hodiē multōs librōs portō.

9. Ō Tiberī, cūr porcōs nunc nōn cūrās? ♦ Ego hodiē aegrōtō. Porcōs equōsque hodiē cūrāre nōn possum. ♦ Ō fīlī, ego porcōs et equōs hodiē cūrāre possum quod tū aegrōtās. Tū in casā manēre potes.

10. Hoc oppidum est parvum. ♦ Ita, nōn habet templa, et nōn habet thermopōlia, et nōn habet popīnās. ♦ Sed bibliothēcam habet.

Answers on page 268.

LESSON 61

NEW WORD **porta, portae**

MEANING *gate*

Porta is a feminine noun of the first declension. This word is related to the verb **portō**, which means *I carry*. Both **porta** and **portō** are related to many English words such as *port, transport, import, portal, portable,* and *report*.

In the ancient world, towns and cities would often have defensive walls, with a gate that could be opened and closed. Therefore, the word **porta** can refer to the gate of a town or city. Here's an example sentence to get you started with this word:

> **Per portās oppidī ambulāmus.** *(We are walking through the gates of the town.)*

EXERCISES

1. **Hoc oppidum magnās portās habet!** ◆ **Oppidum habet magnās portās quod mūrus circum oppidum est magnus. Hic mūrus oppidum servat. Pīrātae oppidum dēlēre nōn possunt quod oppidum habet magnum mūrum.**

2. **Īrātus sum quod per portam ambulāre nōn possum!** ◆ **Cūr tū per portam ambulāre nōn potes?** ◆ **Multōs librōs portō.**

3. **Poēta hodiē est prope portam oppidī.** ◆ **Cūr poēta adest?** ◆ **Hodiē puellīs puerīsque fābulās narrat.** ◆ **Narratne fābulās bonās?** ◆ **Ita. Nunc fābulam dē Neptūnō narrat.** ◆ **Valē! Ad portam nunc properō!**

4. **Ō Fausta, hoc oppidum parvam portam habet. Cūr parvam portam habet?** ◆ **Parvam portam habēmus quod parvum mūrum habēmus. Magnum mūrum ē lignō aedificāre nōn possumus quod multum lignum nōn habēmus.** ◆ **Sed hoc oppidum est prope silvam. Fortasse incolae oppidī lignum ē silvā portāre possunt.** ◆ **Silvam timēmus quod in silvā multae bestiae habitant.**

5. **Puerī puellaeque nunc in silvam ambulant.** ◆ **Cūr?** ◆ **Per silvam ad actam ambulant.** ◆ **Cūr puerī puellaeque circum silvam nōn ambulant?** ◆ **Fortasse bestiās silvae nōn timent.**

6. Ō fīlī, cūr cotīdiē domī cēnāmus? Est nova popīna in oppidō. ♦ Ubi est haec popīna? ♦ Popīna est in oppidō, prope argentāriam. Fortasse cibum bonum habet. ♦ Estne nova popīna prope templum Vulcānī? ♦ Minimē. Popīna est post templum Diānae, inter argentāriam et bibliothēcam.

7. Ō Christophore, cūr ē thermopōliō properās? ♦ Aegrōtō. Hic cibus est malus! ♦ Ego quoque aegrōtō! Hoc thermopōlium est malum!

8. Ō Claudī, cūr pīrātae numquam ad patriam nāvigant? ♦ Nautae validī in scaphīs actam semper servant. ♦ Tūne servās patriam? Num nauta es? ♦ Ita, ego nauta sum. In magnā scaphā actam servō. Pīrātae numquam ad patriam nāvigant quod virī validī et fēminae validae patriam servant. ♦ Fortasse ego quoque in scaphā actam servāre possum. ♦ Habēsne scapham? ♦ Minimē. Bibliothēcāria sum.

9. Incolae oppidī novum templum ē saxō aedificant.

10. Ō Jācōbe, cūr tū ante templum Neptūnī es? ♦ Nauta sum. Interdum dōna ad templum portō. Hodiē per īnsulās pīrātārum nāvigō. ♦ Sunt multī pīrātae inter īnsulās! ♦ Pīrātās timeō!

Answers on page 269.

LESSON 62

HOW TO SAY "THAT" IN LATIN

A few lessons ago, you learned how to say *this* in Latin using **hic**, **haec**, and **hoc**. Now it's time to learn how to say *that*. Like before, let's take it slowly and learn only the nominative singular of each gender so you can get accustomed to these new words.

The masculine form is the word **ille**. This word has two syllables, and sounds something like *IL-leh*. You can use **ille** with masculine nouns, as in these examples:

- **ille vir** (*that man*)

- **ille equus** *(that horse)*
- **ille nauta** *(that sailor)*

The feminine form is the word **illa**, which sounds something like *IL-lah*. You can use **illa** with feminine nouns, as in these examples:

- **illa fēmina** *(that woman)*
- **illa casa** *(that house)*
- **illa rēgīna** *(that queen)*

The neuter form is the word **illud**, which sounds something like *IL-luhd*. You can use **illud** with neuter nouns, as in these examples:

- **illud oppidum** *(that town)*
- **illud scūtum** *(that shield)*
- **illud dōnum** *(that gift)*

Repeat and/or chant these three words in order: **ille**, **illa**, **illud**.

Again, these forms are the nominative singular form of each of the three genders. If we took these nominative forms and put them in a chart, it would look like this:

	MASCULINE	FEMININE	NEUTER
NOMINATIVE (SUBJ./PRED. NOM.)	**ille**	**illa**	**illud**
GENITIVE (POSSESSION)			
DATIVE (IND. OBJECT)			
ACCUSATIVE (DIRECT OBJECT)			
ABLATIVE (MANY USES)			

Since these forms are nominative singular, we will only practice using them in places where they are accompanying a nominative singular noun. We will not study the genitive, dative, accusative, or ablative forms in this book.

HOW <u>NOT</u> TO USE ILLE

Before we move on to the exercises, I want to show you a couple of ways that **ille**, **illa**, **illud** is *not* used in Latin. Hopefully this can help you avoid some confusion. Here's the first way:

> I know <u>that</u> you love broccoli.

Here, the word *that* is a conjunction, joining together two parts of a sentence. **Ille**, **illa**, and **illud** are *not* used in this way. Here's another:

> I didn't eat <u>that</u> much broccoli.

Here, the word *that* is helping to show the amount of broccoli someone ate. **Ille**, **illa** and **illud** are *not* used in this way.

The correct way to use **ille**, **illa**, and **illud** is to specify or point out some person or thing. In these sentences, notice how the word *that* is being used to point out or specify a particular person or thing.

- <u>That man</u> is my father.
- <u>That woman</u> is my sister.
- <u>That shield</u> is my shield.

Words such as *this* and *that* are called *demonstratives* because they demonstrate what specific person or thing you are referring to.

EXERCISES

1. **Ille puer est fīlius Marcī. Hic puer est fīlius Quīntī.**
2. **Illa scapha est magna, sed haec scapha est parva.**
3. **Illud oppidum magnam bibliothēcam habet, sed hoc oppidum bibliothēcam nōn habet.**
4. **Nōnne ille liber est novus? ♦ Ita, hic liber est novus.**
5. **Illa fēmina est Helena. Helena est agricola. Cotīdiē porcōs equōsque cūrat et terram arat.**
6. **Num bibliothēcārius es? ♦ Minimē, agricola sum. Cotīdiē agrōs cūrō. ♦ Habēsne equōs? ♦ Ita, parvum equum habeō.**
7. **Ō Cornēlia, hodiē discipulās docēre nōn possum. ♦ Cūr docēre nōn potes? Magister es! ♦ Aegrōtō hodiē. Fessus sum. ♦ Fortasse tū**

domī manēre potes. Ego discipulās docēre possum. Valē! ◆ Valē, Cornēlia.

8. Interdum ad argentāriam ambulō. ◆ Cūr? Pecūniam nōn habēs. ◆ Pecūniam habeō! Ego cotīdiē in thermopōliō Marcī labōrō. ◆ Tūne labōrās? ◆ Ita. ◆ Ubi est thermopōlium Marcī? ◆ Post templum Vulcānī est. Novum thermopōlium est. ◆ Fortasse hodiē ego in thermopōliō cēnāre possum.

9. Pīrātae per portās oppidī ambulāre nōn possunt. ◆ Cūr? ◆ Portās gladiīs servāmus. ◆ Sed pīrātae quoque gladiōs habent. ◆ Fortasse domī hodiē manēre possum.

10. Ō bibliothēcāria, habēsne librum dē pecūniā? ◆ Ita. Tū in bibliothēcā ades. Multōs librōs dē pecūniā habēmus. Num pecūniam habēs? ◆ Minimē.

Answers on page 269.

LESSON 63

NEW WORD   **lātus, lāta, lātum / angustus, angusta, angustum**

MEANING   *wide / narrow*

Both of our new words for this lesson are first and second declension adjectives. **Lātus, lāta, lātum** is related to our English word *latitude*.

EXERCISES

1. **Illa porta est lāta.** ◆ **Lāta est, sed haec porta est angusta, et ego per portam cum equō ambulāre nōn possum.**
2. **Ō Jūlia, ubi est thermopōlium novum?** ◆ **Inter templum Vulcānī et macellum est.** ◆ **Fortasse hodiē in novō thermopōliō cēnāre possumus.** ◆ **Fortasse, sed pecūniam nōn habēmus.** ◆ **Domī cibum nōn habēmus.**

3. Per angustam portam ambulāre nōn possum quod multum lignum nunc portō. ♦ Ō Aemilia, cūr multum lignum hodiē portās? Num scapham aedificās? ♦ Ita, hodiē parvam scapham ē lignō aedificō. ♦ Cūr scapham aedificās? Tū nōn es nauta. ♦ Ita, nōn sum nauta, sed fortasse nunc nāvigāre possum.

4. Illa puella est discipula bona. ♦ Cūr bona discipula est? ♦ Semper adest, et numquam cum puerīs pugnat. ♦ Nōnne est fīlia Cornēliī? ♦ Ita, est fīlia Cornēliī. In magnā casā habitant prope templum Neptūnī. ♦ Templum Neptūnī est prope argentāriam.

5. Ubi es? Ego ante popīnam sum. ♦ Ante templum Minervae sum. ♦ Fortasse tū ante templum manēre potes. Ad templum nunc properō. Valē. ♦ Valē.

6. Ō Decime, num hodiē obsōnās? ♦ Minimē, hodiē nōn obsōnō. Fessus sum, et domī multum cibum habēmus.

7. Christophorum amō. ♦ Cūr amās Christophorum? Christophorus est poēta. Multam pecūniam nōn habet. ♦ Christophorum amō quod poēta bonus est. Interdum incolīs oppidī in theātrō fābulās narrat. ♦ Sed multam pecūniam nōn habet.

8. Templum vidēre nōn possum. ♦ Cūr? ♦ Est magnus mūrus ante templum. ♦ Post mūrum ambulāre possumus. ♦ Nunc templum vidēre possum.

9. Num īrāta es? ♦ Ita! Īrāta sum! ♦ Cūr? ♦ Īrāta sum quod tū in popīnā hodiē cēnās sed ego domī semper cēnō. ♦ Fortasse tū quoque in popīnā cēnāre potes.

10. Illud templum lātum est.

Answers on page 270.

LESSON 64

ROMAN ROADS

The ancient Romans were famous for their engineering skill. One of their most amazing achievements was the network of thousands of miles of paved roads which connected the various parts of the Roman Empire. The most famous road in ancient Rome was the **Via Appia**, known in English as the *Appian Way*. This long road started in Rome and ran south all the way to the city of Brundisium which was near the eastern tip of Italy. In the city of Rome itself, the **Via Sacra** *(Sacred Road)* ran through the Roman Forum, past many of Rome's most sacred temples—and you can still walk on it even today!

The word **via** is a feminine noun of the first declension. It is often translated into English with words like *road, way,* or *street.* You can use the preposition *in* with the ablative case to say that you are on a road:

> **In viā inter oppidum et actam sumus.** *(We are on the road between the town and the seashore.)*

EXERCISES

1. **Haec via est angusta, sed illa via est lāta.**
2. **Est angusta via in silvā. ♦ Per silvam ambulāre nōn possum. ♦ Num bestiās timēs? ♦ Sunt multī porcī in silvā. Per silvam ambulāre nōn possum quod porcōs timeō. ♦ Nōn sunt porcī in silvā! Fortasse bestiae adsunt, sed porcī in silvā nōn adsunt!**
3. **Ō rēgīna, cūr tū novam viam aedificās? ♦ Ego novam viam aedificō quod viam inter oppidum et actam nōn habēmus. Nautae et agricolae ab oppidō ad actam ambulāre nōn possunt. ♦ Et pīrātae ab actā ad oppidum ambulāre nōn possunt!**
4. **Ille vir est Marcus. Marcus est fīlius Petrī. ♦ Cūr Marcus adest hodiē ante templum Vulcānī? ♦ Hoc templum nōn est templum Vulcānī. Hoc templum est templum Neptūnī. ♦ Cūr Marcus adest hodiē ante templum Neptūnī? ♦ Marcus est nauta. Saepe dōna ad templum Neptūnī portat.**
5. **Mūrum circum oppidum aedificāmus, et portam quoque aedificāmus. ♦ Mūrum aedificāre nōn possumus! ♦ Cūr? ♦ Lignum nōn**

habēmus. Saxa nōn habēmus. Pecūniām nōn habēmus. ◆ Cūr īrātus es?

6. Ō Decime, cūr ad macellum properās? ◆ Nunc obsōnō. Cibum domī nōn habēmus.

7. Ō magister, ubi bestiae habitant? ◆ Nesciō. Fortasse in silvā habitant. ◆ Numquam bestiās in silvā videō. ◆ Ego numquam per silvam ambulō. ◆ Cūr tū per silvam nōn ambulās, ō magister? ◆ Bestiās timeō. Ego semper circum silvam ambulō. Nōn ambulō per silvam.

8. Cūr haec via est angusta? ◆ Haec via nōn est lāta quod magna bibliothēca est post templum. Haec via inter bibliothēcam et templum est.

9. Ō poēta, cūr ante theātrum ades? ◆ Hodiē fābulās in theātrō narrō.

10. Ad bibliothēcam interdum ambulō. ◆ Cūr? Ambulāsne ad bibliothēcam quod librōs amās? ◆ Minimē. Lucrētia est bibliothēcāria. Lucrētiam amō.

Answers on page 270.

LESSON 65

NEW WORD   **longus, longa, longum**

MEANING   *long*

This first and second declension adjective is related to our English words *long* and *longitude.*

EXERCISES

1. Illa via est longa et lāta. Via bona est. ♦ Multās viās bonās habēmus in patriā. ♦ Cūr viae sunt bonae? ♦ Rēgīnam bonam habēmus. Semper viās cūrat.

2. Ō Rūfe, cūr tū pecūniam nōn habēs? Et ubi est scapha? ♦ Longa fābula est. ♦ Num fābula mala est? ♦ Ita, fābula mala est. Fābula est dē pīrātīs, dē gladiīs, et dē īnsulā parvā.

3. Est longa via inter oppidum et actam. ♦ Fortasse ad actam hodiē ambulāre possumus. Numquam ad actam ambulāmus.

4. Illud templum est templum Minervae. ♦ Fortasse ad templum ambulāre possumus. ♦ Fortasse, sed via est angusta, et multī virī adsunt.

5. Est nova popīna in oppidō. Fortasse in popīnā hodiē cēnāre possumus. ♦ Ubi est nova popīna? ♦ Prope portam oppidī, inter templum Neptūnī et magnum macellum.

6. Haec fābula est longa. Cūr longam fābulam narrās, ō Gulielme? ♦ Semper longās fābulās narrō.

7. Ō Quīnte, nōnne magister es? ♦ Minimē, numquam discipulōs doceō. Nunc agricola sum. ♦ Habēsne porcōs? ♦ Ita, habeō porcōs equōsque.

8. Ō Tullia, cūr īrāta es? Cūr fessa es? Cūr discipulās nōn docēs? ♦ Longa fābula est. Fābula dē discipulīs malīs est.

9. Multī pīrātae per portās properant! ♦ Oppidum servāre nōn possumus! ♦ Ubi sunt scūta et gladiī? ♦ Cum pīrātīs pugnāre nōn possumus. ♦ Cūr pugnāre nōn possumus? ♦ Bibliothēcāriī sumus. ♦ Sed bibliothēcāriī validī sumus, et gladiōs habēmus.

10. Ō Rōmule, cūr ante portam oppidī cum equō ades? ♦ Per portam ambulāre nōn possum. ♦ Cūr? ♦ Porta est angusta, sed hic equus est lātus.

Answers on page 270.

LESSON 66

trāns

MEANING   *across, on the other side of*

As English speakers, we see the Latin word **trāns** all the time as part of various English words: *transportation, translation, transcontinental, transplant, transmit, transit, transfer*...the list goes on and on.

Trāns is a preposition that takes the accusative case. It can mean a couple of different things depending on how it is used. When you are talking about something or someone moving somewhere, **trāns** can mean *across*, like in this example:

Trāns viam ambulō. *(I am walking across the street.)*

But if no motion is involved, and something or someone is just sitting still, **trāns** can mean *on the other side of*, as in this example:

Bibliothēca est trāns viam. *(The library is on the other side of the street.)*

The difference is whether something is moving somewhere, or standing still. But either way, **trāns** takes the accusative case.

EXERCISES

1. **Ō nauta, ubi est templum Neptūnī? ♦ Templum Neptūnī est trāns viam, prope portās oppidī. ♦ Nōnne prope magnam bibliothēcam est? ♦ Ita, est prope bibliothēcam. ♦ Valē.**
2. **Ō nauta, cūr trāns īnsulam ambulās? ♦ Scapham nōn habeō. Circum īnsulam nāvigāre nōn possum. ♦ Multum lignum adest quod haec īnsula multās silvās habet. Fortasse tū novam scapham ē lignō aedificāre potes. ♦ Haec īnsula lignum bonum nōn habet. Scapham aedificāre nōn possum.**
3. **Ō Lucrētia, ubi est casa Jūliae? ♦ Trāns viam est. ♦ Habitatne Jūlia in casā prope argentāriam? ♦ Ita, casa Jūliae est post argentāriam, inter templum Minervae et magnum thermōpolium.**
4. **Illa fēmina est valida! ♦ Ita. Illa fēmina est Semprōnia. Agricola est. ♦ Aquam trāns lātum agrum portāre potest! Et multum lignum quoque portāre potest!**

5. Ō nauta, estne oppidum in īnsulā? ♦ Ita, haec īnsula habet magnum oppidum et parvum oppidum. ♦ Ubi est parvum oppidum? ♦ Trāns īnsulam est. ♦ Fortasse circum īnsulam ad parvum oppidum nāvigāre possumus.

6. Ō Rōmule, cūr ambulās per patriam? Tū trāns patriam ambulāre nōn potes quod viae in patriā sunt malae et angustae. ♦ Cūr viae sunt malae? ♦ Viae sunt malae quod incolae patriae numquam viās cūrant. Sunt multa saxa in viīs. Saxa sunt magna, et tū circum saxa ambulāre nōn potes.

7. Salvē, ō bibliothēcāria. Habetne haec bibliothēca librum dē equīs? ♦ Ita, habēmus multōs librōs dē equīs. ♦ Habēsne librōs dē porcīs? ♦ Bibliothēcāria sum. Agricola nōn sum.

8. Num Catharīnam amās, ō Quīnte? ♦ Ita, ego Catharīnam amō. ♦ Ō Quīnte, cūr Catharīnam amās? ♦ Catharīna est bibliothēcāria. Amō librōs. Amō bibliothēcās. Amō bibliothēcāriās. ♦ Fortasse tū dōnum ad bibliothēcam portāre potes. Nōnne pecūniam habēs? ♦ Minimē. Agricola sum. Porcōs habeō. ♦ Fortasse tū Catharīnae porcum dare potes. ♦ Porcus nōn est dōnum bonum.

9. Ego fessa sum. Haec via est longa. Ubi est oppidum? ♦ Portās oppidī nunc videō.

10. Cūr magistrī et discipulī ante theātrum sunt? ♦ Discipulī magistrīque ē scholā ad theātrum ambulant quod poēta hodiē in theātrō fābulās narrat.

Answers on page 271.

LESSON 67

NEW WORD   postulō / postulāre

MEANING   *I demand / to demand*

Postulō is a verb of the first conjugation which is related to the English word *postulate*. Use it with an accusative noun, like this:

Puerī cibum postulant! *(The boys are demanding food!)*

EXERCISES

1. **Ō Marce, cūr magistrī magistraeque pecūniam postulant?** ◆ **Cotīdiē in scholā labōrant. Discipulōs cotīdiē docent et numquam domī manent quod aegrōtant.** ◆ **Fortasse incolae oppidī magistrīs pecūniam dare possunt.** ◆ **Fortasse.**

2. **Ō rēgīna, virī fēminaeque īnsulae cibum postulant.** ◆ **Nōnne cibum habent?** ◆ **Minimē, cibum nōn habent.** ◆ **Fortasse in popīnīs cēnāre possunt.**

3. **Ō fīlī, cūr pecūniam postulās?** ◆ **Nōn habeō pecūniam. Numquam cēnāre possum in popīnā cum Aurēliā et Paulō.** ◆ **Fortasse tū labōrāre potes. Numquam pecūniam habēs quod numquam labōrās.**

4. **Puellae cibum postulant! Habēmusne cibum?** ◆ **Minimē, nōn habēmus cibum.** ◆ **Puellae sunt īrātae!** ◆ **Fortasse hodiē obsōnāre possumus.**

5. **Ō magistra, habēsne librum dē rēgīnīs patriae?** ◆ **Ego librum dē rēgīnīs patriae nōn habeō, sed in bibliothēcā sunt multī librī dē rēgīnīs.** ◆ **Fortasse tū hodiē discipulīs fābulam dē rēgīnā patriae narrāre potes.** ◆ **Ita, multās fābulās dē rēgīnā habeō.**

6. **Ō Fausta, cūr per oppidum properās?** ◆ **Ego ad argentāriam properō quod pecūniam nōn habeō. Ad macellum quoque properō quod cibum nōn habeō. Ego sine pecūniā obsōnāre nōn possum.** ◆ **Ubi est argentāria?** ◆ **Est parva argentāria prope templum Vulcānī, post bibliothēcam. Valē!**

7. **Ō Tiberī, ubi est casa pīrātārum?** ◆ **Illa casa est trāns silvam, prope actam.** ◆ **Fortasse ad casam pīrātārum ambulāre possumus.** ◆ **Minimē! Pīrātae sunt malī!** ◆ **Num cum pīrātīs cēnāre possumus?** ◆ **Minimē!**

8. **Incolae oppidī novōs librōs postulant, sed hoc oppidum bibliothēcam nōn habet.** ◆ **Fortasse magnam bibliothēcam aedificāre possumus!**

9. **Ō Jūlia, cūr ante portās oppidī ades?** ◆ **Oppidum servō.** ◆ **Sed gladium tū nōn habēs.** ◆ **Ego sine gladiō oppidum servāre possum.**

10. **Interdum ad actam ambulō.** ◆ **Cūr? Via inter oppidum et actam est longa et angusta.** ◆ **Actam amō.**

Answers on page 271.

LESSON 68

NEW WORD   **meus, mea, meum**

MEANING   *my*

Possessive adjectives are words like *my, your, his, her, its, our,* and *their.* In this lesson, we are going to start learning how to say this kind of thing in Latin. But don't worry—these are very easy to learn because they are just first and second declension adjectives.

Our new word for this lesson means *my.* Like any other adjective, **meus, mea, meum** will agree with the noun it accompanies in case, number, and gender. Here are a few example sentences to get you started:

- **Tertius est fīlius meus.** *(Tertius is my son.)*
- **Scapha mea est parva.** *(My boat is small.)*
- **Ubi est scūtum meum?** *(Where is my shield?)*

This adjective has a special vocative form for masculine singular nouns: **mī.** For example, if you wanted to say *O, my son!* you would say this:

Ō mī fīlī!

Now that you know how to say *my* in Latin, you may occasionally see two adjectives accompanying one noun. For example, what if you want to say *my small boat* in Latin? You could say it like this:

parva scapha mea *(my small boat)*

So, if you see a noun accompanied by the adjective **meus, mea, meum,** it might have another adjective in addition to that—so pay attention.

EXERCISES

1. **Popīna mea est parva, sed bonum cibum habēmus.** ♦ **Fortasse ego in popīnā hodiē cēnāre possum.** ♦ **Certē! Popīna mea est inter macellum et templum Minervae.**

107

2. Ō mī fīlī, cūr equus cibum nōn habet? Equus est īrātus! ♦ Nesciō. Nōn sum agricola. ♦ Agricolae sumus! ♦ Tū agricola es, sed ego nōn sum agricola. ♦ Nunc ego quoque īrāta sum!

3. Ō rēgīna mea, dōna habēmus. ♦ Ego dōna amō! ♦ Aurum habēmus, et argentum quoque habēmus. ♦ Aurum amō! Laeta sum! ♦ Ego nōn sum laetus, quod nunc aurum meum nōn habeō.

4. Cūr novam casam aedificās, ō Rōmule? ♦ Casa mea nōn est valida. Novam casam meam ē saxō aedificō. Novum mūrum quoque aedificō. ♦ Cūr mūrum aedificās, ō Rōmule? ♦ Mūrum circum casam meam aedificō quod incolās oppidī timeō. Mūrum cum magnīs portīs aedificō.

5. Ō magistra, discipulī sunt īrātī, et novōs librōs postulant. ♦ Pecūniam nōn habēmus. Novōs librōs discipulīs dare nōn possumus. Fortasse trāns viam ad bibliothēcam cum discipulīs ambulāre possumus. ♦ Fortasse. Illa bibliothēca multōs librōs habet.

6. Hodiē valeō. Fortasse ad parvam īnsulam hodiē natāre possum. ♦ Tū prope īnsulam natāre nōn potes. ♦ Cūr? ♦ Illa parva īnsula multōs pīrātās habet. ♦ Minimē, pīrātae in īnsulā nōn habitant. ♦ Incolae īnsulae sunt pīrātae. Ego cotīdiē magnās scaphās pīrātārum videō. ♦ Pīrātās nōn timeō.

7. Ō Semprōnia, cūr ante templum Minervae ades? ♦ Interdum ad templum cum fīliīs meīs ambulō. Nunc ad popīnam properāmus quod fīliī meī cibum postulant.

8. Haec via est longa. Cūr per lātam silvam ambulāmus? ♦ Oppidum est trāns silvam. ♦ Cūr ambulāmus ad oppidum? ♦ Fīlia mea in oppidō habitat. ♦ Cūr in oppidō habitat? ♦ In oppidō habitat quod magnam bibliothēcam habet. Fīlia mea librōs amat.

9. Puerī dōna postulant. ♦ Cūr? ♦ Nesciō. Saepe puerīs dōna damus, sed hodiē dōna postulant. ♦ Nunc pecūniam postulant. ♦ Pecūniam nōn habeō. ♦ Nunc cibum postulant.

10. Ō Jācōbe, cūr trāns angustam viam properās? ♦ Ad bibliothēcam ambulō.

Answers on page 272.

LESSON 69

NEW WORD   **amīcus / amīca**

MEANING   *male friend / female friend*

PRONUNCIATION TIP: In these words, the accent is on the middle syllable, so they sound something like *ah-MEE-kuss* and *ah-MEE-kah*.

Our new words for this lesson are related to the English word *amicable*, which means *friendly*.

A female friend is an **amīca**, which is a feminine noun of the first declension. A male friend is an **amīcus**, which is a masculine noun of the second declension.

- **Lucrētia est amīca mea.** *(Lucretia is my friend.)*
- **Quīntus est amīcus meus.** *(Quintus is my friend.)*

Also, watch out for the vocative form of **amīcus**. Since it ends with **-us**, the vocative form will be **amīce**.

EXERCISES

1. **Salvē, amīca! ♦ Salvēte, amīcī!**
2. **Salvē, amīce! ♦ Nōn sumus amīcī! ♦ Num īrātus es? ♦ Ita, sum īrātus! ♦ Cūr? ♦ Īrātus sum quod tū pecūniam meam habēs!**
3. **Ubi sunt amīcī meī? ♦ Trāns viam sunt, ante macellum. ♦ Cūr ante macellum sunt? ♦ Fortasse nunc obsōnant. ♦ Obsōnāre nōn possum quod pecūniam nōn habeō.**
4. **Hic vir est Marcus. Marcus est amīcus meus. Haec fēmina Fausta est. Fausta quoque est amīca mea.**
5. **Ō Marce, num habitās in oppidō? ♦ Minimē. In īnsulā habitō, sed saepe ad oppidum nāvigō. ♦ Habēsne tū scapham? ♦ Minimē. Haec scapha est scapha amīcōrum meōrum.**
6. **Ō Lāvīnia, habēsne amīcās? ♦ Multās amīcās habeō. ♦ Ubi sunt amīcae tuae? ♦ Amīcae meae sunt in theātrō, sed ego domī sum.**

7. Ō amīce, cūr ab actā properās? ◆ Pīrātae nunc ad actam nāvigant. Pecūniam meam postulant!

8. Ō Rūfe, cūr cum Petrō pugnās? ◆ Īrātus sum quod ille puer meam pecūniam habet! ◆ Ō Petre, num pecūniam Rūfī habēs?

9. Ō amīce, tūne pecūniam habēs? ◆ Semper pecūniam portō. Ego numquam sine pecūniā meā ad oppidum ambulō. ◆ Cūr pecūniam semper portās, ō amīce? ◆ Saepe in oppidō obsōnō, et sine pecūniā obsōnāre nōn possum. Sine cibō, familia mea cēnāre nōn potest. Multās fīliās et multōs fīliōs habeō.

10. Novās viās postulō! ◆ Ō rēgīna, cūr novās viās postulās? ◆ Patria mea viās bonās nōn habet. Viae in patriā meā sunt angustae, et multa saxa habent. Incolae patriae meae trāns patriam ambulāre nōn possunt quod viae sunt malae. ◆ Ō rēgīna, fortasse lātās viās aedificāre possumus.

Answers on page 272.

LESSON 70

NEW WORD   **tuus, tua, tuum**

MEANING   *your*

Our new word for this lesson is a first and second declension adjective, just like **meus**, **mea**, **meum**. Here are a few example sentences:

- **Pūblius est amīcus tuus.** *(Publius is your friend.)*
- **Helena est fīlia tua.** *(Helen is your daughter.)*
- **Scūtum tuum est magnum.** *(Your shield is large.)*

EXERCISES

1. Num saxa in scaphā tuā habēs? ◆ Ita, saxa in scaphā meā habeō. ◆ Cūr? ◆ Ego novam casam in īnsulā aedificō. ◆ Tū ad īnsulam cum saxīs nāvigāre nōn potes! ◆ Sed cotīdiē saxa ā patriā ad īnsulam portō. ◆ Fortasse tū novam casam ē lignō aedificāre potes. Illa īnsula multās silvās habet.

2. Ō Aurēlia, cūr pecūniam tuam nunc numerās? ◆ Ad argentāriam ambulō. ◆ Nōnne argentāria in oppidō est? ◆ Ita. Est parva argentāria inter bibliothēcam et templum Diānae. ◆ Tū multam pecūniam habēs! ◆ Ita. Multam pecūniam habeō quod cotīdiē in macellō labōrō. ◆ Ego quoque cotīdiē labōrō, sed multam pecūniam nōn habeō. ◆ Cūr? ◆ Magister sum.

3. Ō Lūcī, cūr per oppidum cum multīs dōnīs properās? ◆ Ad rēgīnam properō! Rēgīna dōna amat.

4. Ille puer malus tuam pecūniam postulat! Cūr? ◆ Ille puer pecūniam meam postulat quod fīlius meus est.

5. Ō Christophore, cūr cum amīcīs tuīs in thermopōliō nōn cēnās? ◆ Hodiē fessus sum. ◆ Cūr fessus es? ◆ Aegrōtō.

6. Illud templum est magnum! ◆ Illud templum est templum Neptūnī. Interdum ad templum ambulō. ◆ Cūr ad templum interdum ambulās? ◆ Nauta sum.

7. Ō agricola, ubi est casa tua? ◆ Trāns magnum agrum est, prope silvam. ◆ Casa mea est prope casam tuam. Ego in parvā casā in silvā habitō.

8. Haec via est longa et angusta. Ō Tullia, cūr in longā viā ambulāmus? Fessus sum. ◆ Ad oppidum meum ambulāmus! ◆ Cūr? ◆ In oppidō meō est magnum theātrum. Bibliothēca quoque est in oppidō meō. ◆ Nōnne popīna est in oppidō tuō? ◆ Ita, habēmus popīnam bonam. ◆ Fortasse in popīnā cēnāre possumus.

9. Ō amīce, cūr ante argentāriam ades? ◆ Haec argentāria multum argentum habet. ◆ Tū pīrāta es!

10. Num Gulielmus longam fābulam narrat? ◆ Ita. Longam fābulam narrat. ◆ Ō Gulielme, cūr semper longās fābulās narrās?

Answers on page 273.

LESSON 71

NEW WORD   **rēgnum, rēgnī**

MEANING   *kingdom*

Our new word for this lesson is a neuter noun of the second declension. It is related to the Latin word **rēgīna**, which means *queen* (notice that both words start with **rēg-**). It's also related to English words such as *regal* and *regent*.

EXERCISES

1. **Ō rēgīna mea, rēgnum tuum est lātum et longum.** ◆ **Minimē, rēgnum meum est parva īnsula!** ◆ **Nōn est parva īnsula. Haec īnsula est magna!** ◆ **Haec īnsula est parva! Nōnne vidēre potes?** ◆ **Cūr īrāta es?** ◆ **Īrāta sum quod rēgnum meum est parvum!** ◆ **Fortasse magnam īnsulam superāre possumus.**

2. **Salvē, ō rēgīna. Poētae sumus. Trāns rēgnum tuum ambulāmus.** ◆ **Habētisne cibum?** ◆ **Certē. Cibum habēmus, sed pecūniam nōn habēmus.** ◆ **Pecūniam nōn habeō. Fortasse ad argentāriam ambulāre potestis.** ◆ **Tūne rēgīna es, sed pecūniam nōn habēs?** ◆ **Rēgnum meum est parvum.**

3. **In rēgnō meō sunt multa oppida et multae viae. Sed nōn sum laeta quod nōn habeō bibliothēcam in rēgnō meō.** ◆ **Ō rēgīna, ego bibliothēcārius sum. Fortasse novam bibliothēcam in rēgnō tuō aedificāre possumus.**

4. **Incolae rēgnī meī novās viās postulant.** ◆ **Fortasse novās viās ē saxīs aedificāre possumus.** ◆ **Sunt multa saxa in rēgnō meō.**

5. **Haec rēgīna est bona.** ◆ **Cūr bona est?** ◆ **Bona est quod templa cūrat, et viās quoque semper cūrat.**

6. **Ō discipulī, cūr saxa portātis? Cūr labōrātis?** ◆ **Novam viam ē saxīs aedificāmus.** ◆ **Ubi est nova via?** ◆ **Inter oppidum et scholam est. Haec via est angusta, sed bona. Nunc ab oppidō ad scholam ambulāre possumus.**

7. **Ō amīca mea, cūr domī es?** ◆ **Ego domī hodiē maneō quod aegra sum.** ◆ **Tū domī manēre nōn potes!** ◆ **Num īrātus es? Cūr domī manēre nōn possum?** ◆ **Rēgīna multum cibum postulat!** ◆ **Fortasse tū obsōnāre postes.**

8. Novum scūtum ex argentō aurōque aedificō. ♦ Hoc scūtum est
   bonum! ♦ Ita, scūta mea sunt bona et magna. ♦ Cūr magna scūta
   aedificās? ♦ Ego incolīs rēgnī magna scūta dō. Sine scūtīs oppida
   rēgnī servāre nōn possumus. ♦ Fortasse mūrum quoque aedificāre
   possumus. ♦ Hoc rēgnum est magnum. Mūrum circum rēgnum
   aedificāre nōn possumus.
9. Illud thermopōlium est malum. Cibum malum habet. ♦ Sed haec
   popīna cibum bonum habet.
10. Illa fēmina est amīca mea. Salvē, amīca! Valēsne tū hodiē? ♦ Ita,
    valeō hodiē. ♦ Cūr ante argentāriam ades? ♦ Hodiē pecūniam
    meam ad argentāriam portō.

Answers on page 273.

LESSON 72

NEW WORD   **castellum, castellī**

MEANING   *castle, fortress, stronghold*

The word **castellum** is a neuter noun of the second declension. It can mean things
like *fortress, stronghold,* or *castle.* In this book we will translate it as *castle* just for
convenience. And yes, this word is where we get our English word *castle.*

EXERCISES

1. **Illud castellum est magnum, sed hoc castellum est parvum.**
2. **Ō amīce, ubi rēgīna habitat? ♦ Rēgīna in parvō castellō habitat. ♦
   Cūr in parvō castellō habitat? Nōnne magnum castellum habet? ♦
   Minimē. Hoc rēgnum est parvum. Multam pecūniam nōn habēmus.**
3. **Ō Carole, ubi est equus meus? ♦ Equus tuus est post castellum. ♦
   Cūr equus meus est post castellum? ♦ Stabula sunt post castellum.
   Equus tuus est in stabulō.**

113

4. **Ubi sunt amīcae tuae?** ♦ **In novā popīnā prope templum Minervae cēnant.** ♦ **Illa popīna est bona, et cibum bonum habet. Cūr tū cum amīcīs tuīs nōn cēnās?** ♦ **Pecūniam nōn habeō.**

5. **Cūr hic equus ante templum Diānae est?** ♦ **Nesciō. Num est equus Lucrētiae?** ♦ **Est equus Lucrētiae. Fortasse Lucrētia est in templō.**

6. **Salvē, ō Marce. Cūr tū ante portam castellī ades?** ♦ **Ego castellum servō.** ♦ **Cūr castellum servās? Rēgīna abest hodiē.** ♦ **Fīliae rēgīnae in castellō sunt. Familiam rēgīnae servō.**

7. **Ō bibliothēcāria, habēsne librum dē equīs? Fīlius meus equum postulat.** ♦ **Certē, haec bibliothēca multōs librōs dē equīs habet. Hic liber est dē equīs.** ♦ **Tū es bibliothēcāria bona! Valē!**

8. **Haec via est longa et angusta. Fessus sum. Cibum nōn habēmus. Aquam nōn habēmus.** ♦ **Num īrātus es?**

9. **Ō Portia, cūr ad patriam tuam nāvigās?** ♦ **Fīliī meī in patriam habitant.**

10. **Cūr pecūniam postulāmus?** ♦ **Magistrī sumus.**

Answers on page 273.

LESSON 73

Answers on page 273.

NEW WORD   **propter**

MEANING   *on account of, because of*

The word **propter** is a preposition that takes the accusative case. It can mean different things like *near* or *by*. It's related to **prope**, a preposition you already know. But just as often, it means things like *on account of* or *because of*. You can use **propter** to show the reason for something, like this:

Propter bestiās per silvam ambulāre non possum. *(On account of the beasts, I can't walk through the forest.)*

114

In this book, that's the way I will use **propter**, with the meaning *on account of.*

EXERCISES

1. **Propter pīrātās ad īnsulam nāvigāre nōn possumus.**
2. **Silvam timeō. ♦ Cūr silvam timēs? ♦ Numquam per silvam ambulō propter bestiās. Sunt magnī porcī in silvā. ♦ Porcī? Nōn sunt porcī in silvā! ♦ Interdum parvōs porcōs in silvā videō.**
3. **Illud lignum est malum. Propter lignum malum, novam scapham aedificāre nōn possumus. ♦ Fortasse lignum bonum ā silvā portāre possumus. ♦ Illa silva est in rēgnō pīrātārum. ♦ Fortasse, sed novam scapham sine lignō bonō aedificāre nōn possumus.**
4. **Claudia Matthaeum amat, sed Matthaeus Flāviam amat. ♦ Cūr Matthaeus Flāviam amat? ♦ Flāvia popīnam habet. Matthaeus cibum bonum amat.**
5. **Pīrātae īnsulam meam superāre nōn possunt. ♦ Cūr? ♦ Ego et amīcī meī semper īnsulam servāmus.**
6. **Ubi amīcae tuae hodiē cēnant? ♦ Nesciō. Interdum in popīnā cēnant. ♦ Num in thermopōliō cēnant? ♦ Minimē. Numquam in thermopōliō cēnant quod nautae in thermopōliō fābulās malās semper narrant.**
7. **Rūfus puellīs fābulam dē pīrātīs nunc narrat. ♦ Fīliae meae fābulās amant.**
8. **Ō rēgīna, tū magnum castellum in oppidō aedificāre nōn potes. ♦ Cūr? Rēgīna sum! ♦ Hoc oppidum est parvum!**
9. **Virī trāns viam ambulant.**
10. **Virī trāns viam sunt.**

Answers on page 274.

LESSON 74

NEW WORD   **lupus, lupī**

MEANING   *wolf*

A wolf plays an important role in the lore and legends of ancient Rome. According to tradition, Romulus and Remus were twins who had been abandoned (it's a long story) but survived because they were discovered and nursed by a she-wolf. A shepherd found them, and he and his wife raised the two boys. When the boys grew up, they became the founders of the city of Rome. Here is an old photo (in the public domain) of a famous statue which depicts the infants Romulus and Remus being nursed by the she-wolf.

The history of ancient Rome is a fascinating tale—so as you continue your study of Latin, you should read up on the history of the Romans and all that they accomplished.

And by the way, the word **lupus** is a masculine noun of the second declension.

EXERCISES

1. **Ille lupus est magnus!** ♦ **Lupōs timeō!** ♦ **Ego quoque lupōs timeō!** ♦ **Fortasse nunc ē silvā in oppidum properāre possumus.**
2. **Ō magistra, suntne bestiae in silvā?** ♦ **Ita, sunt multī lupī in silvā. In silvam propter lupōs numquam ambulō.**

3. Illud templum est parvum.

4. Rēgīna sum, sed rēgnum meum est parvum. Hoc rēgnum argentāriam nōn habet. Tū quoque es rēgīna, et rēgnum habēs. Nōnne rēgnum tuum habet argentāriam? ♦ Ita, rēgnum meum habet magnam argentāriam, magna templa, et popīnās bonās. ♦ Cūr rēgnum tuum argentāriam et templa habet? ♦ Rēgnum meum est longum et lātum. Multī incolae in rēgnō meō habitant. Est argentum in rēgnō meō, et aurum quoque adest. ♦ Num bibliothēcam habēs? ♦ Ita, est magna bibliothēca in rēgnō meō, cum multīs bibliothēcāriīs librīsque.

5. Tiberius puerīs puellīsque fābulam narrat. ♦ Estne fābula bona? ♦ Ita. Est fābula dē magnō lupō. ♦ Estne illa fābula dē parvīs porcīs quoque? ♦ Ita. Parvī porcī in parvā casā habitant, sed porcī lupum malum nōn timent quod in casā validā habitant.

6. Trāns viam ad argentāriam ambulō. ♦ Ō amīce, cūr ad argentāriam ambulās? ♦ Pecūniam nōn habeō.

7. Ō poēta, puellae puerīque fābulam postulant. Fortasse fābulam narrāre potes. ♦ Fortasse fābulam dē pīrātīs narrāre possum. ♦ Minimē. Illa fābula est mala. ♦ Fābulam dē parvīs porcīs et lupō malō narrāre possum. ♦ Illa fābula est bona!

8. Ō amīcī, cūr estis ante castellum? ♦ Ad rēgīnam dōna portāmus. Nōnne rēgīna in castellō est? ♦ Minimē. Rēgīna hodiē abest.

9. Ō Aemilia, ubi est porcus meus? ♦ Nesciō. Estne porcus post casam? ♦ Minimē. Est magnus lupus post casam, sed porcus abest.

10. Ō Rōmule, cūr fessus es? Cūr manēs domī hodiē? ♦ Longa fābula est.

Answers on page 274.

LESSON 75

NEW WORD   **vīcīnia, vīcīniae**

MEANING   *neighborhood*

Vicinia is a feminine noun of the first declension. It's related to our English word *vicinity*. Here's an example sentence:

> **Sunt multa thermopōlia in vīcīniā tuā.** *(There are many cafes in your neighborhood.)*

EXERCISES

1. **Multī pīrātae in vīcīniā tuā habitant. ♦ Ita. Haec vīcīnia est vīcīnia mala.**
2. **Per vīcīniam tuam ad casam Cornēliī ambulāmus.**
3. **Cūr magnum mūrum circum vīcīniam tuam ē lignō aedificātis? ♦ Nōn aedificāmus mūrum ē lignō. Mūrum ē saxō aedificāmus. ♦ Cūr ē saxō mūrum aedificātis? ♦ Saxa sunt valida. Est silva prope oppidum, et multī lupī in silvā habitant. Mūrum aedificāmus quod lupī in silvā nōn manent.**
4. **Illud thermopōlium est malum. Cūr in thermopōliō malō cum amīcīs tuīs cēnās, ō mī fīlī? Ego in thermopōliō malō propter cibum malum cēnāre nōn possum. ♦ Illud thermopōlium nōn malum est. Amīcī meī interdum in thermopōliō cēnant. ♦ Amīcī tuī sunt puerī malī.**
5. **Nōnne laetus es? ♦ Minimē. Nōn sum laetus. ♦ Cūr tū laetus nōn es? ♦ Fīliam rēgīnae amō, sed agricola sum, et fīlius agricolae sum. Fīlia rēgīnae fīlium agricolae amāre nōn potest. ♦ Cūr? ♦ Ego cotīdiē porcōs cūrō!**
6. **Ō Rōberte, ubi est templum Minervae? ♦ Trāns viam est.**
7. **Ō incola, ubi est oppidum? ♦ Oppidum est trāns silvam.**
8. **Poētae pecūniam postulant! ♦ Cūr? ♦ Fābulās bonās narrant. ♦ Fortasse poētīs pecūniam dare possumus. Habēsne pecūniam? ♦ Minimē. Magistra sum.**
9. **Illud castellum est trāns rēgnum.**
10. **Trāns rēgnum ambulāmus.**

Answers on page 274.

LESSON 76

NEW WORD   **noster, nostra, nostrum**

MEANING   *our*

Our new word for this lesson is an adjective that means *our*. It is a first and second declension adjective, but with the same spelling pattern as the adjective **aeger**, **aegra**, **aegrum**. Here's an example sentence:

Ubi est porcus noster? *(Where is our pig?)*

EXERCISES

1. **Rēgīnam nostram amāmus.** ◆ **Cūr?** ◆ **Rēgīna nostra est fēmina bona. Viās semper cūrat, et agricolīs pecūniam saepe dat.**

2. **Num discipulōs malōs habēmus?** ◆ **Ita. Discipulī nostrī sunt malī. Numquam adsunt in scholā, et semper pugnant.**

3. **Ō Jūlia, ubi sunt fīliī nostrī?** ◆ **In thermopōliō cēnant.** ◆ **Cūr cum nautīs et pīrātīs cēnant? Illud thermopōlium est malum.**

4. **Ubi est pecūnia nostra? Nōnne pecūnia nostra est in argentāriā?** ◆ **Minimē. Pecūnia nostra est domī.**

5. **Ad rēgnum nostrum nāvigāre nōn possumus.** ◆ **Cūr?** ◆ **Sunt multī pīrātae inter īnsulās. Propter pīrātās, per īnsulās nāvigāre nōn possumus.** ◆ **Ego pīrātās nōn timeō.**

6. **Salvēte, ō porcī meī. Valētisne hodiē? Nōnne aquam habētis?** ◆ **Minimē! Aquam nōn habēmus!** ◆ **Cūr aquam nōn habētis?** ◆ **Tū agricola malus es. Fortasse bibliothēca librum dē agricolīs bonīs habet.**

7. **Vīcīnia nostra est mala. Cūr in vīcīniā malā habitāmus?** ◆ **Pīrātae sumus, et amīcī nostrī quoque sunt pīrātae. Vīcīnia nostra est mala propter pīrātās.**

8. **Fortasse hodiē ad theātrum ambulāre possumus.** ◆ **Fortasse.** ◆ **Hodiē poēta in theātrō est. Incolīs oppidī nostrī fābulās narrat.** ◆ **Adsuntne amīcī nostrī in theātrō?** ◆ **Ita.**

9. **Hoc stabulum est angustum. Cūr in stabulō angustō habitō, sed tū in casā habitās?** ◆ **Ego in casā habitō quod agricola sum. Tū in stabulō habitās quod equus es.**

10. **Ille lupus est magnus. Hic lupus est parvus.**

Answers on page 275.

119

LESSON 77

NEW WORD   **vester, vestra, vestrum**

MEANING   *your* (when talking to more than one person)

If you want to say *your* when talking to just one person, you would use the adjective **tuus**, **tua**, **tuum**, like this:

Habēsne librum tuum? *(Do you have your book?)*

In that example, the book was being possessed by only one person. This is clear because the sentence uses the Latin adjective **tuum**, which is used only when something is being possessed by only one person.

But what if you want to ask about an item that is being possessed by more than one person? In English, you could do it like this:

Do you have your book?

In English, the word *you* can refer to one person, or to more than one person. And likewise, the word *your* can refer to an object that is being possessed by one person, or by more than one person. Therefore, the sentence shown above is ambiguous. The speaker could be asking one person if he/she has his/her book. Or, imagine for a moment that two children are sharing one book—the speaker could be asking those two children if they have the book that the two of them share.

This ambiguity is the reason why in the Southeastern United States we have our own special way of differentiating between *your* (possessed by one person) and *your* (possessed by more than one person). If we want to ask one person if he/she has his/her book, we would say it like this:

Do you have your book?

So far so good. But if we want to ask a group of people if they have a book that they share, we say it like this:

120

Do y'all have y'all's book?

For a Southerner (like me) that sentence is very clear. Since we have the word *y'all's* we can specify whether we are addressing one person or more than one person. This removes any ambiguity. This manner of speaking is very colloquial, of course, and I understand that this may sound strange to your ears. But keep reading, and soon you will see the usefulness of this word.

In Latin, unlike English, there is a separate word for *your* (possessed by one person) and *your* (possessed by more than one person). You already know the word for *your* when the object is being possessed by one person—that's the adjective **tuus**, **tua**, **tuum**. But our new word for this lesson is the word that means *your* when something is being possessed by more than one person. That's the first and second declension adjective **vester**, **vestra**, **vestrum**. Observe these examples:

- **liber vester** *(y'all's book)*
- **scapha vestra** *(y'all's boat)*
- **scūtum vestrum** *(y'all's shield)*

Since the adjective **vester**, **vestra**, **vestrum** means *your* when something is being possessed by more than one person, we can use the word *y'all's* as a way to translate that into English. Study and compare these two sentences:

- **Habēsne librum tuum?** *(Do you have your book?)*
- **Habētisne librum vestrum?** *(Do y'all have y'all's book?)*

So, in the answer key, I will translate **tuus**, **tua**, **tuum** as *your*, but I will translate **vester**, **vestra**, **vestrum** as *y'all's*. Again, I am aware that the word *y'all's* might sound silly to you—but try to have fun with it. And remember, as one reviewer of *Getting Started with Latin* wisely commented, that the purpose of the book is to teach you Latin, not English.

EXERCISES

1. **Rēgīna vestra est mala, sed rēgīna nostra est bona magnaque. ◆ Cūr rēgīna vestra est bona magnaque? ◆ Rēgīna nostra semper puerīs puellīsque oppidī cibum dat. Semper rēgnum nostrum servat, et viās semper cūrat. ◆ Rēgīna vestra est bona!**

121

2. Thermopōlium nostrum habet cibum bonum. ♦ Minimē, cibus vester est malus. In thermopōliō vestrō propter cibum malum cēnāre nōn possum.

3. In oppidō nostrō templum Diānae habēmus, et templum Vulcānī quoque habēmus. Nōnne templum in oppidō vestrō habētis? ♦ Minimē. Oppidum nostrum est parvum. Templa nōn habēmus, sed theātrum et popīnās bonās habēmus.

4. Salvē, amīce. Trāns rēgnum tuum ambulāmus. Ubi est castellum rēgīnae? ♦ Castellum est trāns magnam silvam. ♦ Per magnam silvam ambulāre nōn possumus. Fortasse circum silvam ambulāre possumus. ♦ Via circum silvam est longa et angusta, sed via per silvam est lāta, et nōn est longa. ♦ Sunt lupī in silvā. Propter lupōs per silvam ambulāre nōn possumus.

5. Est magna argentāria in oppidō nostrō. ♦ Habetne argentāria aurum et argentum? ♦ Ita. Pīrātae saepe in argentāriam cum multō aurō properant. ♦ Num argentāria pīrātārum est? ♦ Ita, est argentāria pīrātārum!

6. Ō nauta, cūr interdum puerīs fābulās malās tuās narrās? ♦ Puerī saepe fābulās meās postulant. Fābulās malās nōn narrō. Interdum fābulās dē īnsulīs narrō. Interdum fābulās dē pīrātīs narrō. Fābulae meae sunt bonae!

7. Vīcīnia nostra est parva. Cūr aqua est circum vīcīniam nostram? ♦ In parvā īnsulā habitāmus.

8. Ō Tite, cūr bibliothēcārius es? ♦ Bibliothēcārius sum quod librōs bonōs amō. ♦ Suntne librī bonī in bibliothēcā tuā? ♦ In bibliothēcā nostrā librōs bonōs et librōs malōs habēmus.

9. Tū domī hodiē manēre nōn potes. ♦ Cūr? Schola mea est mala, et discipulī sunt malī. ♦ Tū magister es!

10. Cūr multī lupī in vīcīniā vestrā habitant ? ♦ In silvā habitāmus.

Answers on page 275.

LESSON 78

NEW WORD   **fundus, fundī**

MEANING   *farm*

Fundus is a masculine noun of the second declension. It is related to our English word *fundamental*.

In English, we often say the expression *on the farm*. In Latin, you would use the preposition **in** to say that kind of thing. Here's an example sentence.

Tullia et Carolus in fundō habitant. *(Tullia and Charles live on a farm.)*

EXERCISES

1. **Fundus noster est magnus. Multōs equōs habēmus. ♦ Nōnne porcōs habētis? ♦ Ita, sunt multī porcī in fundō nostrō. ♦ Habētisne equōs? ♦ Ita. Multa stabula habēmus. ♦ Fundus vester est magnus!**
2. **Ō agricola, ubi est fundus tuus? ♦ Fundus meus est inter oppidum et actam. ♦ Estne magnus fundus? ♦ Fundus meus est longus et angustus.**
3. **Ō Aurēlia, esne bibliothēcāria? ♦ Minimē, nōn sum bibliothēcāria. Agricola sum. Librōs nōn cūrō. Porcōs cūrō.**
4. **Ō agricola, ubi sunt porcī tuī? ♦ Post casam sunt. ♦ Lupum videō. Cūr lupus est prope porcōs tuōs? ♦ Num lupus adest? ♦ Nunc lupus porcum in silvam portat.**
5. **Ō amīce, ubi est popīna Helenae? ♦ Trāns viam est. ♦ Popīnam vidēre nōn possum quod templum Diānae est ante popīnam. ♦ Ita, popīna Helenae est post templum.**
6. **Ō Claudī, cūr tū nostrīs amīcīs pecūniam semper dās? ♦ Amīcī nostrī pecūniam nōn habent. ♦ Pecūniam nōn habent quod numquam labōrant!**
7. **Ō amīce, cūr circum vīcīniam meam semper ambulās? Cūr tū per vīcīniam meam nōn ambulās? ♦ In vīcīniā malā habitās. ♦ Haec vīcīnia nōn est mala. In vīcīniā nostrā multās popīnās bonās habēmus.**

123

8. Ō rēgīna mea, cūr magnum castellum postulās? ♦ Rēgīna sum, sed in parvō castellō habitō. ♦ Sed castellum tuum est bonum. ♦ Parvum est! Rēgīnae semper in magnīs castellīs habitant! ♦ Rēgīnae interdum in parvīs castellīs habitant.

9. Ō bibliothēcārī, habēsne tū librum dē castellīs? ♦ Tū in bibliothēcā adēs. Multōs librōs dē castellīs habēmus. ♦ Rēgīna nostra novum castellum postulat.

10. Hoc rēgnum viās malās habet. In viīs malīs ambulāre nōn possum! ♦ Trāns rēgnum ambulāre nōn possumus propter viās malās. ♦ Sunt multa saxa in viīs!

Answers on page 276.

LESSON 79

HIS, HER, ITS, AND THEIR

So far, you know the Latin adjectives that mean *my, your, our* and even (GULP) *y'all's.* But you have not yet learned how to say things like *his, her, its,* and *their* in Latin. And that's what we will be working on in this lesson. In Latin, the adjective we need for this kind of thing is the adjective **suus, sua, suum.**

When we study a verb, we put the different forms of the verb into a chart that shows first person, second person, and third person, right? And we can also think of possessive adjectives in this same way. What if we put our possessive adjectives into a chart according to person and number? Here's what it would look like:

	SINGULAR	PLURAL
FIRST PERSON	**meus** *(my)*	**noster** *(our)*
SECOND PERSON	**tuus** *(your)*	**vester** *(y'all's)*
THIRD PERSON	**suus, sua, suum** *(his, her, its, their)*	

Meus, **mea**, **meum** refers to the speaker, and is singular, so we can think of it as being first person singular. **Noster, nostra, nostrum** also refers to the speaker, but is plural, so we can picture it as being first person plural. **Tuus, tua, tuum** refers to the person being spoken to, and is singular, so it is second person singular. **Vester, vestra, vestrum** refers to the people being spoken to, and is plural, so it is second person plural. So far so good.

But in the third person, the adjective **suus, sua, suum** requires a bit of explaining. As English speakers, the way we use this kind of adjective in our native language differs from the way it works in Latin. As you can see from the chart, this adjective covers both the singular *(his, her, its)* and plural *(their)* So, to prevent any confusion, I would like to take some time here to explain a little (or maybe a lot) about how **suus, sua, suum** works in Latin as compared to how *his*, *her*, *its*, and *their* work in English. So…here goes.

In English when you say *his*, *her*, or *its*, it matches the gender of the person possessing the item. Here's an example of what I mean:

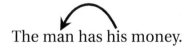
The man has his money.

In this English sentence, the subject of the sentence is the word *man*, which is masculine. Therefore, if we want to say that the money belongs to the man, we use the masculine adjective *his*, and we say *his money*. The adjective looks back to the possessor and gets its gender *from the possessor*.

In Latin, however, the words work together in a different way. Let's convert that entire sentence into Latin using our new adjective **suus, sua, suum** and see if we can learn anything by comparing the English sentence to the Latin sentence. Here's that same sentence in Latin:

125

Vir pecūniam suam habet.

Like any Latin adjective, the adjective **suus, sua, suum** must agree in case, number, and gender with the noun it accompanies—and since **pecuniam** is feminine, the form of **suus, sua, suum** that goes with it must also be feminine. **Suus, sua, suum** can't look back to the person possessing the item to get its gender like it would in an English sentence. **Pecūniam** is accusative, singular, and feminine, so it gets the word **suam** to go with it, which is also accusative, singular, and feminine. So, mentally, you need to think of the gender of the possessor as a separate thing from the gender of the item being possessed.

Now let's talk about how we would translate this kind of sentence into English. When you see **suam** in that sentence, how will you translate it? Now's your chance to look at the gender of the person possessing the item. The person possessing the item is masculine, so we translate **suam** into English as the masculine adjective *his*. When you look at who the possessor is, it gives you the context to know exactly who the adjective **suam** is referring to. Again, think of the gender of the possessor as being a separate thing from the gender of the item being possessed.

But what if a sentence doesn't have a separate word to be the subject? In a Latin sentence, you aren't required to have a separate word to be the subject as you would in an English sentence. What if you see a sentence like this one:

Habet pecūniam suam.

In this Latin sentence, we know that somebody has money, but we don't know who. We could translate **habet** as *he has, she has,* or *it has*. But there is no separate word to be the subject, so we don't know exactly who the verb **habet** is talking about. There isn't enough context here to tell us what the gender of the possessor is, so we really don't know how to translate the sentence. It could mean *He has his money, She has her money,* or *It has its money*.

Just for practice, let's go through this whole process again with a different sentence. This time, it's a sentence in which the person possessing the item is feminine, but the object being possessed is (in Latin at least) a masculine noun.

The woman has her book.

126

In this English sentence, the subject of the sentence is the word *woman*, which is feminine. Therefore, if we want to say that the book belongs to the woman, we use the feminine adjective *her*, and we say *her money*. Again, in English, the adjective looks back to the possessor and gets its gender from the possessor. Now here's that same sentence in Latin:

Fēmina librum suum habet.

Again, as always, the adjective **suus, sua, suum** must agree in case, number, and gender with the noun it accompanies—and since **librum** is masculine, the form of **suus, sua, suum** must also be masculine. **Suus, sua, suum** can't look back to the person possessing the item to get its gender like it would in an English sentence. **Librum** is accusative, singular, and masculine, so it gets the word **suum** to go with it, which is also accusative, singular, and masculine.

And if you translate this sentence into English, how will you know how to translate **suum**? Again, as before, we look back to the subject of the sentence to see what the gender of the person possessing the item is. Since the person possessing the item is feminine, we translate **suum** into English as the feminine adjective *her*. When you look at who the possessor is, it gives you the context to know exactly who the adjective **suum** is referring to.

And again, what happens if there is no separate noun to be the subject? What if you see a sentence like this one:

Habet librum suum.

Here, we know that somebody has a book, but we don't know who. The sentence could mean *He has his book*, *She has her book*, or *It has its book*. But since there is no separate word to be the subject of the sentence, we just don't know who **suum** is referring to.

Here's another situation you might run into. If the possessor is an inanimate object or an animal, you can translate **suus, sua, suum** into English as *its*, like this:

- **Bibliothēca librōs suōs habet.** *(The library has its books.)*
- **Equus cibum suum habet.** *(The horse has its food.)*

In Latin, the noun **bibliothēca** is feminine—but when translating into English, that doesn't matter because it's an inanimate object. Also, the word **equus** is a masculine noun in Latin, but since the possessor is an animal, it is common to just use *its*.

If the item is being possessed by more than one person, you should translate **suus**, **sua**, **suum** into English as *their*. Here's an example:

Nautae scapham suam habent. *(The sailors have their boat.)*

In that sentence, the sailors (**nautae**) are the ones possessing the boat. This means that boat belongs to more than one person. So when you translate the word **suum** into English, translate it as *their*. In English, not only do you look to the possessor to find the gender of the possessive adjective, but the number, too. This is the reason why in the chart at the beginning of this lesson, the bottom row with **suus**, **sua**, **suum** spans both the singular column and the plural column—because in addition to *his*, *her*, and *its*, it can also mean *their*.

LESSON 80

MORE ABOUT SUUS, SUA, SUUM

In this lesson I would like to compare English and Latin a bit more to help you get a sharper picture in your mind of what the adjective **suus**, **sua**, **suum** means (and does not mean) in Latin. I would like you to read the following two paragraphs, paying special attention to the last few words of each one (the part where it says *Fred has his dog*).

1. It's Bring Your Pet Day at the park. Kevin has his cat, Bob has his parrot, and Fred has <u>his</u> dog.

2. Charles is going on a trip, so he asked his friends to let his pets live with them while he is traveling. Kevin has his cat, Bob has his parrot, and Fred has <u>his</u> dog.

Please read those two paragraphs and answer this question: is the word *his* (underlined) at the end of each paragraph referring to the same person, or to two different people?

128

The last few words of each paragraph are the exactly the same—but in each situation, the word *his* is referring to a different person. In the first paragraph, people are at the park with their own pets, and Fred has his own dog. Therefore when it says *Fred has his dog*, the word *his* is referring to Fred. But in the second paragraph, someone named Charles is going on a trip, so Charles is having his dog stay at Fred's house. So when it says *Fred has his dog*, the word *his* is referring to Charles, not Fred. Fred has Charles's dog. So in this way, the English words *his, her,* and *its* can be ambiguous because without sufficient context, you don't know if those words are referring to the subject of the sentence or to somebody else.

But in Latin, we don't have this problem. Why? Because in Latin there is a separate, dedicated word for the way *his* is used in paragraph 1 and another separate, dedicated word for the way *his* is used in paragraph 2. One of them means *his*, as in belonging to the subject of the sentence, and the other means *his* as in belonging to somebody else. So, when you see one of these words in Latin, you know right away who it is referring to, and there is no ambiguity as there might be in a corresponding English sentence.

Here's how it works. The adjective **suus, sua, suum** is the Latin word that works like in paragraph 1. It always refers to the subject of the sentence. So if you have this sentence...

Vir librum suum habet. *(The man has his book.)*

...it means that the man has *his own* book, not somebody else's book.

But there is another word in Latin that can mean *his*, and that is the word **ejus** (pronounced *AAY-yuss*). **Ejus** means *his, her,* or *its*, but in the sense of paragraph 2, belonging to somebody else. So if you see a sentence like this one...

Vir librum ejus habet. *(The man has his/her/its book.)*

...the man does not have his own book—he has somebody else's book. We don't know who the book belongs to, because there isn't really any context to tell us, but what we do know is that in this sentence the book does not belong to the man.

So here's the whole point of this lesson: **suus, sua, suum** always shows that an item belongs to the subject of the sentence, not to somebody else. In this book, we will only work with **suus, sua, suum**, and we will not work with the word **ejus**. But if you continue much further in your Latin studies, you will soon encounter **ejus** again.

LESSON 81

PRACTICING WITH SUUS, SUA, SUUM

For the past two lessons, I've been talking, talking, talking about **suus, sua, suum**. Now, it's time to find out whether or not you paid attention!

For each of the following exercises, I would like for you to answer six (yes, six) questions. Use a notebook or a separate piece of paper so you don't write in this beautiful book!

1. Fill in the blank with the correct form of **suus, sua, suum**.

2. Provide the case, number, and gender of the form you chose.

3. Explain why you chose that particular form. Where did you look to get the information you needed to make your choice?

4. Translate the exercise into English.

5. When you translated **suus, sua, suum** into English, where did you look to find the information you needed to properly translate it?

6. Does the item being possessed belong to the subject of the sentence, or to somebody else?

EXERCISES

1. **Fēmina equum ＿＿＿ habet.**
2. **Vir numquam agrōs ＿＿＿ arat.**
3. **Rēgīna castellum ＿＿＿ aedificat.**
4. **Discipulae bonae semper librōs ＿＿＿ cūrant.**
5. **Rōmulus scūtum ＿＿＿ cūrat.**
6. **Nōnne rēgīna scūtum ＿＿＿ habet?**
7. **Bibliothēcārius librōs ＿＿＿ cūrat.**
8. **Rēgīna semper viās in rēgnō ＿＿＿ cūrat.**
9. **Magister discipulōs ＿＿＿ numquam docet.**
10. **Incolae argentum ＿＿＿ nōn habent.**

Answers on page 276.

LESSON 82

THE ROMAN HOUSE

At this point in the book, I would like to start teaching you the Latin names of the various rooms of a house. But because Roman homes had a somewhat different design that our modern homes, some of these Latin room names won't correspond exactly to English words. So, before we study the names of any specific rooms, let's take a moment to learn about the general design of an ancient Roman house.

The floor plan of a Roman house centered around a large central room with a funnel-shaped hole in the roof. Here's an artist's rendering (as a cross-section) of what this part of the house looked like:

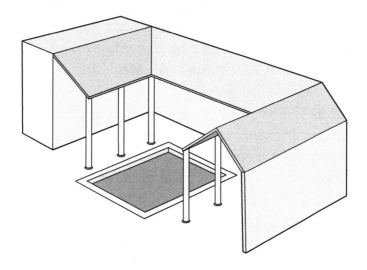

The purpose of the hole in the roof was to allow rain to pour in and collect in a pool which was embedded in the floor. This hole also allowed sunlight into the home. Columns surrounded the pool, supporting the roof and creating a walkway around the pool which connected to the other rooms of the house. As I mentioned above, the rooms of a Roman home may not correspond exactly to the rooms of a modern home. But the Latin language is bigger than just the ancient Romans, and as we try to figure out what to call the various rooms of a house, we can look at later periods of Latin such as the Medieval Period or the Renaissance in order to find suitable words. And, as I always say, try to have fun with it as you go along.

LESSON 83

NEW WORD   **culīna, culīnae**

MEANING   *kitchen*

In Latin, the word for *kitchen* is **culīna**, a feminine noun of the first declension. It's related to our English word *culinary*.

EXERCISES

1. **Haec casa est parva, sed magnam culīnam habet. ♦ Familia nostra in culīnā cēnāre potest.**
2. **Ubi est Tertius? ♦ Tertius in culīnā cēnat.**
3. **Ō rēgīna mea, castellum tuum multās culīnās habet. Cūr novum castellum postulās? ♦ Culīnae meae sunt parvae.**
4. **Obsōnatne nunc Jōsēphus? ♦ Ita, Jōsēphus ad macellum nunc properat. ♦ Ubi est macellum? ♦ Macellum est inter templum Minervae et magnam bibliothēcam.**
5. **In vīcīniā bonā habitāmus. ♦ Ita. Multa castella adsunt. Fortasse rēgīnae quoque in vīcīniā nostrā habitant.**
6. **Ō rēgīna, cūr magnam culīnam in castellō tuō habēs? ♦ Rēgīna sum, et cibum bonum amō. Nōnne culīnam in casā tuā habēs? ♦ Ita, sed culīna parva est. Et in castellō nōn habitō.**
7. **Semprōnia scapham suam habet. ♦ Cūr? ♦ Nesciō. Fortasse hodiē ad īnsulam nāvigat.**
8. **Magistrae cotīdiē discipulōs suōs docent.**
9. **Illa culīna est magna. ♦ Ita. Longa est, sed angusta.**
10. **Estne fundus vester bonus? ♦ Ita. Porcī in fundō nostrō semper sunt laetī, et semper cibum aquamque habent. ♦ Porcōs vestrōs semper cūrātis quod agricolae bonī estis.**

Answers on page 276.

LESSON 84

NEW WORD   **trīclīnium, trīclīniī**

MEANING   *dining room*

PRONUNCIATION TIP: The stress is on the second syllable, so **trīclīnium** sounds something like *tree-CLEAN-nee-uhm.*

The word **trīclīnium** is borrowed from ancient Greek. The **tri-** part of the word means *three*, and the **-clin-** part of the word means *couch* or *bed*. This Greek word is related to English words like *recline, decline,* and *incline.* Therefore the word **trīclīnium** translates literally as *triple-couch.* Because of this large piece of furniture, the entire dining room was called a **trīclīnium.** So you can refer to the dining room in your home as the **trīclīnium.** That's a neuter noun of the second declension.

A **trīclīnium** would have these couches on three sides of the room with one side left open so that food and drink could be brought to the table in the middle. Here's an artist's rendering of what the whole arrangement could have looked like, with some ancient Romans reclining on the couches as they eat.

EXERCISES

1. Ō Rūfe, amīcī tuī in trīclīniō nostrō cēnant. Cūr tū cum amīcīs tuīs nōn cēnās? ♦ In culīnā maneō. ♦ Cūr manēs in culīnā? ♦ Īrātus sum!

2. Semper in trīclīniō cēnāmus. Fortasse interdum in culīnā nostrā cēnāre possumus. ♦ Minimē. Familia nostra est magna. In culīnā nostrā cēnāre nōn possumus.

3. Ō amīca, cūr in oppidum ambulāmus? ♦ Ad macellum nunc ambulāmus. ♦ Cūr nunc obsōnāmus? Tū domī multum cibum habēs! ♦ Ad macellum ambulāmus quod Quīntus in macellō labōrat. ♦ Quīntus? Num fīlius Cornēliī est? ♦ Ita, ille vir est fīlius Cornēliī. ♦ Num Quīntum amās? ♦ Fortasse.

4. Poēta puerīs et puellīs fābulam dē porcīs narrat. ♦ Estne fābula bona? ♦ Ita. In fābulā, parvī porcī in parvā casā habitant. Magnus lupus malus ante casam adest, sed porcī casam suam servant. ♦ Illa fābula est bona!

5. Ō Carole, estne Rūfus fīlius tuus? ♦ Ita, Rūfus est fīlius meus. ♦ Fīlius tuus numquam librum suum habet. Discipulus malus est. Cūr numquam librum suum habet? ♦ Hic liber est magnus. Fortasse Rūfus librum suum portāre nōn potest. ♦ Minimē! Hic liber est parvus!

6. Cūr nōn est bibliothēca in vīcīniā vestrā? ♦ Nesciō. Fortasse incolae vīcīniae nostrae librōs nōn amant.

7. Fessa sum. ♦ Cūr fessa es, ō amīca mea? ♦ Cotīdiē in fundō meō labōrō. ♦ Fundus tuus est magnus. ♦ Ita, hic fundus est lātus et longus. ♦ Fortasse fīliī tuī et fīliae tuae agrōs interdum arāre possunt.

8. Cūr rēgīna in castellō suō hodiē manet? ♦ Fīliī reginae hodiē aegrōtant. Rēgīna nunc fīliōs suōs cūrant. ♦ Rēgīna nostra est fēmina bona. Semper fīliōs suōs et fīliās suās cūrat.

9. Casam vestram amō. ♦ Cūr casam nostram amās? ♦ Casa vestra magnum trīclīnium habet, et magnam culīnam quoque habet.

10. Ego propter bestiās trāns silvam ambulāre nōn possum. ♦ Num lupōs timēs? ♦ Minimē. Magnōs porcōs timeō. Multī porcī in silvā habitant. ♦ Porcī in silvā nōn habitant!

Answers on page 277.

LESSON 85

NEW WORD   **mēnsa, mēnsae / sella, sellae**

MEANING   *table / chair*

Since we are learning about kitchens and dining rooms, let's learn the Latin words for *table* and *chair*. Both of these nouns are feminine nouns of the first declension.

EXERCISES

1. **Mēnsa est in trīclīniō. Sellae quoque in trīclīniō sunt.**
2. **Puer parvam sellam habet, sed ego magnam sellam habeō.**
3. **Ubi est sella mea?** ♦ **Nesciō. Fortasse sella tua in culīnā est.** ♦ **Cūr sellae in culīnā sunt?** ♦ **Rūfus nunc in culīnā cum amīcīs suīs cēnat.** ♦ **Habetne Rūfus amīcōs?**
4. **Cibus noster in mēnsā est. Sellae circum mēnsam sunt.** ♦ **Fortasse nunc cēnāre possumus.** ♦ **Ita. Fīliae nostrae cibum postulant.**
5. **Marcus ē trīclīniō cum cibō nostrō properat!** ♦ **Marcus est puer malus.**
6. **Rēgīna nunc novam sellam postulat.** ♦ **Cūr novam sellam postulat?** ♦ **Rēgīna novam sellam postulat quod sella sua est parva et angusta.**
7. **Ubi est Pūblius?** ♦ **Fundum suum cūrat.** ♦ **Num Pūblius est agricola?** ♦ **Ita, parvum fundum cum porcīs et equīs habet.** ♦ **Ubi est fundus Pūbliī?** ♦ **Fundus Pūbliī nōn est in vīcīniā nostrā. Prope silvam est, inter oppidum et actam.**
8. **Magnus lupus trāns agrum nostrum properat!** ♦ **Ego magnōs lupōs timeō!** ♦ **Ille lupus ad porcōs nostrōs properat! Ubi est gladius meus? Ego porcōs nostrōs gladiō servāre possum.** ♦ **Fortasse ego in casā manēre possum.**
9. **Illud templum nōn est magnum. Cūr templum est parvum?** ♦ **Illud templum nōn est parvum. Angustum est, sed longum est.**
10. **Nōnne bibliothēca in vīcīniā vestrā est?** ♦ **Minimē, sed castellum habēmus.** ♦ **Num castellum est in vīcīniā vestrā?** ♦ **Ita, rēgīna in vīcīniā nostrā habitat.** ♦ **Rēgīna in vīcīniā vestrā nōn habitat!** ♦ **Thermopōlium bonum quoque habēmus.**

Answers on page 277.

135

LESSON 86

NEW WORD **sedeō / sedēre**

MEANING *I sit / to sit*

Sedeō is a verb of the second conjugation. It is related to the English word *sedentary*, which is used to describe people who sit down too much and don't get enough exercise—like me, while I'm sitting here writing this book!

	SINGULAR	PLURAL
FIRST PERSON	**sedeō**	**sedēmus**
SECOND PERSON	**sedēs**	**sedētis**
THIRD PERSON	**sedet**	**sedent**

INFINITIVE	**sedēre**

EXERCISES

1. **In sellā meā sedeō.** ◆ **Illa sella nōn est sella tua. Sella mea est.** ◆ **Minimē! Haec sella est sella mea!** ◆ **Cūr pugnāmus? Sunt multae sellae in trīclīniō.**

2. **Ō Quīnte, cūr in equō tuō cum gladiō sedēs? Num pīrātae ad rēgnum nostrum nāvigant?** ◆ **Hodiē rēgnum nostrum gladiō scūtōque servō.** ◆ **Ego quoque rēgnum servāre possum.** ◆ **Tūne habēs equum?** ◆ **Minimē, sed gladium habeō.** ◆ **Nunc pīrātae rēgnum nostrum superāre nōn possunt.**

3. **Haec discipula est puella bona quod numquam pugnat et semper in sellā suā sedet.** ◆ **Discipulae meae saepe absunt, et domī manent.**

136

4. **Ō Aemilia, cūr hodiē aegrōtās? Cūr domī manēs? ♦ Propter cibum malum aegrōtō. ♦ Tū aegrōtās quod semper in thermopōliīs malīs cēnās.**

5. **Ō Rōberte, cūr in culīnā cum familiā tuā sedēs? ♦ Casa nostra est parva, et trīclīnium nōn habet. Semper in culīnā cēnāmus. ♦ Casa vestra est parva, sed casa bona est. Vīcīnia tua quoque est bona. ♦ Familia mea magnam casam postulat, sed multam pecūniam nōn habeō.**

6. **Cūr in scaphā meā sedēs? ♦ Natāre nōn possum.**

7. **Ō Fausta, cūr in saxō sedēs? ♦ Sellam nōn habeō. ♦ Nōnne saxum est sella mala? ♦ Ita, est sella mala, sed in saxō sedeō quod fessa sum.**

8. **Ō Helena, ubi sunt amīcae tuae? ♦ Amīcae meae in novā popīnā cēnant. ♦ Cūr domī ades? Cūr tū cum amīcīs tuīs nōn cēnās? ♦ Ego ad popīnam nunc properō. Valē!**

9. **Ubi est rēgīna? ♦ Rēgīna in castellō suō cum fīliābus suīs est.**

10. **Ubi sunt Claudia et Pūblius? ♦ In fundō suō labōrant.**

Answers on page 277.

LESSON 87

NEW WORD   **cubiculum, cubiculī / lectus, lectī**

MEANING   *bedroom / bed*

Cubiculum is a neuter noun of the second declension. It is related to our English word *cubicle*. **Lectus** is a masculine noun of the second declension.

EXERCISES

1. **Ubi est Semprōnia? Semprōnia abest. ♦ Semprōnia est in cubiculō suō. ♦ Num aegrōtat? ♦ Minimē, hodiē valet.**

2. **Cūr lectus meus est angustus?** ◆ **Ō fīlia, lectus tuus est angustus quod cubiculum tuum est angustum.** ◆ **Cūr Marcus lātum cubiculum habet?**

3. **Mēnsam et sellam in cubiculō meō habeō.** ◆ **Cūr?** ◆ **Saepe in cubiculō meō labōrō.**

4. **Trīclīnium nostrum nōn est magnum, sed multae sellae in trīclīniō sunt.** ◆ **Cūr multās sellās in trīclīniō vestrō habētis?** ◆ **Saepe in trīclīniō nostrō cum amīcīs nostrīs cēnāmus.** ◆ **Cūr in culīnā vestrā nōn cēnātis?** ◆ **Nōn habēmus mēnsam in culīnā. Sine mēnsā cēnāre nōn possumus.**

5. **Cūr Lūcius ē casā nunc properat?** ◆ **Lūcius nunc obsōnat quod in culīnā nostrā multum cibum nōn habēmus.** ◆ **Cūr Lūcius librōs portat?** ◆ **Ad macellum ambulat. Ad bibliothēcam quoque ambulat.**

6. **Ō Tertī, ubi sunt puellae?** ◆ **In cubiculō suō sunt. Sedent in lectīs suīs.**

7. **Hoc cubiculum est parvum. Cūr cubiculum meum est parvum?** ◆ **Ō fīlia, cubiculum tuum nōn est parvum.** ◆ **Et cūr lectus meus est parvus? Hic lectus est malus!** ◆ **Ō fīlia, lectus tuus nōn est malus! Novus lectus est!**

8. **Num īrātus es?** ◆ **Sum īrātus!** ◆ **Cūr īrātus es?** ◆ **Īrātus sum quod tū equum meum habēs, et pecūniam meam quoque habēs!** ◆ **Sed amīcī sumus.** ◆ **Nōn sumus amīcī!**

9. **In oppidō ambulāmus.**

10. **In oppidum ambulāmus.**

Answers on page 278.

LESSON 88

ROMAN BATHS

These days, most of us bathe at home in our own tubs or showers. But the ancient Romans liked to do their bathing at public bath houses where (for a small fee) you could spend the afternoon in pleasant conversation, exercise, massage, and yes, bathing.

Roman bath houses varied in their size and design, but most of them had the same basic components. There was a dressing room were bathers could undress and store their clothing. Then, there was a warm room where bathers could relax and get accustomed to warmer temperatures. Bathers could then take a dip in either a hot pool or cold pool, or both. While going through the various stages of the bathing process, people could socialize, conduct business, or talk politics.

Depending on the size of the bath house, there could be other amenities such as a courtyard for outdoor exercise, a place to get a massage, a library for studying literature, or a place to get a bite to eat. The afternoon would end with an oily rub-down. Oil and dirt were scraped away with a special tool called a **strigilis**. So you see, the Roman baths weren't just places to get cleaned up—they were a sort of gym, cafe, sauna, day spa, and social club all rolled into one.

Several different Latin terms were used to refer to these public bath houses, depending on the period of Roman history you are talking about: **balneum**, **balnea**, and **thermae**. According to author Harold Whetstone Johnston, the term **balneum** was used first, then the feminine plural term **balneae** was used later to refer to more elaborate baths. Finally, the term **thermae** was used (that, as you already know, is a Greek loan word). The place where you would actually use the toilet was called the **lātrīna**, which is related to our English word *latrine*.

So, if want to talk about the bathroom in your home, you have a couple of choices. If it's a bathroom where there is no bathtub, but just a toilet, you could call it a **lātrīna**. That's a feminine noun of the first declension. But if it's a bathing area, you could call it a **balneum**, which is a neuter noun of the second declension. In the answer key, I will translate both of these words as *bathroom*.

EXERCISES

1. **Ō amīce, ubi est lātrīna?**
2. **Sunt multa cubicula in casā Jūliae. Est magnum balneum quoque in casā. ♦ Illa casa est magna! Cūr casa est magna? ♦ Jūlia multōs fīliōs et multās fīliās habet.**
3. **Carolus abest. Ubi est Carolus? ♦ Carolus est in lātrīnā suā quod aegrōtat.**
4. **Rēgīna magnum trīclīnium habet. Trīclīnium rēgīnae magnam mēnsam habet, et multās sellās quoque habet. Rēgīna cotīdiē cum amīcīs suīs cēnat in trīclīniō suō. ♦ Habetne castellum rēgīnae magnam culīnam? ♦ Ita. Est magna culīna prope trīclīnium.**

5. **Ille puer est fīlius meus. ♦ Habēsne fīliam? ♦ Ita, illa puella est fīlia mea.**

6. **Ō Tertī, cūr in mūrō sedēs? ♦ Semper in mūrō sedeō. Oppidum servō. ♦ Sed scūtum nōn habēs. ♦ Minimē. ♦ Gladium nōn habēs. ♦ Minimē. ♦ Sine gladiō et scūtō tū oppidum servāre nōn potes!**

7. **Ō Fausta, cūr multōs librōs per oppidum portās? ♦ Ego bibliothēcāria sum. Novōs librōs ad bibliothēcam portō. Valē, amīce. ♦ Valē.**

8. **Ō discipulī, habētisne librōs vestrōs? ♦ Ita. Librōs nostrōs habēmus. ♦ Discipulī bonī estis.**

9. **Est via inter oppidum nostrum et oppidum vestrum. ♦ Via est angusta et mala. ♦ Cūr via est mala? ♦ Sunt multa saxa in viā. Ad oppidum vestrum propter saxa ambulāre nōn possum.**

10. **Ubi est Rōmulus? ♦ In cubiculō suō est. In lectō suō sedet.**

Answers on page 278.

LESSON 89

NEW WORD   **hypogaeum, hypogaeī / hortus, hortī**

MEANING   *basement / garden*

PRONUNCIATION TIP: When you convert a word from one alphabet to another, it's called *transliteration*. In Latin, there are many words which are borrowed from the Greek language and transliterated into the Roman alphabet. In these Latin words, the letter *y* is used to represent the Greek letter *upsilon*. It's a long story—but whenever you see the letter *y* in a Latin word, pronounce it like the *u* in *tune* or *fruit*. This means that the word **hypogaeum** will sound something like *hoop-oh-GUY-uhm*.

The word **hypogaeum** is borrowed from ancient Greek. The **hypo-** part of the word means *under* and the **-gae-** part of the word means *earth*. Therefore a **hypogaeum** is a place that is underground, such as a basement or cellar. It's a neuter noun of the second declension.

The word **hortus**, which means *garden*, is related to our English word *horticulture*.

EXERCISES

1. **Ō Gulielme, ubi sunt librī tuī? ♦ Librī meī in hypogaeō meō sunt. Hypogaeum meum est parva bibliothēca. ♦ Habēsne multōs librōs? ♦ Ita. Propter librōs meōs, per hypogaeum meum ambulāre nōn possum. ♦ Cūr multōs librōs habēs? ♦ Librōs amō!**

2. **Ō Jūlia, casam tuam amō! Tū magnam culīnam habēs, et magnum hortum quoque post casam tuam habēs. ♦ Bibliothēcam quoque cum multīs librīs habēmus. ♦ Num bibliothēcam in casā tuā habēs? ♦ Ita, habēmus bibliothēcam in casā nostrā. ♦ Fortasse ego quoque in casā tuā habitāre possum.**

3. **Ubi est Tullia? ♦ Tullia in lectō suō in cubiculō suō est.**

4. **Casa mea hypogaeum nōn habet. ♦ Casa tua hypogaeum nōn habet quod casa tua est magna scapha. Cūr in scaphā habitās? ♦ In magnā scaphā habitō quod nauta sum.**

5. **Ō Rūfe, cūr in hypogaeō Rōbertī habitās? Hoc hypogaeum est parvum et lātrīnam nōn habet. ♦ Multam pecūniam nōn habeō, et Rōbertus est amīcus meus. ♦ Fortasse tū in fundō meō labōrāre potes. ♦ In fundō labōrāre nōn possum. ♦ Cūr? ♦ Porcōs timeō.**

6. **Ō Helena, ubi est hortus tuus? ♦ Hortus meus est post casam meam. ♦ Tū magnum hortum habēs! ♦ Minimē, hortus meus est parvus.**

7. **Cūr puerī cum nautīs sedent? ♦ Nauta puerīs fābulam dē pīrātīs narrat. ♦ Nautae semper fābulās malās narrant.**

8. **Ō fīlia, ubi est liber meus? ♦ Liber tuus in mēnsā in trīcliniō est. ♦ Casa nostra trīclinium nōn habet!**

9. **Cūr trāns viam ambulāmus? ♦ Est popīna bona trāns viam.**

10. **Ō amīcī, cūr in culīnā sedētis? In culīnā nostrā multās sellās nōn habēmus, sed multās sellās in trīcliniō nostrō habēmus.**

Answers on page 278.

LESSON 90

THE ATRIUM

In this lesson, I would like to teach you how to refer to that room of the house where you and your family sit around and relax. Depending on where you live, you might call it a family room, living room, den, great room, sitting room, or parlor. The ancient Romans had places to sit too, but as I mentioned before, the rooms of a Roman home don't match up exactly with the rooms of a modern home.

When we first started talking about the rooms of a house, I showed you a picture of a large room with a hole in the roof for collecting rainwater. That large, central room of the house is called the **ātrium** (that's a neuter noun of the second declension). The funnel-shaped hole in the ceiling was called a **compluvium**. The purpose of this hole was to collect rainwater into the **impluvium**, which was a shallow pool embedded in the floor of the **ātrium**. Water could then drain from the **impluvium** into an underground cistern (a kind of holding tank) for later use. Here's the same picture I showed you a few lessons ago, but with the various parts of the **ātrium** labeled.

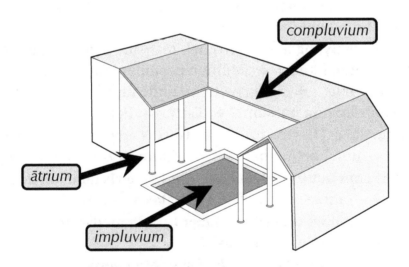

Around the **impluvium** there was a walkway which connected to various side rooms. The **ātrium** could be used for any number of purposes, such as greeting guests.

Here's the point I've been building up to: the word **ātrium** is one of several terms you could possibly use to refer to the sitting room of your home. Let's say, for example, that you have a large room at the front of your house with a skylight, or perhaps a ceiling that extends to the second floor. In that case, the word **ātrium** might be a good word to use to refer to that particular room. Even today, many large buildings have an open area with a high ceiling where you enter the building, and this room is referred to by architects as—you guessed it—an atrium.

But if you have a normal sitting room, such as what we would call a den, family room, living room, or parlor, you probably won't want to call it an **ātrium**. There are several words you could call it, but the best word for this kind of room is probably the second declension neuter noun **exedrium**. This word is related to other English words such as *cathedral* and *dodecahedron* (an object with twelve sides). The *-hedr-* part of each of these words is from the Greek word *hedra* which means *chair*. In the answer key, I will translate **exedrium** as *living room*.

EXERCISES

1. **Jūlia et Fulvia in exedriō cum amīcīs suīs sedent.**
2. **Casa mea ātrium nōn habet. Casa mea est parva.** ♦ **Sed hortum habet.** ♦ **Ita, hortum habēmus post casam. Nōnne tū quoque hortum habēs?** ♦ **Ita, parvum hortum habēmus.**
3. **Ō mī fīlī, cūr tū et amīcī tuī in exedriō nunc sedent?** ♦ **Fessī sumus, et sunt multae sellae in exedriō nostrō.** ♦ **Fortasse tū et amīcī tuī in hypogaeō sedēre potestis.**
4. **Ō lupe, habitāsne in casā?** ♦ **Minimē! Lupus sum. In silvā habitō.**
5. **Possumusne hodiē in trīclīniō cēnāre?** ♦ **Minimē, sellae absunt.**
6. **Haec casa magnum ātrium habet.** ♦ **Cūr in ātriō sumus?** ♦ **Nesciō.** ♦ **Caelum vidēre possum.** ♦ **Ego quoque caelum vidēre possum.**
7. **Ō amīce, cūr tū in scaphā meā ades? Cūr tū pecūniam meam postulās?** ♦ **Nōn sum amīcus tuus.** ♦ **Tūne pīrāta es?** ♦ **Ita. Pīrāta sum.** ♦ **Numquam ego pīrātīs pecūniam dō.**
8. **Ō Lāvīnia, ubi est fīlius tuus?** ♦ **Cornēlius est in fundō suō, cum porcīs suīs.** ♦ **Estne Cornēlius agricola?** ♦ **Ita, Cornēlius est agricola bonus, et magnum fundum habet.** ♦ **Habetne fīlius tuus equōs?** ♦ **Certē. Cornēlius multa stabula et multōs equōs in fundō suō habet.**
9. **Cūr in cubiculō nostrō parvōs lectōs habēmus?** ♦ **Ō fīliae, parvōs lectōs habētis quod parvae puellae estis.** ♦ **Longōs lēctōs postulāmus!**
10. **Ō Paule, cūr in lātrīnā meā ades?** ♦ **Aeger sum.** ♦ **Fortasse in lātrīnā tuā aegrōtāre potes.**

Answers on page 279.

LESSON 91

OVERVIEW OF THE ROMAN HOUSE

Now that you know the names of some of the rooms of a Roman house, let's take a closer look at what a Roman house looked like. Here's a diagram I created which is based on the houses that archaeologists have found at the city of Pompeii.

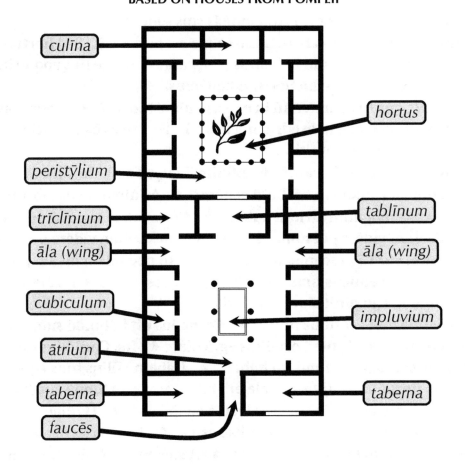

A POSSIBLE
ROMAN HOUSE
BASED ON HOUSES FROM POMPEII

culīna

hortus

peristȳlium

trīclīnium

tablīnum

āla (wing)

āla (wing)

cubiculum

impluvium

ātrium

taberna

taberna

faucēs

Keep in mind that not everybody in ancient Rome lived in a large home like this one—this kind of home would have been owned by a wealthy family. Scholars pay a lot of attention to this kind of home because it can tell us a great deal about Roman society and culture.

144

At the bottom of the diagram, facing the street, you will find the **tabernae.** You may remember that I introduced the word **taberna** to you in *Getting Started with Latin*. The definition I gave you for **taberna** was *store*. Not a terrible definition, but it wasn't a definition that tells exactly what a **taberna** was. You see, a **taberna** was a shop that had an open front facing the street. People could walk into the **taberna** and buy things for sale there. The owners of the home might rent out the **taberna** spaces to someone else, or they might sell things there themselves. The word **taberna** could also refer to an inn, and that particular meaning of the word **taberna** is where we get our English word *tavern*.

Entering the house from the street, you would walk through the front door, between the **tabernae**, and then through the front hallway or entryway. This entryway is called the **faucēs**, which means *throat*, because it's a narrow passage. After passing through the **faucēs**, you would emerge in the **ātrium**, where you would see the **compluvium** and the **impluvium.** Off to the sides there would be various rooms which could be bedrooms, or perhaps dining rooms. At the back of the **ātrium** was the **tablīnum**, where the patriarch of the home (called the **pater familiās**) would keep records and do paperwork. Near the **tablīnum** were side rooms called **ālae** *(wings)* where the business associates and clients of the **pater familiās** would come to greet him each morning. If your house or apartment has an office or study, you could call that room a **tablīnum**. In the exercises, when I use the word **tablīnum**, just translate it as *office*.

Depending on the design, there could be a garden in the rear area of the house. Around this garden there might be a covered walkway, the roof of which could be supported by columns which surround the garden. This kind of area is called a **peristȳlium**. Around the **peristȳlium** there might be rooms which could be used as kitchens, summer dining rooms, or living quarters.

Here is why we know so much about these houses: in Italy, there is a huge volcano called Mount Vesuvius. In ancient times, located near Mount Vesuvius there were two towns called Pompeii and Herculaneum. In the year AD 79 there was a massive eruption of Mount Vesuvius which covered Pompeii and Herculaneum with volcanic ash. But instead of destroying the towns, the volcanic ash hardened, causing the buildings to be perfectly preserved. Over time, archaeologists have dug away the hardened volcanic material, revealing the perfectly preserved Roman towns—which, by the way, you can visit today!

LESSON 92

NEW WORD   **pūrgō / pūrgāre**

MEANING   *I clean up / to clean up*

Our new verb for this lesson is related to the English word *purge*. It means *to clean up*, as in clearing away unwanted stuff. I'm introducing this word to you so you can use it to talk about cleaning up your home. Here's an example sentence using the word **tablīnum** *(office)* which we learned in the last lesson:

Claudia tablīnum suum pūrgat. *(Claudia is cleaning up her office.)*

And, as long as we are talking about cleaning up, let's learn the Latin word for *dirty:* the first and second declension adjective **sordidus**, **sordida**, **sordidum**. It's where we get our English word *sordid*.

EXERCISES

1. **Ō mī fīlī, cubiculum tuum est sordidum.** ♦ **Nunc cubiculum meum pūrgāre nōn possum.** ♦ **Cūr, ō fīlī?** ♦ **Fessus sum.**
2. **Hoc balneum est sordidum. Cūr balneum nōn pūrgās?** ♦ **Hoc balneum nōn est balneum meum.**
3. **Casa mea est magna. Magnum exedrium habēmus, et magnam culīnam quoque habēmus.** ♦ **Sed hypogaeum nōn habētis.**
4. **Ō puellae, stabula nostra sunt sordida. Fortasse stabula hodiē pūrgāre potestis.** ♦ **Propter equōs, stabula pūrgāre nōn possumus.** ♦ **Equī nōn sunt in stabulīs! Equī in agrō sunt!** ♦ **Fessae sumus. Stabula pūrgāre nōn possumus.** ♦ **Minimē!** ♦ **Aegrōtāmus.** ♦ **Valētis! Nōn estis aegrae!**
5. **Ō Christophore, cūr hypogaeum tuum pūrgās?** ♦ **Est aqua in hypogaeō meō.** ♦ **Fortasse in hypogaeō tuō natāre possumus.**
6. **Tablīnum meum est sordidum.** ♦ **Tū numquam tablīnum tuum pūrgās.**
7. **Ō Petre, tū nunc in hypogaeō Christophorī habitāre nōn potes.** ♦ **Cūr?** ♦ **Multa aqua in hypogaeō Christophorī est.** ♦ **Lectus meus est in hypogaeō Christophorī!** ♦ **Nunc lectus tuus est scapha.**

146

8. **Cūr est aqua in exedriō tuō?** ◆ **Nōn sumus in exedriō meō. Sumus in ātriō. Aqua est in impluviō.**

9. **Ubi sunt amīcae meae? Sedentne in exedriō?** ◆ **Minimē. In culīnā sunt quod multus cibus in culīnā est.**

10. **Ō puerī, cūr nōn estis in lectīs vestrīs?** ◆ **Nōn sumus fessī. Tertius est in balneō.**

Answers on page 279.

LESSON 93

THE THIRD DECLENSION

In Latin, there are five patterns of noun endings called *declensions*. You are already familiar with the first and second declensions, but you don't yet know the third, fourth, or fifth declensions. The fourth and fifth declensions have fewer common nouns than the other declensions, so at this point in your Latin studies, you don't really need to know those declensions yet.

But the third declension is a different story! The third declension contains an enormous number of common, useful words—words that no student of Latin can do without. So, the time has come for you to start learning about the third declension.

The third declension is slightly more complicated than the ones you already know, for a couple of reasons. First of all, the third declension includes masculine, feminine, and neuter nouns. This means that you will have to work a little harder to remember what the gender of each noun is. Furthermore, in the third declension there is some variation to the pattern of endings. In other words, the spelling pattern will vary a little depending on the characteristics of each noun.

So really, the third declension is nothing to be afraid of. In this book, I will start you out with some very regular nouns that all share the exact same spelling pattern so you can get accustomed to the endings of the third declension in a nice, gentle way. So, turn the page and let's get started!

LESSON 94

REVIEW OF THE GENITIVE STEM

Before we jump into the third declension, it might be helpful if we review an important concept: the genitive stem. We first talked about the genitive stem in *Getting Started with Latin* when we learned the second declension noun **ager**. This is because **ager** was the first noun we encountered that had a genitive stem which was different from its nominative stem. Other second declension nouns with this same spelling pattern are **puer**, **magister** and **liber**. Furthermore, we have seen several adjectives that have this kind of spelling pattern in their masculine gender: the adjectives **aeger**, **noster**, and **vester**.

So, as a quick review, let's go through the steps of finding and using the genitive stem, using the second declension noun **liber** as an example. Here it is:

liber

First, we find the genitive singular form of the noun:

librī

Now that we have the genitive singular form, we remove the ending:

libr-

Now that we have removed the ending from the genitive singular, we are left with the genitive stem which is **libr-**. Now we can take the various endings of the second declension and stick them to the end of the genitive stem, thereby creating the different forms of that particular noun. For example, if we want to make the genitive plural form of **liber**, we take the genitive stem, and then add the genitive plural ending which is **-ōrum**:

libr + ōrum = librōrum

You may have already mastered the skill of finding and using the genitive stem—but I want to be super-duper sure that you understand this important concept before we jump into the third declension. In the third declension, the genitive stem will be *extremely* important. Most of the nouns you encounter will have a genitive stem that differs from its nominative form. And this means that (as I have probably told you several times by now) whenever you encounter a new noun, you must memorize both the nominative singular *and* the genitive singular. If you don't, you won't know what the genitive stem is, and you won't be able to make all the different forms of the noun.

LESSON 95

NEW WORD   **māter**

MEANING   *mother*

PRONUNCIATION TIP: The accent is on the first syllable, so it sounds something like *MAH-ter*.

This is an exciting lesson because it's time for you to learn your very first noun of the third declension. **Māter** is a feminine noun which means *mother*. It is related to many English words such as *maternal, maternity, matrimony, matrilineal,* and *matriarch.*

As you might have guessed, **māter** is nominative singular. We will start by practicing with this one form, and then I will show you the other forms later. By the way, in the third declension the vocative form is the same as the nominative singular form. So you can use the word **māter** as both nominative singular and vocative singular.

A QUICK WORD ABOUT ADJECTIVES

A first and second declension adjective can modify a noun from any declension—it doesn't matter if the noun and adjective are from different declensions. So go ahead and use first and second declension adjectives with third declension nouns. As always, the adjective must agree in case, number, and gender with the noun it accompanies. Here are a few examples to get you started:

- **māter mea** *(my mother)*
- **māter tua** *(your mother)*
- **māter nostra** *(our mother)*
- **māter vestra** *(y'all's mother)*
- **haec māter** *(this mother)*
- **illa māter** *(that mother)*

149

1. Māter tua est rēgīna. In castellō magnō habitās. ♦ In magnō castellō habitō, sed ego parvum cubiculum habeō.
2. Ō māter, ubi es? ♦ Adsum, mī fīlī!
3. Cūr māter nostra nōn est domī? ♦ Ad thermopōlium cum amīcīs suīs ambulat. ♦ Fortasse domī cēnāre possumus. Estne cibus in culīnā? ♦ Ita, in culīnā cibum habēmus.
4. Māter mea est fessa quod multōs fīliōs habet.
5. Cūr māter vestra numquam per silvam ambulat? ♦ Lupōs timet. Propter lupōs, semper circum silvam ambulat, sed numquam per silvam ambulat.
6. Ubi nunc est māter tua? ♦ In lectō suō est in cubiculō suō.
7. Ō Jācōbe, cūr ante castellum es? ♦ Portās castellī servō.
8. Ō māter, cūr novam casam nostram amās? ♦ Haec casa magnam culīnam habet. Nunc familia nostra in culīnā cēnāre potest. ♦ Mēnsam in culīnā nōn habēmus.
9. Ō māter, cūr balnea nostra pūrgās? ♦ Sordida sunt balnea!
10. Ubi est Rōmulus? Num in exedriō est? ♦ Minimē. Rōmulus est in hypogaeō.

Answers on page 279.

LESSON 96

NEW WORD   **mātris**

MEANING   *mother* (genitive singular)

PRONUNCIATION TIP: The accent is on the first syllable, so it sounds like *MAH-tris.*

Our new word for this lesson, **mātris**, is the genitive singular form of the third declension noun **māter**. Notice that this word is somewhat similar to the second declension noun **ager** because it has an *e* in the nominative singular form that is not there in the genitive singular form.

Let's take the forms of **māter** that you know so far and put them into a declension chart.

THIRD DEC.	SINGULAR	PLURAL
NOMINATIVE (SUBJ./PRED. NOM.)	**māter**	
GENITIVE (POSSESSION)	**mātris**	
DATIVE (IND. OBJECT)		
ACCUSATIVE (DIRECT OBJECT)		
ABLATIVE (MANY USES)		

As I mentioned a couple of lessons ago, whenever you encounter a new third declension noun, you need to memorize both the nominative singular *and* the genitive singular. So, for the noun **māter**, you would chant this over and over: **māter, mātris...māter, mātris...māter, mātris**. In this way, memorize both forms—not only for this noun, but for every third declension noun that you encounter in the future.

Now that you know the genitive singular form of **māter**, we can say that the mother is possessing something.

- **equus mātris** (*the mother's horse*)
- **pecūnia mātris** (*the mother's money*)

And if you put an adjective with **mātris**, it must be genitive, singular, and feminine.

- **Scapham mātris meae videō.** (*I see my mother's boat.*)
- **Popīna mātris tuae cibum bonum habet.** (*Your mother's restaurant has good food.*)

151

EXERCISES

1. Equus mātris meae in stabulō est.

2. Dōnum mātris meae est in exedriō nostrō.

3. Cūr māter tua multōs librōs portat? ◆ Māter mea librōs suōs ad bibliothēcam portat.

4. Frāter mātris meae in hypogaeō nostrō habitat. ◆ Cūr? Nōnne casam habet? ◆ Minimē. In hypogaeō nostrō habitat quod pecūniam nōn habet.

5. Ō māter, ubi est Fredericus? ◆ Nesciō, ō mī fīlī. Fortasse Fredericus cubiculum suum pūrgat. ◆ Minimē! Fredericus numquam cubiculum suum pūrgat.

6. Illa fēmina est amīca mea. ◆ Cūr amīca tua parvam puellam portat? ◆ Amīca mea est māter. Illa puella est fīlia amīcae meae.

7. Ō māter, cūr trāns viam ambulās? ◆ Cibum domī nōn habēmus. Ad macellum properō. ◆ Ego ante templum cum amīcīs meīs manēre possum. Valē, ō māter.

8. Ubi sunt amīcī meī? ◆ Sedent in exedriō. ◆ Fortasse in trīcliniō cēnāre possumus. ◆ Nesciō. Multum cibum nōn habēmus. ◆ Fortasse ad thermopōlium ambulāre possumus. ◆ Fortasse, sed sunt multī nautae in thermopōliō. Fābulās malās interdum narrant. ◆ Fābulās malās saepe narrant.

9. Vīcīnia nostra multa castella habet. Ō māter, esne rēgīna? ◆ Minimē! Nōn sum rēgīna. Agricolae sumus, sed prope castella habitāmus.

10. Ō mī fīlī, cūr cubiculum tuum nōn pūrgās? ◆ Flāvia quoque cubiculum suum nōn pūrgat. ◆ Balnea vestra quoque sunt sordida.

Answers on page 280.

LESSON 97

THE GENITIVE STEM WITH THIRD DECLENSION NOUNS

You now know one noun from the third declension: the word **māter**. You know the nominative singular form and the genitive singular form, which is **mātris**. So far, so good.

Just to make absolutely, positively, double-dog sure that you understand the idea of the genitive stem, I would like to go through the process of finding and using the genitive stem with **māter**. This is the first time you have done this with a third declension noun. Here it is:

māter

First, we take the genitive singular form.

mātris

Next, we remove the genitive singular ending from the genitive singular form. For **mātris**, the genitive singular ending is **-is**, so let's take that away.

mātr-

Now we are left with **mātr-**, which is the genitive stem for this noun. Now that we know the genitive stem, we can add the various endings of the third declension and create the different forms of this noun. But, you don't know any other endings for the third declension yet...but when you do learn some, you'll be ready!

LESSON 98

NEW WORD   **pater, patris**

MEANING   *father*

Our new word for this lesson is a masculine noun of the third declension. It's related to English words like *patriotic, patriarch,* and *patrilineal.*

Observe the nominative singular and genitive singular forms of **pater** in this chart.

THIRD DEC.	SINGULAR	PLURAL
NOMINATIVE (SUBJ./PRED. NOM.)	**pater**	
GENITIVE (POSSESSION)	**patris**	
DATIVE (IND. OBJECT)		
ACCUSATIVE (DIRECT OBJECT)		
ABLATIVE (MANY USES)		

To find the genitive stem, remove the ending from **patris**. This leaves you with **patr-** which is the genitive stem. Later, we will use the genitive stem to create the various forms of this noun.

Also, remember that **pater** is masculine, so you must use masculine adjectives with it as shown in these examples:

- **pater meus** *(my father)*
- **pater tuus** *(your father)*
- **hic pater** *(this father)*
- **ille pater** *(that father)*
- **scapha patris meī** *(my father's boat)*
- **thermopōlium patris nostrī** *(our father's cafe)*

EXERCISES

1. **Ō puer, ubi est pater tuus?** ♦ **Pater meus hodiē domī est.** ♦ **Ubi est casa patris tuī?** ♦ **Inter bibliothēcam et portās oppidī habitāmus.**

2. **Ō pater, in fundō nostrō hodiē labōrāre nōn possum.** ♦ **Cūr, mī fīlī?** ♦ **Fessus sum quod aegrōtō. Fortasse in cubiculō meō manēre possum.**

3. **Ō māter, ubi est argentāria?** ♦ **Cūr? Num pecūniam habēs?** ♦ **Minimē. Amīcī meī in novā popīnā cēnant. Popīna prope argentāriam est. Ubi est argentāria?** ♦ **Argentāria est prope portam oppidī, inter templum Minervae et theātrum.**

4. **Ille vir est pater meus.** ♦ **Cūr pater tuus ad templum Neptūnī properat?** ♦ **Pater meus est nauta. Dōnum ad templum portat. Hodiē per scaphās pīrātārum ad magnam īnsulam nāvigat.**

5. **Ō rēgīna, rēgnum tuum est angustum, sed longum. Fortasse mūrum circum rēgnum tuum aedificāre possumus.** ♦ **Fortasse, sed lignum in rēgnō meō nōn habēmus.** ♦ **Ē saxō mūrum aedificāre possumus.**

6. **Ubi est pater tuus?** ♦ **In exedriō est. Puellīs puerīsque fābulam dē lupō malō et parvīs porcīs narrat.** ♦ **Illa fābula est bona!** ♦ **Ita. Pater meus multās fābulās narrat.**

7. **Culīna nostra est sordida. Īrātus sum quod Rūfus numquam culīnam pūrgat.** ♦ **Rūfus lātrīnam quoque numquam pūrgat.**

8. **Cūr numquam in culīnā nostrā cēnāmus?** ♦ **Numquam in culīnā cēnāmus quod familia nostra est magna! Habēmus multōs fīliōs et multās fīliās.** ♦ **Sed culīna nostra est magna.** ♦ **Ita, sed mēnsa in culīnā nostrā est parva.**

9. **Ō pater, cūr in stabulō habitāmus?** ♦ **In stabulō habitāmus quod equī sumus.**

10. **Cūr multī librī in exedriō sunt?** ♦ **Librī mātris meae sunt. Māter mea librōs amat.**

Answers on page 280.

LESSON 99

NEW WORD   **frāter, frātris**

MEANING   *brother*

Our new word for this lesson, **frāter**, is a masculine noun of the third declension. It's related to English words like *fraternity, fraternal,* and *fraternize.*

The spelling pattern for this noun is the same as for **māter** and **pater**. First, there is an *e* in the nominative singular that is not present in the genitive singular. Also, the genitive singular ending is **-is**. Lastly, the genitive stem is **frātr-**.

THIRD DEC.	SINGULAR	PLURAL
NOMINATIVE (SUBJ./PRED. NOM.)	**frāter**	
GENITIVE (POSSESSION)	**frātris**	
DATIVE (IND. OBJECT)		
ACCUSATIVE (DIRECT OBJECT)		
ABLATIVE (MANY USES)		

EXERCISES

1. **Hic puer est frāter meus, sed ille puer nōn est frāter meus.**
2. **Ō frāter, num in cubiculō meō ades? Cūr in lectō meō sedēs?** ♦ **Īrātus sum quod tū librum meum habēs. Ubi est liber meus?** ♦ **Nesciō. Librum tuum nōn habeō.** ♦ **Minimē! Tū librum meum habēs! Librum meum postulō!**
3. **Haec fēmina est māter mea. Bibliothēcāria est.** ♦ **Labōratne māter tua in bibliothēcā?** ♦ **Ita, librōs cotīdiē cūrat et servat, sed hodiē domī est.** ♦ **Cūr hodiē domī est?** ♦ **Frāter meus hodiē aeger est.**
4. **Cūr multī librī in mēnsā sunt?** ♦ **Librī patris meī sunt. Pater meus librōs amat. Hic liber dē equīs est.**

156

5. **Pater meus pecūniam suam nōn habet. Ō pīrāta, num pecuniam patris meī habēs?** ♦ **Minimē.** ♦ **Cūr multam pecūniam in scaphā tuā habēs?** ♦ **Nesciō.**

6. **Māter mea popīnam habet. Popīna mātris meae cibum bonum habet.** ♦ **Fortasse ego in popīnā mātris tuae hodiē cēnāre possum.** ♦ **Ita. Frāter meus et ego interdum in popīnā mātris meae cēnāmus.**

7. **Cūr īrāta es?** ♦ **Stabula hodiē pūrgāmus. Stabula sunt sordida.** ♦ **Cūr equī stabula sua nōn pūrgant?** ♦ **Equī stabula pūrgāre nōn possunt!**

8. **Ō pater, cūr tū semper in tablīnō tuō sedēs?** ♦ **Ō fīlia mea, ego saepe in tablīnō meō labōrō.** ♦ **Tablīnum tuum est sordidum.**

9. **Ō Helena, cūr in scaphā frātris tuī sedēs?** ♦ **Ad patriam nostram nunc nāvigāmus.** ♦ **Cūr?** ♦ **Frāter mātris meae est aeger. In patriā nostrā habitat.**

10. **Equus mātris tuae est ante argentāriam.** ♦ **Māter mea est in argentāriā.**

Answers on page 280.

LESSON 100

USING THE GENITIVE STEM

At this point you know three nouns from the third declension: **māter**, **pater**, and **frāter**. But for each of these nouns, you only know the nominative singular and genitive singular. The good news is, however, that you know how to find and use the genitive stem. And with that knowledge, you can easily create any other form of the noun.

So, in this lesson, let's put our knowledge of the genitive stem to use and make the nominative plural form of these nouns. In the third declension, the nominative plural ending is **-ēs**. Let's practice this with the noun **māter**.

māter

First, we find the genitive singular form.

mātris

Then, we remove the genitive singular ending, which is **-is**. That leaves us with the genitive stem:

mātr-

Now we have the basic ingredients we need to make the nominative plural form of this noun. We know that the genitive stem is **mātr-**, and we know that in the third declension, the nominative plural ending is **-ēs**. So, let's add the nominative plural ending to the genitive stem and make the nominative plural form of **māter**.

mātr + ēs = mātrēs

Now, we have **mātrēs**, which is the nominative plural form of **māter**. Here's a chart showing the forms of **māter** that you know so far.

THIRD DEC.	SINGULAR	PLURAL
NOMINATIVE (SUBJ./PRED. NOM.)	**māter**	**mātrēs**
GENITIVE (POSSESSION)	**mātris**	
DATIVE (IND. OBJECT)		
ACCUSATIVE (DIRECT OBJECT)		
ABLATIVE (MANY USES)		

Now, repeat those same steps with **pater** and **frāter**, creating the nominative plural form of each of those nouns.

And don't forget: first and second declension adjectives must agree in case, number, and gender with the nouns they accompany, like in these examples:

- **mātrēs bonae** (*good mothers*)

- **patrēs fessī** *(tired fathers)*
- **frātrēs vestrī** *(y'alls brothers)*

EXERCISES

1. **Patrēs et fīliī agrum arant. ♦ Nōnne Rūfus quoque nunc agrum arat? ♦ Minimē, Rūfus numquam agrum arat.**
2. **Mātrēs nostrae ante templum Minervae sunt.**
3. **Frātrēs meī numquam cubicula sua pūrgant.**
4. **Ō Rōberte, ubi sunt frātrēs tuī? ♦ Pater meus et frātrēs meī lignum ē silvā portant.**
5. **Ubi est casa mātris tuae? ♦ Māter mea in silvā habitat. ♦ Cūr in silvā habitat? ♦ Māter mea silvam amat quod nōn prope oppidum est. Stēllās et lūnam vidēre potest. ♦ Ego in silvā habitāre nōn possum quod lupī in silvā adsunt.**
6. **Fīlius patris meī est frāter meus.**
7. **Ubi sunt mātrēs nostrae et patrēs nostrī? ♦ In scholā cum magistrīs sunt.**
8. **Ubi est sella patris meī? ♦ In hypogaeō est. ♦ Cūr? Pater meus numquam in hypogaeō sedet. Semper in exedriō sedet.**
9. **Rēgīna incolīs rēgnī suī pecūniam dat. ♦ Cūr? ♦ Rēgīna est fēmina bona, et semper incolās cūrat. Interdum puerīs puellīsque rēgnī cibum dat.**
10. **Fīlia nostra ab oppidō ad actam cum amicīs suīs ambulat.**

Answers on page 281.

LESSON 101

GENITIVE PLURAL

In the third declension, the genitive plural ending is **-um**. Just for practice, let's go through the steps of forming the genitive plural for each third declension noun that you know. I'm pretty sure that you know the steps by now, but here are those steps again just in case:

1. Find the genitive singular form.
2. Remove the ending, leaving the genitive stem.
3. Add the ending to the genitive stem.
4. *POOF* You have now created the new form of the noun.

If you followed the steps correctly, you should have come up with the following genitive plural forms: **mātrum**, **patrum**, and **frātrum**.

THIRD DEC.	SINGULAR	PLURAL
NOMINATIVE (SUBJ./PRED. NOM.)	pater	patres
GENITIVE (POSSESSION)	patris	patrum
DATIVE (IND. OBJECT)		
ACCUSATIVE (DIRECT OBJECT)		
ABLATIVE (MANY USES)		

Remember that in English, when something is being possessed by more than one person, you usually put the apostrophe after the letter *s*, not before. Here is a chart with three basic rules to help you remember how to handle apostrophes in English.

	RULE	EXAMPLE
RULE #1	To make a noun that does not end in *s* possessive, just add an apostrophe and an *s*.	Lauren always wants to borrow Kate's Latin book.
RULE #2	To make a singular noun that ends in *s* possessive, add an apostrophe and an *s* (just like rule #1).	The class's favorite subject was Latin.
RULE #3	To make a plural noun that ends in *s* possessive, add an apostrophe to the end of the word.	Due to increased interest in Latin, all the books' covers are starting to wear out.

So, if you see this in Latin...

pecūnia nautārum

...the money is being owned or possessed by more than one sailor. So when you translate it into English, you will need to put the apostrophe *after* the letter *s*, like this:

the sailors' money

Of course, you can always translate the genitive case into English using the word *of*, like this:

the money of the sailors

When you translate phrases like this into English, translate them in the way that sounds most natural in English. Here are a few examples to get you started working with third declension genitive plurals.

- **patria mātrum nostrārum** *(our mothers' homeland* OR *the homeland of our mothers)*
- **pecūnia frātrum meōrum** *(my brothers' money* OR *the money of my brothers)*
- **thermopōlium patrum vestrōrum** *(y'all's fathers' cafe* OR *the cafe of y'all's fathers)*

161

1. **Ubi est pecūnia mātrum nostrārum?** ◆ **Pecūnia est in argentāriā.**
2. **Cubicula frātrum meōrum semper sunt sordida.** ◆ **Numquam cubicula sua pūrgant!**
3. **Patrēs nostrī sunt agricolae, sed fundī patrum nostrōrum sunt parvī.** ◆ **Cūr fundī patrum nostrōrum sunt parvī?** ◆ **Parvōs agrōs habent.**
4. **Ō Helena, nōnne māter tua est magistra?** ◆ **Ita. Fessa saepe est quod multōs discipulōs cotīdiē docet.**
5. **Ō pater, multōs librōs in tablīnō tuō habēs.** ◆ **Ita, fīlia mea, librōs amō.** ◆ **Habēsne librum dē porcīs?** ◆ **Minimē, sed multōs librōs dē equīs habeō.**
6. **Ō māter, tū rēgīna es, sed castellum nostrum est parvum. Cūr in parvō castellō habitāmus? Nōnne magnum castellum aedificāre potes?** ◆ **Rēgnum meum est parvum, ō mī fīlī. Propter pecūniam magnum castellum aedificāre nōn possumus. Incolae rēgnī meī multam pecūniam nōn habent.**
7. **Rēgīna nova stabula postulat.** ◆ **Cūr?** ◆ **Rēgīna multōs equōs habet, sed stabula rēgīnae sunt parva.** ◆ **Fortasse magna stabula aedificāre possumus.**
8. **Ubi est equus patris meī?** ◆ **Nōnne in stabulō est?** ◆ **Minimē.**
9. **Cibus frātris meī est in culīnā.**
10. **Ubi est liber mātris tuae?** ◆ **In trīclīniō est.** ◆ **Haec casa trīclīnium nōn habet.**

Answers on page 281.

LESSON 102

ACCUSATIVE SINGULAR

In the third declension, the accusative singular ending is **-em**. Just for practice, take a few moments to go through the process of adding this ending to the third declension nouns you know so far.

Here's a chart with all the third declension forms you know so far, using the noun **frāter**.

THIRD DEC.	SINGULAR	PLURAL
NOMINATIVE (SUBJ./PRED. NOM.)	**frāter**	**frātrēs**
GENITIVE (POSSESSION)	**frātris**	**frātrum**
DATIVE (IND. OBJECT)		
ACCUSATIVE (DIRECT OBJECT)	**frātrem**	
ABLATIVE (MANY USES)		

Here are a few example sentences to get you started.

- **Rēgīna mātrem meam videt.** *(The queen sees my mother.)*
- **Virī patrem meum spectant.** *(The men are watching my father.)*
- **Equus frātrem meum portat.** *(The horse is carrying my brother.)*

EXERCISES

1. **Illa fēmina est māter mea. Mātrem meam amō quod fēmina bona est.**
2. **Frātrem tuum videō. Trāns viam ad templum ambulat.**
3. **Equus patrem meum ad oppidum portat.**
4. **Porcī patrum nostrōrum cibum nōn habent.** ♦ **Patrēs nostrī sunt agricolae malī.**
5. **Multae mātrēs in templō sunt.** ♦ **Ubi sunt dōna mātrum?** ♦ **Dōna in templō sunt.**
6. **Cūr patrēs nostrī ad castellum properant?** ♦ **Rēgīna dōna postulat!** ♦ **Num pecūniam postulat?** ♦ **Minimē, sed aurum argentumque postulat!** ♦ **Illa rēgīna est mala!**
7. **Ō Quīnte, cūr frātrem tuum portās?** ♦ **Frāter meus est aeger et fessus.**
8. **Salvē, ō Aurēlia. Saepe mātrem tuam in macellō meō videō.** ♦ **Salvē, ō Marce. Māter mea interdum in macellō tuō obsōnat.** ♦ **Frāter mātris tuae quoque in macellō meō saepe obsōnat.**
9. **Propter patrem tuum, ego hodiē ad īnsulam nāvigāre nōn possum.** ♦ **Cūr tū nāvigāre nōn potes?** ♦ **Pater tuus scapham meam habet.**
10. **Fundus patris meī est parvus, sed multōs equōs habēmus.** ♦ **Fundus patris meī quoque parvus est, sed porcōs habēmus.**

Answers on page 281.

LESSON 103

ACCUSATIVE PLURAL

In the third declension, the accusative plural ending is **-ēs**.

In the chart below, using **māter** as an example, notice that with its **-ēs** ending, the accusative plural form is the same as the nominative plural form.

THIRD DEC.	SINGULAR	PLURAL
NOMINATIVE (SUBJ./PRED. NOM.)	**māter**	**mātrēs**
GENITIVE (POSSESSION)	**mātris**	**mātrum**
DATIVE (IND. OBJECT)		
ACCUSATIVE (DIRECT OBJECT)	**mātrem**	**mātrēs**
ABLATIVE (MANY USES)		

Since the nominative plural and accusative plural look the same, you will have to use context to tell them apart. For example, the word **frātrēs** could be either nominative plural or accusative singular. In the example sentences below, the word **frātrēs** is nominative plural in one sentence, and accusative plural in the other sentence. Can you figure out which one is which?

- **Agricolae frātrēs meōs spectant.**
- **Frātrēs Christophorī in silvā sunt.**

If you observed the context of the sentence you should have been able to figure out that the word **frātrēs** is accusative plural in the first sentence, and nominative plural in the second sentence. In the first sentence, the word **frātrēs** is being modified by the adjective **meōs**, which you can tell is accusative plural. Logically, that tells you that **frātrēs** must also be accusative plural. In the second sentence, the word **frātrēs** comes first in the sentence, and is really the only good candidate to be the subject of the sentence because it agrees with the plural verb **sunt**. And,

164

if **frātrēs** is nominative, the sentence makes perfect sense. Therefore, **frātrēs** here is nominative plural.

Just for fun, let's end this lesson with a trick question! See what you can do with this one:

Frātrēs spectant.

In this sentence, is **frātrēs** nominative plural or accusative plural? Technically, it could be either. If you read **frātrēs** as nominative plural, the sentence could say *The brothers are watching*. Or, if you read **frātres** as accusative plural, the sentence could say *They are watching the brothers*. There isn't much context here, so there isn't really any way to know for sure. Like I said, it's a trick question!

EXERCISES

1. **Frātrēs meōs videō. Ē silvā properant.**
2. **Rēgīna mātrēs nostrās spectat.** ◆ **Cūr?** ◆ **Mātrēs nostrae dōna ad rēgīnam portant.**
3. **Patria patrum nostrōrum est magna īnsula.**
4. **Dōna mātrum nostrārum in exedriō sunt.**
5. **Numquam frātrēs tuōs in popīnā vidēmus.** ◆ **Frātrēs meī sunt nautae. Semper in thermopōliō malō cēnant et fābulās malās dē pīrātīs narrant.**
6. **Nautae patrēs vestrōs ad novam patriam in scaphā suā portant.**
7. **Haec fēmina est māter mea. In fundō suō habitat.** ◆ **Ubi est fundus mātris tuae?** ◆ **Trāns silvam est.**
8. **Magistra semper frātrēs meōs spectat quod puerī malī sunt.**
9. **Ubi est Marcus hodiē?** ◆ **Ad īnsulam hodiē nāvigat in scaphā mātris suae.** ◆ **Ubi est māter Marcī?** ◆ **Domī est. Māter Marcī ad īnsulam cum Marcō nōn nāvigat.**
10. **Frātrēs meī cubicula sua numquam pūrgant. Cubicula frātrum meōrum sordida sunt.**

Answers on page 281.

LESSON 104

DATIVE SINGULAR AND PLURAL

In this lesson, I'll give you both the dative singular and the dative plural of the third declension. The dative singular ending is **-ī**, and the dative plural ending is **-ibus**. And, as usual, I would like you to go through the process of finding the genitive stem and adding these endings to it to create these new noun forms. When you have finished, compare your results to this chart:

THIRD DEC.	SINGULAR	PLURAL
NOMINATIVE (SUBJ./PRED. NOM.)	pater	patrēs
GENITIVE (POSSESSION)	patris	patrum
DATIVE (IND. OBJECT)	patrī	patribus
ACCUSATIVE (DIRECT OBJECT)	patrem	patrēs
ABLATIVE (MANY USES)		

Here are some example sentences to get you started with third declension dative forms.

- **Nauta patrī meō fābulam malam narrat.** *(The sailor is telling a bad story to my father.)*
- **Puerī mātrī meae dōnum dant.** *(The boys are giving a gift to my mother.)*
- **Agricolae frātribus meīs cibum dant.** *(The farmers are giving food to my brothers.)*

EXERCISES

1. **Frātribus tuīs dōna damus.**
2. **Christophorus mātrī suae fābulam narrat.**
3. **Hic magister patrī meō librum dat.**

166

4. **Ego frātrī meō numquam pecūniam dō. ♦ Cūr? ♦ Frāter meus in exedriō semper sedet. Numquam labōrat.**

5. **Discipulī mātribus nostrīs nunc sellās dant.**

6. **Magistra patribus fābulam dē discipulīs narrat.**

7. **Semprōnia pecūniam mātris meae habet. ♦ Cūr? ♦ Nesciō, sed nunc Semprōnia mātrī meae pecūniam dat.**

8. **Cūr tū frātrī meō librōs dās? ♦ Frāter tuus librōs amat. Bibliothēcārius est.**

9. **Agricola patribus vestrīs pecūniam dat. ♦ Cūr? ♦ Patrēs vestrī in fundō agricolae cotīdiē labōrant.**

10. **Nautae frātribus nostrīs fābulam malam dē pīrātīs narrant. ♦ Cūr nautae semper fābulās malās narrant? ♦ Interdum fābulās bonās narrant, sed saepe fābulās malās narrant.**

Answers on page 282.

LESSON 105

ABLATIVE SINGULAR AND PLURAL

In this lesson, I'll give you both the ablative singular and ablative plural of the third declension. The ablative singular ending is **-e**, and the ablative plural ending is **-ibus** (same as dative plural). And, as usual, I would like you to go through the process of finding the genitive stem and adding these endings to it. When you have finished, observe this chart:

THIRD DEC.	SINGULAR	PLURAL
NOMINATIVE (SUBJ./PRED. NOM.)	**frāter**	**frātrēs**
GENITIVE (POSSESSION)	**frātris**	**frātrum**
DATIVE (IND. OBJECT)	**frātrī**	**frātribus**
ACCUSATIVE (DIRECT OBJECT)	**frātrem**	**frātrēs**
ABLATIVE (MANY USES)	**frātre**	**frātribus**

167

Here are a couple of example sentences to get you started with these third declension ablative forms.

- **Semprōnia ad macellum cum patre suō ambulat.** *(Sempronia is walking to the market with her father.)*
- **Decimus ad īnsulam cum frātribus suīs nāvigat.** *(Decimus is sailing to the island with his brothers.)*

EXERCISES

1. **Ō Lāvīnia, cūr ad actam cum mātre tuā properās?** ♦ **Actam amāmus. Interdum ad actam cum patre meō ambulāmus.** ♦ **Nōnne pater tuus actam amat?** ♦ **Minimē, pater meus aquam timet. Pater meus prope aquam sedet et frātrēs meōs spectat quod natāre nōn potest.**
2. **Ō Rōmule, ubi habitās?** ♦ **In silvā cum frātre meō habitō.** ♦ **Nōnne in casā habitātis?** ♦ **Minimē. Casam nōn habēmus.** ♦ **Cūr in silvā habitātis?** ♦ **Casa patris nostrī est parva.**
3. **Ubi est pater tuus?** ♦ **Pater meus in hypogaeō est cum frātribus meīs.** ♦ **Ubi est māter tua?** ♦ **Māter mea in exedriō cum mātre tuā sedet.**
4. **Ubi nunc est magistra?** ♦ **Magistra in scholā cum mātribus nostrīs et patribus nostrīs est.**
5. **Lucrētia frātrem meum amat, sed frāter meus Cornēliam amat.** ♦ **Frāter tuus Claudiam quoque amat.**
6. **Ubi est pecūnia mātrum nostrārum?** ♦ **In argentāriā est.**
7. **Ego numquam patrēs vestrōs in popīnā videō.** ♦ **Numquam in popīnā cēnant, sed interdum in thermopōliō cēnant.**
8. **Cūr pater meus frātrī meō pecūniam dat?** ♦ **Nesciō. Fortasse frāter tuus in fundō patris tuī labōrat.**
9. **Cūr sella mātris nostrae in culīnā est?** ♦ **Interdum māter nostra sellam suam in culīnam portat.**
10. **Gulielmus patrī meō fābulam longam narrat.** ♦ **Cūr Gulielmus semper fābulās longās narrat?** ♦ **Nesciō, sed fābulae Gulielmī semper longae sunt.**

Answers on page 282.

LESSON 106

MORE ABOUT THE THIRD DECLENSION

Congratulations! You now know all the basic endings of the third declension. We have been practicing with the endings of the third declension by using only three nouns: **māter**, **pater**, and **frāter**.

These three nouns all have the same spelling pattern: they have the letter *e* in the nominative singular, but, like **puer** and **ager** from the second declension, that *e* is not present in the genitive singular. And that's the reason I introduced these three nouns first—since they are so similar, I thought that working with them for a while would allow you to get used to the endings of the third declension more easily.

But not all nouns of the third declension share these same characteristics. As I mentioned before, there is some variety in the spelling patterns of third declension nouns. For example, for some third declension nouns, the nominative singular form is spelled the same as the genitive stem. Other third declension nouns have a nominative singular form which is identical to the genitive singular form. For nouns like these, you have to use the context to figure out what form it is when you are translating. But I won't tell you everything about the third declension here in this book—I don't want to spoil the surprise that you will experience as you advance further in your Latin studies!

Don't worry—it's not as difficult as it sounds, and as with any subject, you get used to it over time. But for now, as you are learning some of this stuff for the first time, the best thing you can do for yourself to help you keep up with it all is to make sure that you memorize the nominative singular *and* genitive singular of every third declension noun. And remembering the gender of each noun won't hurt, either.

LESSON 107

NEW WORD   **soror, sorōris**

MEANING   *sister*

Our new word for this lesson is related to the English word *sorority*. It's a feminine noun of the third declension, but it doesn't have the same spelling pattern as **māter**, **pater**, and **frāter**. Examine the following chart, and see if you can figure out how this noun differs from the third declension nouns you know so far.

THIRD DEC.	SINGULAR	PLURAL
NOMINATIVE (SUBJ./PRED. NOM.)	**soror**	**sorōrēs**
GENITIVE (POSSESSION)	**sorōris**	**sorōrum**
DATIVE (IND. OBJECT)	**sorōrī**	**sorōribus**
ACCUSATIVE (DIRECT OBJECT)	**sorōrem**	**sorōrēs**
ABLATIVE (MANY USES)	**sorōre**	**sorōribus**

Here's what I was hoping you would notice: If you take the genitive singular form, which is **sorōris**, and remove the ending, you are left with the genitive stem, which is **sorōr-**. So, for this particular noun, the genitive stem is spelled the same as the nominative singular form. The only difference is that the *o* in the nominative singular form is a short *o*, while the *o* in the genitive singular form is a long *o*.

So, the point I'm trying to make here is that not every third declension noun will have the same spelling scheme as **māter**, **pater**, and **frāter**. This means that each time you encounter a new third declension noun, you should not assume that it will have the same characteristics as other nouns. Instead, take a fresh look at each new noun, carefully examining the nominative singular and genitive singular.

EXERCISES

1. **Rēgīna est soror mea.** ◆ **Tū frāter rēgīnae es, et rēgīna est soror tua.**
   ◆ **Ita.** ◆ **Habitāsne in castellō cum sorōre tuā?** ◆ **Ita. Parvum
   cubiculum in hypogaeō castellī habeō.** ◆ **Tū in hypogaeō sorōris tuae
   habitās.** ◆ **In castellō sorōris meae habitō.**

2. **Ō pater, puer bonus sum. Cubiculum sorōris meae est sordidum, sed
   ego cubiculum meum semper pūrgō.** ◆ **Ō mī fīlī, lātrīna tua semper
   est sordida. Fortasse lātrīnam interdum pūrgāre potes.**

3. **Puerī interdum in oppidum cum sorōre suā ambulant.**

4. **Amīca sorōris meae in exedriō nostrō sedet.** ◆ **Cūr soror tua nōn est
   in exedriō cum amīcā suā?** ◆ **In cubiculō suō est.**

5. **Poēta sorōribus meīs et frātribus meīs fābulam narrat.**

6. **Soror mea fundum habet.** ◆ **Num fundus sorōris tuae est magnus?** ◆
   Ita. Multa stabula et multī equī in fundō sorōris meae sunt.

7. **Cūr pīrātae patrem meum spectant?** ◆ **Pater tuus ex argentāriā cum
   aurō ambulat.**

8. **Amīcī nostrī patrī meō dōnum dant.**

9. **Cūr soror tua in equō sedet?** ◆ **Equus sorōrem meam ad oppidum
   portat.**

10. **Ego ad bibliothēcam cum sorōribus meīs ambulō.**

Answers on page 282.

LESSON 108

NEW WORD   **rēx, rēgis**

MEANING   *king*

Our new word for this lesson is related to many words both in English and Latin.
Notice that the genitive stem is **rēg-**. That same root is at the beginning of the
words **rēgīna** and **rēgnum**. And, like those Latin words, **rēx** is related to English
words like *regal* and *regent*.

THIRD DEC.	SINGULAR	PLURAL
NOMINATIVE (SUBJ./PRED. NOM.)	rēx	rēgēs
GENITIVE (POSSESSION)	rēgis	rēgum
DATIVE (IND. OBJECT)	rēgī	rēgibus
ACCUSATIVE (DIRECT OBJECT)	rēgem	rēgēs
ABLATIVE (MANY USES)	rēge	rēgibus

EXERCISES

1. Rēx in castellō suō sedet.

2. Ō Carole, cūr frātrēs tuī semper ante castellum sunt? Et cūr rēx frātribus tuīs pecūniam saepe dat? ♦ Rēx pecūniam frātribus meīs dat quod portās castellī servant. ♦ Servāsne tū quoque castellum rēgis? ♦ Minimē. Stabula pūrgō.

3. Ō Quīnte, ubi est rēgīna? ♦ Rēgīna est in castellō cum rēge. Nunc in trīclīniō cēnant. ♦ Ubi rēgīna sedet? ♦ Rēgīna prope rēgem sedet. Soror rēgis quoque adest. Prope frātrem rēgis sedet. Illud trīclīnium est magnum, et magnam mēnsam habet. Familia rēgis circum mēnsam sedet.

4. Ō pater, cūr in castellō habitāmus? ♦ In castellō habitāmus quod ego sum rēx, et māter tua est rēgīna. ♦ Cūr parvum cubiculum habeō? ♦ Castellum nostrum est parvum.

5. Hortus inter casam et mūrum est.

6. Cūr poēta in magnō trīclīniō castellī est? ♦ Virī fēminaeque castellī cum rēge in magnō trīclīniō cēnant. Poēta nunc virīs fēminīsque castellī fābulam narrat. ♦ Rēx fābulās amat. Fortasse rēgī fābulam dē pīrātīs narrāre potest.

7. Frāter rēgis est ante castellum. ♦ Cūr? ♦ Argentum aurumque postulat. ♦ Fortasse rēx frātrī suō pecūniam dare potest. ♦ Minimē. Rēx numquam frātrī suō pecūniam dat.

8. Ubi sunt equī sorōrum meārum? ♦ In stabulīs post castellum sunt.

9. Rōmulus sorōrem meam amat, sed soror mea Rūfum amat. ♦ Cūr soror tua Rūfum amat? Rūfus in hypogaeō mātris suae habitat et pecūniam nōn habet.

10. Propter frātrem tuum, ad patriam patris meī hodiē nāvigāre nōn possum. ♦ Cūr nāvigāre nōn potes? ♦ Frāter tuus pecūniam meam habet.

Answers on page 282.

LESSON 109

NEW WORD   **uxor, uxōris**

MEANING   *wife*

Uxor is a feminine noun of the third declension.

THIRD DEC.	SINGULAR	PLURAL
NOMINATIVE (SUBJ./PRED. NOM.)	uxor	uxōrēs
GENITIVE (POSSESSION)	uxōris	uxōrum
DATIVE (IND. OBJECT)	uxōrī	uxōribus
ACCUSATIVE (DIRECT OBJECT)	uxōrem	uxōrēs
ABLATIVE (MANY USES)	uxōre	uxōribus

As long as we are learning how to say *wife*, let's also learn the second declension masculine noun **marītus** which means *husband*. Here are a couple of practice sentences to get you started with these new words.

- **Rēgīna est uxor rēgis.** *(The queen is the wife of the king.)*
- **Rēx est marītus rēgīnae.** *(The king is the husband of the queen.)*

EXERCISES

1. **Num rēx uxōrem habet?** ♦ **Ita. Lāvīnia est uxor rēgis. Lāvīnia rēgīna est.**
2. **Fēminae scaphās spectant.** ♦ **Cūr scaphās spectant?** ♦ **Uxōrēs nautārum sunt. Marītī uxōrum absunt.**
3. **Uxor mea est bibliothēcāria. Semper librōs in casam nostram portat.** ♦ **Librōs amat.** ♦ **Ita. Librī sunt in culīnā nostrā, et in trīclīniō nostrō, et in cubiculō nostrō, et in mēnsīs, et in sellīs. Propter librōs uxōris meae, per casam ambulāre nōn possum.**

4. **Ō Aemilia, cūr fessa hodiē es? ♦ Hodiē familia mea in casā meā est. Frātrēs meī, sorōrēs meae, māter mea, fīliae meae, et marītus meus hodiē adsunt. ♦ Habēsne multum cibum? ♦ Minimē. Nunc ad macellum properō. ♦ Fortasse ego quoque obsōnāre possum. Ego cibum ad casam tuam portāre possum. ♦ Tū amīcus bonus es!**

5. **Ille vir est marītus meus. ♦ Cūr in bibliothēcam cum multīs librīs properat? ♦ Librōs ad bibliothēcam portat. ♦ Cūr nunc ē bibliothēcā cum multīs librīs ambulat? ♦ Marītus meus librōs amat. Semper in casā nostrā multōs librōs habēmus.**

6. **Ubi est scapha patris tuī? ♦ Pīrātae scapham patris meī habent. Propter pīrātās, pater meus nunc nāvigāre nōn potest.**

7. **Bibliothēcāria sorōribus meīs fābulam narrat.**

8. **Rēgnum nostrum est parvum, sed castellum rēgis est magnum. ♦ Cūr rēx magnum castellum habet? ♦ In vīcīniā bonā habitat.**

9. **Ō Cornēlī, habēsne familiam? ♦ Ita. Ego et uxor mea multās fīliās habēmus. Habēsne tū quoque familiam? ♦ Ita. Marītum habeō, et parvum fīlium. Pater meus quoque in casā nostrā habitat.**

10. **Magistra sorōrum meārum adest.**

Answers on page 283.

LESSON 110

THE ROMAN ARMY

At first, ancient Rome was ruled by kings. Later, the Romans expelled the kings and Rome became a republic. Over time, the Romans began to gain power and influence on both land and sea, and powerful figures fought for military power and glory. The republic fell apart and Rome became an empire. Now, instead of political power being shared by many, political power was concentrated in the hands of the emperor.

As the political situation in Rome changed, so did its army. In the early days, the Roman army was just a militia made up of ordinary citizens who took up arms to defend Rome when needed. But then, around the year 107 BC, a famous Roman named Marius made some fundamental changes to the way the Roman army was organized. Marius turned the army into a professional, organized, standing army. On the surface, this change seemed like a good one—but it brought with it some serious consequences as professional soldiers began to depend on their commanding generals for their livelihood. This meant that soldiers could have a greater loyalty to their commanding generals than to the Roman republic.

In *Getting Started with Latin*, you learned the words **gladius** *(sword)* and **scūtum** *(shield)*. Let me tell you a little more about these weapons, because they have a lot to do with the way the Roman army functioned. The Roman **gladius** was not a long sword with a sharp edge, like the kind of sword a medieval knight might carry. Instead, it was a short sword with a sharp, pointy tip (see bottom left). The **scūtum** we have been taking about is a tall, curved shield that was big enough for a Roman soldier to crouch down behind (see bottom right). He could also put his shield next to the shield of the soldier next to him, forming a shield wall which was difficult for the enemy to penetrate. The discipline, equipment, and tactics of the Roman army made them a very strong fighting force and enabled the Romans to expand their power in every direction. By about AD 100, the Romans controlled the lands on every side of the Mediterranean Sea.

LESSON 111

NEW WORD   **mīles, mīlitis**

MEANING   *soldier*

PRONUNCIATION TIP: **Mīles** has two syllables and sounds something like *MEE-lace*.

Our new word for this lesson is a masculine noun of the third declension. Notice that the genitive stem is **mīlit-**. This word is related to English words like *military*, *militia*, and *militant*.

Here are the forms of **mīles** in a handy chart:

THIRD DEC.	SINGULAR	PLURAL
NOMINATIVE (SUBJ./PRED. NOM.)	mīles	mīlitēs
GENITIVE (POSSESSION)	mīlitis	mīlitum
DATIVE (IND. OBJECT)	mīlitī	mīlitibus
ACCUSATIVE (DIRECT OBJECT)	mīlitem	mīlitēs
ABLATIVE (MANY USES)	mīlite	mīlitibus

EXERCISES

1. **Mīles sum. Frāter meus quoque mīles est. ♦ Estne pater tuus mīles? ♦ Minimē. Pater meus est bibliothēcārius.**
2. **Mīlitēs rēgis pecūniam suam postulant. ♦ Cūr rēx mīlitibus pecūniam nōn dat? ♦ Nesciō. Fortasse rēx pecūniam nōn habet.**
3. **Incolae oppidī mīlitī dōnum dant. ♦ Cūr? ♦ Ille mīles semper portās oppidī servat.**
4. **Ubi est rēx? ♦ Rēx post castellum cum mīlitibus suīs est. ♦ Cūr post castellum sunt? ♦ Scūta et gladiōs cūrant.**

5. **Cūr poēta in magnō trīclīniō cum rēge et amīcīs rēgis adest?** ♦ **Rēx et amīcī suī in magnō trīclīniō cēnant. Poēta fābulās narrat.** ♦ **Adestne uxor rēgis?** ♦ **Minimē. Uxor rēgis est in lectō suō quod hodiē aegrōtat, sed soror rēgis in trīclīniō adest, et prope rēgem sedet.**

6. **Ubi est frāter rēgis?** ♦ **Frāter rēgis est in silvā cum mīlitibus rēgis.** ♦ **Cūr mīlitēs in silvā sunt?** ♦ **Frāter rēgis et mīlitēs per silvam ad actam properant quod pīrātae ad rēgnum nostrum nāvigant.**

7. **Ubi est equus mātris nostrae? Nōn est in stabulō.** ♦ **Māter nostra nunc abest. Fortasse in oppidō est.** ♦ **Fortasse obsōnat.** ♦ **Ita. In casā multum cibum nōn habēmus.**

8. **Ō Rūfe, cūr lectus tuus est in hypogaeō?** ♦ **In hypogaeō habitō.** ♦ **Cūr in hypogaeō patris tuī habitās?** ♦ **Multam pecūniam nōn habeō. Propter pecūniam cum mātre meā et patre meō habitō.**

9. **Ubi est rēx? Nōn est in tablīnō suō.** ♦ **Rēx ad actam cum uxōre suā ambulat.** ♦ **Actam amant.** ♦ **Ita. Castellum rēgis prope actam est.**

10. **Casam nostram cum frātribus meīs pūrgō.** ♦ **Cūr casam pūrgātis?** ♦ **Cubicula nostra sunt sordida.**

Answers on page 283.

LESSON 112

NEW WORD   urbs, urbis

MEANING   *city*

Urbs is a feminine noun of the third declension. It's related to English words like *urban, suburbs,* and *urbane.* The genitive stem is **urb-**.

A few lessons ago, I told you that there would be some variation to the endings of the third declension. Well, now it's time to introduce you to one of those variations. Take a look at the declension chart below for **urbs**, our new word for this lesson, and pay special attention to the genitive plural form.

THIRD DEC. I-STEM	SINGULAR	PLURAL
NOMINATIVE (SUBJ./PRED. NOM.)	urbs	urbēs
GENITIVE (POSSESSION)	urbis	urbium
DATIVE (IND. OBJECT)	urbī	urbibus
ACCUSATIVE (DIRECT OBJECT)	urbem	urbēs
ABLATIVE (MANY USES)	urbe	urbibus

For the noun **urbs**, the genitive singular form is **urbis**, and by removing the ending we find that genitive stem is **urb-**. So far, so good, right?

In the third declension, the ending for the genitive plural is **-um**. So, to make the genitive plural form, we take the genitive stem, add the **-um** ending, and that should give us the genitive plural form, like this:

urb + um = urbum

But wait—according to the declension chart I showed you above, the genitive plural form is **urbium**. Why is the letter *i* there? Why is it **urbium**, and not **urbum**?

The answer is this: some nouns of the third declension are called *i-stem nouns*. It's a long story, but technically, these nouns have the letter *i* at the end of the genitive stem—but sometimes that *i* gets absorbed into or combined with another nearby vowel. But in the genitive plural, the *i* stays put, and so we get an extra *i* before the genitive plural ending, giving us **urbium** instead of **urbum**.

What this means to you is that the genitive plural form of **urbs** is **urbium**. So, if you want to say *of the cities*, you will need to use the word **urbium**, as seen in these examples:

- **incolae urbium** *(the inhabitants of the cities)*
- **fēminae urbium** *(the women of the cities)*
- **mūrī urbium** *(the walls of the cities)*

As we go, I will point out other third declension i-stem nouns. In the meantime, get some practice working with **urbs**.

EXERCISES

1. **Hoc oppidum est magnum.** ♦ **Nōn est oppidum. Magna urbs est. Multī incolae in urbe nunc habitant.** ♦ **Frāter meus in urbe cum uxōre suā habitat.**

2. **Cūr inter urbēs sunt multī mīlitēs?** ♦ **Mīlitēs incolās urbium servant.**

3. **Haec urbs semper multam pecūniam habet. Cūr multam pecūniam habet?** ♦ **Rēx interdum urbibus rēgnī suī pecūniam dat.**

4. **Cūr novam urbem aedificāmus?** ♦ **Sunt multī incolae in rēgnō nostrō.** ♦ **Fessus sum. Novam urbem hodiē aedificāre nōn possum.**

5. **Ubi est soror rēgis?** ♦ **In castellō cum mātre rēgis et fīliābus rēgis est.** ♦ **Rēx noster magnam familiam habet!**

6. **Cūr dat rēx frātribus tuīs pecūniam interdum?** ♦ **Frātrēs meī sunt mīlitēs.**

7. **Ō rēx, sunt multae urbēs in rēgnō tuō. Magnum est rēgnum tuum!** ♦ **Ita, rēgnum meum est longum et lātum, cum multīs urbibus.** ♦ **Tū magnum castellum quoque habēs.** ♦ **Ita, sed balneum meum est parvum.**

8. **Num ab oppidō nostrō ad magnam urbem ambulās?** ♦ **Ita. Ad urbem nunc ambulō.** ♦ **Cūr ad urbem ambulās?** ♦ **Magnae urbēs bibliothēcās bonās habent. Popīnās bonās quoque habent.**

9. **Ille nauta mīlitibus fābulam narrat.**

10. **Cūr amīcae mātris tuae circum mēnsam in trīclīniō nostrō sedent?** ♦ **Māter mea cum amīcīs suīs nunc cēnat.** ♦ **Ubi est cibus? In mēnsā nōn est.** ♦ **Cibus in culīnā est.**

Answers on page 284.

LESSON 113

VERBS THAT WORK WITH THE DATIVE CASE

I would like to show you a common way that the dative case is used in Latin. But to explain it, I need you to think through a few sentences. Consider the following sentence:

I obey the queen.

If you were to analyze the grammar of that sentence, you would conclude that the word *queen* is the direct object. But what if we rearrange the sentence, saying basically the same thing, but in a different way, like this:

I am giving obedience to the queen.

Now, with this wording, the word *queen* is the indirect object instead of being the direct object (*obedience* is the direct object). After all, the queen is the party in the sentence that is receiving or benefiting—in this case, receiving the obedience, or benefiting from the obedience. Now let's try yet another wording for this sentence:

I am being obedient toward the queen.

In this wording, the grammar works differently. Now, the verb is a verb of being, showing a state of being instead of an action. And, as you already know, a verb of being or existing cannot generate a direct object. So again, the word *queen* here is not a direct object.

Here's the point I have been building up to: in Latin, there are some verbs that work along with the dative case to express their meaning. In the type of sentence I showed you above, if we turned that kind of sentence into Latin, the word for *queen* would be in the dative case. The kinds of verbs in Latin that work with the dative case tend to be verbs that express obeying, trusting, helping, forgiving, sparing, etc.

So, just for practice, read these sentences a few times considering the fact that in Latin, the underlined part of the sentence would be in the dative case.

- I am trustful <u>toward the queen</u>.
- I am forgiving <u>toward the queen</u>.
- I am giving obedience <u>to the queen</u>.

As you advance more in your knowledge of Latin, you will start to know just from experience which verbs work with the dative case. But in the meantime, I will start you out slowly in the next lesson with a Latin verb that uses the dative case.

LESSON 114

NEW WORD   **pāreō / pārēre**

MEANING   *I obey / to obey*

In the last lesson you learned that some Latin verbs work with the dative case. Our new word for this lesson is one of those verbs. It's from the second conjugation.

If you want to say *I obey*, just do this:

Pāreō. *(I obey.)*

But if you want to indicate the person who is being obeyed, you need to put that person or thing in the dative case, like this:

Ego semper rēgīnae pāreō. *(I always obey the queen.)*

If this is confusing for you, try to think of it in the ways we examined in the previous lesson: *I am being obedient toward the queen,* or *I am giving obedience to the queen.* Thinking about the sentence in these ways will help you to get the dative feeling of the sentence—the feeling that the queen is the party who is receiving or benefiting in the sentence.

Here are a few more example sentences to get you going with **pāreō** plus the dative case.

- **Decimus magistrō pāret.** *(Decimus is obeying the teacher.)*
- **Mātrī nostrae semper pārēmus.** *(We always obey our mother.)*
- **Mīlitēs rēgī pārent.** *(The soldiers are obeying the king.)*

EXERCISES

1. **Rēx semper rēgīnae pāret.** ♦ **Rēx est marītus bonus!**

181

2. Mīles bonus sum. Ego semper rēgī pāreō. ◆ Ubi nunc sunt mīlitēs rēgis? ◆ In silvā cum rēge sunt. ◆ Cūr tū nōn es in silvā cum rēge et mīlitibus rēgis? ◆ Saepe rēgī pāreō. ◆ Cūr tū domī es? ◆ Interdum rēgī pāreō. ◆ Tū nōn es mīles bonus!

3. Cūr bibliothēcāriae nōn parēs? Tū in bibliothēcā es.

4. Puella bona sum quod mātrī meae pāreō. ◆ Sed tū cubiculum tuum nunc nōn pūrgās. ◆ Mātrī meae saepe pāreō. ◆ Numquam mātrī tuae pārēs.

5. Pūblius numquam patrī suō pāret. ◆ Cūr? Num Pūblius puer malus est? ◆ Puer malus est. Numquam stabula pūrgat, numquam cubiculum suum pūrgat, et porcīs cibum nōn dat.

6. Ō frāter, cūr numquam patrī nostrō pārēs? ◆ Fīlius bonus sum! Semper patrī nostrō pāreō! ◆ Minimē. ◆ Saepe patrī nostrō pāreō. ◆ Minimē. ◆ Interdum patrī nostrō pāreō. ◆ Fortasse.

7. Cubiculum sorōris meae inter cubiculum meum et balneum est. ◆ Cūr sorōrēs tuae magna cubicula habent sed tū parvum cubiculum habēs? Cubicula sorōrum tuārum sunt magna. ◆ Parvum lectum habeō.

8. Bibliothēcārius frātribus meīs novōs librōs dat.

9. Cūr illa fēmina multum aurum habet? Et cūr multum argentum quoque habet? ◆ Nesciō. ◆ Cūr magnam scapham habet? ◆ Nesciō. ◆ Fortasse illa fēmina est pīrāta!

10. Cūr uxōrēs nautārum ad urbem properant? ◆ Ad templum Neptūnī in urbe properant. Dōna ad templum portant quod marītī feminārum hodiē nāvigant.

Answers on page 284.

LESSON 115

NATURAL GENDER AND GRAMMATICAL GENDER

When you classify nouns by gender, there are two kinds of gender to think about: natural gender and grammatical gender. Natural gender is the biological gender that people and animals have. When we think about words that pertain to people or animals, we assume that the word for *man* ought to be masculine, and the word for *woman* ought to be feminine. And they are: **vir** is masculine and **fēmina** is feminine. And much of the time, this is how it works.

Grammatical gender, on the other hand, is the gender that a noun has just as a word—that is, the word itself, not the thing that the word means. This means that sometimes the grammatical gender of a noun can be different from what its gender seems like it ought to be. Here's an example: there is a Latin word that means *manliness.* You would expect that word to be grammatically masculine, right? Since it's a sort of "manly" word? Well, you would be incorrect. The Latin noun **virtūs** (related to the word **vir**) means *manliness*, but is grammatically feminine! Why would the word for *manliness* be feminine? The reason is that grammatical gender is just a way that nouns are classified as having certain characteristics, and does not necessarily have any relationship to biological gender.

So we might ask ourselves, why is a farm (**fundus**) masculine? Why is a library (**bibliothēca**) feminine? Why is a kingdom (**rēgnum**) neuter? Those nouns are classified as having grammatical gender, but we often do not think of them as having a gender because they are inanimate objects. And what about abstract concepts such as patience, intelligence, or patriotism? Should nouns such as these be masculine? Feminine? Maybe neuter because they aren't living things? When you learn Latin nouns like those, it's important to know their grammatical gender because our everday assumptions about gender don't really tell us anything about how these words are used in Latin sentences.

So, the difference between natural gender and grammatical gender can center around expectations. Sometimes the gender of a certain noun matches what you would expect it to be based what the noun means. Other times, the gender of a noun is just a grammatical classification that has nothing to do with what the word means.

LESSON 116

NEW WORD   **fēlēs, fēlis**

MEANING   *cat*

Our new word for this lesson is a feminine noun of the third declension which is related to our English word *feline.* There are a few things to notice about this particular noun. First, notice that **fēlēs** is an i-stem noun, so the genitive plural form will be **fēlium**. And also notice that the nominative singular form, **fēlēs**, is exactly the same as the nominative plural form—and those are both the same as the accusative plural form. So if you see the word **fēlēs**, you will have to examine the context to determine if it is nominative singular, nominative plural, or accusative plural. I told you that there would be a few weird things about the third declension—now do you believe me?

THIRD DEC. I-STEM	SINGULAR	PLURAL
NOMINATIVE (SUBJ./PRED. NOM.)	**fēlēs**	**fēlēs**
GENITIVE (POSSESSION)	**fēlis**	**fēlium**
DATIVE (IND. OBJECT)	**fēlī**	**fēlibus**
ACCUSATIVE (DIRECT OBJECT)	**fēlem**	**fēlēs**
ABLATIVE (MANY USES)	**fēle**	**fēlibus**

In the last lesson we examined the difference between natural gender and grammatical gender. We learned that sometimes the gender of a certain noun matches what you would expect it to be based what the noun means. In other words, since the word **soror** means sister, you would expect to be feminine—and you would be correct. Other times, the gender of a noun is just a grammatical classification that has nothing to do with what the word means. For example, you might expect the word **virtūs** to be masculine because it means *manliness,* but you would be wrong—grammatically, it is feminine.

The reason I'm mentioning this now is because it applies to our new word for this lesson. A cat is a living thing with gender. There are male cats and female cats.

But here's the thing to remember: even if a particular cat is a male cat, the word **fēlēs** is still a feminine noun, grammatically speaking. So if you have a male cat named **Fluffius** (that's a male name from the second declension that I just now made up) and he is a male cat, you could still have a sentence like this:

Fluffius est fēlēs nostra. *(Fluffy is our cat.)*

In this sentence, even though **Fluffius** is a male cat, the noun **fēlēs** is grammatically feminine, and so is being accompanied by the feminine adjective **nostra**. Here's another example:

Haec fēlēs est Fluffius. *(This cat is Fluffy.)*

Notice that in that sentence, again, even though **Fluffius** is a male cat, the noun **fēlēs** is grammatically feminine, and so it is accompanied by the feminine demonstrative **haec**, not the masculine **hic**. This is an example of how natural gender and grammatical gender don't always work together!

EXERCISES

1. **Ō amīce, habēsne fēlem?** ◆ **Ita. Fluffius est fēlēs nostra. In casā nostrā habitat.** ◆ **Haec fēlēs est magna!** ◆ **Ita, Fluffius est fēlēs magna.**
2. **Ō māter, ubi est Fluffius?** ◆ **Fluffius est in cubiculō tuō. In lectō tuō sedet.**
3. **Salvē, ō Fluffī. Valēsne hodiē?** ◆ **Minimē. Cibum nōn habeō. Ubi est cibus meus? Cibum postulō!** ◆ **Tū fēlēs es. Tū cibum postulāre nōn potes.**
4. **Fluffius in culīnā est. In mēnsā sedet.** ◆ **Cūr illa fēlēs nōn pāret? Fluffius in mēnsā sedēre nōn potest.**
5. **Ō bibliothēcāria, cūr fēlēs in bibliothēcā adest?** ◆ **Fēlēs in bibliothēcā nostrā habitat. Bibliothēcam servat et librōs spectat.**
6. **Ō fīlia, cūrāsne fēlem nostram?** ◆ **Ita, ō pater. Fēlī nunc cibum dō.**
7. **Cūr mīlitēs gladiōs habent? Cūr ante portās urbis sunt?** ◆ **Urbem gladiīs scūtīsque servant.**
8. **Cūr est haec fēlēs in casā nostrā?** ◆ **Nesciō. Fēlem nōn habēmus.** ◆ **Nunc haec fēlēs cibum postulat.**
9. **Uxor rēgis et frāter rēgis in trīclīniō pugnant.**
10. **Ubi est scapha sorōrum meārum?**

Answers on page 284.

LESSON 117

MEANING   *mountain*

Our new word for this lesson is a masculine noun of the third declension. It's related to English words like *Montana, piedmont,* and *mount.*

This noun is an i-stem noun, so the genitive plural form will be **montium**. Notice that the letter *o* is long in the nominative singular, but it is short in all the other forms.

THIRD DEC. I-STEM	SINGULAR	PLURAL
NOMINATIVE (SUBJ./PRED. NOM.)	**mōns**	**montēs**
GENITIVE (POSSESSION)	**montis**	**montium**
DATIVE (IND. OBJECT)	**montī**	**montibus**
ACCUSATIVE (DIRECT OBJECT)	**montem**	**montēs**
ABLATIVE (MANY USES)	**monte**	**montibus**

Here's an example sentence to get you going:

> **Sunt multa oppida inter montēs.** *(There are many towns among the mountains.)*

EXERCISES

1. **Ubi est urbs?** ♦ **Urbs est trāns montēs.** ♦ **Per montēs ambulāre nōn possumus.** ♦ **Cūr?** ♦ **Montēs sunt magnī, sed via est angusta.**
2. **Cūr Marcus et Semprōnia in montibus habitant?** ♦ **Montēs amant.** ♦ **Sed magnae fēlēs in montibus habitant.** ♦ **Magnae fēlēs?** ♦ **Ita, magnae fēlēs inter montēs habitant. Ego magnās fēlēs timeō. Timēsne magnās fēlēs montium?**
3. **Ubi habitat Frederīcus?** ♦ **Frederīcus in montibus cum uxōre suā et fīliābus suīs habitat.** ♦ **Cūr Frederīcus in urbe nōn habitat?** ♦

186

Fredericus et uxor sua parvum fundum habent. Equōs habent et porcōs quoque habent.

4. **Propter montem, urbem vidēre nōn possum.** ♦ **Urbs est trāns montem.**

5. **Cūr in magnā casā habitās?** ♦ **Multās sorōrēs habeō. Casa nostra est magna et multa cubicula habet.**

6. **Cūr Tullia in magnā urbe habitat?** ♦ **Marītus Tulliae thermopōlium in urbe habet. Multī virī et multae fēminae in thermopōliō cotīdiē cēnant.**

7. **Cūr incolae montium ad urbem properant?** ♦ **Nesciō. Fortasse ad theātrum properant.**

8. **Claudia mātrī meae fābulam narrat.**

9. **Ō Fluffī, cūr tū numquam pārēs?** ♦ **Fēlēs sum! Ego numquam pāreō.** ♦ **Tū fēlēs mala es.** ♦ **Ubi est cibus meus?**

10. **Sunt multae urbēs inter montēs.**

Answers on page 285.

LESSON 118

NEW WORD   **canis, canis**

MEANING   *dog*

Our new word for this lesson is a third declension noun which is related to the English word *canine*. This noun has a couple of interesting properties. First of all, the nominative singular form is exactly the same as the genitive singular form. Therefore if you are reading an exercise and you see the word **canis**, you will have to use the context of the sentence to decide whether it is nominative singular or genitive singular.

In the past few lessons, we have been discussing the difference between natural gender and grammatical gender. And with that in mind, this particular noun may seem weird to you because it has an unusual characteristic: **canis** can be grammatically either masculine or feminine. This kind of noun is called a *common gender* noun. As with any noun, you simply have to memorize its gender—in this case, the fact that it can be either.

187

And one last thing—**canis** is not an i-stem noun, so the genitive plural form is **canum**.

THIRD DEC.	SINGULAR	PLURAL
NOMINATIVE (SUBJ./PRED. NOM.)	**canis**	**canēs**
GENITIVE (POSSESSION)	**canis**	**canum**
DATIVE (IND. OBJECT)	**canī**	**canibus**
ACCUSATIVE (DIRECT OBJECT)	**canem**	**canēs**
ABLATIVE (MANY USES)	**cane**	**canibus**

In these exercises, you will encounter a male dog named **Fīdus**. I didn't make up this word—it's an actual Latin word that means *loyal*.

EXERCISES

1. **Nōnne rēx multōs canēs habet?** ◆ **Ita. Rēx noster canēs amat.** ◆ **Ubi canēs habitant?** ◆ **Post castellum prope stabula habitant.**
2. **Ō Tertī, habēsne canem?** ◆ **Minimē. Parvam fēlem habeō.**
3. **Ille canis nōn est canis.** ◆ **Num magna fēlēs est?** ◆ **Minimē. Lupus est!** ◆ **Valē!**
4. **Habēsne canem?** ◆ **Ita. Fīdus est canis noster. Fīdus est canis bonus.** ◆ **Cūr canis est bonus?** ◆ **Fīdus est canis bonus quod casam semper servat et numquam cum fēlibus pugnat. Fīdus semper pāret.** ◆ **Fīdus est canis bonus!**
5. **Num rēx abest?** ◆ **Ita, rēx nōn est in castellō.** ◆ **Ubi est rēx?** ◆ **Rēx in montibus cum mīlitibus suīs est. Cum incolīs montium pugnant.**
6. **Mīlitēs nostrī mūrum circum urbem aedificant.** ◆ **Aedificantne mūrum ē lignō?** ◆ **Minimē. Ē saxō mūrum aedificant.**
7. **Cūr Pūblius domī est?** ◆ **Hodiē uxōrem suam cūrat.** ◆ **Cūr? Num aegra est?** ◆ **Ita. Uxor Pūbliī aegra est.** ◆ **Pūblius est marītus bonus!**
8. **Mīlitēs rēgis ad actam cum rēge properant.** ◆ **Cūr ad actam properant?** ◆ **Pīrātae ad īnsulam nostram nāvigant.**
9. **Ō fīlī, cūr pugnās cum sorōribus tuīs?** ◆ **Librum meum habent!**
10. **Urbem gladiō servō.**

Answers on page 285.

LESSON 119

NEW WORD   **quis**

MEANING   *who?*

At this point in the book, you have accumulated quite a bit of practice working with various kinds of questions. You know how to add the **-ne** suffix to the first word of a sentence. You know how to use **nōnne** and **num** to indicate what kind of answer you expect. And, you know how to use words like **ubi** and **cūr**. But there are other kinds of questions that you do not yet know about. Consider this sentence for example:

Who is in the boat?

If you wanted to ask that question in Latin, you would need to use our new word for this lesson which is the word **quis**. **Quis** means *who*. Let's use the word **quis** to ask that same question completely in Latin:

Quis est in scaphā? *(Who is in the boat?)*

Here are a few practice sentences to get you started working with **quis**:

- **Quis est in popīnā?** *(Who is in the restaurant?)*
- **Quis ad actam ambulat?** *(Who is walking to the seashore?)*
- **Quis est ante templum?** *(Who is in front of the temple?)*

EXERCISES

1. **Quis trāns viam properat?** ♦ **Helena trāns viam ad templum Minervae properat.**
2. **Quis per portās urbis ambulat?** ♦ **Cornēlius ad casam frātris suī ambulat.** ♦ **Habitatne frāter Cornēliī in urbe?** ♦ **Ita. Frāter Cornēliī in urbe habitat.**
3. **Quis fēlem nostram cūrat?** ♦ **Tertius fēlem cūrat. Tertius domī est et nunc cibum fēlī dat.**
4. **Videō virum in silvā. Quis in silvā est?** ♦ **Nōn est vir! Lupus est!** ♦ **Valē!**

5. Ō amīcī, per rēgnum vestrum ambulāmus. Quis est rēx vester? ♦ Carolus est rēx noster. ♦ Ubi est rēx? ♦ Rēx noster in magnō castellō habitat. Castellum est trāns silvam, in montibus.

6. Haec bibliothēca est bona. Multōs librōs bonōs habet. ♦ Bibliothēcāria quoque bona est. ♦ Quis est bibliothēcāria? ♦ Aurēlia est bibliothēcāria. Semper librōs servat, et saepe puellīs puerīsque fābulās narrat.

7. Multī montēs circum urbem nostram sunt. ♦ Ita. Montēs urbem servant. Mīlitēs per montēs ambulāre nōn possunt. ♦ Cūr mūrum quoque circum urbem nostram habēmus? ♦ Mūrus quoque urbem nostram servat.

8. Ō uxor, cūr haec fēlēs in mēnsā sedet? ♦ Ō marīte, Fluffius est fēlēs. Semper sedet in sellīs, in mēnsīs, in lectīs. ♦ Numquam Fluffius pāret. ♦ Fīdus, canis noster, numquam in mēnsā sedet. ♦ Fīdus semper pāret. Bonus canis est.

9. Cūr mātrēs nostrae ad argentāriam properant? ♦ Pecūnia mātrum nostrārum est in argentāriā.

10. Poēta rēgibus et rēgīnīs fābulam narrat.

Answers on page 285.

LESSON 120

NEUTER NOUNS OF THE THIRD DECLENSION

As I mentioned before, the third declension contains nouns of all three grammatical genders—but so far, you have only worked with masculine and feminine nouns of the third declension. In the next lesson, you will start working with neuter nouns of the third declension. But before you do, I thought it might be a good idea to review (again) the two rules that apply to all neuter nouns:

1. In the nominative plural, neuter nouns always end in **-a**.

2. For neuter nouns, the accusative forms are the same as the nominative forms.

You already know this stuff because you have been working with neuter nouns of the second declension for a long time: nouns like **dōnum**, **scūtum**, and **oppidum**. But it's always a good idea to review!

LESSON 121

NEW WORD   **flūmen, flūminis**

MEANING   *river*

Our new word for this lesson, **flūmen**, is your first neuter noun of the third declension. Let's talk about the properties of this noun.

First, notice that there is an *e* in the nominative singular which is not present in the genitive singular. The genitive stem is **flūmin-**, with an *i*, not an *e*.

Next, notice that the nominative plural does not end in **-ēs** like masculine and feminine nouns of the third declension. Instead, like every neuter noun, regardless of what declension it is from, the neuter plural form ends in **-a**.

Furthermore, notice that the accusative forms are exactly the same as the nominative forms. Again, this is true for every neuter noun, regardless of declension. So, the accusative singular form has the letter *e* in it, not the letter *i* that is present in the genitive stem.

And finally, notice that **flūmen** is *not* an i-stem noun, so there will not be an extra *i* before the **-um** at the end of the genitive plural. That gives you the genitive plural form **flūminum**.

THIRD DEC.	SINGULAR	PLURAL
NOMINATIVE (SUBJ./PRED. NOM.)	flūmen	flūmina
GENITIVE (POSSESSION)	flūminis	flūminum
DATIVE (IND. OBJECT)	flūminī	flūminibus
ACCUSATIVE (DIRECT OBJECT)	flūmen	flūmina
ABLATIVE (MANY USES)	flūmine	flūminibus

Here are a few example sentences to get you flowing along with this new noun.

- **Hoc flūmen est lātum.** *(This river is wide.)*
- **Urbs est trāns flūmen.** *(The city is on the other side of the river.)*
- **Puellae ā flūmine ad urbem properant.** *(The girls are hurrying from the river to the city.)*

EXERCISES

1. **Hoc flūmen est lātum.** ♦ **Illud flūmen est angustum.**
2. **Ō rēx, mīlitēs tuī sunt trāns flūmen.** ♦ **Habēmusne scapham?** ♦ **Minimē. Fortasse trāns flūmen natāre possumus.** ♦ **Ego natāre nōn possum.** ♦ **Ō rēx, cūr natāre nōn potes?** ♦ **Aquam timeō.**
3. **Sunt multa flūmina in patriā nostrā.**
4. **Quis est in flūmine?** ♦ **Frāter meus in flūmine est. Trāns flūmen natat.** ♦ **Cūr trāns flūmen natat?** ♦ **Helena trāns flūmen habitat.** ♦ **Quis est Helena?** ♦ **Helena puella bona est. Helena in urbe trāns flūmen cum familiā suā habitat. Frāter meus Helenam amat, sed patrem Helenae timet.**
5. **Ō amīce, cūr canis tuus in flūmine natat?** ♦ **Canis meus flūmen amat. Cotīdiē in flūmine natat.**
6. **Propter flūmen, ad urbem ambulāre nōn possumus.** ♦ **Num flūmen est lātum?** ♦ **Ita, flūmen est lātum et longum. Circum flūmen ambulāre nōn possumus.** ♦ **Fortasse trāns flūmen nāvigāre possumus.** ♦ **Minimē. Scaphās nōn habēmus.** ♦ **Fortasse trāns flūmen natāre possumus.**
7. **Amō montēs. Interdum in montibus ambulō.** ♦ **Ego numquam in montibus ambulō quod magnās fēlēs montium timeō.**
8. **Fīliī meī et fīliae meae uxōrī meae semper pārent.**
9. **Ubi sunt pater tuus et pater meus?** ♦ **Patrēs nostrī in popīnā cum amīcīs suīs cēnant.** ♦ **Cūr amīcī patrum nostrōrum porcōs portant?** ♦ **Amīcī patrum nostrōrum agricolae sunt.**
10. **Ō Rūfe, ubi sunt frātrēs tuī? Valentne?** ♦ **Ō magistra, frātrēs meī domī sunt. Hodiē aegrōtant.** ♦ **Quis cūrat nunc frātrēs tuōs?** ♦ **Pater meus et māter mea quoque domī sunt cum frātribus meīs.**

Answers on page 285.

LESSON 122

NEW WORD   **iter, itineris**

MEANING   *journey, trip*

Our new word for this lesson is yet another neuter noun of the third declension. Notice that this word is similar to **flūmen** because it has the letter *e* in the nominative singular, but that letter changes to an *i* in the genitive stem. Therefore the genitive stem is **itiner-**, with an *i*, not an *e*. Also, this noun is not an i-stem noun. It's related to English words like *itinerary* and *itinerant*.

THIRD DEC. NEUTER	SINGULAR	PLURAL
NOMINATIVE (SUBJ./PRED. NOM.)	**iter**	**itinera**
GENITIVE (POSSESSION)	**itineris**	**itinerum**
DATIVE (IND. OBJECT)	**itinerī**	**itineribus**
ACCUSATIVE (DIRECT OBJECT)	**iter**	**itinera**
ABLATIVE (MANY USES)	**itinere**	**itineribus**

The word **iter** can mean different things depending on its context. It can be translated into English as *way, journey, road, trip, march*, etc. For example, if you say that an army is making an **iter**, you could translate it as *march*. Or if someone says that there are many **itinera** through the mountains, you could translate **itinera** as *ways* or *roads*. So you see, it just depends on the context. When you translate this noun, use the translation that sounds best in context.

EXERCISES

1. **Iter tuum nōn est longum.** ♦ **Cūr?** ♦ **Prope urbem habitās.**
2. **Propter longum iter, ad casam tuam ambulāre nōn possum.**
3. **Sunt multa itinera per montēs.**
4. **Per montēs ambulāre nōn possumus.** ♦ **Cūr?** ♦ **Illud iter est longum.**

5. Ō amīce, habēsne canem? ♦ Ita. ♦ Habēsne fēlem? ♦ Minimē. Canis meus cum fēle habitāre nōn potest.

6. Ō Pūblī, habēsne sorōrem? ♦ Minimē, sed multōs frātrēs habeō.

7. Cūr mīlitēs in castellum properant? ♦ Rēgī nōn pārent.

8. Quis est haec puella? ♦ Haec puella est amīca mea.

9. Rēx noster est bonus. Semper mīlitēs suōs cūrat. Rēgīna nostra quoque est bona. ♦ Cūr regīna est bona? ♦ Semper cibum incolīs urbium dat.

10. Pūblius ab oppidō ad magnam urbem hodiē ambulat. ♦ Cūr? Illud iter est longum. Est lātum flūmen inter oppidum et urbem.

Answers on page 286.

LESSON 123

NEW WORD   **quid**

MEANING   *what?*

A few lessons ago, you learned that the word **quis** means *who?* **Quis** can be masculine or feminine. But there is also a neuter form of **quis**, and that is the word **quid**. **Quid** means *what?*

It might help you understand what I'm saying better if we put these words into a chart:

	MASCULINE	FEMININE	NEUTER
NOMINATIVE (SUBJ./PRED. NOM.)	**quis**	**quis**	**quid**
GENITIVE (POSSESSION)			
DATIVE (IND. OBJECT)			
ACCUSATIVE (DIRECT OBJECT)			
ABLATIVE (MANY USES)			

194

Since **quis** can be masculine or feminine, we think of it as being associated with people, and so we translate it as *who*. But since **quid** is neuter, we think of it as being associated with inanimate objects—therefore we translate it into English as *what*. In this book, we will stick to extremely simple sentences with **quid**, just so you can get some basic practice using it. Here are some example sentences to get you going with **quid**.

- **Quid est in scaphā?** *(What is in the boat?)*
- **Quid est trāns montēs?** *(What is on the other side of the mountains?)*
- **Quid est in culīnā nostrā?** *(What is in our kitchen?)*

As with **hic**, **haec**, and **hoc**, we will only use **quis** and **quid** in the nominative case. In this book, you will not learn the genitive, dative, accusative, or ablative forms of **quis** or **quid**.

EXERCISES

1. **Quid est in scaphā?**
2. **Quis est in scaphā?**
3. **Quid est post casam nostram?** ◆ **Novus equus est.** ◆ **Cūr tū novum equum habēs?** ◆ **Agricolae sumus. Equōs in fundō nostrō habēmus.**
4. **Quid est in mēnsā?** ◆ **Dōnum tuum est. Esne laeta?** ◆ **Laeta sum! Dōna amō!**
5. **Quid est in trīclīniō nostrō?** ◆ **Mēnsa et sellae in trīclīniō sunt.**
6. **Quid est in monte? Num casa est?** ◆ **Castellum est. Rēx rēgnī nostrī in monte habitat.** ◆ **Ego castellum vidēre nōn possum.** ◆ **Castellum rēgis est parvum.**
7. **Quis est māter tua?** ◆ **Flāvia est māter mea.** ◆ **Quis est uxor tua?** ◆ **Claudia est uxor mea.** ◆ **Quis est soror tua?** ◆ **Semprōnia est soror mea.** ◆ **Quis est fīlia tua?** ◆ **Catharīna est fīlia mea.** ◆ **Habēsne fīlium?** ◆ **Minimē. Sunt multae fēminae in familiā meā, sed nōn sunt virī!**
8. **Hoc flūmen est lātum et longum.** ◆ **Rēgnum nostrum multa flūmina habet.**
9. **Cūr numquam per silvam ad montēs ambulās?** ◆ **Longum iter est.**
10. **Ō Fluffī, cūr cum canibus semper pugnās?** ◆ **Canēs et fēlēs semper pugnant!**

Answers on page 286.

LESSON 124

NEW WORD   **mare, maris**

MEANING   *sea*

PRONUNCIATION TIP: **Mare** has two syllables, so it sounds something like *MAH-reh*.

Our new noun for this lesson is part of a special class of third declension nouns called *neuter i-stem nouns.* These nouns aren't very common, but as a student of Latin, you should at least be familiar with their characteristics.

For starters, the noun **mare** is unusual because it ends with the letter *e.* But beyond that, because it is an i-stem noun it will have an *i* before the final *a* in the nominative plural and accusative plural (these forms are circled in the chart below). Furthermore, it will have an *i* before the genitive plural ending.

But there's one more thing to know about **mare**. It's a long story, but some third declension i-stem nouns end with the letter *i* in the ablative singular instead of the letter *e* as you would expect (this is also circled in the chart).

THIRD DEC. NEUT. I-STEM	SINGULAR	PLURAL
NOMINATIVE (SUBJ./PRED. NOM.)	mare	maria
GENITIVE (POSSESSION)	maris	marium
DATIVE (IND. OBJECT)	marī	maribus
ACCUSATIVE (DIRECT OBJECT)	mare	maria
ABLATIVE (MANY USES)	marī	maribus

EXERCISES

1. **Hoc mare est magnum et lātum.**
2. **Ō Aurēlia, cūr interdum prope actam sedēs?** ♦ **Mare amō. Saepe prope mare sedeō. Aquam spectō, et scaphās nautārum spectō.** ♦ **Ego quoque mare amō.**

196

3. **Possumusne nāvigāre trāns mare?** ♦ **Minimē. Illud mare est lātum, et multōs pīrātās habet.**

4. **Ō māter, ubi est patria tua?** ♦ **Patria mea trāns mare est.** ♦ **Nāvigāsne tū saepe ad patriam tuam?** ♦ **Interdum ad patriam meam nāvigō quod māter mea in patriā meā habitat.** ♦ **Fortasse ego quoque ad patriam tuam nāvigāre possum.**

5. **Ō pater, ubi est Fluffius?** ♦ **Fluffius est in cubiculō tuō. In lectō tuō sedet.** ♦ **Cūr illa fēlēs semper in lectō meō sedet?**

6. **Quis cibum postulat?** ♦ **Uxōrēs mīlitum cibum postulant.** ♦ **Cūr uxōrēs mīlitum cibum postulant?** ♦ **Rēx noster est malus. Numquam mīlitibus pecūniam dat. Nunc uxōrēs mīlitum cibum nōn habent.** ♦ **Ubi nunc est rēx?** ♦ **Rēx prope mare cum uxōre suā sedet.**

7. **Fluffius semper est fēlēs bona.** ♦ **Cūr Fluffius in mēnsā sedet?** ♦ **Fluffius interdum est fēlēs bona.**

8. **Ō rēx, cūr multae scaphae in flūminibus rēgnī tuī sunt?** ♦ **Pīrātae in rēgnum nostrum in scaphīs suīs nāvigant!** ♦ **Num ad urbem nostram nāvigant?** ♦ **Ita.** ♦ **Ubi sunt mīlitēs nostrī? Ubi est scūtum meum?**

9. **Fīdus est canis bonus.** ♦ **Cūr bonus est?** ♦ **Canis bonus est quod cum fēlibus numquam pugnat, et semper pāret.**

10. **Sunt magnī montēs circum urbem. Iter per montēs est longum, et via est angusta.** ♦ **Quid est trāns montēs?** ♦ **Mare est trāns montēs.**

Answers on page 286.

LESSON 125

MORE ABOUT PRONOUNS

Did you know that we have cases in English? What's that, you say? Cases in English? Yes, we do have them! Let's think for a moment about pronouns like *he* and *she*. Observe them as they serve as the subject of a sentence, as in these examples:

- <u>He</u> is watching the students.
- <u>She</u> is watching the students.

But what happens when these words become direct objects?

- The students are watching <u>he</u>.

- The students are watching <u>she</u>.

Oops—those sentences don't make any sense, do they? That's because the words *he* and *she* can't be direct objects. If you want those words to be direct objects, you have to change them to *him* and *her*. Sound familiar, students of Latin? Here are those same sentences again, but this time with the correct pronouns.

- The students are watching <u>him</u>.
- The students are watching <u>her</u>.

If we wanted to think of these English pronouns the same way we think of Latin pronouns, we could put them into declension charts, like these:

NOMINATIVE (SUBJ./PRED. NOM.)	he
ACCUSATIVE (DIRECT OBJECT)	him

NOMINATIVE (SUBJ./PRED. NOM.)	she
ACCUSATIVE (DIRECT OBJECT)	her

The same thing goes for other pronouns like I, we, and they. For example, you wouldn't say *The students see I.* Instead you would say *The students see me.*

NOMINATIVE (SUBJ./PRED. NOM.)	I
ACCUSATIVE (DIRECT OBJECT)	me

Likewise, you wouldn't say *The students see we.* Instead you would say you would say *The students see us.* And lastly, you wouldn't say *The students see they*, you would say *The students see them.*

NOMINATIVE (SUBJ./PRED. NOM.)	we
ACCUSATIVE (DIRECT OBJECT)	us

NOMINATIVE (SUBJ./PRED. NOM.)	they
ACCUSATIVE (DIRECT OBJECT)	them

So, whether you realize it or not, we do have noun cases in English. Long ago, in the earlier stages of its development, the English language had more cases, but they fell out of use over time. Latin, however, has a full array of pronouns in the various cases, and over the next few lessons you will learn some of them.

LESSON 126

NEW WORD   **mē**

MEANING   *me*

In the previous lesson, you learned that we have cases in English. We learned that the pronoun *I* is nominative, but *me* is accusative.

And the same thing happens in Latin. The word for *I* in Latin is **ego**. But you can't use **ego** as a direct object. Instead, the accusative form of **ego** is the pronoun **mē** (pronounced *may*). Examine this chart:

	SINGULAR
NOMINATIVE (SUBJ./PRED. NOM.)	**ego**
GENITIVE (POSSESSION)	
DATIVE (IND. OBJECT)	
ACCUSATIVE (DIRECT OBJECT)	**mē**
ABLATIVE (MANY USES)	

Here are a couple of example sentences to get you started with **mē**, the accusative form of **ego**.

- **Discipulī mē vident.** *(The students see me.)*
- **Equus mē ad urbem portat.** *(The horse is carrying me to the city.)*

EXERCISES

1. **Ō Aurēlia, amāsne mē?** ♦ **Minimē. Marcum amō.** ♦ **Quis est Marcus?**
2. **Ego lupum videō, sed lupus mē nōn videt.**
3. **Cūr canis noster mē spectat?** ♦ **Cibum postulat.** ♦ **Ō Fīde, tū cibum habēs.**
4. **Ō frāter, ego aegrōtō et hoc iter est longum. Fortasse tū mē portāre potes.** ♦ **Ita, ō soror mea. Sed cūr aegra es?** ♦ **Propter cibum malum aegrōtō.**
5. **Mīlitēs ē montibus properant.** ♦ **Properantne ad urbem nostram?** ♦ **Minimē. Ad castellum rēgis properant.** ♦ **Cūr ad castellum**

properant? Nōnne rēgī pārent? ♦ Minimē. Rēx noster numquam mīlitibus suīs pecūniam dat. Mīlitēs nunc pecūniam ante castellum postulant. ♦ Uxōrēs mīlitum quoque adsunt. ♦ Ita. Uxōrēs mīlitum pecūniam postulant.

6. Interdum in popīnā cum sorōribus meīs cēnō. ♦ Habēsne multās sorōrēs? ♦ Ita. Multās sorōrēs et frātrem quoque habeō.

7. Quid est ante templum Minervae? ♦ Equus est ante templum.

8. Ō pater, cūr trāns lātum mare nāvigāmus? ♦ Ō fīlia mea, ad patriam meam nāvigāmus. Est multum aurum et multum argentum in patriā meā. ♦ Quis est rēx patriae tuae?

9. Tertius et Quīntus puerī bonī sunt. ♦ Cūr bonī sunt? ♦ Cubicula sua et lātrīnam suam nunc pūrgant. Mātrī suae pārent.

10. Per magnōs montēs ambulāre nōn possumus. ♦ Cūr? Nōn est longum iter per montēs. ♦ Ita, iter nōn est longum, sed est lātum flūmen inter urbem et montēs. ♦ Fortasse circum flūmen ambulāre possumus. ♦ Minimē. Illud iter est longum.

Answers on page 287.

LESSON 127

NEW WORD   **mihi**

MEANING   *to me, for me*

PRONUNCIATION TIP: The accent is on the first syllable, so **mihi** sounds something like *MEE-hee*.

In the last lesson, you learned the word **mē**, which is the accusative form of **ego**. Now it's time to learn the dative form, which is **mihi**. Since **mihi** is in the dative case, you can use it in a sentence as an indirect object.

- **Uxor mea mihi dōnum dat.** *(My wife is giving a gift to me.)*
- **Gulielmus mihi longam fābulam narrat.** *(William is telling a long story to me.)*

You can also use **mihi** with verbs that use the dative case, like the verb **pāreō** which means *obey*. Here's an example:

200

Hic canis numquam mihi pāret. *(This dog never obeys me.)*

Here is a chart that shows how **mihi** fits in with the other pronouns you know.

	SINGULAR
NOMINATIVE (SUBJ./PRED. NOM.)	**ego**
GENITIVE (POSSESSION)	
DATIVE (IND. OBJECT)	**mihi**
ACCUSATIVE (DIRECT OBJECT)	**mē**
ABLATIVE (MANY USES)	

EXERCISES

1. **Pater meus numquam mihi pecūniam dat. ♦ Cūr? ♦ Agricolae sumus, sed ego numquam in agrīs labōrō. ♦ Fortasse stabula patris tuī pūrgāre potes.**

2. **Magistra mea mihi librōs bonōs interdum dat. ♦ Librōs mihi numquam dat. ♦ Fortasse tū librōs postulāre potes.**

3. **Ō fēlēs, cūr numquam mihi pārētis? ♦ Fēlēs sumus. Nōn sumus canēs. ♦ Et cūr semper in mēnsā sedētis? ♦ Cibus tuus in mēnsā est.**

4. **Hic vir mīlitibus semper fābulās bonās narrat. ♦ Num nauta est? ♦ Minimē. Nautae fābulās malās semper narrant. Hic vir fābulās bonās narrat.**

5. **Rēx sum, sed mīlitēs mihi numquam pārent. Cūr mihi nōn pārent? ♦ Nesciō. Semper rēgīnae pārent.**

6. **Quid est post castellum? ♦ Stabula rēgis sunt post castellum. Rēx multōs equōs habet.**

7. **Cūr ille pīrāta mē spectat? ♦ Tū nunc aurum per urbem portās. Aurum tuum vidēre potest. ♦ Fortasse ad argentāriam properāre possumus.**

8. **Salvē. Quis es? ♦ Lāvīnia sum. Quis es? ♦ Decimus sum. Labōrāsne in scholā? Esne tū magistra? ♦ Minimē. Bibliothēcāria sum.**

9. **Pīrātae ā marī ad urbem properant. ♦ Illud iter nōn est longum.**

10. **Quis in flūmine natat? ♦ Illa puella est amīca mea. Interdum in flūmine cum sorōribus suīs natat.**

Answers on page 287.

LESSON 128

NEW WORD   **mē**

MEANING   *me (ablative)*

The ablative form of **ego** is **mē**, which looks the same as the accusative form.

	SINGULAR
NOMINATIVE (SUBJ./PRED. NOM.)	**ego**
GENITIVE (POSSESSION)	
DATIVE (IND. OBJECT)	**mihi**
ACCUSATIVE (DIRECT OBJECT)	**mē**
ABLATIVE (MANY USES)	**mē**

Here's how you can use **mē** in a sentence:

- **Amīcī meī sine mē cēnant.** *(My friends are having dinner without me.)*
- **Pater meus fābulam de mē narrat.** *(My father is telling a story about me.)*

If you want to say *with me* in Latin you wouldn't say **cum mē**. Instead, you would use a special word which combines **mē** and **cum**: the word **mēcum**.

> **Christophorus mēcum ad īnsulam nāvigat.** *(Christopher is sailing to the island with me.)*

EXERCISES

1. **Soror mea fābulam dē mē narrat.**
2. **Ō amīce, cur per magnōs montēs ambulās? Via est angusta et iter est longum. ♦ Ad magnam urbem cum frātribus meīs ambulō. ♦ Habētisne cibum? ♦ Ita. ♦ Habētisne pecūniam? ♦ Ita. ♦ Via per montēs angusta est. ♦ Frātrēs meī mēcum ambulant.**

3. **Puer ā mē ad patrem suum ambulat.**
4. **Equus mē ad urbem portat.**
5. **Cūr canis tuus mē spectat? ◆ Cibum habēs.**
6. **Ō amīca, cūr in marī natās? ◆ Ego interdum in marī nātō. Mare amō!**
   ◆ Sed mare est magnum et lātum. Fortasse tū in parvō flūmine natāre
   potes.
7. **Ō māter, cūr mihi pecūniam numquam dās? ◆ Tū mihi numquam**
   pārēs. Cūr cubiculum tuum nōn pūrgās? Cūr balneum tuum nōn
   pūrgās? ◆ Fessus sum.
8. **Cūr incolae montium adsunt? Cūr in montibus nōn sunt? ◆ In**
   montibus habitant, sed hodiē in urbe sunt quod poētae in theātrō
   fābulās narrant. ◆ Iter ā montibus ad urbem est longum.
9. **Quid est ante templum?**
10. **Cūr fēlēs tua in mē semper sedet?**

Answers on page 287.

LESSON 129

THE OTHER FORMS OF TU

Over the past few lessons, I have shown you the dative, accusative, and ablative
forms of the pronoun **ego**. Now it's time to learn those same forms of the pronoun
tū, which means *you*. But instead of giving them to you over several lessons, I'll
give them to you all at once. Observe the following chart:

	SINGULAR
NOMINATIVE (SUBJ./PRED. NOM.)	**tū**
GENITIVE (POSSESSION)	
DATIVE (IND. OBJECT)	**tibi**
ACCUSATIVE (DIRECT OBJECT)	**tē**
ABLATIVE (MANY USES)	**tē**

Here's how you can use **tibi** in a sentence:

- **Agricola tibi cibum dat.** *(The farmer is giving food to you.)*
- **Fēlēs tua tibi numquam pāret.** *(Your cat never obeys you.)*

Here's how you can use **tē** (accusative) in a sentence:

- **Canis tē vidit.** *(The dog sees you.)*

Here's how you can use **tē** (ablative) in a sentence:

- **Fīliī meī ad actam sine mē ambulant.** *(My sons are walking to the seashore without me.)*

And if you want to say *with you* in Latin, you don't say **cum tē**, you say **tēcum**.

Tēcum ad flūmen ambulō. *(I am walking to the river with you.)*

EXERCISES

1. **Amīcī tuī tibi magnum dōnum dant! ◆ Quid est dōnum meum? ◆ Nesciō. Fortasse dōnum tuum est novus equus! ◆ Fortasse dōnum meum est canis! ◆ Canēs amō! ◆ Ego quoque!**
2. **Trāns flūmen natāre nōn possum. Illud flūmen est lātum. ◆ In scaphā meā trāns flūmen tē portāre possum.**
3. **Frātrēs meī semper fābulās bonās dē tē narrant.**
4. **Tē numquam videō in thermopōliō meō, ō amīce. Cūr? ◆ Saepe in popīnā Portiae cēnō. Popīna Portiae cibum bonum habet. ◆ Ego quoque cibum bonum habeō! ◆ Num īrātus es?**
5. **Cūr canis meus tibi pāret, sed mihi nōn pāret? ◆ Canis tuus mē amat!**
6. **Ō Aemilia, tē amō. ◆ Tūne mē amās? ◆ Ita. Et Claudiam quoque amō. Cūr īrāta es?**
7. **Māter tua sine tē ad macellum ambulat.**
8. **Quis est pater tuus? ◆ Pater meus est Cornēlius. ◆ Nōnne pater tuus est tēcum? ◆ Minimē. Domī est.**
9. **Mīlitēs uxōribus suīs dōna dant.**
10. **Cūr post scūtum tuum es? ◆ Tū mē vidēre nōn potes quod ego post scūtum meum sum. ◆ Tē vidēre possum. Scūtum tuum est parvum.**

Answers on page 288.

LESSON 130

THE DATIVE OF POSSESSION

If you want to say in Latin that somebody has something, you can use the verb **habeo** and a direct object, like this:

Equum habeō. *(I have a horse.)*

In that kind of sentence, **habeō** is the verb and **equum** is the direct object—and since **equum** is the direct object, it is in the accusative case. But in Latin, there is another very common way to say that somebody has something. This other way is called the *dative of possession*. And, as you may have guessed, it involves the dative case.

Let me show you in English how a sentence like this will be arranged. If you want to say *I have a horse* in Latin using this method, the first thing we would put in the sentence is *There is...*, like this:

There is...

Next, after *There is...*, we need to say *to me*.

There is to me...

Lastly, you put the thing that is being possessed, which in this case is a horse.

There is to me a horse.

So, that's the basic idea. In Latin, if you say *There is to me a horse*, that's the same as if you said *I have a horse.* Read these English sentences a few times and try to get the feeling of how this kind of sentence flows.

- There is to me a book. (I have a book.)
- There is to me a brother. (I have a brother.)
- There is to me money. (I have money.)

In the next lesson, we will learn how to use the dative of possession in Latin.

LESSON 131

THE DATIVE OF POSSESSION, THIS TIME IN LATIN

In the last lesson, you learned that in Latin you can use a special sentence construction called the dative of possession to say that somebody has something. Using this wording, the sentence *I have a horse* would translate into English literally as *There is to me a horse.* Now that you understand the basic structure of the sentence, let's build that same kind of sentence in Latin.

If we want to say *There is...* in Latin, you can do that by taking the word **est** and putting it first in the sentence.

> **Est...** *(There is...)*

Now comes the dative part of the sentence—whoever is doing the possessing, put that person's name or pronoun in the dative case. In this particular sentence, we need to put the dative form of **ego**, which is **mihi. Mihi** means *to me* or *for me.*

> **Est mihi...** *(There is to me...)*

Pay attention to this next part because it's important: lastly, you put the thing being possessed, but you put it in the *nominative case,* not the accusative case. It can't be accusative because in this kind of sentence construction, it's not the direct object of anything.

> **Est mihi equus.** *(There is to me a horse.)*

Again, this kind of sentence can be used to say that you have something. Word for word, it says *There is to me a horse,* but a smoother, better English translation is *I have a horse.* Either way, it translates into English the same as if the Latin sentence had said **Equum habeō.** So...

> **est mihi equus = equum habeō**

Here are a few simple example sentences for you to study before you try the exercises.

206

- **Est mihi liber.** *(I have a book.)*
- **Est mihi scapha.** *(I have a boat.)*
- **Est mihi soror.** *(I have a sister.)*
- **Est mihi pecūnia.** *(I have money.)*

Try these simple exercises with **mihi**, and in the next lesson we will learn more about the dative of possession.

EXERCISES

1. **Est mihi porcus.** ♦ **Cūr?** ♦ **Agricola sum.**
2. **Est mihi magnum castellum.** ♦ **Cūr?** ♦ **Rēx sum. Rēgēs semper in magnīs castellīs habitant.**
3. **Est mihi soror.** ♦ **Habēsne frātrem?** ♦ **Ita. Est mihi frāter.**
4. **Est mihi magna scapha.** ♦ **Cūr magnam scapham habēs? Num pīrāta es?** ♦ **Minimē, nauta sum. Trāns mare interdum nāvigō.**
5. **Haec urbs est magna.** ♦ **Multī incolae in urbe habitant. Frāter meus in urbe habitat.** ♦ **Est mihi frāter, sed mēcum in urbe nōn habitat. Frāter meus in fundō habitat.**
6. **Ō mī fīlī, tū puer bonus es.** ♦ **Ō māter, cūr puer bonus sum?** ♦ **Tū semper mihi pārēs.** ♦ **Fortasse mihi pecūniam dare potes.**
7. **Ō Rūfe, interdum tē in thermopōliō malō cum pīrātīs videō. Cūr cēnās cum pīrātīs?** ♦ **Bonās fābulās narrant.**
8. **Ō pīrāta, quid est in scaphā tuā?** ♦ **Argentum et aurum sunt in scaphā meā.**
9. **Ō pater, ubi est fēlēs nostra?** ♦ **Fluffius in culīnā est. In mēnsā sedet.** ♦ **Cūr Fluffius tibi nōn pāret?** ♦ **Fluffius est fēlēs. Nōn est canis.**
10. **Nāvigāsne hodiē ad īnsulam?** ♦ **Ita. Haec scapha mē ad īnsulam portat.** ♦ **Quis tēcum nāvigat?** ♦ **Cum sorōribus meīs et mātre meā nāvigō.**

Answers on page 288.

LESSON 132

MORE ABOUT THE DATIVE OF POSSESSION

In the last lesson, we practiced working with the dative of possession in sentences like this:

Est mihi equus. *(I have a horse.)*

That kind of sentence was a nice, simple way to get started working with the dative of possession. Now that you have the basic idea of how the dative of possession works, in this lesson I would like to show you a few simple variations of this kind of sentence.

First of all, you can negate the sentence by putting the word **nōn** in front of **est**, like this:

Nōn est mihi equus. *(I do not have a horse.)*

With the word **nōn** there, the sentence now says *There is not to me a horse*, but we will translate it into English as *I don't have a horse.*

Next, if you are talking to someone, and you want to say that the person you are talking to has someting, you can use the word **tibi** (the dative form of **tū**) to say that.

Est tibi equus. *(You have a horse.)*

A word-for-word translation would say *There is to you a horse*, but we will translate it into English as *You have a horse.*

And finally, the thing that the person is possessing could be plural. For example, what if the someone has more than one horse? Then, you would use the word **sunt** instead of **est**, and then use the word **equī**, which is plural, instead of **equus**.

Sunt mihi equī. *(I have horses.)*

208

In that sentence, instead of the word **est** meaning *There is*, we have the word **sunt** meaning *There are*. So, a word-for-word translation would be *There are to me horses*, but we will translate it into English as *I have horses*.

The dative of possession can be used in more ways than the ways I am showing you here in this lesson. You can put other nouns in the dative case to show that things belong to them. I will show you more about this later as we go along.

EXERCISES

1. **Nōn est mihi fundus. Nōn sum agricola.**
2. **Ō Claudia, nōnne māter es?** ◆ **Ita, māter sum. Sunt mihi multae fīliae.**
3. **Rēx sum, sed nōn est mihi castellum.** ◆ **Cūr nōn est tibi castellum?** ◆ **Habeō parvum rēgnum. In rēgnō meō nōn sunt multī incolae. In parvā casā habitō.** ◆ **Tū es rēx, sed in parvā casā habitās? Fortasse tū magnam casam aedificāre potes.**
4. **Ō puer, quis est pater tuus?** ◆ **Ego fīlius Rōbertī sum, et Aurēlia est māter mea.**
5. **Trāns flūmen natāre nōn possumus.** ◆ **Cūr? Cotīdiē natāmus. Validī sumus.** ◆ **Hoc flūmen est lātum!** ◆ **Est mihi scapha. Scapha mea mē trāns flūmen portāre potest.** ◆ **Fortasse ego tēcum nāvigāre possum.**
6. **Hoc iter nōn est longum quod equum habeō.**
7. **Ō nauta, cūr mihi fābulam malam narrās?** ◆ **Nauta sum. Semper tibi fābulās malās narrō!** ◆ **Fortasse interdum fābulam bonam narrāre potes.** ◆ **Nōn sunt mihi fābulae bonae.**
8. **Ō pater, cūr obsōnās?** ◆ **Obsōnō quod cibum in casā nostrā nōn habēmus. Hodiē in trīclīniō nostrō cum sorōribus meīs cēnāmus. Sunt mihi multae sorōrēs.**
9. **Ō rēx, cūr tū in trīclīniō nōn sedēs? Amīcī tuī in magnō trīclīniō sine tē cēnant.** ◆ **Īrātus sum.** ◆ **Cūr īrātus es? Cūr manēs in cubiculō tuō?** ◆ **Soror mea in sellā meā sedet, et frāter meus fābulās dē mē narrat.**
10. **In hypogaeō patris meī habitō.**

Answers on page 288.

LESSON 133

NEW WORD   **nōmen, nōminis**

MEANING   *name*

Our new word for this lesson is a neuter noun of the third declension. Like **flūmen** and **iter**, it has the letter *e* in the nominative singular, but that letter changes to an *i* in the genitive stem. This noun is related to English words like *nomination, nominal,* and *nomenclature.*

THIRD DEC. NEUTER	SINGULAR	PLURAL
NOMINATIVE (SUBJ./PRED. NOM.)	**nōmen**	**nōmina**
GENITIVE (POSSESSION)	**nōminis**	**nōminum**
DATIVE (IND. OBJECT)	**nōminī**	**nōminibus**
ACCUSATIVE (DIRECT OBJECT)	**nōmen**	**nōmina**
ABLATIVE (MANY USES)	**nōmine**	**nōminibus**

Over the past few lessons, you have been learning about the dative of possession—and that's good, because you'll be needing the dative of possession as you work with the word **nōmen**. The reason for this is that in Latin, the dative of possession is the most stylistically correct way to say what someone's name is. Let me explain.

If you want, you can say this:

Nōmen meum est Gulielmus.

And that's fine—it translates into English as *My name is William,* but it's not really the way ancient Roman authors wrote. The best way to say what someone's name is in Latin is by using the dative of possession, like this:

Nōmen mihi est Gulielmus.

210

Here, using the dative of possession, the sentence says *The name to me is William*, but you would translate that into English as *My name is William*.

This next part could be tricky for you, so pay attention: when you are saying what someone else's name is, the dative case is used in the same way. Observe:

Quid est nōmen mātrī tuae?

Here, **mātrī** and **tuae** are in the dative case, so the sentence says *What is the name to your mother?* But you should translate it into English as *What is your mother's name?*

So, the point to remember here is that whenever you see the word **nōmen**, be on the lookout for a nearby word in the dative case. That dative word is very likely to tell you who the name belongs to.

EXERCISES

1. **Salvē. Nōmen mihi est Gulielmus.** ♦ **Salvē, ō Gulielme. Nōmen mihi est Claudia.** ♦ **Ō Claudia, tūne bibliothēcāria es?** ♦ **Ita, in bibliothēcā librōs curō, et puerīs puellīsque interdum fābulās narrō.**
2. **Quid est nōmen rēgī?** ♦ **Nōmen rēgī est Rōbertus.**
3. **Salvē, ō nauta. Quis es?** ♦ **Salvē. Nōmen mihi est Quīntus.**
4. **Salvē, ō bibliothēcāria. Nōmen mihi est Christophorus.** ♦ **Salvē, ō Christophore.** ♦ **Habēsne librōs dē flūminibus?** ♦ **Certē. Bibliothēca nostra multōs librōs dē flūminibus habet.**
5. **Ō amīce, habēsne canem?** ♦ **Ita. Nōmen canī meō est Fīdus.** ♦ **Habēsne fēlem?** ♦ **Ita, fēlem quoque habeō. Nōmen fēlī meae est Fluffius.**
6. **Ō Pūblī, habēsne sorōrem?** ♦ **Ita, sorōrem habeō. Nōmen sorōrī meae est Portia.**
7. **Cūr mīlitēs in castellum properant?** ♦ **Rēgī nōn pārent.**
8. **Quis est haec fēmina?** ♦ **Haec fēmina est amīca mea.**
9. **Rēx noster est bonus. Semper incolīs urbium cibum dat. Uxor rēgis quoque est bona.** ♦ **Cūr uxor rēgis est bona?** ♦ **Semper fīliōs fīliāsque mīlitum cūrat.**
10. **Quid est nōmen fīliō tuō?** ♦ **Nōmen fīliō meō est Titus.**

Answers on page 288.

LESSON 134

NEW WORD   **arbor, arboris**

MEANING   *tree*

Now that you know "tree" declensions, it's time to branch out and learn a new noun: the word **arbor**, which means *tree*. It's a feminine noun of the third declension. It is not an i-stem, so the genitive plural form is **arborum**.

In English, we have several words related to **arbor**. An *arborist* is a person who specializes in trees. An *arboretum* is a special garden dedicated to trees. In many countries, there is a special holiday called *Arbor Day* on which people are encouraged to plant trees.

THIRD DEC.	SINGULAR	PLURAL
NOMINATIVE (SUBJ./PRED. NOM.)	**arbor**	**arborēs**
GENITIVE (POSSESSION)	**arboris**	**arborum**
DATIVE (IND. OBJECT)	**arborī**	**arboribus**
ACCUSATIVE (DIRECT OBJECT)	**arborem**	**arborēs**
ABLATIVE (MANY USES)	**arbore**	**arboribus**

EXERCISES

1. **Propter arborēs, casam tuam vidēre nōn possum.** ◆ **Sunt multae arborēs ante casam nostram.** ◆ **Cūr habētis multās arborēs ante casam vestram?** ◆ **In silvā habitāmus.**

2. **Ō amīce, scapham aedificāre nōn possumus.** ◆ **Cūr? Nōnne lignum habēmus?** ◆ **Minimē. Lignum nōn habēmus.** ◆ **Sunt multae arborēs in silvā. Fortasse arborēs ē silvā portāre possumus.** ◆ **Ō amīce, validī sumus, sed magnās arborēs portāre nōn possumus.**

3. **Ō marīte, ubi est fēlēs nostra? Ubi est Fluffius?** ◆ **Nesciō, ō uxor mea.** ◆ **Quid est in arbore nostrā?** ◆ **Nesciō. Num Fluffius in arbore est?** ◆ **Ita, Fluffius est in arbore!**

4. **Quīntus scapham ex arboribus aedificat.** ◆ **Cūr scapham aedificat?** ◆ **Rēx noster novās scaphās postulat. Rēgī pāret.** ◆ **Cūr rēx scaphās**

postulat? Rēgnum est magna silva. Rēgnum nōn est prope mare, et nōn habet flūmina. ◆ Quīntus semper rēgī pāret quod mīles est.

5. Vīcīniam vestram amō quod haec vīcīnia multās arborēs habet.

6. Ō Semprōnia, ubi est marītus tuus? ◆ Marītus meus in hypogaeō sedet. ◆ Cūr semper in hypogaeō sedet? ◆ Hypogaeum nostrum est tablīnum marītī meī.

7. Salvē. Quid est nōmen tibi? ◆ Salvē. Nōmen mihi est Catharīna.

8. Tū mē vidēre nōn potes. ◆ Tē vidēre possum. ◆ Post arborem sum. Tū mē vidēre nōn potes. ◆ Illa arbor est angusta. Tē vidēre possum.

9. Ō Aemilia, cūr domī manēs? Amīcae tuae ad actam ambulant. Numquam ad actam sine tē ambulant. ◆ In cubiculō meō maneō quod fessa sum. ◆ Cūr fessa es? ◆ Hodiē aegrōtō.

10. Cūr ab urbe ad montēs ambulāre nōn possumus? Hoc iter nōn est longum. ◆ Est lātum flūmen inter urbem et montēs. Scapham non habēmus.

Answers on page 289.

LESSON 135

NEW WORD   **pōns, pontis**

MEANING   *bridge*

Our new word for this lesson is a masculine noun of the third declension which is related to the English word *pontificate*.

THIRD DEC. I-STEM	SINGULAR	PLURAL
NOMINATIVE (SUBJ./PRED. NOM.)	**pōns**	**pontēs**
GENITIVE (POSSESSION)	**pontis**	**pontium**
DATIVE (IND. OBJECT)	**pontī**	**pontibus**
ACCUSATIVE (DIRECT OBJECT)	**pontem**	**pontēs**
ABLATIVE (MANY USES)	**ponte**	**pontibus**

Because **pōns** is an i-stem noun, the genitive plural form will be **pontium**. Also notice that the *o* in the nominative singular form is long, but in the other forms the *o* is short.

EXERCISES

1. **Cūr rēx rēgīnaque novum pontem aedificant?** ◆ **Rēgnum nostrum est prope mare. Est īnsula prope actam, sed nōn est pōns inter īnsulam et actam. Nunc rēx rēgīnaque novum pontem postulant.** ◆ **Illa īnsula est parva. Quid est in īnsulā?** ◆ **Īnsula est parva, sed in īnsulā est magnum castellum.**

2. **Ō Semprōnia, cūr tū trāns flūmen semper natās? Cūr trāns pontem nōn ambulās?** ◆ **Ille pōns est angustus. Ego timeō angustōs pontēs, sed natāre amō.**

3. **Quid est nōmen novō pontī?** ◆ **Nōmen est "Pōns Rēgis."** ◆ **Cūr nōmen est "Pōns Rēgis?"** ◆ **Nōmen est "Pōns Rēgis" quod mīlitēs rēgis pontem aedificant et arborēs ē silvā rēgis portant.**

4. **Quid est in flūmine?** ◆ **Parva scapha est.** ◆ **Quis est in scaphā?** ◆ **Vir est in scaphā.** ◆ **Quis est vir?** ◆ **Nesciō. Virum vidēre nōn possum.** ◆ **Cūr tū virum vidēre nōn potes?** ◆ **Scapha virī post arborem est.** ◆ **Fortasse ad flūmen ambulāre possumus.** ◆ **Nunc virum vidēre possum. Ille vir est Rūfus.** ◆ **Cūr Rūfus est in scaphā suā?** ◆ **Nesciō. Fortasse trāns flūmen nāvigat.** ◆ **Videtne Rūfus tē?** ◆ **Minimē. Rūfus mē nōn videt, sed ego Rūfum vidēre possum.**

5. **Ō Rōmule, potesne mēcum ad actam ambulāre?** ◆ **Hodiē tēcum ad actam ambulāre possum, sed in marī natāre nōn possum.** ◆ **Cūr?** ◆ **Mare timeō.**

6. **Hic pōns est longus et angustus.** ◆ **Cūr trāns pontem ambulāmus?** ◆ **Trāns flūmen ambulāmus.** ◆ **Cūr trāns flūmen ambulāmus?** ◆ **Ad urbem ambulāmus.**

7. **Fēlēs nostra semper in mēnsā sedet. Haec fēlēs mihi nōn pāret.** ◆ **Cūr tibi nōn pāret?** ◆ **Fēlēs est. Nōn est canis.**

8. **Salvē, ō Flāvia.** ◆ **Salvē, ō Quīnte.** ◆ **Quis est tēcum hodiē?** ◆ **Amīca mea mēcum est.** ◆ **Quid est nōmen amīcae tuae?** ◆ **Nōmen amīcae meae est Tullia.**

9. **Cūr amīcī meī sine mē in popīnā cēnant?** ◆ **Numquam sine tē cēnant.**

10. **Ō fīlia, cūr cubiculum tuum pūrgās?** ◆ **Fortasse mihi pecūniam dare potes.**

Answers on page 289.

LESSON 136

I LIKE IT, I LIKE IT!

Over the next few lessons, I'm going to teach you how to say that you like something in Latin. In English, here's how we say what we like something:

> I like the boat.

In that sentence, the word *I* is the subject of the sentence, the word *like* is the verb, and the word *boat* is the direct object. But in Latin, this kind of sentence has a different structure. Observe this sentence:

> The boat to me is pleasing.

In that sentence, the words are doing different things than in the previous sentence. Here, the word *boat* is the subject, not the word *I*. And the verb is not *like*, but *is pleasing*. And the part that says *to me* is the indirect object—that's the person that is liking something. In Latin, this part of the sentence will be in the dative case.

So literally, in Latin the sentence will say *The boat to me is pleasing*, but we will translate it into English as *I like the boat*.

Here are some examples to get you accustomed to this kind of sentence structure:

- The food to me is pleasing. (I like the food.)
- These shoes to me are pleasing (I like these shoes.)
- Coffee to me is pleasing. (I like coffee.)
- My job to me is pleasing. (I like my job.)

Read through these example sentences a few times and try to get the feeling of this kind of sentence. You could even make up sentences of your own, saying them with the Latin sentence structure, then English sentence structure just for practice. When you're ready, go on to the next lesson and we will start to put together this kind of sentence in Latin.

LESSON 137

I LIKE IT! (THIS TIME IN LATIN)

In the last lesson, we talked about the kind of sentence structure that we use to say that we like something In Latin. That kind of sentence is worded like this:

The boat to me is pleasing.

But right now, you don't know a Latin verb that means *it is pleasing*. So it's time to learn a new verb: the verb **placeō**, which is from the second conjugation. Observe the chart below.

	SINGULAR	PLURAL
FIRST PERSON	(unnecessary)	(unnecessary)
SECOND PERSON	(unnecessary)	(unnecessary)
THIRD PERSON	placet	placent

In the chart, I only displayed the third person singular and third person plural forms because those are the only forms we need. **Placet** means *he, she,* or *it is pleasing*, and **placent** means *they are pleasing*.

Using the new verbs we just learned, let's start putting together our Latin sentence. If we want to say *I like the boat* in Latin, we would start with the word for *boat*, like this:

Scapha... *(The boat...)*

Next, we need to use the dative case to show to whom the boat is pleasing. For this, we will need the word **mihi**, which is the dative form of **ego**.

Scapha mihi... *(The boat to me...)*

216

Finally, we need to add in the verb **placet**.

Scapha mihi placet. *(The boat to me is pleasing.)*

Now our sentence is complete. Literally, the sentence says *The boat to me is pleasing*, but we will translate it into English as *I like the boat*.

If the thing that you like is plural, you will need to use the plural verb **placent** instead of the singular **placet**.

Equī mihi placent. *(Horses to me are pleasing.)*

Literally, that sentence says *Horses to me are pleasing*, but we will translate it into English as *I like horses*.

You can also make this kind of sentence with **tibi**:

Hic liber tibi placet. *(This book to you is pleasing.)*

Literally, that sentence says *This book to you is pleasing*. But we will translate it into English as *You like this book*.

So that's the basic idea. Work through some more practice sentences, and then you'll be ready to go on to the exercises.

- **Castella mihi placent.** *(I like castles.)*
- **Frāter meus tibi placet.** *(You like my brother.)*
- **Illud templum tibi placet.** *(You like that temple.)*

EXERCISES

1. **Haec casa mihi placet.**
2. **Equus tuus mihi placet.**
3. **Haec sella tibi placet.**
4. **Bibliothēcae mihi placent.**
5. **Canēs tibi placent.**
6. **Haec fēlēs mihi placet.** ♦ **Illa fēlēs nōn est fēlēs.** ♦ **Quid est?** ♦ **Parvus canis est.**

7. **Ubi est templum Minervae?** ♦ **Trāns viam est.** ♦ **Templum vidēre nōn possum.** ♦ **Cūr templum vidēre nōn potes?** ♦ **Sunt multae arborēs ante templum. Templum vidēre nōn possum propter arborēs.**

8. **Cūr mīlitēs nunc absunt?** ♦ **Aegrī sunt propter cibum malum.** ♦ **Quis urbem servat?** ♦ **Nesciō. Fortasse tū urbem servāre potes.** ♦ **Ego urbem servāre nōn possum quod nōn est mihi gladius.** ♦ **Tibi gladium meum dare possum.**

9. **Ō Rūfe, ubi es? Tē vidēre nōn possum.** ♦ **Post arborem sum.** ♦ **Cūr post arborem es?** ♦ **Magister meus adest.**

10. **Quid est nōmen tibi?** ♦ **Nōmen mihi est Decimus.**

Answers on page 289.

LESSON 138

I DONT LIKE IT!

If you want to say that you don't like something, just put the word **nōn** in front of **placet** or **placent**, like this:

Gladius tuus mihi nōn placet.

Literally, this sentence says *Your sword to me is not pleasing.* But we will translate it into English as *I don't like your sword.*

EXERCISES

1. **Haec popīna mihi nōn placet. ◆ Cūr? ◆ Hic cibus est malus. ◆ Mimime. Hic cibus est bonus! ◆ Fortasse frātribus meīs cibum dare possum.**

2. **Illa īnsula mihi nōn placet. ◆ Cūr? ◆ Multī pīrātae in īnsulā habitant.**

3. **Fēlēs patris meī mihi nōn placet. ◆ Cūr? ◆ Mihi numquam pāret, et in mē semper sedet. ◆ Num illa fēlēs in tē sedet? ◆ Ita. Interdum in exedriō sedeō, et fēlēs in mē sedet.**

4. **Haec sella mihi placet. ◆ Mihi quoque placet. ◆ Cūr tibi placet? ◆ Mihi placet quod lāta est.**

5. **Hoc castellum mihi nōn placet. ◆ Ō rēx, cūr hoc castellum tibi nōn placet? ◆ Hoc castellum mihi nōn placet quod cubiculum meum est parvum, et balneum nōn est prope cubiculum meum. ◆ Fortasse novum balneum aedificāre possumus, ō rēx.**

6. **Ō māter, cūr trāns pontem tēcum ambulō? ◆ Ad urbem ambulāmus, sed urbs trāns flūmen est. ◆ Cūr ad urbem ambulāmus? ◆ Sorōrēs meae in urbe habitant. Interdum sorōribus meīs cibum dō.**

7. **Canis tuus mihi nōn placet. ◆ Cūr? ◆ Mē semper spectat. ◆ Est tibi cibus. Tē spectat quod cibum habēs. ◆ Fortasse tū cānī cibum dare potes.**

8. **Hic pōns mihi nōn placet. ◆ Cūr? ◆ Hic pōns est angustus. Angustī pontēs mihi nōn placent.**

9. **Numquam sine tē obsōnō. ◆ Cūr? ◆ Tū pecūniam semper habēs.**

10. **Cūr uxor tua semper in hortō labōrat? ◆ Hortus noster multās arborēs habet. Uxor mea arborēs amat.**

Answers on page 290.

LESSON 139

DO YOU LIKE IT?

If you want to say *You like the seashore*, you can say it like this:

Acta tibi placet. *(You like the seashore.)*

But what if you want to ask someone whether or not they like the seashore? If you want to say "Do you like the seashore?" you can do it by putting the word **placet** first, along with the special **-ne** suffix. That turns the sentence into a question, like this:

Placetne tibi acta? *(Do you like the seashore?)*

In that sentence, since the verb **placet** has the **-ne** suffix, **placetne** is asking the question *Is it pleasing?* Besides that, the words are the same as before, but in a different order.

Also, if you are asking if someone likes more than one thing, you should put the word **placent** first, along with the **-ne** suffix:

Placentne tibi canēs? *(Do you like dogs?)*

In that sentence, since the verb **placent** has the **-ne** suffix, **placentne** is asking the question *Are they pleasing?* Besides that, the words are the same as before, but in a different order.

Here are a few more example sentences for practice

- **Placetne tibi cibus?** *(Do you like the food?)*
- **Placetne tibi ille liber?** *(Do you like that book?)*
- **Placentne tibi equī?** *(Do you like horses?)*

EXERCISES

1. **Nōmen fēlī meae est Fluffius. Placetne tibi fēlēs mea? ♦ Minimē. Fluffius semper in mē sedet, et mihi nōn pāret.**

2. **Placentne tibi montēs?** ♦ **Ita. Interdum per montēs ambulō.** ♦ **Montēs mihi nōn placent propter magnās fēlēs montium.**
3. **Placentne flūmina?** ♦ **Ita. Interdum in flūminibus natō.**
4. **Placetne tibi hoc thermopōlium?** ♦ **Ita. Hic cibus est bonus. Saepe in thermopōliō cēnō.**
5. **Placentne tibi lupī?** ♦ **Minimē. Lupōs timeō. Propter lupōs, numquam per silvam ambulō.**
6. **Arborēs mihi placent.** ♦ **Mihi quoque placent. Est mihi hortus. In hortō meō sunt multae arborēs.**
7. **Lupōs videō, sed lupī mē nōn vident.** ♦ **Lupī tē nunc vident!**
8. **Soror mea novum canem habet.** ♦ **Quid est nōmen canī sorōris tuae?** ♦ **Nōmen canī est Fīdus. Sed Fīdus numquam sorōrī meae pāret.** ♦ **Tūne habēs canem?** ♦ **Minimē. Est mihi fēlēs.**
9. **Ubi est rēx? Num in castellō est?** ♦ **Minimē. Rēx in montibus cum mīlitibus suīs est.**
10. **Quis trāns pontem ambulat?** ♦ **Christophorus trāns pontem ambulat.** ♦ **Cūr Christophorus fēlem suam portat?** ♦ **Fēlēs Christophorī aegrōtat. Christophorus fēlem suam ad urbem portat.**

Answers on page 290.

LESSON 140

THE THIRD CONJUGATION

It is now time for you to learn about the third conjugation. But before we do, let's take a moment to review some general information about conjugations so you can think about the third conjugation in context with what you already know.

In Latin, there are four main patterns of verb endings called *conjugations*. The first conjugation, second conjugation, third conjugation, and fourth conjugation each have certain characteristics. In the following chart, observe the differences between the first conjugation and the second conjugation using the verbs **portō** and **doceō** as examples. As you observe the infinitive form and third person singular form of each verb, pay special attention to the letters indicated by arrows.

	INFINITIVE	3RD PERSON SING.
1ST CONJ.	**portāre**	**portat**
2ND CONJ.	**docēre**	**docet**

Notice that in the first conjugation, the infinitive ends in **-āre**. If you remove the **-re** from the end of the infinitive, you get the stem of the verb which is **portā-**. Then, we add the personal endings to the stem, giving us forms like **portās**, **portat**, **portāmus**, **portātis**, and **portant**. Notice that the letter *a* that comes before the personal endings is sometimes long, with a macron over it, and sometimes short (in the third person forms).

In the second conjugation, we see a similar pattern. In the second conjugation, the infinitive ends in **-ēre**. If you remove the **-re** from the end of the infinitive, you get the stem of the verb which is **docē-**. Then, we add the personal endings to the stem, giving us forms like **docēs**, **docet**, **docēmus**, **docētis**, and **docent**. And, similar to what we saw in the first conjugation, the letter *e* that comes before the personal endings is sometimes long, with a macron over it, and sometimes short (in the third person forms).

Now that we have reviewed the first and second conjugations, it's time to talk about the third conjugation. When you study the third conjugation, you have to take note of a big difference in the way the personal endings are added to the stem. You see, we can't do that thing where we remove the **-re** from the end of the infinitive, get the stem, and then start adding personal endings. In the third conjugation, the vowel that is at the end of the stem is not the same letter that comes before the personal endings.

In the chart below, I provide you with the same first and second conjugation examples from the previous chart, but I have added a row for the third conjugation so you can compare them. The new verb here from the third conjugation is the verb **currō** which means *I run*. Study the infinitive form and third person singular form of this verb in the chart below, paying special attention to the letters indicated by arrows.

	INFINITIVE	3RD PERSON SING.
1ST CONJ.	**portāre**	**portat**
2ND CONJ.	**docēre**	**docet**
3RD CONJ.	**currere**	**currit**

There are two things I would like you understand here. First of all, notice that in the infinitive form of **currō**, which is **currere**, the letter *e* three letters from the end is a short *e*, not a long *e* (that letter is indicated by an arrow). Unlike what you see in the second conjugation, there is no macron over that letter. This is important because it changes how this infinitive is pronounced. According to the rules of Latin pronunciation, since that *e* there (three letters from the end) is short, the accent or stress will move away from that syllable to the first syllable of the word. Therefore, **currere** will *not* be pronounced *kurr-AY-reh*, with the accent or stress on the second syllable. Instead, it will be pronounced like *KURR-eh-reh*, with the stress on the first syllable. Please take note of this important pronunciation difference between the second and third conjugations. Just because both infinitives end with the same letters doesn't mean that they are pronounced the same. Whether the *e* is long or short makes a big difference!

The other big thing to notice here is the fact that when you remove the **-re** from the end of **currere**, you get **curre-** as the stem. But the letter *e* which you see there at the end of the stem is *not* the letter that will come before the personal endings. Instead, when you make the present tense forms of **currō**, the letter *i* will come before the personal endings, giving you forms such as the third person singular form **currit** which you see displayed in the chart.

Here's a quick review of the main points I want you to remember about the third conjugation.

- In a third conjugation infinitive, the *e* is short, unlike the long *e* found in a second conjugation infinitive.
- Because the *e* in the infinitive is short, the accent moves away from that syllable.
- The letter that comes before the personal ending is the letter *i*, not the letter *e*.

In the next lesson, we will continue our study of the third conjugation by putting together some Latin sentences with the verb **currō**.

LESSON 141

NEW WORD   **currō / currere**

MEANING   *I run / to run*

PRONUNCIATION TIP: Notice that in these third conjugation verb forms, the stress or accent may not fall on the syllable you expect it to. The infinitive **currere** sounds like *KURR-eh-reh*. **Currimus** and **curritis** both have the stress on the first syllable, sounding like *KURR-ih-mus* and *KURR-ih-tiss*.

In the last lesson we took some time to review some basic information about how conjugations work in Latin, and we began to observe the characteristics of the third conjugation, comparing them to the other conjugations you know. You learned that in the third conjugation, the infinitive has a short *e*, not a long *e*. You also learned that the vowel at the end of the verb stem changes from *e* to *i* when we add the personal endings. So far so good.

But there is one more thing I need to tell you before we start using the third conjugation in sentences: in the third person plural form, the letter that comes before the personal ending will be the letter *u*, not the letter *i*. This is indicated by an arrow in the chart below.

	SINGULAR	PLURAL
FIRST PERSON	**currō**	**currimus**
SECOND PERSON	**curris**	**curritis**
THIRD PERSON	**currit**	**currunt**

INFINITIVE	**currere**

224

So, when it comes to the third conjugation, you really have to keep track of your vowels! You get a short *e* in the infinitive, the letter *i* before most of the personal endings, and the letter *u* before the personal ending in the third person plural.

Here are a few example sentences to get you up and running (heh heh) with the third conjugation.

- **Ad actam currō.** *(I am running to the seashore.)*
- **Cūr per urbem curris?** *(Why are you running through the city?)*
- **Quis in scholā currit?** *(Who is running in the school?)*
- **Trans pontem currimus.** *(We are running across the bridge.)*
- **Cūr ex urbe curritis?** *(Why are y'all running out of the city?)*
- **Equī ē stabulīs currunt!** *(The horses are running out of the stables!)*
- **Ego per silvam hodiē currere nōn possum.** *(I cannot run through the forest today.)*

EXERCISES

1. **Cum cane meō cotīdiē currō.**
2. **Cūr fēlēs ā cane currit?** ♦ **Fēlēs canem timet.**
3. **Sorōrēs meae trāns pontem cotīdiē currunt.** ♦ **Ille pōns est longus et angustus.** ♦ **Ita. Ego numquam trāns pontem ambulō quod pontem timeō, sed sorōrēs meae pontem nōn timent.**
4. **Fēlēs tua mihi placet. Quid est nōmen fēlī tuae?** ♦ **Nōmen fēlī meae est Fluffius. Fluffius semper est fēlēs bona.** ♦ **Cūr Fluffius est fēlēs bona?** ♦ **Fluffius numquam cum cane nostrō pugnat.** ♦ **Sed Fluffius saepe in mēnsā sedet.** ♦ **Fluffius interdum est fēlēs bona.**
5. **Placetne tibi rēx noster?** ♦ **Ita. Rēx noster mihi placet. Semper mīlitibus pecūniam dat, et uxōribus mīlitum cibum dat.** ♦ **Mihi quoque rēx noster placet.** ♦ **Cūr rēx tibi placet?** ♦ **Sunt multa flūmina in rēgnō nostrō. Rēx noster novōs pontēs trāns flūmina aedificant.**
6. **Fēlēs mihi placent. In casā meā multās fēlēs habeō.** ♦ **Habēsne magnam casam?** ♦ **Minimē. Ego et fēlēs meae in parvā casā habitāmus. Sunt fēlēs in culīnā, in exedriō, et in cubiculō meō.** ♦ **Habēsne hypogaeum?** ♦ **Ita. Fīlius meus in hypogaeō nostrō habitat.**
7. **Cūr canēs nostrī in casam currunt?** ♦ **Cibus canum in casā est.**
8. **Quis ex argentāriā cum aurō currit?** ♦ **Ille vir argentum quoque portat.** ♦ **Nunc ad scapham suam currit.** ♦ **Ille vir est pīrāta!**

9. **Nōn est mihi fēlēs.** ♦ **Cūr?** ♦ **Canēs habeō.**
10. **Semper ā pīrātīs currō.**

Answers on page 290.

LESSON 142

NEW WORD   **dūcō /dūcere**

MEANING   *I lead / to lead*

PRONUNCIATION TIP: **Dūcere**, **dūcimus** and **dūcitis** all have the stress on the first syllable.

Our new word for this lesson is another verb from the third conjugation. It is related to a huge number of English words such as *conductor, duct, reduction,* and *production.*

Remember the characteristics of the third conjugation: there is a short *e* in the infinitive, the letter *i* comes before the personal endings, and the letter *u* comes before the personal ending in the third person plural.

	SINGULAR	PLURAL
FIRST PERSON	**dūcō**	**dūcimus**
SECOND PERSON	**dūcis**	**dūcitis**
THIRD PERSON	**dūcit**	**dūcunt**

INFINITIVE	**dūcere**

Here are some example sentences to get you started.

- **Rēx mīlitēs dūcit.** *(The king is leading the soldiers.)*
- **Equum in stabulum dūcō.** *(I am leading the horse into the stable.)*
- **Num tū mē trāns pontem dūcis?** *(You aren't leading me across the bridge, are you?)*

EXERCISES

1. **Quis mīlitēs trāns flūmen dūcit?** ◆ **Rēx mīlitēs dūcit.** ◆ **Rēx mīlitēs trāns flūmen dūcere nōn potest quod flūmen pontem nōn habet.** ◆ **Fortasse rēx et mīlitēs novum pontem aedificāre possunt. Multae arborēs sunt prope flūmen.** ◆ **Fortasse trāns flūmen natāre possunt.**
2. **Puellās puerōsque ad scholam dūcimus.**
3. **Quīntus uxōrem suam et fīliōs suōs ad urbem dūcit.** ◆ **Cūr?** ◆ **Māter Quīntī in urbe habitat.**
4. **Cūr magistrae discipulās ē scholā dūcunt?** ◆ **Discipulae hodiē ad theātrum ambulant.** ◆ **Cūr ad theātrum ambulant?** ◆ **Hodiē poēta in theātrō fābulās narrat.** ◆ **Quis est poēta?** ◆ **Petrus est poēta. Petrus in urbe nostrā fābulās hodiē narrat.**
5. **Discipulī ē scholā currunt.**
6. **Salvē, ō Tullia. Marītus tuus est amīcus meus.** ◆ **Quis es?** ◆ **Nōmen mihi est Pūblius. Agricola sum.** ◆ **Salvē, ō Pūblī. Habitāsne in fundō?** ◆ **Interdum in fundō meō habitō, sed casam in urbe habeō. Interdum in urbe habitō.** ◆ **Cūr in urbe interdum habitās? Placetne tibi haec urbs?** ◆ **Ita, haec urbs mihi placet.** ◆ **Quis fundum tuum nunc cūrat?** ◆ **Frāter meus nunc fundum meum cūrat.**
7. **Cūr mīlitēs rēgis ē castellō currunt? Pārentne rēgī?** ◆ **Ita. Portās castellī servant.**
8. **Ō uxor mea, cūr porcum nostrum spectās?** ◆ **Porcus noster currit.** ◆ **Porcus noster numquam currit. Cūr currit?** ◆ **Lupus adest! Porcus noster ā lupō currit!**
9. **Hodiē mīlitēs dūcere nōn possum.** ◆ **Sed rēx es!** ◆ **Tū rēgīna es. Fortasse tū mīlitēs dūcere potes.** ◆ **Fēmina valida sum. Mīlitēs dūcere possum!**
10. **Quid nōmen est tibi?** ◆ **Nōmen mihi est Portia. Quid nōmen est tibi?** ◆ **Salvē, ō Portia. Nōmen mihi est Tertius.** ◆ **Salvē, ō Tertī.**

Answers on page 291.

LESSON 143

NEW WORD   **legō / legere**

MEANING   *I read / to read*

Our new word for this lesson is yet another verb of the third conjugation. It is related to English words like *legible* and *illegible*.

	SINGULAR	PLURAL
FIRST PERSON	**legō**	**legimus**
SECOND PERSON	**legis**	**legitis**
THIRD PERSON	**legit**	**legunt**

INFINITIVE	**legere**

Here are some example sentences to get you started.

- **Librum de equīs legō.** *(I am reading a book about horses.)*
- **Soror mea cotīdiē librōs in bibliothēcā legit.** *(My sister reads books every day at the library.)*
- **Librōs patris nostrī legimus.** *(We are reading our father's books.)*

EXERCISES

1. **Cūr Paulus in exedriō semper sedet?** ◆ **Librōs in exedriō nostrō semper legit.**
2. **Sum discipulus malus.** ◆ **Cūr?** ◆ **Numquam librōs meōs legō.**

228

3. **Ego librum dē porcīs legō.** ♦ **Cūr?** ♦ **Porcī mihi placent.** ♦ **Nōnne porcōs amās?** ♦ **Fortasse.**

4. **Placentne tibi librī?** ♦ **Ita. Semper librōs in cubiculō meō legō.**

5. **Cūr Fausta et Christophorus puellās et puerōs ad bibliothēcam dūcunt?** ♦ **Bibliothēcārius puellīs et puerīs novōs librōs hodiē dat.** ♦ **Haec bibliothēca mihi placet. Multōs librōs bonōs habet.**

6. **Tē saepe in thermopōliō Quīntī videō.** ♦ **Ita. Illud thermopōlium mihi placet.**

7. **Quid est in scaphā tuā, ō pīrāta?** ♦ **Argentum habeō. Habēsne aurum?** ♦ **Minimē! Valē!**

8. **Ō Claudia, cūr canis tuus tibi nōn pāret?** ♦ **Nesciō. Fīdus est canis bonus, sed hodiē fessus est.**

9. **Ō Rōmule, cūr ab actā curris?** ♦ **Ā pīrātīs currō!**

10. **Quis pecūniam meam habet?**

Answers on page 291.

LESSON 144

PHRASES THAT USE THE VERB "AGO"

PRONUNCIATION TIP: **Agō** sounds like *AAAH-go*, with the stress on the first syllable. **Agimus**, **agitis**, and **agere** also have the stress on the first syllable.

Our new word for this lesson is a third conjugation verb which is used often in various Latin idioms, phrases, and greetings. It's the verb **agō**. It is related to English words like *agent, agency, action, act, agitate,* and *agenda.*

The verb **agō** is a versatile verb. Study its forms in the chart below, and then we will talk about how to use it.

	SINGULAR	PLURAL
FIRST PERSON	**agō**	**agimus**
SECOND PERSON	**agis**	**agitis**
THIRD PERSON	**agit**	**agunt**

INFINITIVE	**agere**

As I mentioned above, the verb **agō** is rather versatile and can be used in many contexts. When it is translated into English, here are a few of the words it gets translated with: *do, drive, make, guide, push*...it's a long list.

When I think about **agō**, it reminds me of the English verb *do*. The verb *do* is so versatile, you can use it to say all kinds of things. Read these English sentences and think about just how versatile the English verb *do* can be.

- Sorry, Dad—I didn't have time to <u>do</u> the lawn.
- I don't have time to <u>do</u> my hair.
- They want our company to <u>do</u> the advertising for their new product.
- I don't want to <u>do</u> planning committee again this year.
- Before you go to your friend's house, you must <u>do</u> your homework.
- During our senior year, we want to <u>do</u> a play.

In the sentences above, the word *do* meant a variety of things such as *take care of, make, fix up, work on, complete, participate in,* and *perform*. That's a broad range of meanings! And it's the same thing in Latin with the verb **agō**. Let's examine a couple of the ways that this particular verb can be used in Latin phrases and greetings.

If you want to say *thank you* in Latin, you can use the verb **agō** to do it. Observe:

Grātiās tibi agō.

The word **grātia** is a first declension noun that means things like *grace* or *thanks*. In this particular phrase, it's in the accusative plural because it is the direct object.

You already know that **tibi** means *to you*. Here, **agō** means something like *I give*. A word-for-word translation would be *Thanks to you I give*. But we will translate it into English simply as *Thank you*. **Gratiās tibi agō** is a good phrase to memorize because it is so useful in conversations.

Here's another good phrase that involves **agō**:

Quid agis?

You already know that **quid** means *what*. **Agis** is the second person singular form of **agō**. In this particular phrase, **agō** means *do*. So **Quid agis** literally means *What are you doing?* In Latin, this phrase is used as a greeting to say something like *What are you up to?* or *What's up?* This is another good one to learn so you can use it in conversations.

EXERCISES

1. **Ō mī fīlī, tibi pecūniam dare possum. ♦ Grātiās tibi agō, ō māter.**
2. **Salvē, Jācōbe. Quid agis? ♦ Salvē. Hodiē cubiculum meum pūrgō. ♦ Cūr cubiculum tuum pūrgās, ō amīce? ♦ Cubiculum meum sordidum est.**
3. **Salvē, ō Lāvīnia. Quid agis? ♦ Hodiē ad urbem currō. ♦ Cūr ad urbem curris? ♦ Pater meus aegrōtat. In urbe habitat. ♦ Ego tēcum ad urbem currere possum. ♦ Grātiās tibi agō! Tū amīcus bonus es.**
4. **Salvē, ō Gulielme. Quid agis? ♦ Carolus puerīs puellīsque fābulam dē porcīs narrat. ♦ Illa fābula mihi placet. ♦ Mihi quoque placet. ♦ In fābulā, parvī porcī in casā validā habitant. ♦ Et magnus lupus malus ante casam adest.**
5. **Salvē, ō Jūlia. Quid agis? ♦ Librum dē arboribus legō. ♦ Cūr librum dē arboribus legis? ♦ Sunt multae arborēs in hortō nostrō.**
6. **Salvē, ō mīles. Quid agis? ♦ Rēx mīlitēs per montēs dūcit. ♦ Cūr? ♦ Ad rēgnum pīrātārum ambulāmus.**
7. **Ō mī marīte, num frātrī tuō pecūniam dās? ♦ Ō uxor mea, frāter meus pecūniam nōn habet. ♦ Sed in hypogaeō nostrō habitat!**
8. **Est mihi gladius. ♦ Est mihi scūtum. ♦ Urbem gladiō scūtōque servāre possumus.**
9. **Placentne tibi fēlēs? ♦ Minimē. Fēlēs semper in mē sedent.**
10. **Est mihi magnus fundus. ♦ Ubi est fundus tuus? ♦ Fundus meus est inter urbem et actam.**

Answers on page 291.

LESSON 145

NEW WORD   **discō / discere**

MEANING   *I learn / to learn*

Our new word for this lesson is yet another verb from the third conjugation. It's related to English words like *disciple* and *discipline*, and it's also related to the Latin words **discipulus** and **discipula**. It is *not* related to the English word *disco* (a club where people go to dance).

	SINGULAR	PLURAL
FIRST PERSON	**discō**	**discimus**
SECOND PERSON	**discis**	**discitis**
THIRD PERSON	**discit**	**discunt**

INFINITIVE	**discere**

As long as we are talking about learning things, let me show you how to say (in Latin) that you are learning Latin. You'll need the first declension feminine noun **lingua**, which means *tongue* or *language*. So, you could say this:

Novam linguam discō. *(I am learning a new language.)*

The word **Latīnus, Latīna, Latīnum** is a first and second declension adjective which means *Latin*. So you can refer to the Latin language as **Lingua Latīna**, like this:

Linguam Latīnam discō. *(I am learning the Latin language.)*

232

Here are a few more practice sentences for you to study before you move on to the exercises.

- **Lingua Latīna mihi placet!** *(I like the Latin language!)*
- **Librum dē linguā Latīnā legimus.** *(We are reading a book about the Latin language.)*
- **Cūr linguam Latīnam discis?** *(Why are you learning the Latin language?)*

EXERCISES

1. **Ō Rūfe, cūr linguam Latīnam discis? ◆ Lingua Latīna mihi placet. ◆ Ego quoque linguam Latīnam discō. ◆ Cūr? ◆ Lingua Latīna est lingua bona.**

2. **Claudia librōs dē linguā Latīnā saepe legit. ◆ Cūr? ◆ Claudia linguam Latīnam discit.**

3. **Illa schola est mala. ◆ Cūr? ◆ Discipulī linguam Latīnam nōn discunt, et magistrī linguam Latīnam nōn docent.**

4. **Ō Pūblī, esne tū magister? ◆ Ita. Cotīdiē linguam Latīnam doceō. Discipulī meī linguam Latīnam discunt. ◆ Ego quoque magistra sum, sed in scholā meā linguam Latīnam nōn docēmus. ◆ Cūr nōn docētis linguam Latīnam in scholā vestrā? ◆ Schola mea est parva.**

5. **Ō Quīnte, cūr tū linguam Latīnam nōn discis? ◆ Nōn habeō librum dē linguā Latīnā. ◆ Ego multōs librōs dē linguā Latīnā habeō. Librum tibi dare possum. ◆ Grātiās tibi agō! Lingua Latīna mihi placet.**

6. **Est liber dē linguā Lātīna in mēnsā. Quis linguam Latīnam discit? ◆ Ego et sorōrēs meae linguam Latīnam discimus.**

7. **Ō magistra, linguam Latīnam hodiē discere nōn possum. ◆ Cūr, ō discipule? ◆ Fessus sum.**

8. **Cūr rēx hodiē mīlitēs nōn dūcit? ◆ Rēx hodiē aegrōtat. In cubiculō suō hodiē manet. ◆ Fortasse uxor rēgis mīlitēs dūcere potest. ◆ Uxor rēgis est rēgīna valida! Rēgīna in equō suō sedēre potest et mīlitēs dūcere potest.**

9. **Ō Claudia, cūr tū semper cum cane tuō curris? ◆ Fēlēs mea mēcum currere nōn potest.**

10. **Salvē, ō Helena. Quid agis? ◆ Hodiē ad theātrum cum frātribus meīs ambulō.**

Answers on page 291.

LESSON 146

NEW WORD   **volō / velle**

MEANING   *I want / to want*

PRONUNCIATION TIP: In classical Latin pronunciation, the letter *v* sounds like a *w*. But in ecclesiastical pronunciation, it sounds like a *v*.

Our new word for this lesson is related to English words like *volunteer, voluntary,* and *volition* (notice that those words all begin with *vol-*).

Technically, **volō** is from the third conjugation, but the forms are so irregular that it's hardly recongizable as a third conjugation verb. This means that you will simply have to memorize the forms of **volō**. But if you are speaking Latin, you will probably learn them quickly just from frequent use (that's one of the advantages of speaking Latin).

	SINGULAR	PLURAL
FIRST PERSON	**volō**	**volumus**
SECOND PERSON	**vīs**	**vultis**
THIRD PERSON	**vult**	**volunt**

INFINITIVE	**velle**

You can use **volō** to say you want a thing, like these example sentences:

- **Volō novum equum.** *(I want a new horse.)*
- **Canis meus cibum vult.** *(My dog wants food.)*

- **Vultisne novam scapham?** *(Do y'all want a new boat?)*

You can also use **volō** with a complementary infinitive, as seen in these sentences:

- **Volumus ambulāre ad flūmen.** *(We want to walk to the river.)*
- **Domī hodiē manēre volunt.** *(They want to stay at home today.)*

EXERCISES

1. **Fīliae meae canem volunt.** ♦ **Cūr?** ♦ **Canēs amant.** ♦ **Fortasse fēlem habēre possunt.**
2. **Salvē, amīca. Quid agis?** ♦ **Ad templum Minervae nunc ambulāre volumus.**
3. **Ille nauta pecūniam nostram vult!** ♦ **Ille nauta est pīrāta!** ♦ **Pīrātīs numquam pecūniam dō. Pugnāre volō!** ♦ **Ego volō currere!**
4. **Fundum volō.** ♦ **Cūr?** ♦ **Agrōs arāre volō, et equōs cūrāre volō.**
5. **Novam sellam volō.** ♦ **Cūr?** ♦ **Haec sella mihi nōn placet.**
6. **Salvē, ō rēx!** ♦ **Salvē, agricola.** ♦ **Ō rēx, est mihi fundus, sed porcōs nōn habeō. Fortasse tū mihi porcōs dare potes.** ♦ **Ita. Tibi porcōs dare possum.** ♦ **Grātiās tibi agō, ō rēx. Tū es rēx bonus.**
7. **Quis vult librum?** ♦ **Ō bibliothēcāria, ego librum volō. Linguam Latīnam discō, sed librum dē linguā Latīnā nōn habeō.** ♦ **Librum tibi dē linguā Latīnā dare possum.** ♦ **Grātiās tibi agō!**
8. **Hoc castellum mihi nōn placet. Novum castellum aedificāre volō.** ♦ **Ō rēx, castellum tuum est magnum. Cūr novum castellum vīs?** ♦ **Hoc castellum parvās lātrīnās habet. Parvae lātrīnae mihi nōn placent.** ♦ **Sed magnum trīclīnium habēs.**
9. **Cūr tū librum dē fundīs legis?** ♦ **Fundum aedificāre volō.** ♦ **Habēsne agrum?** ♦ **Ita.** ♦ **Habēsne equum?** ♦ **Ita.** ♦ **Habēsne porcum?** ♦ **Minimē, sed porcum volō.**
10. **Mīlitēs equōs in stabula dūcunt.**

Answers on page 292.

LESSON 147

NEW WORD   **nōlō / nōlle**

MEANING   *I do not want / to not want*

Our new word for this lesson is just like **volō**, except negative—so it means to *not* want something. And if you thought **volō** was a weird verb, just wait until you see the different forms of this one!

	SINGULAR	PLURAL
FIRST PERSON	**nōlō**	**nōlumus**
SECOND PERSON	**nōn vīs**	**nōn vultis**
THIRD PERSON	**nōn vult**	**nōlunt**

INFINITIVE	**nōlle**

The various forms of **nōlō** are really just the word **nōn** combined with the various forms of **volō**. Sometimes, **nōn** and **volō** get smushed together into one word, like in the forms **nōlō**, **nōlumus**, and **nōlunt**. Other times, **nōn** and **volō** stay separate, as seen in the forms **nōn vīs**, **nōn vult**, and **nōn vultis**.

And, as with **volō**, you'll need to try to memorize these forms. But if you can start using them in conversation, you'll master them quickly just from frequent usage.

EXERCISES

1. **Pecūniam tuam nōlō.**
2. **Currere hodiē nōn vīs. Cūr?** ♦ **Fessus sum.**
3. **Illa discipula librum suum legere nōn vult.**

4. **Balneum nostrum pūrgāre nōlumus.** ♦ **Cūr?** ♦ **Nōn est sordidum.**
♦ **Balneum vestrum est sordidum!**

5. **Cūr linguam Latīnam discere nōn vultis?** ♦ **Volumus linguam Latīnam discere, sed librum dē linguā Latīnā nōn habēmus.** ♦ **Multōs librōs dē linguā Latīnā habeō.**

6. **Canem nōlunt.** ♦ **Cūr?** ♦ **Fēlem volunt.**

7. **Ō pater, nōlumus cubicula nostra pūrgāre.** ♦ **Cūr?** ♦ **Librōs legere volumus.**

8. **Jūlia discipulōs ē bibliothēcā ad scholam dūcit.**

9. **Placetne tibi haec popīna?** ♦ **Ita. Hic cibus est bonus, et pīrātae absunt.**

10. **Salvē, ō Rūfe. Quid agis?** ♦ **Currō ad fundum nostrum quod māter mea aegrōtat.** ♦ **Ego tēcum currere possum!** ♦ **Grātiās tibi agō. Tū bona amīca es.**

Answers on page 292.

LESSON 148

MORE GREETINGS AND PHRASES

As we draw closer to the end of this book, I would like to give you a few more phrases that you can use in everyday Latin conversations.

YOU'RE WELCOME

If someone says to you **Grātiās tibi agō** *(Thank you)*, and you want to say *You're welcome*, you can say this:

Libenter.

Libenter is an adverb that means something like *gladly* or *willingly*, but you can use it to say *You're welcome*. The stress is on the second syllable, so it sounds something like *lib-BENT-terr*.

HOW ARE YOU?

If you want to say *How are you?* in Latin, you have a few choices. You can say this:

Valēsne?

You already know this word—it's just the second person singular form of the verb **valeō**. With the **-ne** suffix at the end, it means something like *Are you strong?* or *Are you well?* You can also say this:

Quōmodo tē habēs?

The word **quōmodo** means *how?* The other two words in this phrase are words you already know: **tē** means *you* (here it's in the accusative case) and **habēs** means *you have*. Literally, it says *How do you have you?* with the sense of *How do you hold yourself?* But it translates into English as something like *How are you?* or *How are you doing?*

I'M DOING WELL

If somebody asks you how you are doing, you can respond like this:

Bene.

The word **bene** is an adverb that means things like *well, fine,* or *good.* The stress is on the first syllable, so it sounds something like *BEH-neh.* You can also say this:

Valeō.

Valeō, as you know, means *I am strong* or *I am well.* You can also say this:

Bene mē habeō.

This sentence literally says *Well do I hold me*, in the sense of *I hold myself well.* It basically means *I'm doing well.*

I'M DOING POORLY

If you are not doing well, you can express it like this:

Male mē habeō.

This sentence is the opposite of **Bene me habeo**. The word **male** is an adverb (related to the adjective **malus, mala, malum**) which means *badly*. It sounds like *MAH-leh*. Therefore this sentence literally says *Badly do I hold me*, in the sense of *I hold myself poorly*. It basically means *I'm doing poorly*.

I'M SORRY

If you want to say *I'm sorry*, you can do it like this:

Mē paenitet.

The word **paenitet** is the third person singular form of the verb **paeniteō**, which means things like *regret, repent*, or *to be sorry*. It's a long story, but when you put **mē** and **paenitet** together in this phrase, it literally means something like *It causes me to regret*. **Mē paenitet** is for when you are apologizing for something you did, not for offering condolences to someone.

FORGIVE ME / EXCUSE ME

To say *Forgive me!* or *Excuse me!* in Latin, use this phrase:

Ignōsce mihi.

The verb **ignōscō** means *I forgive*. The word **ignōsce** is what is called an *imperative*—that is, a verb that issues a command. Therefore **ignosce** is a command that means *Forgive!* or *Excuse!* It is singular, so you are saying the command to only one person. This verb is one of those verbs that works with the dative case, so instead of using **mē**, which is accusative, we use **mihi**, which is dative. Therefore **Ignōsce mihi** means something like *Be forgiving to me!* or *Be excusing toward me!* But just think of it a way to say *Forgive me* or *Excuse me*. If you want to say **Ignōsce mihi** to more than one person, it changes to **Ignōscite mihi.**

PLEASE

In Latin, there are few different ways to say *please*. Here are a couple of simple ways, just to get you started.

- **quaesō**
- **obsecrō**

Quaesō is a verb that means *I ask* or *I beg*. **Obsecrō** is a verb that means *I beseech*. But they can both be used in conversation to mean *please*.

LESSON 149

THE FOURTH CONJUGATION

There are four conjugations in Latin, and you know three of them. Now it's time to learn about the fourth conjugation. But don't worry—it's not too hard, and it's somewhat similar to the third conjugation.

In the fourth conjugation, the infinitive ends in **-īre**. This means that unlike the third conjugation, we can remove the **-re** from the end of the infinitive, get the stem, and then start adding personal endings. In the chart below I have given you your very first verb from the fourth conjugation: the verb **veniō** which means *I come*. Study the infinitive form and third person singular form of this verb in the chart below, paying special attention to the letters indicated by arrows.

	INFINITIVE	3RD PERSON SING.
1ST CONJ.	**portāre**	**portat**
2ND CONJ.	**docēre**	**docet**
3RD CONJ.	**currere**	**currit**
4TH CONJ.	**venīre**	**venit**

Notice that the infinitive form of **veniō** has a long *i* three letters from the end (that letter is indicated by an arrow). This infinitive will be pronounced *wen-EEER-eh* (or *ven-EEER-eh* in ecclesiastical pronunciation) with the stress or accent on the second syllable. Also notice that the letter *i* is the letter you will see before the personal endings. This *i* will be a long *i* in the first person and second person forms, but short in the third person forms, as you see here in the form **venit**.

Let's look at all the present tense forms of **veniō** in this chart. Notice that the letter *u* comes before the personal ending in the third person plural, just as it did in the third conjugation.

240

	SINGULAR	PLURAL
FIRST PERSON	**veniō**	**venīmus**
SECOND PERSON	**venīs**	**venītis**
THIRD PERSON	**venit**	**veniunt**

INFINITIVE	**venīre**

Even though these verb forms look somewhat similar to third conjugation forms, they are very different because of vowel length. In the third conjugation, the letter *i* before the personal endings is always short. But here, since the letter *i* is long in some forms, the stress or accent will fall on that syllable.

For example, **venīmus** has a long *i*, so the accent will fall on the second syllable: *wenn-EEE-mus.* In Latin, the accent can never fall on the final syllable of a word. Therefore, for any verb with two syllables (such as **venīs** and **venit**) the stress falls on the first syllable. For **veniunt**, the *i* is short, so the accent moves back to the first syllable: *WENN-eee-unt.*

Here are a few example sentences with **veniō**:

- **Ad popīnam nunc veniō.** *(I am coming to the restaurant now.)*
- **Venīsne ad casam meam?** *(Are you coming to my house?)*
- **Pīrātae numquam ad urbem nostram veniunt.** *(Pirates never come to our city).*
- **Hodiē ad fundum venīre nōn possum.** *(I can't come to the farm today.)*
- **Nōlō ad urbem venīre hodiē.** *(I do not want to come to the city today.)*

EXERCISES

1. **Salvē, ō Gulielme. Quōmodo tē habēs?** ♦ **Bene. Quōmodo tē habēs, ō Jūlia?** ♦ **Bene mē habeō.** ♦ **Cūr venīs hodiē ad macellum meum?** ♦ **Obsōnō quod hodiē marītus meus domī cum sorōribus suīs et frātribus suīs cēnat.**

241

2. Ō amīce, ubi es? Ante bibliothēcam sum. ◆ Ad bibliothēcam nunc veniō. ◆ Cūr tū abes? ◆ Ignōsce mihi. Ad bibliothēcam properō!

3. Cūr tū numquam ad urbem meam venīs? ◆ Rēx urbis tuae mihi nōn placet. ◆ Rēx noster est malus, sed haec urbs est bona. Urbs nostra multās arborēs, bonās popīnās, et magnum macellum habet.

4. Salvē, ō Cornēlī. Estne soror tua domī? ◆ Ō Tullia, cūr cotīdiē ad casam meam venīs? ◆ Soror tua est amīca mea.

5. Salvē, ō Portia. Quōmodo tē habēs? ◆ Bene mē habeō. ◆ Tibi dōnum dare volō. ◆ Quid est dōnum? Dōna mihi placent! ◆ Liber est. ◆ Grātiās tibi agō! Librōs amō! Saepe librōs legō. ◆ Libenter. Liber dē porcīs est. ◆ Nōn sum agricola!

6. Agricola novōs equōs ad fundum suum dūcit.

7. Salvē, ō Rōberte. Quid agis? ◆ Hodiē ad actam tēcum venīre nōn possum. ◆ Cūr mēcum venīre nōn potes? ◆ Acta mihi placet, sed hodiē aegrōtō.

8. Linguam Latīnam discere volō. ◆ Cūr? ◆ Lingua Latīna mihi placet. ◆ Habēsne librum dē linguā Latīnā? ◆ Minimē. ◆ Fortasse ego tibi librum dare possum. Librum meum legere potes. ◆ Grātiās tibi agō. ◆ Libenter.

9. Rēx mīlitēs suōs ad mare dūcit. ◆ Fortasse ad īnsulam pīrātārum nāvigāre volunt! ◆ Fortasse. Mīlitēs multās scaphās habent. ◆ Rēx et mīlitēs cum pīrātīs pugnāre volunt!

10. Ō discipulī, cūr ē scholā curritis? ◆ Nōlumus discere hodiē linguam Latīnam!

Answers on page 292.

LESSON 150

NEW WORD   **audiō / audīre**

MEANING   *I hear / to hear*

Our new word for this lesson is another verb of the fourth conjugation. It is related to English words like *audio, audible, auditory, audit, auditorium,* and *audition.*

	SINGULAR	PLURAL
FIRST PERSON	**audiō**	**audīmus**
SECOND PERSON	**audīs**	**audītis**
THIRD PERSON	**audit**	**audiunt**

INFINITIVE	**audīre**

Here are a few example sentences to study:

- **Lupōs audiō!** *(I hear wolves!)*
- **Audīsne mē?** *(Do you hear me?)*
- **Mare audīre possum.** *(I can hear the sea.)*

EXERCISES

1. **Canem meum audiō. Audīsne canem meum? ♦ Ita. Cibum vult!**
2. **Ō rēx, potesne audīre incolās urbis? ♦ Nōnne cibum habent? ♦ Minimē. Cibum postulant. ♦ Cūr cibum postulant? ♦ Uxōrēs mīlitum tuōrum cibum postulant quod tū numquam marītīs feminārum pecūniam dās. ♦ Mīlitēs meī sunt malī. Numquam mihi pārent.**

243

3. Per silvam ambulāre nōlō. ♦ Cūr? ♦ Lupōs in silvā audiō.

4. Ō fēlēs mea, quōmodo tē habēs? ♦ Male mē habeō! Cibum nōn habeō! Volō cibum! ♦ Nunc cibum tibi dō. ♦ Grātiās tibi agō. Hic cibus mihi placet. ♦ Libenter.

5. Ō magistra, librōs nostrōs hodiē legere nōlumus. ♦ Ō discipulī malī, cūr librōs vestrōs hodiē legere nōn vultis? ♦ Ad actam ambulāre volumus. ♦ Ego quoque ad actam ambulāre volō.

6. Hic discipulus numquam magistrō pāret. ♦ Fortasse ille discipulus magistrum nōn audīre potest.

7. Salvē, ō mī canis. Quōmodo tē habēs? ♦ Male mē habeō. ♦ Cūr, ō Fluffī? ♦ Īrātus sum. Canis sum, sed nōmen mihi est "Fluffius." Novum nōmen volō. ♦ Fortasse tibi novum nōmen dare possum. ♦ "Fīdus" est nōmen bonum.

8. Salvē, ō Tullia. Quid agis? ♦ Ad urbem cum sorōre meā ambulō. ♦ Cūr ad urbem ambulātis? ♦ Ad bibliothēcam ambulāmus quod novōs librōs volumus. ♦ Ego ad mare cum frātribus meīs ambulō. Frātrēs meī in marī natāre volunt.

9. Ō puella, ubi linguam Latīnam discis? ♦ In scholā meā linguam Latīnam discimus.

10. Cotīdiē puellās ad scholam dūcimus.

Answers on page 293.

LESSON 151

NEW WORD   **eō / īre**

MEANING   *I go / to go*

PRONUNCIATION TIP: The word **eō** sounds like *EH-oh,* and **īre** sounds like *EEE-ray.*

Our new word for this lesson is yet another verb of the fourth conjugation. It's kind of a weird, irregular verb because the first person singular and third person plural forms start with the letter *e,* but the other forms start with the letter *i.* Familiarize yourself with the various forms of **eō** with this chart.

	SINGULAR	PLURAL
FIRST PERSON	eō	īmus
SECOND PERSON	īs	ītis
THIRD PERSON	it	eunt

INFINITIVE	īre

You can use **eō** just like you would use the word *go* in English, as seen in these examples:

- **Ad theatrum eō.** *(I am going to the theater.)*
- **Tullia ad templum Minervae it.** *(Tullia is going to the temple of Minerva.)*
- **Equī in stabulum eunt.** *(The horses are going into the stable.)*
- **Ego hodiē ad scholam īre nōlō.** *(I do not want to go to school today.)*

245

EXERCISES

1. **Ad lātrīnam eō.**

2. **Ō Semprōnia, cūr per silvam īs? Sunt multī lupī in silvā. Potesne lupōs audīre?** ◆ **Ita. Lupōs audiō, sed lupōs nōn timeō.** ◆ **Ego semper circum silvam eō quod lupōs timeō.** ◆ **Circum silvam īre nōlō. Ego per silvam īre volō.**

3. **Ad macellum sine pecūniā numquam eō.**

4. **Ō pater, fābulam audīre volō.** ◆ **Ego tibi fābulam dē parvīs porcīs narrāre possum. Placetne tibi illa fābula?** ◆ **Grātiās tibi agō, ō pater. Illa fābula mihi placet.** ◆ **Libenter, fīlia mea.**

5. **Multae fēlēs in viā sunt. Cūr fēlēs per urbem nostram currunt?** ◆ **Fēlēs ad casam Rōbertī eunt.** ◆ **Cūr ad casam Rōbertī eunt?** ◆ **Rōbertus fēlibus cotīdiē cibum dat.**

6. **Salvē, ō Aemilia. Quid agis? Cūr es in bibliothēcā?** ◆ **Ad bibliothēcam interdum veniō.** ◆ **Ego quoque. Saepe in bibliothēcā sedeō et librōs legō. Nunc librum dē maribus legō.**

7. **Linguam Latīnam discere volō, sed nōn possum.** ◆ **Cūr?** ◆ **In scholā meā, magistrī linguam Latīnam nōn docent et discipulī linguam Latīnam nōn discunt.**

8. **Semper ad thermopōlium tuum veniō quod tū cibum bonum habēs.**

9. **Ō rēx, mīlitēs tuī cum incolīs oppidī pugnāre nōlunt.** ◆ **Cūr?** ◆ **Incolae oppidī sunt amīcī mīlitum.**

10. **Salvē, ō nauta. Quid est nōmen tibi?** ◆ **Nōmen mihi est Cornēlius.** ◆ **Cūr multae fēlēs in scaphā tuā adsunt?** ◆ **Fēlēs meae semper mēcum nāvigant. Mare amant.**

Answers on page 293.

LESSON 152

IMPERATIVES

An imperative is a verb that issues a command. In each of the following examples, the imperative is underlined:

- <u>Clean</u> your room!
- <u>Get</u> your jacket!
- <u>Come</u> here!

In Latin, imperatives are easy. All you really have to do is remove the **-re** from the end of the infinitive. Just for practice, let's make an imperative out of the first conjugation verb **portō**.

portō

First, you find the infinitive:

portāre

Then you remove the **-re** from the end of the infinitive, leaving the stem:

portā

And that's all there is to it! **Portā** is an imperative that means *Carry!* Here's an example sentence with the imperative verb **portā**:

Portā saxum! *(Carry the rock!)*

No matter what conjugation a verb is from, just remove the **-re** from the infinitive, and that's the imperative. See, I told you it was easy! Here are examples from each conjugation.

- **properāre ⟶ properā**
- **docēre ⟶ docē**

- **legere** ⟶ **lege**
- **venīre** ⟶ **venī**

Notice that there will be a macron over the last letter of the imperative, except for imperatives from the third conjugation.

Here's an example sentence with each of these verbs.

- **Properā ad bibliothēcam!** *(Hurry to the library!)*
- **Docē linguam Latīnam!** *(Teach the Latin language!)*
- **Lege librum tuum!** *(Read your book!)*
- **Venī ad popīnam meam!** *(Come to my restaurant!)*

By the way, one of the verbs you know has an irregular imperative. That's the verb **dūcō**, which means *I lead*. The imperative form of **dūcō** is **dūc**. Here's an example sentence:

Dūc mīlitēs! *(Lead the soldiers!)*

And the verb **dō** is irregular. Even though the infinitive of **dō** is **dare**, with a short *a*, the imperative has a long *a*.

Dā mihi pecūniam! *(Give money to me!)*

Note also that for the verb **eō** the infinitive is **īre**. Therefore the imperative is just the letter *i* (with a macron over it).

Ī ad scholam! *(Go to school!)*

The imperative verbs that I have shown you in this lesson are singular imperatives—that is, they are for when you are telling just one person to do something. In the next lesson, I will show you how to tell a group of people to do something.

EXERCISES

1. **Ō māter, dā mihi pecūniam!**
2. **Curre ad urbem!** ♦ **Cūr?** ♦ **Pīrātae nunc veniunt!**
3. **Dā mihi novum gladium!**

248

4. **Disce linguam Latīnam!** ◆ **Nōlō discere linguam Latīnam. Volō īre ad actam.**
5. **Est aqua in scaphā nostrā.** ◆ **Natā ad actam!**
6. **Lege librum tuum.**
7. **Dā mihi pecūniam tuam!** ◆ **Numquam ego pīrātīs pecūniam dō.**
8. **Ō discipule, sedē in sellā tuā!**
9. **Curre ex oppidō!**
10. **Portā lignum!**

Answers on page 293.

LESSON 153

PLURAL IMPERATIVES

In the last lesson, we learned about singular imperatives. We learned that to make a singular imperative, you simply remove the **-re** from the end of the infinitive form. Not too hard, eh?

To make a plural imperative, it's almost as easy. All you have to do is take away the **-re** from the end of the infinitive and add the suffix **-te**. Let's use the first conjugation verb **portō** again as an example. Here's the infinitive form of **portō**:

portāre

Now we remove the **-re** from the end and add the suffix **-te** in its place:

portāte

The accent is on the second syllable, so it sounds something like *por-TAH-teh*.

The only exception to this process is with third conjugation verbs. (Have you noticed yet that the third conjugation doesn't play well with others?) For a third conjugation verb such as **currō**, first you take the infinitive...

currere

...and you remove not just the **-re** from the end, but three letters: **-ere**.

curr-

Now you add **-ite** to the end of that, and you get this:

currite

Notice that there is no macron over the letter *i* here, so the accent moves to the first syllable and it sounds like *CURR-ih-te*.

Here are example sentences with plural imperatives from each of the four conjugations.

- **Ō nautae, aedificāte novam scapham!** *(Sailors, build a new boat!)*
- **Sedēte, ō discipulī!** *(Sit down, students!)*
- **Ō discipulī, legite librōs tuōs!** *(Students, read your books!)*
- **Ō incolae urbis, audīte rēgem!** *(Inhabitants of the city, hear the king!)*

EXERCISES

1. **Portāte aquam ad stabula!**
2. **Ō puerī, sedēte in sellīs tuīs!**
3. **Ō fīliī et fīliae, pūrgāte cubicula vestra!**
4. **Ō puellae, in casam currite!**
5. **Ō mīlitēs, ambulāte ad castellum!**
6. **Ō puerī, cūrāte equōs. Date equīs aquam cibumque!**
7. **Ō mīlitēs, pugnāte cum pīrātīs!**
8. **Discite linguam Latīnam!**
9. **Īte in urbem!**
10. **Properāte ad theātrum!**

Answers on page 293.

LESSON 154

NEGATIVE IMPERATIVES

So far you know how to make a singular imperative, for telling one person what to do, and a plural imperative, for telling multiple people what to do. Now, let's learn how to make a negative imperative—that is, how to tell someone *not* to do something.

In Latin, telling someone not to do something has a kind of strange sentence structure. Here is literally what you will say to someone if you want to tell them not to carry a sword:

Do not <u>want</u> to carry a sword!

The sentence structure here is different from the way we would say it in English. In English we would say *Do not carry a sword!* But in Latin you tell the person not to *want* to carry the sword. I know, it's weird, but it's really not difficult once you get this basic concept.

The way we tell someone not to want something in Latin is using the imperative forms of the irregular verb **nōlō**, which means *I do not want*. The imperative forms of the **nōlō** look like this:

- **nōlī**
- **nōlīte**

So, **nōlī** says, *Hey, you singular person, don't want!* And **nōlīte** says *Hey you plural people, don't want!*

All you have to do now to make a negative imperative is to take either **nōlī** or **nōlīte**, and add an infinitive to them, like this:

- **Nōlī portāre!** *(Don't want* (singular) *to carry!)*
- **Nōlīte portāre!** *(Don't want* (plural) *to carry!)*

Literally, both of these sentences say *Don't want to carry!* But we will translate them into English as *Don't carry!* The only difference is that one is singular and one is plural.

Here are a few practice sentences to get you accustomed to working with these negative imperatives.

- **Nōlī sedēre in fēle!** *(Don't sit on the cat!)*
- **Nōlīte currere in casā!** *(Don't run in the house!)*
- **Nōlī pugnāre cum sorōre tuā!** *(Don't fight with your sister!)*
- **Nōlīte īre per silvam!** *(Don't go through the forest!)*

EXERCISES

1. **Nōlī currere per scholam!**
2. **Nōlīte cēnāre in thermopoliīs malīs cum nautīs!**
3. **Nōlī arāre agrōs. Ī in stabulum et cūrā equōs.**
4. **Nōlīte natāre in marī! Natāte in flūmine!**
5. **Ō fēlēs, nōlī sedēre in mēnsā.** ◆ **Sed semper in mēnsā sedeō. Haec mēnsa mihi placet.** ◆ **Cūr tū mihi numquam pārēs?** ◆ **Nōn sum canis. Sum fēlēs.**
6. **Ō frātrēs meī, nōlīte pugnāre. Pārēte mātrī nostrae.**
7. **Nōlī dūcere mīlitēs in castellum.**
8. **Nōlīte nāvigāre ad īnsulam pīrātārum!**
9. **Nōlī aedificāre scapham.** ◆ **Cūr?** ◆ **Prope flūmen nōn habitāmus.**
10. **Nōlīte īre ad thermopōlium sine mē.**

Answers on page 294.

A FEW FINAL THOUGHTS

Congratulations! You have made it to the end of this book. Now that you have finished the book, I'd like to say a few words about what I had in mind while I was writing it. My goal was to create a language learning experience for you with one foot in the past and one foot in the present. I wanted to give you words and sentences that an ancient Roman might have said, but that could still be meaningful today in modern life. It was (mostly) possible because of one important fact: no matter where you go, no matter the time period, no matter the ethnicity, nationality, or religion, people are just people. We all eat, drink, sleep, go shopping, go to school, go to work, live in homes, take care of our families, and want the best for our children. We have a lot in common—and hopefully that human connection that we all share made it possible for me to take a language from the ancient world and make it somehow relevant to your life here in the modern world.

In *Getting Started with Latin*, I was trying to teach you the very basics of the Latin language. But here, in *Keep Going with Latin*, I wanted to take you a bit further and teach you...

- Some good ol' fashioned Latin grammar knowledge
- Nuggets of information about the culture of the ancient Romans which I thought might stir up your curiosity for further study
- How to speak Latin with your friends, family, teachers, students, or colleagues

Hopefully, if I have done my job right, you have gained confidence in your Latin abilities, become more curious about Roman (and Greek) culture, and have started to speak some Latin. You, the reader, will be the judge of whether or not I have succeeded.

As we finish, I would like to leave you with a thought that I think is crucial for anyone who seeks to learn a new language. Whenever you set out to learn a new language, it can be easy to become goal-oriented, viewing knowledge of the language as some kind of destination or goal which must be reached. But I would like you to envision your study of Latin differently. Imagine your study of Latin not as a destination, but as a journey. No matter how much you learn about Latin, there will always be more to learn. So don't stop here—keep going further down the road. And always remember to have fun along the way. If you have fun while you learn, you'll be more motivated, and you'll learn more. So be sure to enjoy the journey!

ANSWER KEY

LESSON FIVE

1. Julia often walks from the forest to the town.
2. Mark and Claudia are building a large house.
3. Paul and Fausta often work in the fields.
4. Christopher's sons are guarding the town.
5. Flavia's daughter has much silver.
6. Quintus often gives money to Joseph.
7. We are watching Cornelius.
8. The boys are in the boat with Romulus.
9. Charles has Claudius's sword.
10. Catherine is plowing the soil with Helen.

LESSON SIX

1. Where is the farmer?
2. Where is Aurelia?
3. Where are the shield and sword?
4. Julia and Publius are in the house, but where is Claudius?
5. The boys are walking with Julius from the town to the forest.
6. The queen is building a large wall around the town.
7. The girls are carrying rocks.
8. Mark's son loves Lucretia, but Lucretia loves Publius.
9. Without wood, we cannot build a boat.
10. Helen is giving food to the girl.

LESSON SEVEN

1. Boy, where are the farmers?
2. Tullia, where is Lucius?
3. Son, where is Aurelia?
4. Claudia, where is Lucretia?
5. Claudius, where is Mark's money?
6. Lavinia often swims around the island.
7. Rufus and Helen are fighting!
8. Mark, where is the sailors' food?
9. Decimus often tells a story to the girls.
10. The inhabitants of the island never give money to the queen.

LESSON EIGHT

1. Quintus, why are you walking to the forest?
2. Why are we sailing around the island? We are not sailors!
3. Lavinia, why is Diana in the town?
4. Bad boys, why are y'all fighting?
5. Tullia, where are the men's swords?
6. Why are we plowing the fields? We are not farmers!

7. Why are Cornelius's daughters sailing to the large island with the sailors?
8. Sailor, why do you always tell bad stories to the boys?
9. Tiberius can't walk in the forest because he fears the beasts.
10. Flavia is building a house with rocks and wood.

LESSON NINE

1. Paula, where is Lucretia? ♦ Lucretia is swimming to the island with Julia and Fausta.
2. The queen's daughter always gives money to the farmers.
3. The men of the island are fighting with swords and shields. ♦ They are destroying the town!
4. Where is Portia? ♦ Portia is carrying large rocks from the fields. ♦ Portia is strong!
5. Men of the island! Why are the sailors conquering the island? ♦ The sailors are conquering the island because we don't have swords.
6. I cannot see the boat. Girl, where is Robert's boat?
7. Why is Peter not plowing the soil? ♦ Peter is not a farmer.
8. Why is Fulvia happy? ♦ She has much money. ♦ Where is Fulvia? ♦ She is counting the money in the house.
9. Why are we plowing the fields? We are not farmers. ♦ We are farmers!
10. I always give food to the boys and girls.

LESSON TEN

1. Hello, Tullia and Peter! ♦ Hello, Cornelia!
2. Hello, Robert! ♦ Hello, Claudia!
3. Hello, Julia and Julius! ♦ Hello, Rufus!
4. Hello, Sempronia! Where is Lavinia? ♦ She is in the house with the girls and boys.
5. Hello, sailor! You can't sail to the homeland without food. ♦ I don't have food, but I have money.
6. Aurelia is a strong woman! ♦ Why is she a strong woman? ♦ She is strong because she carries water to the house daily.
7. Publius, where is the queen? ♦ She is in the town. She is giving food to the boys and girls.
8. Hello, sailors. Where is the boat? ♦ We don't have a boat. ♦ Why? ♦ We are farmers.
9. Mark, where is the moon? ♦ The moon is in the sky!
10. I can't stay in the boat, but I can't swim!

LESSON ELEVEN

1. *Decimus, where is Julia?* ♦ *I don't know.*
2. *Fausta, where is Joseph?* ♦ *I don't know, but Tiberius is in the house.*
3. *Hello Robert! Where is the wood?* ♦ *I don't know.*
4. *Fulvia, where is the sword?* ♦ *In the boat.*
5. *The sailor never sails to the island without food and money.*
6. *Why are you building a wall with wood?* ♦ *Wood is strong.*
7. *Why are y'all sailing to the homeland?* ♦ *We are sailing to the homeland because we are longing for the homeland.*
8. *Sempronia, where is Charles?* ♦ *Charles is with the queen. Charles is giving a gift to the queen.*
9. *We fear the island.* ♦ *Why?* ♦ *The island has many beasts!*
10. *Hello, Rufus and Christopher. Why are y'all swimming to the island?* ♦ *We don't have a boat.*

LESSON TWELVE

1. *Claudius is at home.*
2. *Tiberius, where is Julius?* ♦ *He is at home.*
3. *Julia, where are you?* ♦ *I am at home.*
4. *Where is Charles?* ♦ *I don't know, but Portia is in the field.*
5. *Sempronia, where is Cornelia?* ♦ *She is at home.*
6. *Hello, Robert and Claudia.* ♦ *Hello, Tullia!*
7. *The girls often walk from the seashore to the forest.*
8. *Aurelia, why do y'all have a gift?* ♦ *We often give gifts to the girls of the town.* ♦ *I never give gifts because I don't have money.*
9. *Romulus, why do you have Tiberius's sword?* ♦ *I am guarding the town because we do not have a wall around the town.*
10. *The inhabitants of the town are building a wall with rocks.*

LESSON 13

1. *I do not live in the town. I live in the forest.* ♦ *There are large beasts in the forest! I fear the beasts!*
2. *Matthew lives on the island, but he longs for the homeland.* ♦ *Why?* ♦ *He loves the homeland.*
3. *Joseph, where do you live?* ♦ *I live on the island.*
4. *We never sail to the homeland. We always stay on the island.*
5. *We always guard the town with swords and shields.* ♦ *Why?* ♦ *We love the town because we live in the town.*

6. *Quintus is not a farmer, but he plows the fields because he does not have food.* ♦ *Quintus is a farmer!*
7. *We don't have money.* ♦ *Y'all don't have money because y'all never work!*
8. *Fulvia is not happy.* ♦ *Why?* ♦ *She is plowing a large field.*
9. *Hello, girl. Where is Helen?* ♦ *I don't know.*
10. *Rufus is a bad boy!* ♦ *Why?* ♦ *He always fights with Quintus!*

LESSON 14

1. *Goodbye, farmers!* ♦ *We are not farmers. We are sailors.*
2. *Goodbye, Portia and Sempronia.* ♦ *Goodbye, Christopher.*
3. *Goodbye, Romulus. I am sailing to the island.* ♦ *Goodbye, Mark.*
4. *Hello, Fausta and Aurelia.* ♦ *Hello, Decimus. Where is Paul?* ♦ *I don't know.*
5. *Boy, where do you live?* ♦ *I live in a house near the seashore.*
6. *Where are Cornelia and Publius?* ♦ *They are at home.*
7. *Claudius, why do you not have a sword?* ♦ *I never have a sword, but I always carry a shield.*
8. *Where do y'all live?* ♦ *We are inhabitants of the large islands.*
9. *Men of the homeland, why are y'all building a wall?* ♦ *We are building a wall because we are guarding the homeland.*
10. *I never swim to the island.* ♦ *Why?* ♦ *I can't swim.*

LESSON 15

1. *Hello. Where is Titus?* ♦ *Titus is not at home today.* ♦ *Why?* ♦ *I don't know.* ♦ *Goodbye.*
2. *Why are Peter and Titus working today? They never plow the fields.* ♦ *I don't know.*
3. *Fulvia and Cornelia are working in the fields today. They are plowing the soil.*
4. *The sailors are not sailing to the island today.* ♦ *Why?* ♦ *They are staying in the homeland.*
5. *Aemilia, where is Rufus today?* ♦ *He is at home.* ♦ *Why is he at home?* ♦ *He is working in the house.*
6. *The girls and boys are walking from the town to the seashore today.* ♦ *Why?* ♦ *They live in the town, but they long for the seashore.* ♦ *I can't walk to the seashore today.*
7. *The men have shields, but they do not have swords.* ♦ *We can give swords to the men.*
8. *We cannot guard the town.* ♦ *Why?* ♦ *There is not a wall around the town.* ♦ *We can build a wall today with wood and rocks.*

9. *Lucretia's son cannot swim to the island.*
10. *The girls walk from the school to the house daily.*

LESSON 16

1. *Is Aurelia at home? ♦ Aurelia is walking to the seashore today. Aurelia loves the seashore!*
2. *Sailor, are you telling a bad story to the boys? ♦ I always tell bad stories! ♦ Why? ♦ I am a sailor!*
3. *Am I a sailor? ♦ I don't know. Do you have a boat? ♦ I have many boats. ♦ Do you sail? ♦ I sail to the homeland daily. ♦ You are a sailor!*
4. *Am I a farmer? ♦ I don't know. Do you have fields? ♦ I have fields. ♦ Do you plow the fields? ♦ Daily. ♦ You are a farmer!*
5. *Hello, Tullia. Where are Joseph's daughters? ♦ They live in the forest with Sempronia and Cornelia.*
6. *Do you have money? ♦ I don't have money, but I have silver and gold.*
7. *Do we have food? Do we have water? ♦ We have food and water.*
8. *Julius is fighting with Rufus! ♦ Why? ♦ Rufus has Julius' money. ♦ Rufus is a bad boy!*
9. *Sailor, there is water in the boat! ♦ We can't sail to the island! ♦ Goodbye!*
10. *Romulus, where is the men's food? They don't have food. ♦ I don't know. We give food to the men daily. ♦ Why? ♦ The inhabitants of the homeland do not have food.*

LESSON 18

1. *You live in the town.*
2. *You live in the town.*
3. *Do you live in the town?*
4. *Do you live in the town?*
5. *Son, I plow the fields daily, but you always stay in the house. ♦ I can't work today. Goodbye.*
6. *Aemilia, why are you swimming to the island? ♦ I don't have a boat! ♦ I have a boat but I fear the water.*
7. *We are not walking to school. We are staying at home today. ♦ Y'all are bad boys!*
8. *The strong men are plowing the fields, and they are carrying rocks from the fields.*
9. *The queen always gives money and food to Fausta's daughters. ♦ Why? ♦ The queen is a good woman. ♦ Where do Fausta's daughters live? ♦ They live in the forest.*
10. *Hello, Tullia. Do you have a boat? ♦ Hello. I have many boats. ♦ Why do you have many boats? Do you often sail to the islands? ♦ I sail to the islands daily.*

LESSON 19

1. *The horse is not in the stable. Where is the horse? ♦ I don't know. Am I a farmer?*
2. *Hello, farmer. Why do you have many horses? ♦ I am not a farmer. I am a sailor. I have boats.*
3. *Hello, Julia. Where is Lucretia? ♦ I don't know, but Cornelius is in the stable with the horses. ♦ Goodbye.*
4. *Robert, where is the boat today? ♦ We are carrying the boat to the water. ♦ Why are y'all carrying the boat? ♦ Today we are sailing to the islands with swords and shields. ♦ Y'all can't fight with the men of the islands!*
5. *The horse is not in the field. Where is the horse? ♦ The horse is carrying the farmer to the town today.*
6. *Where is the moon? Where are the stars? ♦ They are in the sky!*
7. *Is there a wall around the town? ♦ The queen is building a wall with rocks.*
8. *The daughters of the queen are not happy. ♦ Why? ♦ Cornelia is not telling a story to the girls today.*
9. *The strong men and the strong women are guarding the town, but the town does not have a wall. Without a wall, they can't guard the town. ♦ Do they have swords? ♦ They have shields, but they do not have swords.*
10. *Lucretia, you can't give silver and gold to the queen! ♦ Why can't I give a gift to the queen? ♦ We are farmers! We don't have gold! We don't have silver!*

LESSON 20

1. *Do you have money? ♦ Certainly!*
2. *Is there a school in the town? ♦ There is.*
3. *Are we in a boat? ♦ We are. ♦ Why? I am not a sailor, and I fear water. ♦ We are sailing to the homeland today.*
4. *Do you see the horse? ♦ Not at all. ♦ Where is the horse? Is the horse in the stable? ♦ I don't know.*
5. *Quintus, do you have a horse? ♦ Not at all. I do not have a horse, I do not have a boat, I do not have money, and I do not have food!*
6. *Hello, Sempronia. Where is Robert's house? Does Robert live in the town? ♦ Yes, Robert lives in the town. Robert's house is near the school. ♦ Goodbye.*
7. *Girls, can y'all swim? ♦ Certainly. We swim daily. We can swim around the island! ♦ Y'all are strong girls! ♦ Yes. We are strong because we swim daily.*
8. *Is Lucretia at home today? ♦ She is. Lucretia is working near the house today. ♦ Why? ♦ Lucretia is building a boat today.*

9. *Joseph, do you have a boat? ♦ Yes. I have a large boat. ♦ Where is the boat? ♦ The sons of Romulus have the boat today. The boat is carrying the sons of Romulus to the island.*

10. *Cornelia, are you happy? ♦ I am not happy! ♦ Why are you not happy, Cornelia? ♦ I love Publius, but Publius loves Aurelia. ♦ Does Publius love Aurelia? ♦ Yes. He loves Aurelia. ♦ Do you love Publius? ♦ Certainly. ♦ Why do you love Publius? Publius is a poet, and he does not have money.*

LESSON 21

1. *The bad sailors never take care of the boats!*
2. *Helen and Tiberius always take care of the horses.*
3. *Robert, can you take care of the boys and girls today? ♦ Certainly. I have many sons and daughters.*
4. *Decimus and Rufus are bad boys. ♦ Why are they bad boys? ♦ The boys are bad because they do not take care of the horses! ♦ Where are the horses? ♦ In the stable. ♦ We can give food to the horses.*
5. *Decimus, do you live in the forest? ♦ Not at all. I live in a house near the seashore. ♦ Why do you live near the seashore? ♦ I love the seashore. I have many boats.*
6. *Where is Claudius today? Is he working in the fields? ♦ Not at all, Claudius can't work today. ♦ Why? ♦ I don't know. ♦ Goodbye.*
7. *Hello, Sempronia and Romulus. Do y'all have horses? ♦ Yes. We have strong horses because we are farmers.*
8. *Farmer, why are you giving a horse to Joseph? ♦ I am giving a horse to Joseph because Joseph is a farmer, but he does not have a horse.*
9. *Where do the boys live? ♦ The boys live in the town. ♦ Do you live in the town? ♦ Not at all, I live in the forest.*
10. *Why are the boys near the boats? ♦ The sailors are telling stories today. ♦ Bad sailors, why do you always tell bad stories to the boys?*

LESSON 22

1. *Matthew is a good farmer because he always takes care of the fields.*
2. *Claudia is a good girl. ♦ Why is she a good girl? ♦ The girl is good because she works in the field daily and she takes care of the horses in the stable. ♦ Claudia is a good and strong girl!*
3. *Paul and Romulus are good sons. ♦ Why are they good sons? ♦ They never fight, and they always work in the fields. ♦ They are good boys! ♦ Yes. But Lucius is a bad boy because he never*

takes care of the horses. ♦ *Does Lucius carry wood from the forest? ♦ Not at all.*

4. *The queen of the homeland is good because she always guards the homeland and often gives food to the men and women of the homeland.*
5. *Farmers, we are good girls and good boys because we always take care of the horses. ♦ We have horses? ♦ Y'all are not good farmers.*
6. *Rufus and Claudia are taking care of the girls and boys.*
7. *Tertius, where are the women today? ♦ I don't know. They are not at home. ♦ Is William at home? ♦ Not at all. ♦ Is Rufus at home? ♦ He is. He is working in the house today. ♦ Goodbye.*
8. *The girls and boys walk to the school daily. They are good girls and good boys.*
9. *The queen's daughter is a good girl. ♦ Why is she a good girl? ♦ She often gives food to the girls of the town.*
10. *We live in a bad house. ♦ Why is the house bad? ♦ The house is bad because it is in the forest near the beasts! ♦ Are there beasts in the forest? ♦ Certainly! There are many beasts in the forest! ♦ We live in a bad house.*

LESSON 23

1. *Hello, Sempronia. Are you a farmer? ♦ Yes. I have many pigs and horses.*
2. *Peter, why do you have a pig? Are you a farmer? ♦ Not at all. I am carrying the pig to a farmer. ♦ Why? ♦ The farmer has many pigs.*
3. *I fear the island. ♦ Why do you fear the island? ♦ There are large pigs on the island. ♦ Do you fear pigs? ♦ I fear large pigs.*
4. *Hello, pigs. Do y'all have food? ♦ Not at all! We do not have food!*
5. *I have much money, but you do not have money. ♦ Why do you have money? ♦ I have money because I always work in the fields!*
6. *Where is Rufus? Is he working in the stables? ♦ Not at all. Rufus is walking to the seashore. He is not at home.*
7. *Aemilia, can you see the boats? ♦ Not at all. I cannot see the boats because the moon is not in the sky.*
8. *Christopher, why are you a farmer? ♦ I am a farmer because I love the soil. I am happy because I take care of the pigs and horses daily. ♦ Are you a good farmer? ♦ Certainly, I am a good farmer. ♦ Goodbye.*
9. *Helen is walking in the forest.*
10. *Helen is walking into the forest.*

LESSON 24

1. *Christopher is absent. Where is Christopher? ♦ I don't know.*

2. Where is Peter? ♦ He is absent. ♦ Where does Peter live? ♦ I don't know.
3. Where is Aemilia ? ♦ I don't know. ♦ Is Rufus at home? ♦ Yes.
4. Is Aurelia at home? ♦ Not at all, Aurelia is absent. ♦ Where is Aurelia? ♦ She is in the town.
5. The girls are absent. Where are the girls? ♦ Today the girls are walking to the forest. ♦ Why are they walking to the forest? ♦ They love the forest!
6. Where is Sempronia? ♦ She is taking care of the horses in the stables. ♦ Sempronia is a good woman.
7. Are you Claudia? ♦ I am Claudia. ♦ Hello, Claudia!
8. The bad boys are not taking care of the horses! ♦ Why? Where are the boys? ♦ They are absent. ♦ They are not good farmers.
9. Girls, why do y'all walk to the seashore daily? ♦ We love the seashore! ♦ Today y'all cannot walk to the seashore because we are farmers and we have many pigs. Do the pigs have food today?
10. Hello, Charles. ♦ Hello, Helen and Peter. Why are y'all not at home? ♦ We are in the town today because we do not have food. ♦ Do y'all have money? ♦ Yes. ♦ Goodbye!

LESSON 25

1. Bad pirates are sailing to the homeland! ♦ Do we have swords? ♦ Yes. ♦ Do we have shields? ♦ Yes, we have shields. ♦ We can fight with the pirates!
2. Sailor, are you a pirate? ♦ Not at all. I am a good sailor. ♦ Why do you have much gold? ♦ I do not have much gold. ♦ Why do you have much silver? ♦ I don't know. ♦ You are a pirate!
3. Romulus, why do you fear the island? ♦ I fear the island because many pirates live on the island. They are bad men! I never sail to the island. ♦ You never sail to the island because you don't have a boat.
4. We never give money to pirates. ♦ Why? ♦ We do not have money.
5. Farmer, the horses are absent. Where are the horses? ♦ I don't have horses. I have pigs.
6. Why is Sempronia absent today? ♦ I don't know. ♦ Where is Sempronia? ♦ She is at home.
7. Do you have a horse, Cornelius? ♦ Yes, I have many horses. ♦ I have a large pig.
8. Hello, pirate. ♦ Hello. Do you have money? Do you have gold? Do you have silver? ♦ Not at all! Goodbye!
9. Tertius is a good son. ♦ Why? ♦ He is a good son because he never fights with bad boys, and he takes care of the pigs daily. ♦ Tertius is a good boy!

10. The pirates have gold and silver.

LESSON 26

1. Tiberius can't work in the field today because he is sick.
2. Hello, Aemilia. Why are you absent? Are you sick today? ♦ Not at all. I am walking to school.
3. Boy, why aren't you walking to school? ♦ I am not a bad boy. I am sick today.
4. Farmer, we can't take care of the pigs today. ♦ Why? ♦ We are sick. ♦ Perhaps y'all can stay at home today. I can give food to the pigs.
5. Mark, why are you counting the horses? ♦ We have many horses in the stables.
6. Quintus's daughter loves Rufus. ♦ Why does she love Rufus? ♦ Rufus is a good man. He always takes care of the fields, and he never tells bad stories to the boys, and he often guards the homeland. ♦ Rufus is a good farmer and a good man!
7. Are the girls at home? ♦ Not at all. They are absent. The girls are walking from the seashore to the forest. ♦ Why? ♦ They love the forest.
8. I see a large pig. ♦ Where is the large pig? ♦ In the field. ♦ Do we have pigs? ♦ Not at all, we have horses. ♦ Why is the pig in the field? ♦ I don't know.
9. Why are the men of the island fighting with the men of the town? ♦ I don't know, but they are destroying the town! ♦ Do you have a shield? Do you have a sword? ♦ Not at all. ♦ Without swords and shields we cannot fight! ♦ Goodbye.
10. Hello, Portia. Where does Julia live? Does Julia live in the forest with the beasts? ♦ Yes, Julia lives in the forest.

LESSON 27

1. Do you live in the town now? ♦ Not at all, I live in the forest. ♦ Why do you live in the forest? ♦ I love the forest. ♦ I cannot live in the forest because I fear the beasts.
2. Hello, James and Lucretia. Where is Tullia now? ♦ Tullia is absent. ♦ Is Tullia sick? ♦ Tullia is absent now because she is taking care of boys and girls.
3. Am I at home? ♦ Not at all, you are in a boat! We are sailing now to the homeland. ♦ I cannot sail to the homeland. I am sick!
4. Decimus is a strong man. ♦ Why? ♦ He is a strong man because daily he carries wood, water, and rocks. ♦ Why does Decimus carry wood? ♦ He is now building a wall with wood.
5. Charles, why do you have much money now? ♦ I have money because I work in the fields daily and I take care of pigs. Now I am counting the money.

258

6. *Are Quintus's daughters working in the fields?*
   ♦ *Yes, now they are plowing the soil.* ♦ *Do the horses have food in the stables?* ♦ *Not at all, but I can take care of the horses and the pigs today.*
7. *Rufus, do you love Fausta?* ♦ *Yes. I love Fausta. And I love Claudia.*
8. *You can't carry large rocks in the boat!* ♦ *But the boat is large!*
9. *Why is Romulus building a wall today?* ♦ *The town doesn't have a wall. Without a wall we can't guard the town.* ♦ *Why is Romulus building a wall around the town? Romulus doesn't live in the town.* ♦ *I don't know.*
10. *Why are you sick now?* ♦ *We are in a boat!* ♦ *You are a pirate! You can't be sick!* ♦ *But I am sick.* ♦ *You are not a good pirate.*

LESSON 28

1. *Paul is absent. Where is Paul now?* ♦ *I don't know. Perhaps he is staying home because he is sick.*
2. *Hello. Lucretia and Sempronia are absent. Where are they now?* ♦ *I don't know, but perhaps they are in the town.* ♦ *Goodbye.*
3. *The strong farmer is carrying rocks from the fields.* ♦ *Why?* ♦ *There are many rocks in the field. The farmer cannot plow a field with many rocks.*
4. *William is absent. Where is William?* ♦ *Perhaps he is in the forest.* ♦ *William is not in the forest. William never walks in the forest because he fears the beasts.*
5. *Where are we? Where is the boat? Are we on an island?* ♦ *Perhaps. I see land, and water is around the land. Are we on an island?* ♦ *You are not a good sailor.*
6. *Robert's son is absent and is not plowing the field. Where is Robert's son now?* ♦ *I don't know.* ♦ *Robert's son is a bad boy!*
7. *The horse is not strong. It cannot carry the boy from the town to the forest.* ♦ *Perhaps the boy can walk to the forest.* ♦ *The boy cannot walk to the forest without food and water.* ♦ *Perhaps the pig can carry the boy?* ♦ *The pig cannot carry the boy!*
8. *Today Cornelia and Portia are carrying gifts into the town. Why are they carrying gifts to the town?* ♦ *Today the queen is present in the town. Often Cornelia and Portia give gifts to the queen because they love the queen.*
9. *Christopher always guards the homeland with sword and shield.*
10. *Do the pigs have food today?* ♦ *Do we have pigs?* ♦ *Certainly! We have many pigs! You are a bad farmer!*

LESSON 29

1. *Where is Julia? Why is Julia absent today?* ♦ *Julia is sick today.*
2. *Is Tiberius at home today? Is he sick?* ♦ *Yes. Tiberius is sick today.*
3. *Publius, where is the horse? It is not in the stable.* ♦ *I don't know. I am taking care of the pigs now.*
4. *I can't see.* ♦ *You can't see because the moon is not in the sky.* ♦ *Why are we in the forest? I fear the beasts of the forests!* ♦ *I don't fear the beasts because I have a sword.*
5. *Charles, where is Cornelia today? Is she sick?* ♦ *Not at all. Cornelia is never sick. She is at home, but she is not sick.*
6. *Tullia, can you work today?* ♦ *Yes, I am not sick. I can take care of the fields and I can give food to the pigs.*
7. *Hello farmers! Do y'all have a horse?* ♦ *We are not farmers. We are poets.* ♦ *Perhaps y'all have a good story.* ♦ *Certainly, we have many good stories. We are good poets!*
8. *Does the queen have much money?* ♦ *Yes, the queen has much money.* ♦ *Does the queen have gold?* ♦ *Certainly. The queen has much gold and much silver.*
9. *The poet is telling a good story now to Sempronia's daughters.* ♦ *Sempronia's daughters love stories.*
10. *Lavinia, why are you at home with Claudia?* ♦ *Today I am taking care of Claudia because she is sick.* ♦ *You are a good woman!*

LESSON 30

1. *Where is William?* ♦ *I am present!*
2. *Hello boys. Why is Tiberius absent?* ♦ *I don't know. Perhaps he is sick today.* ♦ *Tiberius is not sick today. He is at home, but he is not sick.*
3. *The girls are present, but the boys are absent. Where are the boys? Are the boys sick?* ♦ *Yes. The boys are at home because they are sick.*
4. *Hello, boys! Julius, is Matthew present?* ♦ *Not at all, Matthew is absent.* ♦ *Where is Matthew?* ♦ *I don't know. Perhaps Matthew is now working with the farmers in the fields.* ♦ *Matthew never works in the fields.*
5. *Quintus is absent. Where is Quintus?* ♦ *Perhaps he is guarding the wall of the town.* ♦ *Do we have a wall?* ♦ *Yes. We have a large wall around the town.*
6. *Can I stay in the house today?* ♦ *Certainly, you can stay in the house.*
7. *James, why don't the pigs have food?* ♦ *The bad farmers are not taking care of the pigs.* ♦ *Bad farmers, why don't you give food to the pigs?*

259

8. *Hello, Romulus. Why is Claudius absent? Is he sick?* ♦ *Yes, today Claudius is sick. I am taking care of Claudius at home.* ♦ *You are a good man. Goodbye.*

9. *Joseph, why are you happy today?* ♦ *I love Lucretia!* ♦ *Why do you love Lucretia?* ♦ *Lucretia is a good woman. She is always happy, and she always gives food to the boys and girls of the town.* ♦ *Lucretia is a good woman!* ♦ *Yes, I love Lucretia because she is a good woman.*

10. *Hello, Tullia. Why are you watching the boats?* ♦ *I watch the boats daily because I love boats.* ♦ *I see pirates!*

LESSON 31

1. *Catherine, are you sick today?* ♦ *Not at all, I am well!*

2. *The farmer can't take care of the horses today.* ♦ *The farmer is sick, but we are well. Perhaps we can take care of the horses.*

3. *I am taking care of the boys because they are sick. Is Claudia sick today?* ♦ *Not at all, Claudia is well. She is working in the house now.*

4. *We can't walk to school today. We are sick!* ♦ *Bad girls! Y'all are not sick, but y'all are well. Y'all can't stay home today.* ♦ *Perhaps we can walk to the seashore.*

5. *The girls and boys are absent now. Where are they? Are the boys and girls sick?* ♦ *I don't know, but Cornelia and Matthew are present.*

6. *Portia, I love Christopher.* ♦ *Do you love Christopher?* ♦ *Yes, he is a good boy.* ♦ *I love Christopher.* ♦ *Do you love Christopher?* ♦ *Yes.* ♦ *We love Christopher, but Christopher loves Helen.*

7. *You can't build a boat, Publius.* ♦ *Why?* ♦ *You don't have wood.* ♦ *But we are near the forest. Perhaps we can carry wood from the forest.* ♦ *Perhaps, but large beasts live in the forests.* ♦ *Perhaps the beasts are absent today.*

8. *Aemilia, do you live near the seashore?* ♦ *Not at all, I live in the town.* ♦ *Do you have a house?* ♦ *Yes, I have a house near the wall of the town.*

9. *Is Romulus present?* ♦ *Not at all. Romulus is walking into the forest with Rufus.*

10. *Where is Paul's son?* ♦ *Paul's son is now taking care of the pigs, and he is giving food to the horses.*

LESSON 32

1. *Hello, Romulus. Where are the students?* ♦ *The students are at school, but Charles is not at school. Charles is absent.* ♦ *Why is Charles absent?* ♦ *Charles is sick. He is at home.*

2. *The students are absent.* ♦ *Perhaps they are walking to the seashore. The students love the seashore!* ♦ *They are bad students!*

3. *The students are present, but they do not have food. Why don't they have food?* ♦ *I don't know, but now we are giving food to the students.*

4. *The students are absent. Where are they?* ♦ *I don't know. Perhaps the students are at home.*

5. *Claudia is absent. Where is Claudia?* ♦ *She is walking to the forest with the students.*

6. *Tullia, why is Claudius walking into the forest now?* ♦ *He is carrying wood from the forest to the town.* ♦ *Why is he carrying wood?* ♦ *The inhabitants of the town are building a wall around the town with wood.* ♦ *Why are they building a wall?* ♦ *There are many pirates near the town.*

7. *Aurelia, are you a student?* ♦ *Yes, I am a student. I walk to school daily.*

8. *Hello, Titus. Are you well today?* ♦ *Yes, I am well today, but Mark's daughter is sick.* ♦ *Why is Mark's daughter sick?* ♦ *I don't know, but she is at home today.* ♦ *Goodbye, Titus.* ♦ *Goodbye.*

9. *Where is the pig?* ♦ *Do we have a pig?* ♦ *Yes. We have a pig, but it is now absent. Where is the pig?* ♦ *I don't know.* ♦ *You are a bad farmer.*

10. *Hello, students. I am present today, but Tiberius is absent.* ♦ *Why is Tiberius absent? Is Tiberius well?* ♦ *Not at all. Tiberius is sick.* ♦ *Is Tiberius at home?* ♦ *Yes, he is at home. The sons and daughters of Tiberius are taking care of Tiberius.*

LESSON 33

1. *Portia and Cornelia are now teachers.* ♦ *Why are they teachers?* ♦ *They love the students. They love the school.* ♦ *They are good teachers!*

2. *Is Claudius a teacher?* ♦ *Not at all, Claudius is student.*

3. *Sempronia, are you a student?* ♦ *Not at all. I am a teacher now, but I do not have a school.* ♦ *Perhaps the men and women of the town can build a school.* ♦ *Perhaps. I am a good teacher!*

4. *Is Peter present?* ♦ *I am present! Hello, teacher!* ♦ *Hello, student!*

5. *Men of the town, why do y'all carry wood from the forest daily?* ♦ *We are building a school.* ♦ *Why?* ♦ *The teacher has many students, but he does not have a school.* ♦ *Y'all are good men!*

6. *Horses, are y'all well today? Do y'all have food?* ♦ *We are well, and we have food.*

7. *Rufus, why do you never sail to the island?* ♦ *I often sail to the island.* ♦ *Do you have a boat?* ♦ *Not at all. I sail in Robert's boat. Robert is a good sailor. I am sailing to the island with Robert today.*

8. *Cornelia is walking into the forest. She does not fear the beasts.*
9. *Mark, can you swim?* ♦ *Yes, I can swim, but I never swim because I fear the pirates.*
10. *The teacher often tells stories to the students.*

LESSON 34

1. *I am a teacher. I teach students daily.*
2. *Are you a teacher?* ♦ *Not at all, I don't teach students.*
3. *Are we teachers? Do we teach students?* ♦ *Yes, we teach students daily. We are teachers.* ♦ *Can we stay at home today?*
4. *The school has many students, but it doesn't have teachers.* ♦ *Why?* ♦ *The school does not have money.* ♦ *Perhaps I can teach the students.*
5. *Cornelia, where is the teacher? The teacher is absent.* ♦ *I don't know. Perhaps she is walking to the seashore now.* ♦ *The teacher is bad! Perhaps you can teach the students today.*
6. *Good students walk to school daily, but bad students are always absent.*
7. *I see Rufus, Cornelia, and Joseph…but where is Titus?* ♦ *I don't know. Is Titus absent?* ♦ *Yes. Perhaps Titus is sick at home.* ♦ *Not at all, Titus is not sick. He is a bad student, but he is not sick.*
8. *Lavinia, do you love Romulus?* ♦ *Not at all, I love Quintus.* ♦ *Quintus is a good man, but he is a teacher and does not have money.* ♦ *Perhaps, but he has a large house with horses and stables.*
9. *I live in the town. Do y'all live in the forest?* ♦ *Not at all! We cannot live near the beasts.*
10. *Are you sailing to the homeland?* ♦ *Yes. Today I am sailing to the homeland.* ♦ *Why are you sailing to the homeland?* ♦ *I am sailing because I can't swim.*

LESSON 35

1. *The school is small, but we have many students.* ♦ *Perhaps the queen can build a large school.* ♦ *Perhaps. The queen has much money, but we do not have money.*
2. *I don't fear the beasts of the island.* ♦ *Why?* ♦ *The beasts of the island are small. I don't fear small beasts.* ♦ *Do you fear large beasts?* ♦ *Yes. I never walk in the forest because large beasts live in the forest.*
3. *Cornelius is a teacher. He teaches in a small school.* ♦ *Why is Cornelius's school small?* ♦ *Cornelius does not have many students.*
4. *Julia is a good woman.* ♦ *Why?* ♦ *She always takes care of the horses in the stables. She gives food and water to the horses daily.*

5. *Aemilia, why are you absent? The students are present today, but you are absent.* ♦ *Today I am staying at home. I am happy at home.* ♦ *You can't stay at home!* ♦ *Why can't I stay at home?* ♦ *You can't stay at home because you are a teacher! You teach the students!*
6. *Where is Catherine today?* ♦ *I am present!* ♦ *Hello, Catherine!* ♦ *Hello, teacher.*
7. *Cornelia and Helen, y'all are good girls.* ♦ *Why?* ♦ *Y'all are good girls because y'all never fight with boys, y'all always take care of the pigs, y'all walk to school daily, and y'all are good students.*
8. *Goodbye, inhabitants of the town. We are walking now to the homeland.*
9. *You are a good horse.* ♦ *I am not horse. I am pig!* ♦ *Are you a pig?* ♦ *You are a bad farmer.*
10. *The inhabitants of the town are building a wall with rocks.* ♦ *Why?* ♦ *They fear the pirates. Pirates often sail from the islands to the town.*

LESSON 36

1. *This horse is large.*
2. *This woman is the daughter of Tiberius.*
3. *This town is small, but it has many inhabitants.*
4. *This boy is bad!* ♦ *Why?* ♦ *He never takes care of the horses, and always fights with girls!*
5. *This boat is small, but strong.* ♦ *Yes, but you can't carry rocks in the boat.*
6. *This wood is strong.*
7. *This school is small, but it has many students.* ♦ *But they are bad students.*
8. *This man is watching the boats.* ♦ *Why is he watching the boats?* ♦ *Perhaps he is a sailor.* ♦ *This man is not a sailor! He is a pirate!*
9. *This teacher teaches many students.*
10. *Teacher, I have a good story. Perhaps I can tell the story to the students.* ♦ *Not at all, Rufus. You always tell bad stories to the students. You can't tell a bad story.* ♦ *I often tell bad stories, teacher, but this story is good.*

LESSON 37

1. *Peter, is there a library in the town?* ♦ *Yes, there is a small library in the town. It is near the school.* ♦ *I love libraries! Perhaps we can walk to the library.*
2. *Sempronia, are you a librarian?* ♦ *Yes, I am a librarian. I work at the library.*
3. *James, why is Rufus walking to the library now? And why is he carrying a gift?* ♦ *Aurelia is a librarian at the library. Rufus loves Aurelia.*
4. *Fulvia, this boat is large.* ♦ *Not at all, this boat is small.* ♦ *This boat can carry many sailors!*

5. *Tullia, where does this boy live? ♦ This boy lives in the town.*
6. *The students are walking from the school to the library.*
7. *Is Mark present? Is he well today? ♦ Not at all, Mark is absent. ♦ Where is Mark? ♦ I don't know. Perhaps he is at home. ♦ Perhaps he is sick.*
8. *The good men are guarding the island, but they don't have shields. ♦ Do the men have swords? ♦ Yes, they have swords. ♦ Where are the men? ♦ The men are in the boats now. They are sailing around the island.*
9. *This bad teacher never teaches the students. ♦ Why? ♦ I don't know. He is always absent. ♦ Perhaps we can teach the students. ♦ Not at all! We are not teachers!*
10. *Peter, why are we in a boat? ♦ We are guarding the island. ♦ Why are we guarding the island? ♦ We are guarding the island because many pirates are sailing to the island with swords now. ♦ Do we have swords? ♦ We do not have swords. ♦ Perhaps I can stay at home, and you can guard the island.*

LESSON 38

1. *This theater is large!*
2. *Aurelia, where is Claudia now? ♦ Claudia is at the theater. ♦ Claudia loves the theater!*
3. *Rufus, where is the theater? ♦ We do not have a theater in the homeland. ♦ Perhaps the queen can build a theater. ♦ Perhaps, but the inhabitants of the homeland don't have much money.*
4. *Teacher, where are the students today? ♦ Many students are at home today because they are sick, but you are present because you are well. ♦ Yes, I am well, but perhaps today I can stay at home. Goodbye, teacher.*
5. *This pig is large! Why is this pig large? ♦ The farmer gives much food to the pig daily.*
6. *Where is Publius? ♦ He is in the stable. He is taking care of the horse. ♦ Why is Publius taking care of the horse? Publius is not a farmer.*
7. *Helen, are you a teacher? ♦ Yes, I teach students daily.*
8. *Is Quintus a teacher? ♦ Not at all. Quintus is a bad student! ♦ Quintus isn't a bad student, is he? ♦ Yes, he is a bad student. He is absent daily, and often stays at home.*
9. *The girls and boys are walking into the forest.*
10. *This library is small. Where is the librarian? ♦ I don't know.*

LESSON 39

1. *This book is bad! ♦ Why? ♦ It has a bad story.*

2. *Why are y'all walking to the library? ♦ We are carrying books to the library. We love good books.*
3. *This library is small, but it has many books. ♦ This library is small, but good.*
4. *Why is the teacher giving books to the students today? ♦ Without books, the teacher cannot teach the students.*
5. *The teacher is telling a story to the queen's daughters. ♦ Why? ♦ The girls love stories.*
6. *Are you taking care of the horses today? ♦ Yes. I am a farmer, and I take care of horses daily.*
7. *Fausta, why are you always present in the library? Do you love books? ♦ Not at all. I love Mark. Mark is the librarian.*
8. *Does Sempronia have a horse? ♦ Not at all, but she has a boat. ♦ Why? ♦ Sempronia often sails to the homeland. ♦ Why does she sail to the homeland? ♦ Sempronia's daughter lives in the homeland.*
9. *Where is the poet today? ♦ The poet is at the theater. Today he is telling stories to the girls and boys. ♦ The girls and boys love stories!*
10. *Librarian, do you have a good book? ♦ You are in a library. This library has many books. ♦ Perhaps this book is good.*

LESSON 40

1. *I have a new book. ♦ I love new books. ♦ Why? ♦ I am a librarian.*
2. *This town has a new library. ♦ Where is the new library? ♦ It is near the school.*
3. *Woman, is there a library in the town? ♦ Yes, and I am the new librarian! We have many books. I take care of the books daily.*
4. *Son, why is James absent? ♦ I don't know. Perhaps James is in the field. He often works in the fields. ♦ James is not working today. He is at the theater now!*
5. *Where is Joseph? ♦ He is guarding the town with a sword and shield. ♦ Why? ♦ We don't have a wall around the town. ♦ Perhaps y'all can build a new wall. ♦ We have many rocks. ♦ Perhaps y'all can build a wall with rocks.*
6. *Why is Decimus not swimming to the island with the boys and girls? Does he fear the water? ♦ Yes, Decimus fears the water.*
7. *Are we in a boat? ♦ We are. ♦ Why? ♦ Today we are sailing to the homeland. ♦ I am sick. I can't sail today.*
8. *Cornelia, do you have a pig? ♦ Yes. I have many pigs.*
9. *Am I a farmer? ♦ I don't know. Do you plow the fields? ♦ Yes. ♦ Do you take care of horses? ♦ Daily. ♦ You are a farmer.*

10. *We can't teach the students.* ♦ *Why?* ♦ *This school does not have books.* ♦ *We are near the library. Perhaps you and the students can walk to the library. The library has many books.*

LESSON 41

1. *Charles, why are you hurrying to school now?* ♦ *I am a teacher. I teach students daily.* ♦ *But you are sick today. You can stay at home today.* ♦ *I am not sick! I am well today! Goodbye!*
2. *Son, why are you hurrying?* ♦ *I am hurrying to school because I am a good student. Goodbye!*
3. *Sailor, why are we hurrying to the island?* ♦ *Many pirates are sailing to the island now.* ♦ *Perhaps we can sail from the island.* ♦ *Do you fear the pirates?*
4. *Am I a teacher?* ♦ *I don't know. Do you teach students daily?* ♦ *Yes.* ♦ *You are a teacher.*
5. *Women, why are y'all hurrying to the school?* ♦ *We are teachers.* ♦ *Goodbye, teachers.*
6. *Where is Rufus?* ♦ *I don't know. Rufus is absent.* ♦ *Why is Rufus absent?* ♦ *I don't know. Perhaps Rufus is at home.* ♦ *Perhaps Rufus is at the theater.* ♦ *This town does not have a theater.*
7. *Do you work at the new library?* ♦ *Yes. I take care of the books daily because I am a librarian.* ♦ *Where is new library?* ♦ *In the town, near the house of Romulus.*
8. *The girls and boys are hurrying to the seashore.* ♦ *Why?* ♦ *They love the seashore!*
9. *Teacher, do you have new books?* ♦ *This school does not have new books. Without new books, we cannot teach the students.*
10. *Decimus, I have a new pig now.* ♦ *Is it a large pig?* ♦ *Yes, this pig is large. I give much food to the pig daily.*

LESSON 42

1. *The farmers are hurrying out of the town to the fields.* ♦ *Why?* ♦ *They are plowing the fields today.* ♦ *Perhaps we can work in the fields today.* ♦ *Not at all. We are not farmers!*
2. *Aemilia is hurrying out of the school into the library.* ♦ *Why?* ♦ *Aemilia is a librarian. She works in the library daily. She takes care of the books, and always tells stories to the girls and boys.* ♦ *Aemilia is a good librarian!*
3. *The farmers are carrying wood out of the forest.* ♦ *Why are they carrying wood?* ♦ *Today they are building a small house out of wood.* ♦ *Why are they building a house?* ♦ *Charles does not have a house. Charles lives in the forest, but now he can live in a house.*
4. *I live in the library.* ♦ *Not at all, you do not live in the library.* ♦ *But I am always present in the library.* ♦ *You are a librarian. You work in the library, but you do not live in the library!*
5. *Claudius is hurrying out of the new library with many books. He loves books!* ♦ *Yes, Claudius is a good student.*
6. *Flavia, are you a teacher?* ♦ *Certainly. I teach students daily.*
7. *This town is large now.* ♦ *Yes, it is large. This town has a large school, a new library, and a large wall.* ♦ *Many men and many women live in the town now.* ♦ *They are building a new theater out of wood now.*
8. *Hello, pigs!* ♦ *Hello, farmer.* ♦ *Are y'all well today?* ♦ *Yes. We are well today.* ♦ *Do y'all have food?* ♦ *Yes. We have food, and this food is good. You are a good farmer.*
9. *Robert, are Aemilia and Christopher sick today? They are absent today.* ♦ *Not at all, they are well.* ♦ *Why are they absent?* ♦ *I don't know. Perhaps they are at home.*
10. *The men and women are building a new town.* ♦ *Why?* ♦ *This town is small, and they have many sons and daughters.* ♦ *Where is the new town?* ♦ *It is near the forest.*

LESSON 43

1. *This market is bad!* ♦ *Why?* ♦ *It is bad because it does not have good food.*
2. *Romulus, why are you hurrying to the market?* ♦ *I do not have food.* ♦ *Why do you not have food, Romulus?* ♦ *I have many sons and many daughters.*
3. *Hello, Sempronia! Why are you hurrying to the library?* ♦ *I love good books.*
4. *We do not have food.* ♦ *This town has many markets, but we do not have money.* ♦ *We do not have money, but we have a pig. Perhaps...* ♦ *Not at all!*
5. *Where is the teacher? And why is this woman present?* ♦ *The teacher is absent because she is sick. This woman is the teacher today.*
6. *Am I present?* ♦ *Yes, you are present.* ♦ *Where am I?* ♦ *You are at home. You are sick.*
7. *I am the queen.* ♦ *Lucretia, you are not a queen. You are a librarian.* ♦ *I am queen of books. I always take care of and guard the books.* ♦ *You are not a queen! You are a librarian!* ♦ *I am the queen of the library.*
8. *Quintus, do you love Aurelia?* ♦ *Not at all, I love Claudia.* ♦ *Claudia loves Tiberius.* ♦ *Why does Claudia love Tiberius?* ♦ *Tiberius has much money, and he has a large house.* ♦ *I have many pigs.*
9. *Daughter, where is the new book? The book is absent.* ♦ *I don't know. Perhaps Mark is carrying the new book to the library now.*

10. *The boy is hurrying into the library.* ♦ *Now he is hurrying out of the library with many books.*

LESSON 44

1. *We never have food in the house.* ♦ *Why?* ♦ *We never grocery shop!* ♦ *Perhaps today we can grocery shop.* ♦ *We don't have money!*
2. *Tullia, where is Charles now?* ♦ *Charles is grocery shopping now because we do not have food.*
3. *I can't grocery shop because this market is small and bad.*
4. *Hello, Publius. Where do you work now?* ♦ *I work at the market.* ♦ *Where is the market?* ♦ *In the town, near Helen's house.*
5. *The sailors are sailing from the island with much silver and much gold.* ♦ *Perhaps they are pirates!* ♦ *Not at all, they are good sailors.*
6. *This town does not have a theater.* ♦ *Perhaps we can build a new theater out of wood. We live near the forest, and we have much wood.* ♦ *We can carry wood out of the forest to the town.*
7. *Tullia, you are a good daughter, and you are a good girl.* ♦ *Am I a good girl?* ♦ *Yes. You never fight with boys, and you are a good student. You always take care of the horses and you give food to the pigs daily.*
8. *James, why are we walking to the market?* ♦ *We are grocery shopping.*
9. *Is this woman a librarian?* ♦ *Yes. She is a librarian. She works at the new library. She takes care of the books and counts the books daily.*
10. *Why are the men and boys hurrying out of the town?* ♦ *They are hurrying to the boats.* ♦ *Why are they hurrying to the boats now?* ♦ *Bad pirates are sailing out of the islands to the homeland. The men and boys are guarding the homeland with boats.* ♦ *They are farmers! They can't sail!* ♦ *They are farmers, but they can sail. They are farmers and sailors.*

LESSON 45

1. *Robert, why is Paul angry?* ♦ *Paul is angry because he does not have money.* ♦ *Paul never works.*
2. *Cornelia, why is Sempronia angry?* ♦ *Sempronia is angry because this library is small and does not have good books.* ♦ *Perhaps we can walk to the theater.*
3. *Why is this farmer angry?* ♦ *The new horse is absent.* ♦ *Where is the horse? Is the horse in the stable?* ♦ *Not at all. The horse is not in the stable.*
4. *I see Aurelia. She is hurrying out of the library with many books.* ♦ *Aurelia always carries many books out of the library. She loves books!*
5. *This girl is Tullia.* ♦ *Is she Mark's daughter?* ♦ *Yes, Tullia is Mark's daughter.* ♦ *Is she a student?* ♦ *Yes. Tullia is a good student. She never stays at home, but hurries to school daily.*
6. *Where is Rufus?* ♦ *Rufus is hurrying to the market. He is grocery shopping in the town because we do not have food.*
7. *This librarian is angry!* ♦ *Why?* ♦ *He is angry because bad students are destroying books in the library!* ♦ *Good students never destroy books.*
8. *Are you angry?* ♦ *Not at all. I am happy.* ♦ *Why?* ♦ *I am happy today because I have a new book.*
9. *Daughter, why are we building a wall around the town?* ♦ *We live near the forest. There are many beasts in the forest.* ♦ *Where is the wood?*
10. *Hello, Helen. I am the new teacher.* ♦ *Hello.* ♦ *Do we have good students?* ♦ *This school is a school of girls. We do not have boys, but many girls are present.* ♦ *Are the girls good students? I can't teach bad students.* ♦ *Yes. They are always present, and they never fight.*

LESSON 46

1. *Aemilia is working in the fields. Lavinia also is working in the fields.* ♦ *Why?* ♦ *They are many rocks in the fields. Lavinia and Aemilia are carrying the rocks out of the field.*
2. *The moon is now in the sky, and the stars are also present.* ♦ *Perhaps we can count the stars!* ♦ *Not at all, we can't count the stars.*
3. *You have a new book! Why do you have a new book?* ♦ *I am a teacher, and I teach many students.* ♦ *Do you have a school?* ♦ *Not at all, I do not have a school. I teach students at the library.*
4. *I often walk to the new library.* ♦ *I also. I love books.* ♦ *I often walk to the library because I love Julia. Julia is a librarian. She works in the library.*
5. *Hello, Cornelia. Are you well today?* ♦ *Yes, I am well.* ♦ *Why are you hurrying to the town?* ♦ *I am grocery shopping. I am hurrying to the market now because we don't have food in the house, but we have many sons and many daughters.*
6. *This town is small, but this library is large.*
7. *This town does not have a wall.* ♦ *Why, Lucretia?* ♦ *We don't have wood.* ♦ *Perhaps we can carry wood out of the forest.* ♦ *Perhaps, but I am not strong.* ♦ *Not at all! You are strong! You can carry wood out of the forest, and I also can carry wood.*

8. *This man is Christopher. Christopher is a librarian.*
9. *I am angry. ♦ I also! ♦ Why are you angry? ♦ I am angry because this town does not have a theater. Why are you angry? ♦ I am angry because this town does not have a library.*
10. *Son, why is the pig in the house! ♦ Are you angry? ♦ Yes! I am angry! Why is the pig in the house? ♦ The pig is sick. I am taking care of the pig in the house.*

LESSON 47

1. *Where is the cafe? ♦ The cafe is near Robert's house.*
2. *This town does not have a cafe. ♦ Why? ♦ It is a small town.*
3. *Where we are? In the town? In the forest? ♦ We are in a boat! ♦ Why are we in a boat? ♦ We are in a boat because we are pirates! ♦ Am I a pirate? I fear pirates! ♦ You are a bad pirate.*
4. *We do not have food at home. Perhaps we can walk to the market. We can grocery shop. ♦ We have money. Perhaps we can walk to the cafe. Claudia's cafe has good food!*
5. *Tertius is angry. ♦ Why? ♦ He does not have food, and he does not have money. ♦ Perhaps we can give money to Tertius. ♦ Not at all!*
6. *Why are you angry? ♦ I am angry because we are in the library, but I do not see the librarian. Where is the librarian? Where are the new books? ♦ I don't know. ♦ This library is bad.*
7. *Fausta, is Julia a teacher? Does she teach students? ♦ Not at all. Julia is a librarian. She takes care of and guards the books daily.*
8. *The horses are angry! ♦ Why? ♦ They do not have food in the stables. ♦ Rufus is not taking care of the horses! ♦ Perhaps Rufus is sick. ♦ Not at all! Rufus is at the theater!*
9. *Romulus, why are you hurrying to the town? ♦ I am hurrying to the theater. I love the theater. ♦ I also love the theater. Perhaps I also can walk to the theater. ♦ Yes, you also can.*
10. *The girls are hurrying out of the town. ♦ Why? ♦ I don't know. Perhaps they are hurrying to the seashore.*

LESSON 48

1. *I am tired. ♦ Why? ♦ I am a teacher. I teach students. ♦ I also am tired.*
2. *I can't grocery shop today. ♦ Why? Are you tired? ♦ Yes. I am tired. I am staying at home.*
3. *This town is small. ♦ This town does not have a market. ♦ This town does not have a good cafe. ♦ Why are we present? ♦ It has a large library with many books.*

4. *I can't grocery shop today. ♦ Why? We do not have food at home. ♦ I can't grocery shop because I am tired. I am staying at home today.*
5. *Helen, do you have sons? ♦ Yes. I am always tired because I have many sons and daughters.*
6. *Hello, students. ♦ Goodbye, teacher. ♦ Why are y'all hurrying out of the school?*
7. *This farmer has many pigs, but he does not have horses. ♦ Why? ♦ He does not have a stable.*
8. *Hello, Aurelia. Are you well today? Are you tired? ♦ Not at all, I am well today. I am not tired.*
9. *This boy is Tullia's son.*
10. *This horse can't carry Julia to the town. ♦ Why? ♦ It is tired. ♦ Perhaps Julia can walk to the town. ♦ Julia is also tired.*

LESSON 50

1. *Hello, Peter! You have food, right? ♦ Yes. I have food.*
2. *This library has many books, right? ♦ Yes. this library is large, and has many books.*
3. *There is a cafe in the town, right? ♦ Yes. There is a good cafe near Sempronia's house.*
4. *You are a student, right? ♦ Yes, I am a student. And you? ♦ I also am a student.*
5. *You take care of the horses daily, right? ♦ Certainly, I always take care of the horses. I give food to the horses daily.*
6. *The farmers are tired, right? ♦ Yes. The farmers are tired because today they are plowing the soil.*
7. *The sailors are present, right? ♦ Not at all. They are absent.*
8. *Hello. Are we near the library? ♦ Yes. You can see the library. ♦ Yes, now I can see the library.*
9. *Are Decimus and Tullia grocery shopping now? ♦ Yes, they are hurrying to the market now.*
10. *Hello, horses. Y'all have food, right? ♦ Not at all! The pigs have food, but we do not have food! ♦ Y'all have water, right? ♦ Not at all! ♦ I am a bad farmer.*

LESSON 51

1. *You aren't a pirate, are you?*
2. *You are a pirate, right?*
3. *You aren't tired, are you? ♦ I am tired and angry! ♦ Why are you tired? Why are you angry? ♦ I am angry because we do not have a horse. Why are we walking to the town? ♦ I also am tired. We are walking to the town because the market is in the town. We do not have food. ♦ I can't grocery shop today. ♦ Why? We do not have food! ♦ I am tired!*
4. *You are a pirate, right? ♦ Yes, I am a pirate. ♦ I don't have gold!*

5. *You aren't a teacher, are you? ◆ Not at all. I am not a teacher. I am a librarian. ◆ You work at a library, right? ◆ Yes, I work at a large library. I take care of and guard the books daily.*

6. *Tertius doesn't live in the forest, does he? ◆ Not at all, Tertius does not live in the forest. Tertius lives in a large house in the town.*

7. *This horse doesn't have food, does it? ◆ Not at all. The horse does not have food. ◆ Why? ◆ The horse does not have food because Mark is a bad boy! Mark never takes care of the horses!*

8. *The queen isn't sailing to the island, is she? ◆ Not at all. The queen always stays in the homeland. She never sails to the island. ◆ Why does the queen never sail to the island? ◆ Bad pirates live on the island!*

9. *Flavia doesn't love Robert, does she? ◆ Not at all, Flavia loves Decimus. ◆ Why? ◆ Decimus is a good man. He has a large house, and has money also.*

10. *Is Quintus grocery shopping? ◆ Yes, Quintus is grocery shopping because we do not have food in the house.*

LESSON 52

1. *Where is Lucretia's house? ◆ Lucretia's house is between the seashore and the forest. ◆ Lucretia's house isn't near the seashore, is it? ◆ Not at all. Lucretia lives near the forest.*

2. *Girl, where is the library? ◆ The library is between the school and the market. ◆ The library has good books, right? ◆ Certainly, the library has many good books. ◆ I love books. I am walking to the library now.*

3. *They are many boats between the homeland and the island. ◆ They are not pirates, are they? ◆ Not at all, they are not pirates.*

4. *Lucretia, why are you hurrying to Quintus's cafe? ◆ Quintus's cafe has good food!*

5. *You aren't angry, are you?*

6. *You are angry, right? ◆ Yes. I am angry because I am tired. I hurry to the market daily because we have many daughters and many sons. I grocery shop daily.*

7. *You aren't sick, are you, Mark? ◆ Not at all, I am well today.*

8. *This island is bad. ◆ Why is this island bad? ◆ It is an island of pirates! Many pirates live on the island. ◆ I fear pirates! ◆ I also fear pirates. Perhaps now we can sail to the homeland. ◆ Yes. There are many pirates among the islands!*

9. *There is a library in the town, right? ◆ Yes, this town has a new library, but the library is small. ◆ Does the town have a theater? ◆ Not at all. The inhabitants of the town love books, but they do not love theaters.*

10. *Aurelia is present, Sempronia is present, Tullia is present. ◆ Claudia is absent. ◆ Where is Claudia? Claudia isn't sick, is she? ◆ I don't know. Perhaps Claudia is at home.*

LESSON 53

1. *This restaurant has bad food, right? ◆ Yes. This food is bad. ◆ Perhaps we can give the food to the horses. ◆ Perhaps we can give the food to the pigs.*

2. *Cornelia, does this town have a good restaurant? ◆ Certainly. There is a good restaurant near Robert's house. It is between the wall of the town and the library.*

3. *You can't work in the restaurant today because you are sick. ◆ I am not sick! I am well today! ◆ Not at all, you are sick. You can stay at home today.*

4. *Son, where is the school? ◆ I don't know. ◆ You are a student, right? ◆ Yes, I am a student. ◆ You are a bad student.*

5. *Why does Lucretia walk to the library daily? ◆ Lucretia loves books, and she loves the librarian, too. ◆ I also love good books.*

6. *Rufus is hurrying out of the new restaurant with good food!*

7. *The new teacher isn't sick, is she? ◆ Not at all, the teacher is well and is present today. The students also are present.*

8. *Daughters, why are we hurrying to the market now? ◆ We are grocery shopping because we do not have food. ◆ Perhaps we can walk to a restaurant. Quintus's restaurant has good food. ◆ Not at all! Pirates and bad men are always present in Quintus's restaurant, and they often tell bad stories. ◆ But…it has good food.*

9. *We are walking out of the town now. ◆ Why? ◆ We are walking into the large forest. ◆ Y'all don't fear the beasts, do you? ◆ Not at all, we do not fear the beasts of the forest because we have swords and shields.*

10. *Poet, perhaps you can tell a good story to the boys and girls. ◆ I never tell bad stories!*

LESSON 54

1. *Why do we never have dinner at the restaurant, Christopher? ◆ We never have money! ◆ Perhaps we can have dinner at home.*

2. *We can have dinner at the cafe, right? ◆ Perhaps, but bad men are often present at the cafe. ◆ Are pirates present? ◆ Yes. Pirates are present, and they always tell bad stories in the cafe.*

3. *Teacher, where is William today? ◆ William is at home because he is sick. ◆ William is not*

sick. He is absent because he is a bad student and he is a bad boy, too!

4. *Hello, Catherine. ♦ Hello, Publius. ♦ You are well today, right? ♦ Yes, I am well. I am walking to the library. ♦ Why are you walking to the library? You aren't a librarian, are you? ♦ Yes, I am a librarian. I work in the library daily. I guard and take care of the books.*

5. *Charles, why do you have a large house? ♦ I have many sons and many daughters! ♦ You are tired, right? ♦ Yes, I am always tired.*

6. *Daughter, why are you not at home? You are sick, right? ♦ Not at all, I am not sick. I am well. I am walking to the seashore now with Cornelius's daughters. Are you angry? ♦ Not at all, I am not angry. Goodbye, daughter.*

7. *Where are we? We aren't in a boat, are we? ♦ Not at all, we are walking out of the restaurant. ♦ I am sick.*

8. *You are a teacher, right? ♦ Yes, I am a teacher. I teach students daily. I am also a librarian. ♦ Do you work in the new library? ♦ Yes, I take care of the books daily. ♦ Where is the new library? ♦ The new library is near the wall of the town, between the school and Romulus's house.*

9. *Robert, I love Tiberius. ♦ You don't love Tiberius, do you? Tiberius is a pirate! ♦ Tiberius is not a pirate! ♦ Tiberius is a pirate. Why does Tiberius have much gold and silver? ♦ I don't know. Perhaps he has much money. ♦ And why does he have a large boat? ♦ I don't know. Perhaps he builds boats. Perhaps he is a sailor. ♦ Not at all! Tiberius is a bad pirate!*

10. *Paul, why are you building a boat out of wood? ♦ I can't build a boat out of rock.*

LESSON 55

1. *Today I am teaching the students about pigs.*
2. *Librarian, this book is not about boats. ♦ I am not a librarian. You are in a cafe.*
3. *Mark is telling a story about the strong women of the homeland.*
4. *We can't have dinner now because we don't have food in the house. ♦ There is a restaurant in the town. ♦ I have money. Perhaps we can have dinner in the restaurant. You don't have money, do you? ♦ Not at all. But you have money.*
5. *You aren't mad, are you? ♦ Not at all. I am happy. ♦ Why are you happy? ♦ I am happy because James is absent. ♦ James is a bad boy!*
6. *Romulus, do you have horses? ♦ Yes, I have many horses. I have pigs, too.*
7. *This market is large! ♦ Yes. It has much food.*
8. *Claudia, where is the new cafe? ♦ The new cafe is in the town, between the large market and*

the theater. ♦ The theater is small, isn't it? ♦ Yes, the theater is small.

9. *Julius can't grocery shop now because he is sick. ♦ Julius isn't sick, is he? ♦ Yes, he is sick. ♦ I do not have food in the house. Perhaps you can grocery shop. ♦ I am a pirate. I never grocery shop.*

10. *Why do we never swim? ♦ There are many pirates among the islands. ♦ Perhaps, but today I do not see the pirates. We can swim now!*

LESSON 56

1. *Sometimes we have dinner at a restaurant.*
2. *I can't walk in the forest. ♦ Why? ♦ I fear the beasts of the forest. Perhaps we can walk around the forest. ♦ I am tired. I can't walk around the forest.*
3. *Sometimes I teach about the theater.*
4. *This library is large! ♦ Yes, this library has many books. I am the librarian. I take care of the books. ♦ Why are you a librarian? ♦ I love good books.*
5. *Tiberius, are you a farmer? ♦ Yes. ♦ Do you take care of pigs? ♦ Sometimes I take care of pigs, and sometimes I take care of horses.*
6. *The beasts are hurrying out of the forest! ♦ I fear the beasts. Goodbye!*
7. *Where is Claudia today? She isn't sick, is she? ♦ She is present. Claudia is not sick, but Tertius and Decimus are at home because they are sick.*
8. *The pirates are hurrying out of the town with much silver. ♦ There are many pirates among the towns.*
9. *We have a new library in the town! ♦ Perhaps the new library has new books. ♦ Perhaps. Where is the new library? ♦ I don't know. It is new.*
10. *Helen, why do you never grocery shop at the market? ♦ Sometimes I grocery shop at the market, but often I have dinner in cafes because I do not live near the market.*

LESSON 57

1. *This bank is small, but it has much money! ♦ And it has much silver, too! ♦ Perhaps it has gold, too!*
2. *Rufus, why are you hurrying to the bank now? ♦ I do not have money. ♦ Why do you not have money? ♦ I am a teacher. ♦ Perhaps the queen can give money to the teachers. The queen has much money.*
3. *Claudia, where is bank? ♦ The bank is in the town, between library and Mark's cafe.*
4. *Where are the sailors? ♦ They are having dinner in the restaurant. They are telling bad stories. ♦*

Why do they always tell bad stories? ♦ *Sailors always tell bad stories.*

5. *Fred, you often walk to the seashore, right?* ♦ *Yes. Sometimes I walk to the seashore. Sometimes I walk in the forest.*
6. *The pirates are building a new bank in the town.* ♦ *Why are they building a bank?* ♦ *They have much money, and they also have gold. The pirates' boats can't sail with much gold.*
7. *Charles, why are you not grocery shopping today?* ♦ *Cornelia, I can't grocery shop today. I am sick today. I am tired. Perhaps you can grocery shop today.* ♦ *You are not sick!* ♦ *You aren't angry, are you?* ♦ *I am angry because you are not sick!*
8. *Hello, girls and boys.* ♦ *Why you are present? You aren't the new teacher, are you?* ♦ *Yes, I am the new teacher.*
9. *This town is small. We don't have a library. We don't have good restaurants. We don't have a bank!* ♦ *Y'all have a market, right?* ♦ *Not at all!*
10. *Aemilia, do you have a new book?* ♦ *Yes. This book is about theaters.*

LESSON 58

1. *There are temples in the town, right?* ♦ *Yes, there is a temple in the town. It is the temple of Diana.* ♦ *Is the temple of Diana large?* ♦ *Not at all, the temple is small.*
2. *Where is the restaurant?* ♦ *In the town, near the temple of Vulcan.*
3. *Quintus, why are sailors in the temple of Neptune?* ♦ *Sailors sometimes carry gifts to the temple.* ♦ *Why do sailors carry gifts to the temple of Neptune?* ♦ *The sailors are sailing to the islands today. There are many pirates among the islands.*
4. *Why is this small temple in the forest?* ♦ *I don't know. Perhaps it is the temple of Diana.* ♦ *There are not many temples in the forest.*
5. *They are many men and many women in the temple today.* ♦ *Why?* ♦ *I don't know.* ♦ *Is it the temple of Minerva?* ♦ *Yes, this temple is the temple of Minerva.* ♦ *Now they are walking out of the temple.*
6. *Son, where is temple of Vulcan?* ♦ *I don't know. Perhaps the temple of Vulcan is near the bank.*
7. *This temple is large!* ♦ *Yes, it is the temple of Minerva!*
8. *The bank is not small, is it?* ♦ *Not at all, this bank is large because it has much silver.* ♦ *I see the silver.* ♦ *I see gold also.*
9. *Aurelia, where are we having dinner today?* ♦ *I am tired. Perhaps we can have dinner in the new restaurant.* ♦ *Where is this new restaurant?* ♦ *The new restaurant is near temple of*

Neptune, between the market and the bank.

10. *Lucretia is walking to the market now, right?* ♦ *Yes, Lucretia is grocery shopping now. She is walking to the market and to the library also.* ♦ *Does Lucretia have a book?* ♦ *Yes, she has a book about horses, but today Lucretia is carrying the book to the library.*

LESSON 59

1. *We are in front of the cafe. Where are you?* ♦ *I am behind the cafe.*
2. *The students are in front of the school, but where is Publius? Publius and Claudia are absent.* ♦ *I don't know. Perhaps they are in the library. Publius and Claudia love books.* ♦ *The library is behind the school, right?* ♦ *Yes, the library is behind the school.*
3. *Cornelia, why are sailors in front of temple of Neptune?* ♦ *I don't know. Perhaps they are carrying gifts to the temple.*
4. *Mark's horse is in front of the restaurant. Perhaps Mark is in the restaurant.* ♦ *Yes, Mark is having dinner in the restaurant now.*
5. *The inhabitants of the town are building a large temple.* ♦ *They aren't building the temple out of wood, are they?* ♦ *Not at all, they are building the temple out of gold!* ♦ *The inhabitants of the town have much gold!*
6. *Son, where is the horse? It is not in the stable. The horse is absent.* ♦ *Perhaps the horse is behind the house.* ♦ *Not at all, son. The horse is not behind the house.* ♦ *Perhaps the horse is carrying money to the bank.* ♦ *Not at all! Horses don't have money!* ♦ *Perhaps the horse is in the temple of Neptune.* ♦ *Now I am angry!*
7. *Why are the teachers tired?* ♦ *The teachers are tired today because the students are bad.*
8. *Portia sometimes walks into the library without books and hurries out of the library with many books. Portia loves books!* ♦ *Portia is a good student. Now Portia has a book about the queens of the homeland.*
9. *This student isn't sick, is he?* ♦ *Not at all, this student is well. He can stay at school.*
10. *The sailors do not have food. Perhaps you and I can carry food to the sailors.* ♦ *Yes, but we do not have food!* ♦ *Perhaps we can walk to the market now.*

LESSON 60

1. *Why are we walking through the town? We aren't walking to the new library, are we?* ♦ *Yes, we are walking to the new library now.* ♦ *Why?* ♦ *Helen is the librarian.* ♦ *You don't love Helen, do you?* ♦ *Perhaps.*

2. *Boys, why are y'all walking through the forest? This forest has many beasts!* ♦ *We do not fear the beasts!* ♦ *But the beasts of the forest are large! Perhaps y'all can walk around the forest.*

3. *Julia, why are you hurrying through the fields? ♦ I am hurrying to school. ♦ You are a good student! Goodbye!*

4. *This woman is a pirate!* ♦ *Not at all, this woman is not a pirate. ♦ Why does she have a book about pirates? ♦ She has a book about pirates because she is a librarian. This woman is not a pirate.*

5. *I am walking through the school, but I do not see students. Where are the students? The students aren't sick today, are they? ♦ Not at all. The students are in the library.*

6. *Tullia, why are you a librarian? ♦ I am a librarian because I love books. ♦ I also love books. Today I have a new book. ♦ Is it a good book? ♦ Yes, this book is good.*

7. *This horse does not have water. Why? ♦ Rufus is a bad boy. He never takes care of the horse. ♦ Where is Rufus now? ♦ I don't know.*

8. *Quintus, why are you carrying large books today? You aren't walking to the library, are you? ♦ Not at all, I am walking to school now. Today I am carrying many books.*

9. *Tiberius, why are you not taking care of the pigs now? ♦ I am sick today. I can't take care of the pigs and horses today. ♦ Son, I can take care of the pigs and horses today because you are sick. You can stay in the house.*

10. *This town is small. ♦ Yes, it does not have temples, and it does not have cafes, and it does not have restaurants. ♦ But it has a library.*

LESSON 61

1. *This town has large gates!* ♦ *The town has large gates because the wall around the town is large. This wall guards the town. Pirates can't destroy the town because the town has a large wall.*

2. *I am angry because I can't walk through the gate!* ♦ *Why can't you walk through the gate? ♦ I am carrying many books.*

3. *A poet is near the gate of the town today. ♦ Why is the poet present? ♦ Today he is telling stories to the girls and boys. ♦ Is he telling good stories? ♦ Yes. Now he is telling a story about Neptune. ♦ Goodbye! I am hurrying to the gate now!*

4. *Fausta, this town has a small gate. Why does it have a small gate? ♦ We have a small gate because we have a small wall. We can't build a large wall out of wood because we do not have much wood. ♦ But this town is near the forest. Perhaps the inhabitants of the town can carry wood out of the forest. ♦ We fear the forest*

because many beasts live in the forest.

5. *The boys and girls are walking into the forest now. ♦ Why? ♦ They are walking through the forest to the seashore. ♦ Why aren't the boys and girls walking around the forest? ♦ Perhaps they do not fear the beasts of the forest.*

6. *Son, why do we have dinner at home daily? There is a new restaurant in the town. ♦ Where is this restaurant? ♦ The restaurant is in the town, near the bank. Perhaps it has good food. ♦ Is the new restaurant near the temple of Vulcan? ♦ Not at all. The restaurant is behind temple of Diana, between the bank and library.*

7. *Christopher, why are you hurrying out of the cafe? ♦ I am sick. This food is bad! ♦ I am also sick! This cafe is bad!*

8. *Claudius, why do pirates never sail to the homeland? ♦ Strong sailors always guard the seashore in boats. ♦ Are you guarding the homeland? You aren't a sailor, are you? ♦ Yes, I am a sailor. I guard the seashore in a large boat. Pirates never sail to the homeland because strong men and strong women guard the homeland. ♦ Perhaps I also can guard the seashore in a boat. ♦ Do you have a boat? ♦ Not at all. I am a librarian.*

9. *The inhabitants of the town are building a new temple out of rock.*

10. *James, why are you in front of the temple of Neptune? ♦ I am a sailor. Sometimes I carry gifts to the temple. Today I am sailing through the islands of the pirates. ♦ There are many pirates among the islands! ♦ I fear the pirates!*

LESSON 62

1. *That boy is Mark's son. This boy is Quintus's son.*

2. *That boat is large, but this boat is small.*

3. *That town has a large library, but this town does not have a library.*

4. *That book is new, right? ♦ Yes, this book is new.*

5. *That woman is Helen. Helen is a farmer. She takes care of the pigs and horses daily and plows the soil.*

6. *You're not a librarian, are you? ♦ Not at all, I am a farmer. I take care of the fields daily. ♦ Do you have horses? ♦ Yes, I have a small horse.*

7. *Cornelia, I can't teach the students today. ♦ Why can't you teach? You are a teacher! ♦ I am sick today. I am tired. ♦ Perhaps you can stay at home. I can teach the students! Goodbye! ♦ Goodbye, Cornelia.*

8. *Sometimes I walk to the bank. ♦ Why? You don't have money. ♦ I have money! I work daily in Mark's cafe. ♦ You work? ♦ Yes. ♦ Where is Mark's cafe? ♦ It is behind the temple of Vulcan.*

It is a new cafe. ♦ *Perhaps today I can have dinner in the cafe.*

9. *Pirates can't walk through the gates of the town.* ♦ *Why?* ♦ *We are guarding the gates with swords.* ♦ *But the pirates also have swords.* ♦ *Perhaps I can stay at home today.*

10. *Librarian, do you have book about money?* ♦ *Yes. You are present in a library. We have many books about money. You don't have money, do you?* ♦ *Not at all.*

LESSON 63

1. *That gate is wide.* ♦ *It is wide, but this gate is narrow, and I can't walk through the gate with a horse.*

2. *Julia, where is the new cafe?* ♦ *It is between the temple of Vulcan and the market.* ♦ *Perhaps we can have dinner today in the new cafe.* ♦ *Perhaps, but we do not have money.* ♦ *We do not have food at home.*

3. *I can't walk through the narrow gate because I am carrying much wood.* ♦ *Aemilia, why are you carrying much wood today? You aren't building a boat, are you?* ♦ *Yes, today I am building a small boat out of wood.* ♦ *Why are you building a boat? You are not a sailor.* ♦ *Yes, I am not a sailor, but perhaps now I can sail.*

4. *That girl is a good student.* ♦ *Why is she a good student?* ♦ *She is always present, and never fights with boys.* ♦ *She is Cornelius's daughter, right?* ♦ *Yes, she is Cornelius's daughter. They live in a large house near the temple of Neptune.* ♦ *The temple of Neptune is near the bank.*

5. *Where are you? I am in front of the restaurant.* ♦ *I am in front of the temple of Minerva.* ♦ *Perhaps you can stay in front of the temple. I am hurrying to the temple now. Goodbye.* ♦ *Goodbye.*

6. *Decimus, you aren't grocery shopping today, are you?* ♦ *Not at all, today I am not grocery shopping. I am tired, and we have much food at home.*

7. *I love Christopher.* ♦ *Why do you love Christopher? Christopher is a poet. He does not have much money.* ♦ *I love Christopher because he is a good poet. Sometimes he tells stories to the inhabitants of the town at the theater.* ♦ *But he does not have much money.*

8. *I can't see the temple.* ♦ *Why?* ♦ *There is a large wall in front of the temple.* ♦ *We can walk behind the wall.* ♦ *Now I can see the temple.*

9. *You aren't angry, are you?* ♦ *Yes! I am angry!* ♦ *Why?* ♦ *I am angry because you are having dinner at a restaurant today, but I always have dinner at home.* ♦ *Perhaps you also can have*

dinner at the restaurant.

10. *That temple is wide.*

LESSON 64

1. *This road is narrow, but that road is wide.*

2. *There is a narrow road in the forest.* ♦ *I can't walk through the forest.* ♦ *You don't fear the beasts, do you?* ♦ *They are many pigs in the forest. I can't walk through the forest because I fear the pigs.* ♦ *There are not pigs in the forest! Perhaps beasts are present, but pigs are not present in the forest!*

3. *Queen, why are you building a new road?* ♦ *I am building a new road because we do not have a road between the town and the seashore. Sailors and farmers can't walk from the town to the seashore.* ♦ *And pirates can't walk from the seashore to the town!*

4. *That man is Mark. Mark is Peter's son.* ♦ *Why is Mark present today in front of the temple of Vulcan?* ♦ *This temple is not the temple of Vulcan. This temple is the temple of Neptune.* ♦ *Why is Mark present today in front of the temple of Neptune?* ♦ *Mark is a sailor. He often carries gifts to the temple of Neptune.*

5. *We are building a wall around the town, and we are building a gate also.* ♦ *We can't build a wall!* ♦ *Why?* ♦ *We do not have wood. We do not have rocks. We do not have money.* ♦ *Why are you angry?*

6. *Decimus, why are you hurrying to the market?* ♦ *I am grocery shopping now. We do not have food at home.*

7. *Teacher, where do beasts live?* ♦ *I don't know. Perhaps they live in the forest.* ♦ *I never see beasts in the forest.* ♦ *I never walk through the forest.* ♦ *Why don't you walk through the forest, teacher?* ♦ *I fear the beasts. I always walk around the forest. I don't walk through the forest.*

8. *Why is this road narrow?* ♦ *This road is not wide because a large library is behind the temple. This road is between the library and the temple.*

9. *Poet, why are you present in front of theater?* ♦ *Today I am telling stories at the theater.*

10. *Sometimes I walk to the library.* ♦ *Why? Do you walk to the library because you love books?* ♦ *Not at all. Lucretia is the librarian. I love Lucretia.*

LESSON 65

1. *That road is long and wide. It is a good road.* ♦ *We have many good roads in the homeland.* ♦ *Why are the roads good?* ♦ *We have a good queen. She always takes care of the roads.*

2. *Rufus, why do you not have money? And where is the boat? ♦ It's a long story. ♦ It's not a bad story, is it? ♦ Yes, it is a bad story. The story is about pirates, about swords, and about a small island.*

3. *There is a long road between the town and the seashore. ♦ Perhaps today we can walk to the seashore. We never walk to the seashore.*

4. *That temple is the temple of Minerva. ♦ Perhaps we can walk to the temple. ♦ Perhaps, but the road is narrow, and many men are present.*

5. *There is a new restaurant in the town. Perhaps we can have dinner at the restaurant today. ♦ Where is the new restaurant? ♦ It is near the gate of the town, between the temple of Neptune and the large market.*

6. *This story is long. Why are you telling a long story, William? ♦ I always tell long stories.*

7. *Quintus, you are a teacher, right? ♦ Not at all, I never teach students. Now I am a farmer. ♦ Do you have pigs? ♦ Yes, I have pigs and horses.*

8. *Tullia, why are you angry? Why are you tired? Why are you not teaching students? ♦ It's a long story. It's a story about bad students.*

9. *Many pirates are hurrying through the gates! ♦ We can't guard the town! ♦ Where are the shields and swords? ♦ We can't fight with pirates. ♦ Why can't we fight? ♦ We are librarians. ♦ But we are strong librarians, and we have swords.*

10. *Romulus, why are you present in front of the gate of the town with a horse? ♦ I can't walk through the gate. ♦ Why? ♦ The gate is narrow, but this horse is wide.*

LESSON 66

1. *Sailor, where is temple of Neptune? ♦ The temple of Neptune is on the other side of the road, near the gates of the town. ♦ It is near the large library, right? ♦ Yes, it is near the library. ♦ Goodbye.*

2. *Sailor, why are you walking across the island? ♦ I don't have a boat. I can't sail around the island. ♦ Much wood is present because this island has many forests. Perhaps you can build a new boat out of wood. ♦ This island does not have good wood. I can't build a boat.*

3. *Lucretia, where is Julia's house? ♦ It is on the other side of the road. ♦ Does Julia live in a house near the bank? ♦ Yes, Julia's house is near the bank, between the temple of Minerva and the large cafe.*

4. *That woman is strong! ♦ Yes. That woman is Sempronia. She is a farmer. ♦ She can carry water across the wide field! And she can carry much wood, too!*

5. *Sailor, is there a town on the island? ♦ Yes, this island has a large town and small town. ♦ Where is the small town? ♦ It is on the other side of the island. ♦ Perhaps I can sail around the island.*

6. *Romulus, why are you walking through the homeland? You can't walk across the homeland because the roads in the homeland are bad and narrow. ♦ Why are the roads bad? ♦ The roads are bad because the inhabitants of the homeland never take care of the roads. There are many rocks on the roads. The rocks are large and you can't walk around the rocks.*

7. *Hello, librarian. Does this library have a book about horses? ♦ Yes, we have many books about horses. ♦ Do you have books about pigs? ♦ I am a librarian. I am not a farmer.*

8. *You don't love Catherine, do you Quintus? ♦ Yes, I love Catherine. ♦ Quintus, why do you love Catherine? ♦ Catherine is a librarian. I love books. I love libraries. I love librarians. ♦ Perhaps you can carry a gift to the library. You have money, right? ♦ Not at all. I am a farmer. I have pigs. ♦ Perhaps you can give a pig to Catherine. ♦ A pig is not a good gift.*

9. *I am tired. This road is long. Where is the town? ♦ I see the gates of the town now.*

10. *Why are the teachers and students in front of theater? ♦ The students and teachers are walking out of the school to the theater because a poet is telling stories today at the theater.*

LESSON 67

1. *Mark, why are the teachers demanding money? ♦ They work at the school daily. They teach the students daily and never stay at home because they are sick. ♦ Perhaps the inhabitants of the town can give money to the teachers. ♦ Perhaps.*

2. *Queen, the men and women of the island are demanding food. ♦ They have food, right? ♦ Not at all, they don't have food. ♦ Perhaps they can have dinner in restaurants.*

3. *Son, why are you demanding money? ♦ I do not have money. I can never eat at the restaurant with Aurelia and Paul. ♦ Perhaps you can work. You never have money because you never work.*

4. *The girls are demanding food! Do we have food? ♦ Not at all, we do not have food. ♦ The girls are angry! ♦ Perhaps today we can grocery shop.*

5. *Teacher, do you have a book about the queens of the homeland? ♦ I don't have a book about the queens of the homeland, but at the library there are many books about queens. ♦ Perhaps today you can tell a story about the queen of the homeland to the students. ♦ Yes, I have many stories about the queen.*

271

6. *Fausta, why are you hurrying through the town? ♦ I am hurrying to the bank because I don't have money. I am hurrying to the market also because I don't have food. I can't grocery shop without money. ♦ Where is the bank? ♦ There is a small bank near temple of Vulcan, behind the library. Goodbye!*
7. *Tiberius, where is the pirates' house? ♦ That house is on the other side of the forest, near the seashore. ♦ Perhaps we can walk to the pirates' house. ♦ Not at all! The pirates are bad! ♦ We can't have dinner with the pirates, can we? ♦ Not at all!*
8. *The inhabitants of the town are demanding new books, but this town does not have a library. ♦ Perhaps we can build a large library!*
9. *Julia, why are you present in front of gates of the town? ♦ I am guarding the town. ♦ But you don't have a sword. ♦ I can guard the town without a sword.*
10. *Sometimes I walk to the seashore. ♦ Why? The road between the town and the seashore is long and narrow. ♦ I love the seashore.*

LESSON 68

1. *My restaurant is small, but we have good food. ♦ Perhaps I can have dinner today in the restaurant. ♦ Certainly! My restaurant is between the market and the temple of Minerva.*
2. *My son, why doesn't the horse have food? The horse is angry! ♦ I don't know. I am not farmer. ♦ We are farmers! ♦ You are a farmer, but I am not a farmer. ♦ Now I also am angry!*
3. *My queen, we have gifts. ♦ I love gifts! ♦ We have gold, and we have silver, too. ♦ I love gold! I am happy! ♦ I am not happy, because now I don't have my gold.*
4. *Why are you building a new house, Romulus? ♦ My house is not strong. I am building my new house out of rock. I am building a new wall, too. ♦ Why are you building a wall, Romulus? ♦ I am building a wall around my house because I fear the inhabitants of the town. I am building a wall with large gates.*
5. *Teacher, the students are angry, and they are demanding new books. ♦ We do not have money. We can't give new books to the students. Perhaps we can walk with the students across the road to the library. ♦ Perhaps. That library has many books.*
6. *I am well today. Perhaps I can swim to the small island today. ♦ You can't swim near the island. ♦ Why? ♦ That small island has many pirates. ♦ Not at all, pirates do not live on the island. ♦ The inhabitants of the island are pirates. I see the pirates' large boats daily. ♦ I do not fear pirates.*

7. *Sempronia, why are you present in front of the temple of Minerva? ♦ Sometimes I walk to the temple with my sons. Now we are hurrying to the restaurant because my sons are demanding food.*
8. *This road is long. Why are we walking through the wide forest? ♦ The town is on the other side of the forest. ♦ Why are we walking to the town? ♦ My daughter lives in the town. ♦ Why does she live in the town? ♦ She lives in the town because it has a large library. My daughter loves books.*
9. *The boys are demanding gifts. ♦ Why? ♦ I don't know. We give gifts to the boys often, but today they are demanding gifts. ♦ Now they are demanding money. ♦ I do not have money. ♦ Now they are demanding food.*
10. *James, why are you hurrying across the narrow road? ♦ I am walking to the library.*

LESSON 69

1. *Hello, friend! ♦ Hello, friends!*
2. *Hello, friend! ♦ We are not friends! ♦ You aren't angry, are you? ♦ Yes, I am angry! ♦ Why? ♦ I am angry because you have my money!*
3. *Where are my friends? ♦ They are on the other side of the road, in front of the market. ♦ Why are they in front of the market? ♦ Perhaps they are grocery shopping now. ♦ I can't grocery shop because I don't have money.*
4. *This man is Mark. Mark is my friend. This woman is Fausta. Fausta also is my friend.*
5. *Mark, you don't live in the town, do you? ♦ Not at all. I live on the island, but I often sail to the town. ♦ Do you have a boat? ♦ Not at all. This boat is my friends' boat.*
6. *Lavinia, do you have friends? ♦ I have many friends. ♦ Where are your friends? ♦ My friends are at the theater, but I am at home.*
7. *Friend, why are you hurrying from the seashore? ♦ Pirates are sailing now to the seashore. They are demanding my money!*
8. *Rufus, why are you fighting with Peter? ♦ I am angry because that boy has my money! ♦ Peter, you don't have Rufus's money, do you?*
9. *Friend, do you have money? ♦ I always carry money. I never walk to the town without my money. ♦ Why do you always carry money, friend? ♦ I often grocery shop in the town, and I can't grocery shop without money. Without food, my family can't have dinner. I have many daughters and many sons.*
10. *I demand new roads! ♦ Queen, why are you demanding new roads? ♦ My homeland does not have good roads. The roads in my homeland are narrow, and they have many rocks. The inhabitants of the homeland can't*

walk across the homeland because the roads are bad. ♦ Queen, perhaps we can build wide roads.

LESSON 70

1. *You don't have rocks in your boat, do you? ♦ Yes, I have rocks in my boat. ♦ Why? ♦ I am building a new house on the island. ♦ You can't sail to the island with rocks! ♦ But I carry rocks daily from the homeland to the island. ♦ Perhaps you can build the new house out of wood. That island has many forests.*

2. *Aurelia, why are you counting your money now? ♦ I am walking to the bank. ♦ There is a bank in the town, right? ♦ Yes. There is a small bank between the library and the temple of Diana. ♦ You have much money! ♦ Yes. I have much money because I work daily at the market. ♦ I also work daily, but I do not have much money. ♦ Why? ♦ I am a teacher.*

3. *Lucius, why are you hurrying through the town with many gifts? ♦ I am hurrying to the queen! The queen loves gifts.*

4. *That bad boy is demanding your money! Why? ♦ That boy is demanding my money because he is my son.*

5. *Christopher, why aren't you having dinner at the cafe with your friends? ♦ I am tired today. ♦ Why are you tired? ♦ I am sick.*

6. *That temple is large! ♦ That temple is the temple of Neptune. Sometimes I walk to the temple. ♦ Why do you sometimes walk to the temple? ♦ I am a sailor.*

7. *Farmer, where is your house? ♦ It is on the other side of the large field, near the forest. ♦ My house is near your house. I live in a small house in the forest.*

8. *This road is long and narrow. Tullia, why are we walking on a long road? I am tired. ♦ We are walking to my town. ♦ Why? ♦ In my town is a large theater. A library also is in my town. ♦ There is a restaurant in your town, right? ♦ Yes, we have a good restaurant. ♦ Perhaps we can have dinner at the restaurant.*

9. *Friend, why are you present in front of the bank? ♦ This bank has much silver. ♦ You are a pirate!*

10. *William isn't telling a long story, is he? ♦ Yes. He is telling a long story. ♦ William, why do you always tell long stories?*

LESSON 71

1. *My queen, your kingdom is wide and long. ♦ Not at all, my kingdom is a small island! ♦ It is not a small island. This island is large! ♦ This island is small! You can see, right? ♦ Why are*

you angry? ♦ I am angry because my kingdom is small! ♦ Perhaps we can conquer a large island.

2. *Hello, queen. We are poets. We are walking across your kingdom. ♦ Do y'all have food? ♦ Certainly. We have food, but we do not have money. ♦ I don't have money. Perhaps you can walk to the bank. ♦ You are the queen, but you don't have money? ♦ My kingdom is small.*

3. *In my kingdom there are many towns and many roads. But I am not happy because I do not have a library in my kingdom. ♦ Queen, I am a librarian. Perhaps we can build a new library in your kingdom.*

4. *The inhabitants of my kingdom are demanding new roads. ♦ Perhaps we can build new roads out of rocks. ♦ There are many rocks in my kingdom.*

5. *This queen is good. ♦ Why is she good? ♦ She is good because she takes care of the temples, and she always takes care of the roads also.*

6. *Students, why are y'all carrying rocks? Why are y'all working? ♦ We are building a new road out of rocks. ♦ Where is the new road? ♦ It is between the town and the school. This road is narrow, but good. Now we can walk from the town to the school.*

7. *My friend, why are you at home? ♦ I am staying at home today because I am sick. ♦ You can't stay at home! ♦ You aren't angry, are you? Why can't I stay at home? ♦ The queen is demanding much food! ♦ Perhaps you can grocery shop.*

8. *I am building a new shield out of silver and gold. ♦ This shield is good! ♦ Yes, my shields are good and large. ♦ Why are you building large shields? ♦ I give large shields to the inhabitants of the kingdom. Without shields we can't guard the towns of the kingdom. ♦ Perhaps we can build a wall also. ♦ This kingdom is large. We can't build a wall around the kingdom.*

9. *That cafe is bad. It has bad food. ♦ But this restaurant has good food.*

10. *That woman is my friend. Hello, friend! Are you well today? ♦ Yes, I am well today. ♦ Why are you present in front of the bank? ♦ Today I am carrying my money to the bank.*

LESSON 72

1. *That castle is large, but this castle is small.*

2. *Friend, where does the queen live? ♦ The queen lives in a small castle. ♦ Why does she live in a small castle? She has a large castle, right? ♦ Not at all. This kingdom is small. We do not have much money.*

3. *Charles, where is my horse? ♦ Your horse is behind the castle. ♦ Why is my horse behind the castle? ♦ The stables are behind the castle. Your*

horse is in the stable.

4. *Where are your friends?* ♦ *They are having dinner at the new restaurant near the temple of Minerva.* ♦ *That restaurant is good, and it has good food. Why aren't you having dinner with your friends?* ♦ *I do not have money.*
5. *Why is this horse in front of the temple of Diana?* ♦ *I don't know. It is not Lucretia's horse, is it?* ♦ *It is Lucretia's horse. Perhaps Lucretia is in the temple.*
6. *Hello, Mark. Why are you present in front of the gate of the castle?* ♦ *I am guarding the castle.* ♦ *Why are you guarding the castle? The queen is absent today.* ♦ *The queen's daughters are in the castle. I am guarding the queen's family.*
7. *Librarian, do you have a book about horses? My son is demanding a horse.* ♦ *Certainly, this library has many books about horses. This book is about horses.* ♦ *You are a good librarian! Goodbye!*
8. *This road is long and narrow. I am tired. We don't have food. We don't have water.* ♦ *You aren't angry, are you?*
9. *Portia, why are you sailing to your homeland?* ♦ *My sons live in the homeland.*
10. *Why are you demanding money?* ♦ *We are teachers.*

LESSON 73

1. *We can't sail to the island on account of pirates.*
2. *I fear the forest.* ♦ *Why do you fear the forest?* ♦ *I never walk through the forest on account of the beasts. There are large pigs in the forest.* ♦ *Pigs? There aren't pigs in the forest!* ♦ *Sometimes I see small pigs in the forest.*
3. *That wood is bad. On account of bad wood, we can't build a new boat.* ♦ *Perhaps we can carry good wood from the forest.* ♦ *That forest is in the kingdom of the pirates.* ♦ *Perhaps, but we can't build a new boat without good wood.*
4. *Claudia loves Matthew, but Matthew loves Flavia.* ♦ *Why does Matthew love Flavia?* ♦ *Flavia has a restaurant. Matthew loves good food.*
5. *Pirates can't conquer my island.* ♦ *Why?* ♦ *I and my friends always guard the island.*
6. *Where are your friends having dinner today?* ♦ *I don't know. Sometimes they have dinner at the restaurant.* ♦ *They don't have dinner in the cafe, do they?* ♦ *Not at all. They never have dinner in the cafe because sailors are always telling bad stories in the cafe.*
7. *Rufus is telling a story now about pirates to the girls.* ♦ *My daughters love stories.*
8. *Queen, you can't build a large castle in the town.* ♦ *Why? I am the queen!* ♦ *This town is*

small!

9. *The men are walking across the road.*
10. *The men are on the other side of the road.*

LESSON 74

1. *That wolf is large!* ♦ *I fear the wolves!* ♦ *I also fear wolves!* ♦ *Perhaps now we can hurry out of the forest into the town.*
2. *Teacher, are there beasts in the forest?* ♦ *Yes, they are many wolves in the forest. I never walk into the forest on account of the wolves.*
3. *That the temple is small.*
4. *I am a queen, but my kingdom is small. This kingdom does not have a bank. You also are a queen, and you have a kingdom. Your kingdom has a bank, right?* ♦ *Yes, my kingdom has a large bank, large temples, and good restaurants.* ♦ *Why does your kingdom have a bank and temples?* ♦ *My kingdom is long and wide. Many inhabitants live in my kingdom. There is silver in my kingdom, and gold also is present.* ♦ *You don't have a library, do you?* ♦ *Yes, there is a large library in my kingdom, with many librarians and books.*
5. *Tiberius is telling a story to the boys and girls.* ♦ *Is it a good story?* ♦ *Yes. It is a story about a large wolf.* ♦ *Is that story about little pigs, too?* ♦ *Yes. Small pigs live in a small house, but the pigs do not fear the bad wolf because they live in a strong house.*
6. *I am walking across the road to the bank.* ♦ *Friend, why are you walking to the bank?* ♦ *I do not have money.*
7. *Poet, the girls and boys are demanding a story. Perhaps you can tell a story.* ♦ *Perhaps I can tell a story about pirates.* ♦ *Not at all. That story is bad.* ♦ *I can tell a story about little pigs and a bad wolf.* ♦ *That story is good!*
8. *Friends, why are y'all in front of castle?* ♦ *We are carrying gifts to the queen. The queen is in the castle, right?* ♦ *Not at all. The queen is absent today.*
9. *Aemilia, where is my pig?* ♦ *I don't know. Is the pig behind the house?* ♦ *Not at all. There is a large wolf behind the house, but the pig is absent.*
10. *Romulus, why are you tired? Why are you staying at home?* ♦ *It's a long story.*

LESSON 75

1. *Many pirates live in your neighborhood.* ♦ *Yes. This neighborhood is a bad neighborhood.*
2. *We are walking through your neighborhood to Cornelius's house.*
3. *Why are y'all building a large wall around your neighborhood out of wood?* ♦ *We are not*

274

building a wall out of wood. We are building a wall out of rock. ♦ Why are y'all building a wall out of rock? ♦ Rocks are strong. There is a forest near the town, and many wolves live in the forest. We are building a wall because the wolves don't stay in the forest.

4. *That cafe is bad. Why do you have dinner in the bad cafe with your friends, my son? I can't have dinner in the bad cafe on account of the bad food. ♦ That cafe is not bad. My friends sometimes have dinner in the cafe. ♦ Your friends are bad boys.*

5. *You are happy, right? ♦ Not at all. I am not happy. ♦ Why aren't you happy? ♦ I love the queen's daughter, but I am a farmer, and I am the son of a farmer. The queen's daughter can't love a farmer's son. ♦ Why? ♦ I take care of pigs daily!*

6. *Robert, where is the temple of Minerva? ♦ It is on the other side of the road.*

7. *Inhabitant, where is the town? ♦ The town is on the other side of the forest.*

8. *The poets are demanding money! ♦ Why? ♦ They are telling good stories. ♦ Perhaps we can give money to the poets. Do you have money? ♦ Not at all. I am a teacher.*

9. *That castle is on the other side of the kingdom.*

10. *We are walking across the kingdom.*

LESSON 76

1. *We love our queen. ♦ Why? ♦ Our queen is a good woman. She always takes care of the roads, and often gives money to the farmers.*

2. *We don't have bad students, do we? ♦ Yes. Our students are bad. They are never present at the school, and they always fight.*

3. *Julia, where are our sons? ♦ They are having dinner at the cafe. ♦ Why are they having dinner with sailors and pirates? That cafe is bad.*

4. *Where is our money? Our money is in the bank, right? ♦ Not at all. Our money is at home.*

5. *We can't sail to our kingdom. ♦ Why? ♦ There are many pirates among the islands. On account of pirates, we can't sail through the islands. ♦ I do not fear pirates.*

6. *Hello, my pigs. Are y'all well today? Y'all have water, right? ♦ Not at all! We do not have water! ♦ Why don't y'all have water? ♦ You are a bad farmer. Perhaps the library has a book about good farmers.*

7. *Our neighborhood is bad. Why do we live in a bad neighborhood? ♦ We are pirates, and our friends are also pirates. Our neighborhood is bad on account of pirates.*

8. *Perhaps we can walk to the theater today. ♦*

Perhaps. ♦ Today a poet is at the theater. He is telling stories to the inhabitants of our town. ♦ Are our friends at the theater? ♦ Yes.

9. *This stable is narrow. Why do I live in a narrow stable, but you live in a house? ♦ I live in the house because I am a farmer. You live in the stable because you are a horse.*

10. *That wolf is large. This wolf is small.*

LESSON 77

1. *Y'all's queen is bad, but our queen is good and great. ♦ Why is y'all's queen good and great? ♦ Our queen always gives food to the boys and girls of the town. She always guards our kingdom, and she always takes care of the roads. ♦ Y'all's queen is good!*

2. *Our cafe has good food. ♦ Not at all, y'all's food is bad. I can't have dinner in y'all's cafe on account of the bad food.*

3. *We have a temple of Diana in our town, and we also have a temple of Vulcan. Do y'all have a temple in y'all's town? ♦ Not at all. Our town is small. We don't have temples, but we have a theater and good restaurants.*

4. *Hello, friend. We are walking across your kingdom. Where is the queen's castle? ♦ The castle is on the other side of the large forest. ♦ We can't walk through the large forest. Perhaps we can walk around the forest. ♦ The road around the forest is long and narrow, but the road through the forest is wide, and is not long. ♦ There are wolves in the forest. We can't walk through the forest on account of the wolves.*

5. *There is a large bank in our town. ♦ Does the bank have gold and silver? ♦ Yes. Pirates often hurry into the bank with much gold. ♦ It isn't a bank of pirates, is it? ♦ Yes, is a bank of pirates!*

6. *Sailor, why do you sometimes tell your bad stories to the boys? ♦ The boys often demand my stories. I don't tell bad stories. Sometimes I tell stories about islands. Sometimes I tell stories about pirates. My stories are good!*

7. *Our neighborhood is small. Why is there water around our neighborhood? ♦ We live on a small island.*

8. *Titus, why are you a librarian? ♦ I am a librarian because I love good books. ♦ Are there good books in your library? ♦ In our library we have good books and bad books.*

9. *You can't stay at home today. ♦ Why? My school is bad, and the students are bad. ♦ You are a teacher!*

10. *Why do many wolves live in y'all's neighborhood? ♦ We live in the forest.*

LESSON 78

1. *Our farm is large. We have many horses.* ♦ *Y'all have pigs, right?* ♦ *Yes, they are many pigs on our farm.* ♦ *Do y'all have horses?* ♦ *Yes. We have many stables.* ♦ *Y'all's farm is large!*

2. *Farmer, where is your farm?* ♦ *My farm is between the town and the seashore.* ♦ *Is it a large farm?* ♦ *My farm is long and narrow.*

3. *Aurelia, are you a librarian?* ♦ *Not at all, I am not a librarian. I am a farmer. I do not take care of books. I take care of pigs.*

4. *Farmer, where are your pigs?* ♦ *They are behind the house.* ♦ *I see a wolf. Why is a wolf near your pigs?* ♦ *A wolf isn't present, is it?* ♦ *Now the wolf is carrying a pig into the forest.*

5. *Friend, where is Helen's restaurant?* ♦ *It is on the other side of the road.* ♦ *I can't see the restaurant because the temple of Diana is in front of restaurant.* ♦ *Yes, Helen's restaurant is behind the temple.*

6. *Claudius, why do you always give money to our friends?* ♦ *Our friends do not have money.* ♦ *They don't have money because they never work!*

7. *Friend, why do you always walk around my neighborhood? Why don't you walk through my neighborhood?* ♦ *You live in a bad neighborhood.* ♦ *This neighborhood is not bad. We have many good restaurants in our neighborhood.*

8. *My queen, why are you demanding a large castle?* ♦ *I am the queen, but I live in a small castle.* ♦ *But your castle is good.* ♦ *It is small! Queens always live in large castles!* ♦ *Queens sometimes live in small castles.*

9. *Librarian, do you have a book about castles?* ♦ *You are present in a library. We have many books about castles.* ♦ *Our queen is demanding a new castle.*

10. *This kingdom has bad roads. I can't walk on bad roads!* ♦ *We can't walk across the kingdom on account of the bad roads.* ♦ *There are many rocks in the roads!*

LESSON 81

1. ❶ **suum** ❷ accusative, singular, masculine ❸ it agrees with **equum** ❹ *The woman has her horse.* ❺ at **fēmina** ❻ the subject

2. ❶ **suōs** ❷ accusative, plural, masculine ❸ because it agrees with **agrōs** ❹ *The man never plows his fields.* ❺ at **vir** ❻ the subject

3. ❶ **suum** ❷ accusative, singular, neuter ❸ because it agrees with **castellum** ❹ *The queen is building her castle.* ❺ at **rēgīna** ❻ the subject

4. ❶ **suōs** ❷ accusative, plural, masculine ❸ because it agrees with **librōs** ❸ *The good students always takes care of their books.* ❹ at **discipulae** ❺ the subject

5. ❶ **suum** ❷ accusative, singular, neuter ❸ because it agrees with **scūtum** ❹ *Romulus is taking care of his shield.* ❺ at **Rōmulus** ❻ the subject

6. ❶ **suum** ❷ accusative, singular, neuter ❸ because it agrees with **scūtum** ❹ *The queen has her shield, right?* ❺ at **rēgīna** ❻ the subject

7. ❶ **suōs** ❷ accusative, plural, masculine ❸ because it agrees with **librōs** ❹ *The librarian is taking care of his books.* ❺ at **bibliothēcārius** ❻ the subject

8. ❶ **suō** ❷ ablative, singular, neuter ❸ because it agrees with **rēgnō** ❹ *The queen always takes care of the roads in her kingdom.* ❺ at **rēgīna** ❻ the subject

9. ❶ **suōs** ❷ accusative, plural, masculine ❸ because it agrees with **discipulōs** ❹ *The teacher never teaches his students.* ❺ at **magister** ❻ the subject

10. ❶ **suum** ❷ accusative, singular, neuter ❸ because it agrees with **argentum** ❹ *The inhabitants don't have their silver.* ❺ at **incolae** ❻ the subject

LESSON 83

1. *This house is small, but it has a large kitchen.* ♦ *Our family can have dinner in the kitchen.*

2. *Where is Tertius?* ♦ *Tertius is having dinner in the kitchen.*

3. *My queen, your castle has many kitchens. Why are you demanding a new castle?* ♦ *My kitchens are small.*

4. *Is Joseph grocery shopping now?* ♦ *Yes, Joseph is hurrying to the market now.* ♦ *Where is the market?* ♦ *The market is between the temple of Minerva and the large library.*

5. *We live in a good neighborhood.* ♦ *Yes, many castles are present. Perhaps queens also live in our neighborhood.*

6. *Queen, why do you have a large kitchen in your castle?* ♦ *I am a queen, and I love good food. You have a kitchen in your house, right?* ♦ *Yes, but it is a small kitchen. And I don't live in a castle.*

7. *Sempronia has her boat.* ♦ *Why?* ♦ *I don't know. Perhaps today she is sailing to the island.*

8. *The teachers teach their students daily.*

9. *That kitchen is large.* ♦ *Yes. It is long, but narrow.*

10. *Is y'all's farm good?* ♦ *Yes. The pigs on our farm are always happy, and they always have food*

and water. ♦ Y'all always take care of y'all's pigs because y'all are good farmers.

LESSON 84

1. *Rufus, your friends are having dinner in our dining room. Why are you not having dinner with your friends? ♦ I am staying in the kitchen. ♦ Why are you staying in the kitchen? ♦ I am angry!*

2. *We always have dinner in the dining room. Perhaps sometimes we can have dinner in our kitchen. ♦ Not at all. Our family is large. We can't have dinner in our kitchen.*

3. *Friend, why are we walking into the town? ♦ We are walking to the market now. ♦ Why are we grocery shopping now? You have much food at home! ♦ We are walking to the market because Quintus works at the market. ♦ Quintus? He isn't Cornelius's son, is he? ♦ Yes, that man is Cornelius's son. ♦ You don't love Quintus, do you? ♦ Perhaps.*

4. *The poet is telling a story about pigs to the boys and girls. ♦ Is it a good story? ♦ Yes. In the story, small pigs live in a small house. A large, bad wolf is present in front of the house, but the pigs are guarding their house. ♦ That story is good!*

5. *Charles, is Rufus your son? ♦ Yes, Rufus is my son. ♦ Your son never has his book. He is a bad student. Why does he never have his book? ♦ This book is large. Perhaps Rufus can't carry his book. ♦ Not at all! This book is small!*

6. *Why is there not a library in y'all's neighborhood? ♦ I don't know. Perhaps the inhabitants of our neighborhood do not love books.*

7. *I am tired. ♦ Why are you tired, my friend? ♦ I work on my farm daily. ♦ Your farm is large. ♦ Yes, this farm is wide and long. ♦ Perhaps your sons and daughters can plow the fields sometimes.*

8. *Why is the queen staying in her castle today? ♦ The queen's sons are sick today. The queen is taking care of her sons now. ♦ Our queen is a good woman. She always takes care of her sons and her daughters.*

9. *I love y'all's house. ♦ Why do you love our house? ♦ Why? ♦ Y'all's house has a large dining room, and it has a large kitchen, too.*

10. *I can't walk across the forest on account of the beasts. ♦ You don't fear the wolves, do you? ♦ Not at all. I fear the large pigs. Many pigs live in the forest. ♦ Pigs don't live in the forest!*

LESSON 85

1. *The table is in the dining room. The chairs are also in the dining room.*

2. *The boy has a small chair, but I have a large chair.*

3. *Where is my chair? ♦ I don't know. Perhaps your chair is in the kitchen. ♦ Why are the chairs in the kitchen? ♦ Rufus is having dinner now in the kitchen with his friends. ♦ Does Rufus have friends?*

4. *Our food is on the table. The chairs are around the table. ♦ Perhaps now we can have dinner. ♦ Yes. Our daughters are demanding food.*

5. *Mark is hurrying from the dining room with our food! ♦ Mark is a bad boy.*

6. *The queen is demanding a new chair now. ♦ Why is she demanding a new chair? ♦ The queen is demanding a new chair because her chair is small and narrow.*

7. *Where is Publius? ♦ He is taking care of his farm. ♦ Publius isn't a farmer, is he? ♦ Yes, he has a small farm with pigs and horses. ♦ Where is Publius's farm? ♦ Publius's farm is not in our neighborhood. It is near the forest, between the town and the seashore.*

8. *A large wolf is hurrying across our field. ♦ I fear large wolves. ♦ That wolf is hurrying to our pigs! Where is my sword? I can guard our pigs with a sword! ♦ Perhaps I can stay in the house.*

9. *That temple isn't large. Why is the temple small? ♦ That temple isn't small. It is narrow, but it is long.*

10. *There is a library in y'all's neighborhood, right? ♦ Not at all, but we have a castle. ♦ There isn't a castle in y'all's neighborhood, is there? ♦ Yes, the queen lives in our neighborhood. ♦ The queen does not live in y'all's neighborhood! ♦ We also have a good cafe.*

LESSON 86

1. *I am sitting in my chair. ♦ That chair is not your chair. It is my chair. ♦ Not at all! This chair is my chair! ♦ Why are we fighting? There are many chairs in the dining room.*

2. *Quintus, why are you sitting on your horse with a sword? Pirates aren't sailing to our kingdom, are they? ♦ I am guarding our kingdom today with sword and shield. ♦ I also can guard the kingdom. ♦ Do you have a horse? ♦ Not at all, but I have a sword. ♦ Now pirates cannot conquer our kingdom.*

3. *This student is a good girl because she never fights and she always sits in her chair. ♦ My students are often absent, and they stay at home.*

4. *Aemilia, why are you sick today? Why are you staying at home? ♦ I am sick on account of bad food. ♦ You are sick because you always have dinner in bad cafes.*

5. *Robert, why are you sitting in the kitchen with your family? ♦ Our house is small, and it does not have a dining room. We always have dinner in the kitchen. ♦ Y'all's house is small, but it is a good house. Y'all's neighborhood also is good. ♦ My family is demanding a large house, but I don't have much money.*

6. *Why are you sitting in my boat? ♦ I can't swim.*

7. *Fausta, why are you sitting on a rock? ♦ I don't have a chair. ♦ A rock is a bad chair, isn't it? ♦ Yes, it is a bad chair, but I am sitting on a rock because I am tired.*

8. *Helen, where are your friends? ♦ My friends are having dinner at the new restaurant. ♦ Why are you at home? Why are you not having dinner with your friends? ♦ I am hurrying to the restaurant now. Goodbye!*

9. *Where is the queen? ♦ The queen is in her castle with her daughters.*

10. *Where are Claudia and Publius? ♦ They are working on their farm.*

LESSON 87

1. *Where is Sempronia? Sempronia is absent. ♦ Sempronia is in her bedroom. ♦ She isn't sick, is she? ♦ Not at all, she is well today.*

2. *Why is my bed narrow? ♦ Daughter, your bed is narrow because your bedroom is narrow. ♦ Why does Mark have a wide bedroom?*

3. *I have a table and a chair in my bedroom. ♦ Why? ♦ I often work in my bedroom.*

4. *Our dining room is not large, but many chairs are in the dining room. ♦ Why do y'all have many chairs in y'all's dining room? ♦ Often we have dinner in our dining room with our friends. ♦ Why don't y'all have dinner in y'all's kitchen? ♦ We don't have a table in the kitchen. We can't have dinner without a table.*

5. *Why is Lucius hurrying out of the house now? ♦ Lucius is now grocery shopping because we do not have much food in our kitchen. ♦ Why is Lucius carrying books? ♦ He is walking to the market. He is walking to the library, too.*

6. *Tertius, where are the girls? ♦ They are in their bedroom. They are sitting on their beds.*

7. *This bedroom is small. Why is my bedroom small? ♦ Daughter, your bedroom is not small. ♦ And why is my bed small? This bed is bad! ♦ Daughter, your bed is not bad! It is a new bed!*

8. *You aren't angry, are you? ♦ I am angry! ♦ Why are you angry? ♦ I'm angry because you have my horse and you have my money, too! ♦ But we are friends. ♦ We are not friends!*

9. *We are walking in the town.*

10. *We are walking into the town.*

LESSON 88

1. *Friend, where is the bathroom?*

2. *There are many bedrooms in Julia's house. There is a large bathroom also in the house. ♦ That house is large! Why is the house large? ♦ Julia has many sons and many daughters.*

3. *Charles is absent. Where is Charles? ♦ Charles is in his bathroom because he is sick.*

4. *The queen has a large dining room. The queen's dining room has a large table, and it has many chairs, too. The queen has dinner with her friends in the dining room daily. ♦ Does the queen's castle have a large kitchen? ♦ Yes. There is a large kitchen near the dining room.*

5. *That boy is my son. ♦ Do you have a daughter? ♦ Yes, that girl is my daughter.*

6. *Tertius, why are you sitting on the wall? ♦ I always sit on the wall. I am guarding the town. ♦ But you don't have a shield. ♦ Not at all. ♦ You don't have a sword. ♦ Not at all. ♦ You can't guard the town without a sword and a shield!*

7. *Fausta, why are you carrying many books through the town? ♦ I am a librarian. I am carrying new books to the library. Goodbye, friend. ♦ Goodbye.*

8. *Students, do y'all have y'all's books? ♦ Yes. We have our books. ♦ Y'all are good students.*

9. *There is a road between our town and y'all's town. ♦ The road is narrow and bad. ♦ Why is the road bad? ♦ There are many rocks in the road. I can't walk to y'all's town on account of the rocks.*

10. *Where is Romulus? ♦ He's in his bedroom. He is sitting on his bed.*

LESSON 89

1. *William, where are your books? ♦ My books are in my basement. My basement is a small library. ♦ Do you have many books? ♦ Yes. On account of my books, I can't walk through my basement. ♦ Why do you have many books? ♦ I love books!*

2. *Julia, I love your house! You have a large kitchen, and you have a large garden also behind your house. ♦ We have a library also, with many books. ♦ You don't have a library in your house, do you? ♦ Yes, we have a library in our house. ♦ Perhaps I also can live in your house.*

3. *Where is Tullia? ♦ Tullia is in her bed, in her bedroom.*

4. *My house doesn't have a basement. ♦ Your house doesn't have a basement because your house is a large boat. Why do you live on a boat? ♦ I live on a large boat because I am a sailor.*

5. *Rufus, why do you live in Robert's basement? This basement is small and doesn't have a bathroom. ♦ I do not have much money, and Robert is my friend. ♦ Perhaps you can work on my farm. ♦ I can't work on a farm. ♦ Why? ♦ I fear pigs.*
6. *Helen, where is your garden? ♦ My garden is behind my house. ♦ You have a large garden! ♦ Not at all, my garden is small.*
7. *Why are the boys sitting with the sailors? ♦ A sailor is telling a story about pirates to the boys. ♦ Sailors always tell bad stories.*
8. *Daughter, where is my book? ♦ Your book is on the table in the dining room. ♦ Our house doesn't have a dining room!*
9. *Why are we walking across the road? ♦ There is a good restaurant on the other side of the street.*
10. *Friends, why are y'all sitting in the kitchen? We don't have many chairs in our kitchen, but we have many chairs in our dining room.*

LESSON 90

1. *Julia and Fulvia are sitting in the living room with their friends.*
2. *My house doesn't have an atrium. My house is small. ♦ But it has a garden. ♦ Yes, we have a garden behind the house. You also have a garden, right? ♦ Yes, we have a small garden.*
3. *My son, why are you and your friends sitting in the living room now? ♦ We are tired, and there are many chairs in our living room. ♦ Perhaps you and your friends can sit in the basement.*
4. *Wolf, do you live in a house? ♦ Not at all! I am a wolf. I live in the forest.*
5. *Can we eat dinner in the dining room today? ♦ Not at all, the chairs are absent.*
6. *This house has a large atrium. ♦ Why are we in the atrium? ♦ I don't know. ♦ I can see the sky. ♦ I also can see the sky.*
7. *Friend, why are you present in my boat? Why are you demanding my money? ♦ I am not your friend. ♦ Are you a pirate? ♦ Yes. I'm a pirate. ♦ I never give money to pirates.*
8. *Lavinia, where is your son? ♦ Cornelius is on his farm, with his pigs. ♦ Is Cornelius a farmer? ♦ Yes, Cornelius is a good farmer, and he has a large farm. ♦ Does your son have horses? ♦ Certainly. Cornelius has many stables and many horses on his farm.*
9. *Why do we have small beds in our bedroom? ♦ Daughters, y'all have small beds because y'all are small girls. ♦ We demand long beds!*
10. *Paul, why are you present in my bathroom? ♦ I am sick. ♦ Perhaps you can be sick in your bathroom.*

LESSON 92

1. *My son, your bedroom is dirty. ♦ I can't clean my bedroom now. ♦ Why, son? ♦ I am tired.*
2. *This bathroom is dirty. Why aren't you cleaning the bathroom? ♦ This bathroom is not my bathroom.*
3. *My house is large. We have a large living room, and we have a large kitchen, also. ♦ But y'all don't have a basement.*
4. *Girls, our stables are dirty. Perhaps y'all can clean the stables today. ♦ On account of the horses, we can't clean the stables. ♦ The horses are not in the stables! The horses are in the field. ♦ We are tired. We can't clean the stables. ♦ Not at all! ♦ We are sick! ♦ Y'all are well! Y'all are not sick!*
5. *Christopher, why are you cleaning your basement? ♦ There is water in my basement. ♦ Perhaps we can swim in your basement.*
6. *My office is dirty. ♦ You never clean your office.*
7. *Peter, you can't live in Christopher's basement. ♦ Why? ♦ Much water is in Christopher's basement. ♦ My bed is in Christopher's basement! ♦ Now your bed is a boat.*
8. *Why is there water in your living room? ♦ We are not in my living room. We are in the atrium. The water is in the impluvium.*
9. *Where are my friends? Are they sitting in the living room? ♦ Not at all. They are in the kitchen because much food is in the kitchen.*
10. *Boys, why are y'all not in y'all's beds? ♦ We're not tired. Tertius is in the bathroom.*

LESSON 95

1. *Your mother is the queen. You live in a large castle. ♦ I live in a large castle, but I have a small bedroom.*
2. *Mother, where are you? ♦ I am present, my son!*
3. *Why is our mother not at home? ♦ She is walking to the cafe with her friends. ♦ Perhaps we can have dinner at home. Is there food in the kitchen? ♦ Yes, we have food in the kitchen.*
4. *My mother is tired because she has many sons.*
5. *Why does y'all's mother never walk through the forest? ♦ She fears the wolves. On account of the wolves, she always walks around the forest, but never walks through the forest.*
6. *Where is your mother now? ♦ She is in her bed, in her bedroom.*
7. *James, why are you in front of the castle? ♦ I am guarding the gates of the castle.*
8. *Mother, why do you love our new house? ♦ This house has a large kitchen. Now our family can have dinner in the kitchen. ♦ We do not have a table in the kitchen.*

9. *Mother, why are you cleaning our bathrooms?*
   ♦ The bathrooms are dirty!
10. *Where is Romulus? He isn't in the living room,*
    is he? ♦ Not at all. Romulus is in the basement.

LESSON 96

1. *My mother's horse is in the stable.*
2. *My mother's gift is in our living room.*
3. *Why is your mother carrying many books? ♦ My*
   mother is carrying her books to the library.
4. *My mother's brother lives in our basement. ♦*
   Why? He has a house, right? ♦ Not at all. He
   lives in our basement because he does not have
   money.
5. *Mother, where is Fred? ♦ I don't know, my son.*
   Perhaps Fred is cleaning his bedroom. ♦ Not at
   all! Fred never cleans his bedroom.
6. *That woman is my friend. ♦ Why is your friend*
   carrying a small girl? ♦ My friend is a mother.
   That girl is my friend's daughter.
7. *Mother, why are you walking across the street?*
   ♦ We don't have food at home. I am hurrying to
   the market. ♦ I can stay in front of the temple
   with my friends. Goodbye, Mother.
8. *Where are my friends? ♦ They are sitting in the*
   living room. ♦ Perhaps we can have dinner in
   the dining room. ♦ I don't know. We do not
   have much food. ♦ Perhaps we can walk to the
   cafe. ♦ Perhaps, but there are many sailors in
   the cafe. They sometimes tell bad stories. ♦ They
   often tell bad stories.
9. *Our neighborhood has many castles. Mother,*
   are you a queen? ♦ Not at all! I am not a queen.
   We are farmers, but we live near castles.
10. *My son, why aren't you cleaning your bedroom?*
    ♦ Flavia also is not cleaning her bedroom. ♦
    Y'all's bathrooms are also dirty.

LESSON 98

1. *Boy, where is your father? ♦ My father is at*
   home today. ♦ Where is your father's house? ♦
   We live between the library and the gates of the
   town.
2. *Father, I can't work on our farm today. ♦ Why,*
   my son? ♦ I am tired because I am sick. Perhaps
   I can stay in my bedroom.
3. *Mother, where is the bank? ♦ Why? You don't*
   have money, do you? ♦ Not at all. My friends
   are having dinner at the new restaurant. The
   restaurant is near the bank. Where is the bank?
   ♦ The bank is near the gate of the town,
   between the temple of Minerva and the theater.
4. *That man is my father. ♦ Why is your father*
   hurrying to the temple of Neptune? ♦ My father
   is a sailor. He is carrying a gift to the temple.

Today he is sailing through pirates' boats to the
large island.
5. *Queen, your kingdom is narrow, but long.*
   Perhaps we can build a wall around your
   kingdom ♦ Perhaps, but we don't have wood in
   my kingdom. ♦ We can build the wall out of
   rock.
6. *Where is your father? ♦ He's in the living room.*
   He is telling a story about a bad wolf and small
   pigs to the girls and boys. ♦ That story is good! ♦
   Yes. My father tells many stories.
7. *Our kitchen is dirty. I am angry because Rufus*
   never cleans the kitchen. ♦ Rufus never cleans
   the bathroom, also.
8. *Why do we never have dinner in our kitchen? ♦*
   We never have dinner in our kitchen because
   our family is large! We have many sons and
   many daughters. ♦ But our kitchen is large. ♦
   Yes, but the table in our kitchen is small.
9. *Father, why do we live in a stable? ♦ We live in a*
   stable because we are horses.
10. *Why are there many books in the living room?*
    ♦ They are my mother's books. My mother loves
    books.

LESSON 99

1. *This boy is my brother, but that boy is not my*
   brother.
2. *Brother, you aren't present in my bedroom, are*
   you? Why are you sitting on my bed? ♦ I'm
   angry because you have my book. Where is my
   book? ♦ I don't know. I don't have your book. ♦
   Not at all! You have my book! I demand my
   book!
3. *This woman is my mother. She is a librarian. ♦*
   Does your mother work at the library? ♦ Yes, she
   takes care of the books and guards the books
   daily, but today she is at home. ♦ Why is she at
   home today? ♦ My brother is sick today.
4. *Why are many books on the table? ♦ They are*
   my father's books. My father loves books. This
   book is about horses.
5. *My father doesn't have his money. Pirate, you*
   don't have my father's money, do you? ♦ Not at
   all. ♦ Why do you have much money in your
   boat? ♦ I don't know.
6. *My mother has a restaurant. My mother's*
   restaurant has good food. ♦ Perhaps I can have
   dinner at your mother's restaurant today. ♦ Yes.
   My brother and I sometimes eat at my mother's
   restaurant.
7. *Why are you mad? ♦ We are cleaning the stables*
   today. The stables are dirty. ♦ Why don't the
   horses clean their stables? ♦ Horses can't clean
   stables!
8. *Father, why do you always sit in your office? ♦*

My daughter, I often work in my office. ♦ Your office is dirty.

9. *Helen, why are you sitting in your brother's boat? ♦ We are sailing to our homeland now. ♦ Why? ♦ My mother's brother is sick. He lives in our homeland.*
10. *Your mother's horse is in front of the bank. ♦ My mother is at the bank.*

LESSON 100

1. *The fathers and sons are plowing the field. ♦ Rufus also is plowing the field now, right? ♦ Not at all, Rufus never plows the field.*
2. *Our mothers are in front of the temple of Minerva.*
3. *My brothers never clean their bedrooms.*
4. *Robert, where are your brothers? ♦ My father and my brothers are carrying wood from the forest.*
5. *Where is your mother's house? ♦ My mother lives in the forest. ♦ Why does she live in the forest? ♦ My mother loves the forest because it is not near the town. She can see the stars and the moon. ♦ I can't live in the forest because wolves are present in the forest.*
6. *My father's son is my brother.*
7. *Where are our mothers and our fathers? ♦ They are in the school with the teachers.*
8. *Where is my father's chair? ♦ It is in the basement. ♦ Why? My father never sits in the basement. He always sits in the living room.*
9. *The queen is giving money to the inhabitants of her kingdom. ♦ Why? ♦ The queen is a good woman, and she always takes care of the inhabitants. Sometimes she gives food to the boys and girls of the kingdom.*
10. *Our daughter is walking from the town to the seashore with her friends.*

LESSON 101

1. *Where is our mothers' money? ♦ The money is in the bank.*
2. *My brothers' bedrooms are always dirty. ♦ They never clean their bedrooms!*
3. *Our fathers are farmers, but our fathers' farms are small. ♦ Why are our fathers' farms small? ♦ They have small fields.*
4. *Helen, your mother is a teacher, right? ♦ Yes. She is often tired because she teaches many students daily.*
5. *Father, you have many books in your office. ♦ Yes, my daughter, I love books. ♦ Do you have a book about pigs? ♦ Not at all, but I have many books about horses.*
6. *Mother, you are a queen, but our castle is small. Why do we live in a small castle? You can build*

a large castle, right? ♦ My kingdom is small, my son. We can't build a large castle on account of money. The inhabitants of my kingdom don't have much money.
7. *The queen is demanding new stables. ♦ Why? ♦ The queen has many horses, but the queen's stables are small. ♦ Perhaps we can build large stables.*
8. *Where's my father's horse? ♦ It's in the stable, right? ♦ Not at all.*
9. *My brother's food is in the kitchen.*
10. *Where is your mother's book? ♦ It is in the dining room. ♦ This house doesn't have a dining room.*

LESSON 102

1. *That woman is my mother. I love my mother because she is a good woman.*
2. *I see your brother. He is walking across the road to the temple.*
3. *The horse is carrying my father to the town.*
4. *Our fathers' pigs don't have food. ♦ Our fathers are bad farmers.*
5. *Many mothers are in the temple. ♦ Where are the mother's gifts? ♦ The gifts are in the temple.*
6. *Why are our fathers hurrying to the castle? ♦ The queen is demanding gifts! ♦ She isn't demanding money, is she? ♦ Not at all, but she is demanding gold and silver! ♦ That queen is bad!*
7. *Quintus, why are you carrying your brother? ♦ My brother is sick and tired.*
8. *Hello, Aurelia. I often see your mother at my market. ♦ Hello, Mark. My mother sometimes grocery shops at your market. ♦ Your mother's brother also grocery shops at my market often.*
9. *On account of your father, I can't sail to the island today. ♦ Why can't you sail? ♦ Your father has my boat.*
10. *My father's farm is small, but we have many horses. ♦ My father's farm is also small, but we have pigs.*

LESSON 103

1. *I see my brothers. They are hurrying out of the forest.*
2. *The queen is watching our mothers. ♦ Why? ♦ Our mothers are carrying gifts to the queen.*
3. *Our fathers' homeland is a large island.*
4. *Our mothers' gifts are in the living room.*
5. *We never see your brothers at the restaurant. ♦ My brothers are sailors. They always have dinner at the bad cafe and they tell bad stories about pirates.*

6. *The sailors are carrying y'all's fathers to a new homeland in their boat.*
7. *This woman is my mother. She lives on her farm. ♦ Where is your mother's farm? ♦ It is on the other side of the forest.*
8. *The teacher always watches my brothers because they are bad boys.*
9. *Where is Mark today? ♦ He is sailing to the island today in his mother's boat. ♦ Where is Mark's mother? ♦ She is at home. Mark's mother is not sailing to the island with Mark.*
10. *My brothers never clean their bedrooms. My brothers' bedrooms are dirty.*

LESSON 104

1. *We are giving gifts to your brothers.*
2. *Christopher is telling a story to his mother.*
3. *This teacher is giving a book to my father.*
4. *I never give money to my brother. ♦ Why? ♦ My brother always sits in the living room. He never works.*
5. *The students are giving chairs to our mothers now.*
6. *The teacher is telling a story about the students to the fathers.*
7. *Sempronia has my mother's money. ♦ Why? ♦ I don't know, but now Sempronia is giving money to my mother.*
8. *Why are you giving books to my brother? ♦ Your brother loves books. He is a librarian.*
9. *The farmer is giving money to y'all's fathers. ♦ Why? ♦ Y'all's fathers work daily on the farmer's farm.*
10. *The sailors are telling a bad story about pirates to our brothers. ♦ Why do the sailors always tell bad stories? ♦ Sometimes they tell good stories, but often they tell bad stories.*

LESSON 105

1. *Lavinia, why are you hurrying to the seashore with your mother? ♦ We love the seashore. Sometimes we walk to the seashore with my father. ♦ Your father loves the seashore, right? ♦ Not at all, my father fears the water. My father sits near the water and watches my brothers because he can't swim.*
2. *Romulus, where do you live? ♦ I live in the forest with my brother. ♦ Y'all live in a house, right? ♦ Not at all. We do not have a house. ♦ Why do y'all live in the forest? ♦ Our father's house is small.*
3. *Where is your father? ♦ My father is in the basement with my brothers. ♦ Where is your mother? ♦ My mother is sitting in the living room with your mother.*

4. *Where is the teacher now? ♦ The teacher is in the school with our mothers and our fathers.*
5. *Lucretia loves my brother, but my brother loves Cornelia. ♦ Your brother loves Claudia, too.*
6. *Where is our mothers' money? ♦ It is in the bank.*
7. *I never see y'all's fathers at the restaurant. ♦ They never have dinner in the restaurant, but sometimes they have dinner at the cafe.*
8. *Why is my father giving money to my brother? ♦ I don't know. Perhaps your brother works on your father's farm.*
9. *Why is our mother's chair in the kitchen? ♦ Sometimes our mother carries her chair into the kitchen.*
10. *William is telling a long story to my father. ♦ Why does William always tell long stories? ♦ I don't know, but William's stories are always long.*

LESSON 107

1. *The queen is my sister. ♦ You are the queen's brother, and the queen is your sister. ♦ Yes. ♦ Do you live in a castle with your sister? ♦ Yes. I have a small bedroom in the basement of the castle. ♦ You live in your sister's basement. ♦ I live in my sister's castle.*
2. *Father, I am a good boy. My sister's bedroom is dirty, but I always clean my bedroom. ♦ My son, your bathroom is always dirty. Perhaps you can clean your bathroom sometimes.*
3. *Sometimes the boys walk into the town with their sister.*
4. *My sister's friend is sitting in our living room. ♦ Why is your sister not in the living room with her friend? ♦ She is in her bedroom.*
5. *The poet is telling a story to my sisters and my brothers.*
6. *My sister has a farm. ♦ Your sister's farm isn't large, is it? ♦ Yes. Many stables and many horses are on my sister's farm.*
7. *Why are the pirates watching my father? ♦ Your father is walking out of the bank with gold.*
8. *Our friends are giving a gift to my father.*
9. *Why is your sister sitting on a horse? ♦ The horse is carrying my sister to the town.*
10. *I am walking to the library with my sisters.*

LESSON 108

1. *The king is sitting in his castle.*
2. *Charles, why are your brothers always in front of the castle? And why does the king often give money to your brothers? ♦ The king gives money to my brothers because they guard the gates of the castle. ♦ Do you also guard the king's castle? ♦ Not at all. I clean the stables.*

282

3. *Quintus, where is the queen?* ♦ *The queen is in the castle with the king. They are having dinner in the dining room now.* ♦ *Where is the queen sitting?* ♦ *The queen is sitting near the king. The king's sister is also present. She is sitting near the king's brother. That dining room is large, and it has a large table. The king's family is sitting around the table.*

4. *Father, why do we live in a castle?* ♦ *We live in a castle because I am a king, and your mother is a queen.* ♦ *Why do I have a small bedroom?* ♦ *Our castle is small.*

5. *The garden is between the house and the wall.*

6. *Why is a poet in the castle's large dining room?* ♦ *The men and women of the castle are having dinner with the king in the large dining room. The poet is telling a story now to the men and women of the castle.* ♦ *The king loves stories. Perhaps he can tell a story about pirates to the king.*

7. *The king's brother is in front of the castle.* ♦ *Why?* ♦ *He is demanding silver and gold.* ♦ *Perhaps the king can give money to his brother.* ♦ *Not at all. The king never gives money to his brother.*

8. *Where are my sisters' horses?* ♦ *They are in the stables behind the castle.*

9. *Romulus loves my sister, but my sister loves Rufus.* ♦ *Why does your sister love Rufus? Rufus lives in his mother's basement and doesn't have money.*

10. *On account of your brother, I can't sail to my father's homeland today.* ♦ *Why can't you sail?* ♦ *Your brother has my money.*

LESSON 109

1. *The king doesn't have a wife, does he?* ♦ *Yes. Lavinia is the king's wife. Lavinia is the queen.*

2. *The women are watching the boats.* ♦ *Why are they watching the boats?* ♦ *They are the wives of the sailors. The wives' husbands are absent.*

3. *My wife is a librarian. She always carries books into our house.* ♦ *She loves books.* ♦ *Yes. Books are in our kitchen, and in our dining room, and in our bedroom, and on the tables, and on the chairs. On account of my wife's books, I can't walk through the house.*

4. *Aemilia, why are you tired today?* ♦ *My family is in my house today. My brothers, my sisters, my mother, my daughters, and my husband are present today.* ♦ *Do you have much food?* ♦ *Not at all. I am hurrying to the market now.* ♦ *Perhaps I can grocery shop also. I can carry the food to your house.* ♦ *You are a good friend!*

5. *That man is my husband.* ♦ *Why is he hurrying into the library with many books?* ♦ *He is carrying books to the library.* ♦ *Why is he now walking out of the library with many books?* ♦ *My husband loves books. We always have many books in our house.*

6. *Where is your father's boat?* ♦ *Pirates have my father's boat. On account of the pirates, my father can't sail now.*

7. *The librarian is telling a story to my sisters.*

8. *Our kingdom is small, but the king's castle is large.* ♦ *Why does the king have a large castle?* ♦ *He lives in a good neighborhood.*

9. *Cornelius, do you have a family?* ♦ *Yes. I and my wife have many daughters. Do you also have a family?* ♦ *Yes. I have a husband, and a small son. My father also lives in our house.*

10. *My sisters' teacher is present.*

LESSON 111

1. *I am a soldier. My brother also is a soldier.* ♦ *Is your father a soldier?* ♦ *Not at all. My father is a librarian.*

2. *The king's soldiers are demanding their money.* ♦ *Why is the king not giving money to the soldiers?* ♦ *I don't know. Perhaps the king doesn't have money.*

3. *The inhabitants of the town are giving a gift to the soldier.* ♦ *Why?* ♦ *That soldier always guards the gates of the town.*

4. *Where is the king?* ♦ *The king is behind the castle with his soldiers.* ♦ *Why are they behind the castle?* ♦ *They are taking care of their shields and swords.*

5. *Why is a poet present in the large dining room with the king and the king's friends?* ♦ *The king and his friends are having dinner in the large dining room. The poet is telling stories.* ♦ *Is the king's wife present?* ♦ *Not at all. The king's wife is in her bed because she is sick today, but the king's sister is present in the dining room, and she is sitting near the king.*

6. *Where is the king's brother?* ♦ *The king's brother is in the forest with the king's soldiers.* ♦ *Why are the soldiers in the forest?* ♦ *The king's brother and the soldiers are hurrying through the forest to the seashore because pirates are sailing to our kingdom.*

7. *Where is our mother's horse? It is not in the stable.* ♦ *Our mother is absent now. Perhaps she is in the town.* ♦ *Perhaps she is grocery shopping.* ♦ *Yes. We don't have much food in the house.*

8. *Rufus, why is your bed in the basement?* ♦ *I live in the basement.* ♦ *Why do you live in your father's basement?* ♦ *I don't have much money. On account of money I live with my mother and my father.*

9. *Where is the king? He is not in his office. ♦ The king is walking to the seashore with his wife. ♦ They love the seashore. ♦ Yes. The king's castle is near the seashore.*
10. *I am cleaning our house with my brothers. ♦ Why are y'all cleaning the house? ♦ Our bedrooms are dirty.*

LESSON 112

1. *This town is large. ♦ It is not a town. It is a large city. Many inhabitants live in the city now. ♦ My brother lives in the city with his wife.*
2. *Why are there many soldiers among the cities? ♦ The soldiers are guarding the inhabitants of the cities.*
3. *This city always has much money. Why does it have much money? ♦ The king sometimes gives money to the cities of his kingdom.*
4. *Why are we building a new city? ♦ There are many inhabitants in our kingdom. ♦ I'm tired. I can't build a new city today.*
5. *Where is the king's sister? ♦ She is in the castle with the king's mother and the king's daughters. ♦ Our king has a large family!*
6. *Why does the king sometimes give money to your brothers? ♦ My brothers are soldiers.*
7. *King, there are many cities in your kingdom. Your kingdom is large! ♦ Yes, my kingdom is long and wide, with many cities. ♦ You have a large castle, too. ♦ Yes, but my bathroom is small.*
8. *You aren't walking from our town to the large city, are you? ♦ Yes. I am walking to the city now. ♦ Why are you walking to the city? ♦ Large cities have good libraries. They have good restaurants, too.*
9. *That sailor is telling a story to the soldiers.*
10. *Why are your mother's friends sitting around the table in our dining room? ♦ My mother is having dinner with her friends now. ♦ Where is the food? It is not on the table. ♦ The food is in the kitchen.*

LESSON 114

1. *The king always obeys the queen. ♦ The king is a good husband!*
2. *I am a good soldier. I always obey the king. ♦ Where are the king's soldiers now? ♦ They are in the forest with the king. ♦ Why are you not in the forest with the king and the king's soldiers? ♦ I often obey the king. ♦ Why are you at home? ♦ I sometimes obey the king. ♦ You are not a good soldier!*
3. *Why are you not obeying the librarian? You are in a library.*

4. *I am a good girl because I obey my mother. ♦ But you are not cleaning your bedroom now. ♦ I often obey my mother. ♦ You never obey your mother.*
5. *Publius never obeys his father. ♦ Why? Publius isn't a bad boy, is he? ♦ He is a bad boy. He never cleans the stables, he never cleans his bedroom, and he never gives food to the pigs.*
6. *Brother, why do you never obey our father? ♦ I am a good son! I always obey our father! ♦ Not at all. ♦ I often obey our father. ♦ Not at all. ♦ I sometimes obey our father. ♦ Perhaps.*
7. *My sister's bedroom is between my bedroom and the bathroom. ♦ Why do your sisters have large bedrooms but you have a small bedroom? Your sisters' bedrooms are large. ♦ I have a small bed.*
8. *The librarian is giving new books to my brothers.*
9. *Why does that woman have much gold? And why does she have much silver also? ♦ I don't know. ♦ Why does she have a large boat? ♦ I don't know. ♦ Perhaps that woman is a pirate!*
10. *Why are the sailors' wives hurrying to the city? ♦ They are hurrying to the temple of Neptune in the city. They are carrying gifts to the temple because the women's husbands are sailing today.*

LESSON 116

1. *Friend, do you have a cat? ♦ Yes. Fluffy is our cat. He lives in our house. ♦ This cat is large! ♦ Yes, Fluffy is a large cat.*
2. *Mother, where is Fluffy? ♦ Fluffy is in your bedroom. He is sitting on your bed.*
3. *Hello, Fluffy. Are you well today? ♦ Not at all. I don't have food. Where is my food? I demand food! ♦ You are a cat. You can't demand food.*
4. *Fluffy is in the kitchen. He is sitting on the table. ♦ Why does that cat not obey? Fluffy can't sit on the table.*
5. *Librarian, why is a cat present in the library? ♦ The cat lives in our library. He guards the library and watches the books.*
6. *Daughter, are you taking care of our cat? ♦ Yes, father. I am giving food to the cat now.*
7. *Why do the soldiers have swords? Why are they in front of the gates of the city? ♦ They are guarding the city with swords and shields.*
8. *Why is this cat in our house? ♦ I don't know. We don't have a cat. ♦ Now this cat is demanding food.*
9. *The king's wife and the king's brother are fighting in the dining room.*
10. *Where is my sisters' boat?*

LESSON 117

1. *Where is the city? ♦ The city is on the other side of the mountains. ♦ We can't walk through the mountains. ♦ Why? ♦ The mountains are large, but the road is narrow.*
2. *Why do Mark and Sempronia live in the mountains? ♦ They love the mountains. ♦ But large cats live in the mountains. ♦ Large cats? ♦ Yes, large cats live among the mountains. I fear large cats. Do you fear the large cats of the mountains?*
3. *Where does Fred live? ♦ Fred lives in the mountains with his wife and his daughters. ♦ Why does Fred not live in the city? ♦ Fred and his wife have a small farm. They have horses and they have pigs also.*
4. *On account of the mountain, I can't see the city. ♦ The city is on the other side of the mountain.*
5. *Why do you live in a large house? ♦ I have many sisters. Our house is large and it has many bedrooms.*
6. *Why does Tullia live in the large city? ♦ Tullia's husband has a cafe in the city. Many men and many women have dinner in the cafe daily.*
7. *Why are the inhabitants of the mountains hurrying to the city? ♦ I don't know. Perhaps they are hurrying to the theater.*
8. *Claudia is telling a story to my mother.*
9. *Fluffy, why do you never obey? ♦ I am a cat! I never obey. ♦ You are a bad cat. ♦ Where is my food?*
10. *There are many cities among the mountains.*

LESSON 118

1. *The king has many dogs, right? ♦ Yes. Our king loves dogs. ♦ Where do the dogs live? ♦ They live behind the castle near the stables.*
2. *Tertius, do you have a dog? ♦ Not at all. I have a small cat.*
3. *That dog is not a dog. ♦ It isn't a large cat, is it? ♦ Not at all. It's a wolf! ♦ Goodbye!*
4. *Do you have a dog? ♦ Yes. Fidus is our dog. Fidus is a good dog. ♦ Why is the dog good? ♦ Fidus is a good dog because he always guards the house and never fights with cats. Fidus always obeys. ♦ Fidus is a good dog!*
5. *The king isn't absent, is he? ♦ Yes, the king is not in the castle. ♦ Where is the king? ♦ The king is in the mountains with his soldiers. They are fighting with the inhabitants of the mountains.*
6. *Our soldiers are building a wall around the city. ♦ Are they building the wall out of wood? ♦ Not at all. They are building the wall out of rock.*
7. *Why is Publius at home? ♦ He is taking care of his wife today. ♦ Why? She isn't sick, is she? ♦*

Yes. Publius's wife is sick. ♦ Publius is a good husband!
8. *The king's soldiers are hurrying to the seashore with the king. ♦ Why are they hurrying to the seashore? ♦ Pirates are sailing to our island.*
9. *Son, why are you fighting with your sisters? ♦ They have my book!*
10. *I am guarding the city with a sword.*

LESSON 119

1. *Who is hurrying across the road? ♦ Helen is hurrying across the road to the temple of Minerva.*
2. *Who is walking through the gates of the city? ♦ Cornelius is walking to his brother's house. ♦ Does Cornelius's brother live in the city? ♦ Yes. Cornelius's brother lives in the city.*
3. *Who is taking care of our cat? ♦ Tertius is taking care of the cat. Tertius is at home and he is now giving food to the cat.*
4. *I see a man in the forest. Who is in the forest? ♦ It's not a man! It's a wolf! ♦ Goodbye!*
5. *Friends, we are walking through y'all's kingdom. Who is y'all's king? ♦ Charles is our king. ♦ Where is the king? ♦ Our king lives in a large castle. The castle is on the other side of the forest, in the mountains.*
6. *This library is good. It has many good books. ♦ The librarian also is good. ♦ Who is the librarian? ♦ Aurelia is the librarian. She always guards the books, and often tells stories to the girls and boys.*
7. *Many mountains are around our city. ♦ Yes. The mountains guard the city. Soldiers can't walk through the mountains. ♦ Why do we have a wall also around our city? ♦ The wall also guards our city.*
8. *Wife, why is this cat sitting on the table? ♦ Husband, Fluffy is a cat. He always sits on the chairs, on the tables, on the beds. ♦ Fluffy never obeys. ♦ Fidus, our dog, never sits on the table. ♦ Fidus always obeys. He is a good dog.*
9. *Why are our mothers hurrying to the bank? ♦ Our mothers' money is in the bank.*
10. *The poet is telling a story to the kings and queens.*

LESSON 121

1. *This river is wide. ♦ That river is narrow.*
2. *King, your soldiers are on the other side of the river. ♦ Do we have a boat? ♦ Not at all. Perhaps we can swim across the river. ♦ I can't swim. ♦ King, why can't you swim? ♦ I fear the water.*
3. *There are many rivers in our kingdom.*
4. *Who is in the river? ♦ My brother is in the river. He is swimming across the river. ♦ Why is he*

285

swimming across the river? ♦ *Helen lives on the other side of the river.* ♦ *Who is Helen?* ♦ *Helen is a good girl. Helen lives in the city on the other side of the river with her family. My brother loves Helen, but he fears Helen's father.*

5. *Friend, why is your dog swimming in the river?* ♦ *My dog loves the river. He swims in the river daily.*
6. *On account of the river, we can't walk to the city.* ♦ *The river isn't wide, is it?* ♦ *Yes, the river is wide and long. We can't walk around the river.* ♦ *Perhaps we can sail across the river.* ♦ *Not at all. We don't have boats.* ♦ *Perhaps we can swim across the river.*
7. *I love the mountains. Sometimes I walk in the mountains.* ♦ *I never walk in the mountains because I fear the large cats of the mountains.*
8. *My sons and my daughters always obey my wife.*
9. *Where are your father and my father?* ♦ *Our fathers are having dinner at the restaurant with their friends.* ♦ *Why are our fathers' friends carrying pigs?* ♦ *Our fathers' friends are farmers.*
10. *Rufus, where are your brothers? Are they well?* ♦ *Teacher, my brothers are at home. They are sick today.* ♦ *Who is taking care of your brothers now?* ♦ *My father and my mother also are at home with my brothers.*

LESSON 122

1. *Your journey is not long.* ♦ *Why?* ♦ *You live near the city.*
2. *On account of the long journey, I can't walk to your house.*
3. *There are many ways through the mountains.*
4. *We can't walk through the mountains.* ♦ *Why?* ♦ *That journey is long.*
5. *Friend, do you have a dog?* ♦ *Yes.* ♦ *Do you have a cat?* ♦ *Not at all. My dog can't live with a cat.*
6. *Publius, do you have a sister?* ♦ *Not at all, but I have many brothers.*
7. *Why are the soldiers hurrying into the castle?* ♦ *They are not obeying they king.*
8. *Who is this girl?* ♦ *This girl is my friend.*
9. *Our king is good. He always takes care of his soldiers. Our queen also is good.* ♦ *Why is the queen good?* ♦ *She always gives food to the inhabitants of the cities.*
10. *Publius is walking from the town to the large city.* ♦ *Why? That journey is long. There is a wide river between the town and the city.*

LESSON 123

1. *What is in the boat?*

2. *Who is in the boat?*
3. *What is behind our house?* ♦ *It is a new horse.* ♦ *Why do you have a new horse?* ♦ *We are farmers. We have horses on our farm.*
4. *What is on the table?* ♦ *It is your gift. Are you happy?* ♦ *I am happy! I love gifts!*
5. *What is in our dining room?* ♦ *A table and chairs are in our dining room.*
6. *What is on the mountain? It's not a house, is it?* ♦ *It's a castle. The king of our kingdom lives on the mountain.* ♦ *I can't see the castle.* ♦ *The king's castle is small.*
7. *Who is your mother?* ♦ *Flavia is my mother.* ♦ *Who is your wife?* ♦ *Claudia is my wife.* ♦ *Who is your sister?* ♦ *Sempronia is my sister.* ♦ *Who is your daughter?* ♦ *Catherine is my daughter.* ♦ *Do you have a son?* ♦ *Not at all. There are many women in my family, but there are not men!*
8. *This river is wide and long.* ♦ *Our kingdom has many rivers.*
9. *Why do you never walk through the forest to the mountains?* ♦ *It's a long journey.*
10. *Fluffy, Why do you always fight with dogs?* ♦ *Cats and dogs always fight!*

LESSON 124

1. *This sea is large and wide.*
2. *Aurelia, why do you sometimes sit near the seashore?* ♦ *I love the sea. I often sit near the sea. I watch the water, and I watch the sailors' boats.* ♦ *I also love the sea.*
3. *Can we sail across the sea?* ♦ *Not at all. That sea is wide, and it has many pirates.*
4. *Mother, where is your homeland?* ♦ *My homeland is on the other side of the sea.* ♦ *Do you often sail to your homeland?* ♦ *Sometimes I sail to my homeland because my mother lives in my homeland.* ♦ *Perhaps I also can sail to your homeland.*
5. *Father, where is Fluffy?* ♦ *Fluffy is in your bedroom. He is sitting on your bed.* ♦ *Why does that cat always sit on my bed?*
6. *Who is demanding food?* ♦ *The wives of the soldiers are demanding food.* ♦ *Why are the wives of the soldiers demanding food?* ♦ *Our king is bad. He never gives money to the soldiers. Now the wives of the soldiers do not have food.* ♦ *Where is the king now?* ♦ *The king is sitting near the sea with his wife.*
7. *Fluffy is always a good cat.* ♦ *Why is Fluffy sitting on the table?* ♦ *Fluffy is sometimes a good cat.*
8. *King, why are many boats in the rivers of your kingdom?* ♦ *Pirates are sailing into our kingdom in their boats!* ♦ *They aren't sailing to*

our city, are they? ♦ *Yes.* ♦ *Where are our soldiers? Where is my shield?*

9. *Fidus is a good dog.* ♦ *Why is he good?* ♦ *He is a good dog because he never fights with cats, and he always obeys.*

10. *There are large mountains around the city. The journey through the mountains is long, and the road is narrow.* ♦ *What is on the other side of the mountains?* ♦ *The sea is on the other side of the mountains.*

LESSON 126

1. *Aurelia, do you love me?* ♦ *Not at all. I love Mark.* ♦ *Who is Mark?*

2. *I see the wolf, but the wolf does not see me.*

3. *Why is our dog watching me?* ♦ *He is demanding food.* ♦ *Fidus, you have food.*

4. *Brother, I am sick and this journey is long. Perhaps you can carry me.* ♦ *Yes, my sister. But why are you sick?* ♦ *I am sick on account of bad food.*

5. *The soldiers are hurrying out of the mountains.* ♦ *Are they hurrying to our city?* ♦ *Not at all. They are hurrying to the king's castle.* ♦ *Why are they hurrying to the castle? They are obeying the king, right?* ♦ *Not at all. Our king never gives money to his soldiers. The soldiers now are demanding money in front of the castle.* ♦ *The wives of the soldiers are present also.* ♦ *Yes. The wives of the soldiers are demanding money.*

6. *Sometimes I have dinner at a restaurant with my sisters.* ♦ *Do you have many sisters?* ♦ *Yes. I have many sisters and a brother also.*

7. *What is in front of the temple of Minerva?* ♦ *A horse is in front of the temple.*

8. *Father, why are we sailing across the wide sea?* ♦ *My daughter, we are sailing to my homeland. There is much gold and much silver in my homeland.* ♦ *Who is the king of your homeland?*

9. *Tertius and Quintus are good boys.* ♦ *Why are they good?* ♦ *They are cleaning their bedrooms and bathroom now. They are obeying their mother.*

10. *We can't walk through the large mountains.* ♦ *Why? It is not a long journey through the mountains.* ♦ *Yes, the journey is not long, but there is a wide river between the city and the mountains.* ♦ *Perhaps we can walk around the river.* ♦ *Not at all. That journey is long.*

LESSON 127

1. *My father never gives money to me.* ♦ *Why?* ♦ *We are farmers, but I never work in the fields.* ♦ *Perhaps you can clean your father's stables.*

2. *My teacher sometimes gives good books to me.* ♦ *She never gives books to me.* ♦ *Perhaps you can demand books.*

3. *Cats, why do y'all never obey me?* ♦ *We are cats. We are not dogs.* ♦ *And why do y'all always sit on the table?* ♦ *Your food is on the table.*

4. *This man always tells good stories to the soldiers.* ♦ *He isn't a sailor, is he?* ♦ *Not at all. Sailors always tell bad stories. This man is telling good stories.*

5. *I am the king, but the soldiers never obey me. Why do they not obey me?* ♦ *I don't know. They always obey the queen.*

6. *What is behind the castle?* ♦ *The king's stables are behind the castle. The king has many horses.*

7. *Why is that pirate watching me?* ♦ *You are carrying gold through the city now. He can see your gold.* ♦ *Perhaps we can hurry to the bank.*

8. *Hello. Who are you?* ♦ *I am Lavinia. Who are you?* ♦ *I am Decimus. Do you work at the school? Are you a teacher?* ♦ *Not at all. I am a librarian.*

9. *The pirates are hurrying from the sea to the city.* ♦ *That journey is not long.*

10. *Who is swimming in the river?* ♦ *That girl is my friend. Sometimes she swims in the river with her sisters.*

LESSON 128

1. *My sister is telling a story about me.*

2. *Friend, why are you walking through the large mountains? The road is narrow and the journey is long.* ♦ *I am walking to the large city with my brothers.* ♦ *Do y'all have food?* ♦ *Yes.* ♦ *Do y'all have money?* ♦ *Yes.* ♦ *The road through the mountains is narrow.* ♦ *My brothers are walking with me.*

3. *The boy is walking from me to his father.*

4. *The horse is carrying me to the city.*

5. *Why is your dog watching me?* ♦ *You have food.*

6. *Friend, why are you swimming in the sea?* ♦ *I sometimes swim in the sea. I love the sea!* ♦ *But the sea is large and wide. Perhaps you can swim in a small river.*

7. *Mother, why do you never give money to me?* ♦ *You never obey me. Why are you not cleaning your bedroom? Why are you not cleaning your bathroom?* ♦ *I am tired.*

8. *Why are the inhabitants of the mountains present? Why are they not in the mountains?* ♦ *They live in the mountains, but today they are in the city because poets are telling stories at the theater.* ♦ *The journey from the mountains to the city is long.*

9. *What is in front of the temple?*

10. *Why does your cat always sit on me?*

LESSON 129

1. *Your friends are giving you a large gift! ♦ What is my gift? ♦ I don't know. Perhaps your gift is a new horse! ♦ Perhaps my gift is a dog! ♦ I love dogs! ♦ I also!*
2. *I can't swim across the river. That river is wide. ♦ I can carry you across the river in my boat.*
3. *My brothers always tell good stories about you.*
4. *I never see you in my cafe, friend. Why? ♦ I often have dinner at Portia's cafe. Portia's cafe has good food. ♦ I also have good food! ♦ You aren't angry, are you?*
5. *Why does my dog obey you, but he doesn't obey me? ♦ Your dog loves me!*
6. *Aemilia, I love you. ♦ Do you love me? ♦ Yes. And I love Claudia also. Why are you angry?*
7. *Your mother is walking to the market without you.*
8. *Who is your father? ♦ My father is Cornelius. ♦ Your father is with you, right? ♦ Not at all. He is at home.*
9. *The soldiers are giving gifts to their wives.*
10. *Why are you behind your shield? ♦ You can't see me because I am behind my shield. ♦ I can see you. Your shield is small.*

LESSON 131

1. *I have a pig. ♦ Why? ♦ I am a farmer.*
2. *I have a large castle. ♦ Why? ♦ I am a king. Kings always live in large castles.*
3. *I have a sister. ♦ Do you have a brother? ♦ Yes. I have a brother.*
4. *I have a large boat. ♦ Why do you have a large boat? You aren't a pirate, are you? ♦ Not at all, I am a sailor. Sometimes I sail across the sea.*
5. *This city is large. ♦ Many inhabitants live in the city. My brother lives in the city. ♦ I have a brother, but he does not live with me in the city. My brother lives on a farm.*
6. *My son, you are a good boy. ♦ Mother, why am I a good boy? ♦ You always obey me. ♦ Perhaps you can give money to me.*
7. *Rufus, sometimes I see you at the bad cafe with pirates. Why do you have dinner with pirates? ♦ They tell good stories.*
8. *Pirate, what is in your boat? ♦ Silver and gold are in my boat.*
9. *Father, where is our cat? ♦ Fluffy is in the kitchen. He is sitting on the table. ♦ Why does Fluffy not obey you? ♦ Fluffy is a cat. He is not a dog.*
10. *Are you sailing to the island today? ♦ Yes. This boat is carrying me to the island. ♦ Who is*

sailing with you? ♦ I am sailing with my sisters and my mother.

LESSON 132

1. *I don't have a farm. I am not a farmer.*
2. *Claudia, you are a mother, right? ♦ Yes, I am a mother. I have many daughters.*
3. *I am a king, but I don't have a castle. ♦ Why don't you have a castle? ♦ I have a small kingdom. There are not many inhabitants in my kingdom. I live in a small house. ♦ You are the king, but you live in a small house? Perhaps you can build a large house.*
4. *Boy, who is your father? ♦ I am Robert's son, and Aurelia is my mother.*
5. *We can't swim across the river. ♦ Why? We swim daily. We are strong. ♦ This river is wide! ♦ I have a boat. My boat can carry me across the river. ♦ Perhaps I can sail with you.*
6. *This journey is not long because I have a horse.*
7. *Sailor, why are you telling a bad story to me? ♦ I am a sailor. I always tell bad stories to you! ♦ Perhaps sometimes you can tell a good story. ♦ I don't have good stories.*
8. *Father, why are you grocery shopping? ♦ I am grocery shopping because we do not have food in our house. Today we are having dinner in our dining room with my sisters. I have many sisters.*
9. *King, why aren't you sitting in the dining room? Your friends are having dinner in the large dining room without you. ♦ I am angry. ♦ Why are you angry? Why are you staying in your bedroom? ♦ My sister is sitting in my chair, and my brother is telling stories about me.*
10. *I live in my father's basement.*

LESSON 133

1. *Hello. My name is William. ♦ Hello, William. My name is Claudia. ♦ Claudia, are you a librarian? ♦ Yes, I take care of the books at the library, and sometimes I tell stories to the boys and girls.*
2. *What is the king's name? ♦ The king's name is Robert.*
3. *Hello, sailor. Who are you? ♦ Hello. My name is Quintus.*
4. *Hello, librarian. My name is Christopher. ♦ Hello, Christopher. ♦ Do you have books about rivers? ♦ Certainly. Our library has many books about rivers.*
5. *Friend, do you have a dog? ♦ Yes. My dog's name is Fidus. ♦ Do you have a cat? ♦ Yes, I have a cat, too. My cat's name is Fluffy.*
6. *Publius, do you have a sister? ♦ Yes, I have a sister. My sister's name is Portia.*

7. *Why are the soldiers hurrying into the castle?* ♦ *They are not obeying the king.*
8. *Who is this woman?* ♦ *This woman is my friend.*
9. *Our king is good. He always gives food to the inhabitants of the cities. The king's wife also is good.* ♦ *Why is the king's wife good?* ♦ *She always takes care of the sons and daughters of the soldiers.*
10. *What is your son's name?* ♦ *My son's name is Titus.*

LESSON 134

1. *On account of the trees, I can't see your house.* ♦ *There are many trees in front of our house.* ♦ *Why do y'all have many trees in front of y'all's house?* ♦ *We live in the forest.*
2. *Friend, we can't build a boat.* ♦ *Why? We have wood, right?* ♦ *Not at all. We don't have wood.* ♦ *There are many trees in the forest. Perhaps we can carry trees from the forest.* ♦ *Friend, we are strong, but we can't carry large trees.*
3. *Husband, where is our cat? Where is Fluffy?* ♦ *I don't know, my wife.* ♦ *What is in our tree?* ♦ *I don't know. Fluffy isn't in the tree, is he?* ♦ *Yes, Fluffy is in the tree!*
4. *Quintus is building a boat out of trees.* ♦ *Why is he building a boat?* ♦ *Our king is demanding new boats. He is obeying the king.* ♦ *Why is the king demanding boats? The kingdom is a large forest. The kingdom is not near the sea, and does not have rivers.* ♦ *Quintus always obeys the king because he is a soldier.*
5. *I love y'all's neighborhood because this neighborhood has many trees.*
6. *Sempronia, where is your husband?* ♦ *My husband is sitting in the basement.* ♦ *Why does he always sit in the basement?* ♦ *Our basement is my husband's office.*
7. *Hello. What is your name?* ♦ *Hello. My name is Catherine.*
8. *You can't see me.* ♦ *I can see you.* ♦ *I am behind a tree. You can't see me.* ♦ *That tree is narrow. I can see you.*
9. *Aemilia, why are you staying at home? Your friends are walking to the seashore. They never walk to the seashore without you.* ♦ *I am staying in my bedroom because I am tired.* ♦ *Why are you tired?* ♦ *I am sick today.*
10. *Why can't we walk from the city to the mountains? This journey is not long.* ♦ *There is a wide river between the city and the mountains. We don't have a boat.*

LESSON 135

1. *Why are the king and queen building a new bridge?* ♦ *Our kingdom is near the sea. There is an island near the seashore, but there is not a bridge between the island and the seashore. Now the king and queen are demanding a new bridge.* ♦ *That island is small. What is on the island?* ♦ *The island is small, but on the island is a large castle.*
2. *Sempronia, why do you always swim across the river?* ♦ *Why don't you walk across the bridge?* ♦ *That bridge is narrow. I fear narrow bridges, but I love to swim.*
3. *What is new bridge's name?* ♦ *The name is "King's Bridge."* ♦ *Why is the name "King's Bridge?"* ♦ *The name is "King's Bridge" because the king's soldiers are building the bridge and they are carrying trees out of the king's forest.*
4. *What is in the river?* ♦ *It is a small boat.* ♦ *Who is in the boat?* ♦ *A man is in the boat.* ♦ *Who is the man?* ♦ *I don't know. I can't see the man.* ♦ *Why can't you see the man?* ♦ *The man's boat is behind a tree.* ♦ *Perhaps we can walk to the river.* ♦ *Now I can see the man. That man is Rufus.* ♦ *Why is Rufus in his boat?* ♦ *I don't know. Perhaps he is sailing across the river.* ♦ *Does Rufus see you?* ♦ *Not at all. Rufus does not see me, but I can see Rufus.*
5. *Romulus, can you walk with me to the seashore?* ♦ *I can walk with you today to the seashore, but I can't swim in the sea.* ♦ *Why?* ♦ *I fear the sea.*
6. *This bridge is long and narrow.* ♦ *Why are we walking across the bridge?* ♦ *We are walking across the river.* ♦ *Why are we walking across the river?* ♦ *We are walking to the city.*
7. *Our cat always sits on the table. This cat does not obey me.* ♦ *Why does he not obey you?* ♦ *He is a cat. He is not a dog.*
8. *Hello, Flavia.* ♦ *Hello, Quintus.* ♦ *Who is with you today?* ♦ *My friend is with me.* ♦ *What is your friend's name?* ♦ *My friend's name is Tullia.*
9. *Why are my friends having dinner at the restaurant without me?* ♦ *They never have dinner without you.*
10. *Daughter, why are you cleaning your bedroom?* ♦ *Perhaps you can give money to me.*

LESSON 137

1. *I like this house.*
2. *I like your horse.*
3. *You like this chair.*
4. *I like libraries.*
5. *You like dogs.*
6. *I like this cat.* ♦ *That cat isn't a cat.* ♦ *What is it?* ♦ *It's a small dog.*
7. *Where is the temple of Minerva?* ♦ *It is on the other side of the road.* ♦ *I can't see the temple.* ♦

Why can't you see the temple? ♦ *There are many trees in front of the temple. I can't see the temple on account of the trees.*

8. *Why are the soldiers absent now?* ♦ *They are sick on account of bad food.* ♦ *Who is guarding the city?* ♦ *I don't know. Perhaps you can guard the city.* ♦ *I can't guard the city because I don't have a sword.* ♦ *I can give my sword to you.*

9. *Rufus, where are you? I can't see you.* ♦ *I am behind a tree.* ♦ *Why are you behind a tree?* ♦ *My teacher is present.*

10. *What is your name?* ♦ *My name is Decimus.*

LESSON 138

1. *I don't like this restaurant.* ♦ *Why?* ♦ *This food is bad.* ♦ *Not at all. This food is good!* ♦ *Perhaps I can give the food to my brothers.*

2. *I don't like that island.* ♦ *Why?* ♦ *Many pirates live on the island.*

3. *I don't like my father's cat.* ♦ *Why?* ♦ *He never obeys me, and he always sits on me.* ♦ *That cat doesn't sit on you, does he?* ♦ *Yes. Sometimes I sit in the living room and the cat sits on me.*

4. *I like this chair.* ♦ *I also like it.* ♦ *Why do you like it?* ♦ *I like it because it is wide.*

5. *I don't like this castle.* ♦ *King, why don't you like this castle?* ♦ *I don't like this castle because my bedroom is small, and the bathroom is not near my bedroom.* ♦ *Perhaps we can build a new bathroom, king.*

6. *Mother, why am I walking across the bridge with you?* ♦ *We are walking to the city, but the city is on the other side of the river.* ♦ *Why are we walking to the city?* ♦ *My sisters live in the city. Sometimes I give food to my sisters.*

7. *I don't like your dog.* ♦ *Why?* ♦ *He always watches me.* ♦ *You have food. He is watching you because you have food.* ♦ *Perhaps you can give food to the dog.*

8. *I don't like this bridge.* ♦ *Why?* ♦ *This bridge is narrow. I don't like narrow bridges.*

9. *I never grocery shop without you.* ♦ *Why?* ♦ *You always have money.*

10. *Why does your wife always work in the garden?* ♦ *Our garden has many trees. My wife loves trees.*

LESSON 139

1. *My cat's name is Fluffy. Do you like my cat?* ♦ *Not at all. Fluffy always sits on me, and does not obey me.*

2. *Do you like the mountains?* ♦ *Yes. Sometimes I walk through the mountains.* ♦ *I don't like the mountains on account of the large cats of the mountains.*

3. *Do you like rivers?* ♦ *Yes. Sometimes I swim in rivers.*

4. *Do you like this cafe?* ♦ *Yes. This food is good. I often have dinner at the cafe.*

5. *Do you like wolves?* ♦ *Not at all. I fear wolves. On account of wolves, I never walk through the forest.*

6. *I like trees.* ♦ *I like them, too. I have a garden. In my garden are many trees.*

7. *I see wolves but the wolves don't see me.* ♦ *The wolves see you now!*

8. *My sister has a new dog.* ♦ *What is the name of your sister's dog?* ♦ *The dog's name is Fidus. But Fidus never obeys my sister.* ♦ *Do you have a dog?* ♦ *Not at all. I have a cat.*

9. *Where is the king? He's not in the castle, is he?* ♦ *Not at all. The king is in the mountains with his soldiers.*

10. *Who is walking across the bridge?* ♦ *Christopher is walking across the bridge.* ♦ *Why is Christopher carrying his cat?* ♦ *Christopher's cat is sick. Christopher is carrying his cat to the city.*

LESSON 141

1. *I run with my dog daily.*

2. *Why is the cat running from the dog?* ♦ *The cat fears the dog.*

3. *My sisters run across the bridge daily.* ♦ *That bridge is long and narrow.* ♦ *Yes. I never walk across the bridge because I fear the bridge, but my sisters do not fear the bridge.*

4. *I like your cat. What is your cat's name?* ♦ *My cat's name is Fluffy. Fluffy is always a good cat.* ♦ *Why is Fluffy a good cat?* ♦ *Fluffy never fights with our dog.* ♦ *But Fluffy often sits on the table.* ♦ *Fluffy is sometimes a good cat.*

5. *Do you like our king?* ♦ *Yes. I like our king. He always gives money to the soldiers, and he gives food to the wives of the soldiers.* ♦ *I also like our king.* ♦ *Why do you like the king?* ♦ *There are many rivers in our kingdom. Our king is building new bridges across the rivers.*

6. *I like cats. In my house I have many cats.* ♦ *Do you have a large house?* ♦ *Not at all. I and my cats live in a small house. There are cats in the kitchen, in the living room, and in my bedroom.* ♦ *Do you have a basement?* ♦ *Yes. My son lives in our basement.*

7. *Why are our dogs running into the house?* ♦ *The dogs' food is in the house.*

8. *Who is running out of the bank with gold?* ♦ *That man is carrying silver, too.* ♦ *Now he is running to his boat.* ♦ *That man is a pirate!*

9. *I don't have a cat.* ♦ *Why?* ♦ *I have dogs.*

10. *I always run from pirates.*

LESSON 142

1. *Who is leading the soldiers across the river? ♦ The king is leading the soldiers. ♦ The king can't lead the soldiers across the river because the river does not have a bridge. ♦ Perhaps the king and the soldiers can build a new bridge. Many trees are near the river. ♦ Perhaps they can swim across the river.*
2. *We are leading the girls and boys to school.*
3. *Quintus is leading his wife and his sons to the city. ♦ Why? ♦ Quintus's mother lives in the city.*
4. *Why are the teachers leading the students out of the school? ♦ The students are walking to the theater today. ♦ Why are they walking to the theater? ♦ Today a poet is telling stories at the theater. ♦ Who is the poet? ♦ Peter is the poet. Peter is telling stories in our city today.*
5. *The students are running out of the school.*
6. *Hello, Tullia. Your husband is my friend. ♦ Who are you? ♦ My name is Publius. I am a farmer. ♦ Hello, Publius. Do you live on a farm? ♦ Sometimes I live on my farm, but I have a house in the city. Sometimes I live in the city. ♦ Why do you sometimes live in the city? Do you like this city? ♦ Yes, I like this city. ♦ Who is taking care of your farm now? ♦ My brother is taking care of my farm now.*
7. *Why are the king's soldiers running out of the castle? Are they obeying the king? ♦ Yes. They are guarding the gates of the castle.*
8. *My wife, why are you watching our pig? ♦ Our pig is running. ♦ Our pig never runs. Why is he running? ♦ A wolf is present! Our pig is running from a wolf!*
9. *I can't lead the soldiers today. ♦ But you are the king! ♦ You are the queen. Perhaps you can lead the soldiers. ♦ I am a strong woman. I can lead the soldiers!*
10. *What is your name? ♦ My name is Portia. What is your name? ♦ Hello, Portia. My name is Tertius. ♦ Hello, Tertius.*

LESSON 143

1. *Why does Paul always sit in the living room? ♦ He always reads books in our living room.*
2. *I am a bad student. ♦ Why? ♦ I never read my books.*
3. *I am reading a book about pigs. ♦ Why? ♦ I like pigs. ♦ You love pigs, right? ♦ Perhaps.*
4. *Do you like books? ♦ Yes. I always read books in my bedroom.*
5. *Why are Fausta and Christopher leading the girls and boys to the library? ♦ The librarian is giving new books to the girls and boys today. ♦ I like this library. It has many good books.*
6. *I often see you at Quintus's cafe. ♦ Yes. I like that cafe.*
7. *What is in your boat, pirate? ♦ I have silver. Do you have gold? ♦ Not at all! Goodbye!*
8. *Claudia, why does your dog not obey you? ♦ I don't know. Fidus is a good dog, but today he is tired.*
9. *Romulus, why are you running from the seashore? ♦ I am running from pirates!*
10. *Who has my money?*

LESSON 144

1. *My son, I can give money to you. ♦ Thank you, Mother.*
2. *Hello, James. What's up? ♦ Hello. Today I am cleaning my bedroom. ♦ Why are you cleaning your bedroom, friend? ♦ My bedroom is dirty.*
3. *Hello, Lavinia. What's up? ♦ I am running to the city today. ♦ Why are you running to the city? ♦ My father is sick. He lives in the city. ♦ I can run to the city with you. ♦ Thank you! You are a good friend.*
4. *Hello, William. What's up? ♦ Charles is telling a story about pigs to the boys and girls. ♦ I like that story. ♦ I like it, too. ♦ In the story, small pigs live in a strong house. ♦ And a large, bad wolf is present in front of the house.*
5. *Hello, Julia. What's up? ♦ I am reading a book about trees. ♦ Why are you reading a book about trees? ♦ There are many trees in our garden.*
6. *Hello, soldier. What's up? ♦ The king is leading the soldiers through the mountains. ♦ Why? ♦ We are walking to the kingdom of the pirates.*
7. *My husband, you aren't giving money to your brother, are you? ♦ My wife, my brother does not have money. ♦ But he lives in our basement!*
8. *I have a sword. ♦ I have a shield. ♦ We can guard the city with sword and shield.*
9. *Do you like cats? ♦ Not at all. Cats always sit on me.*
10. *I have a large farm. ♦ Where is your farm? ♦ My farm is between the city and the seashore.*

LESSON 145

1. *Rufus, why are you learning the Latin language? ♦ I like the Latin language. ♦ I also am learning the Latin language. ♦ Why? ♦ The Latin language is a good language.*
2. *Claudia often reads books about the Latin language. ♦ Why? ♦ Claudia is learning the Latin language.*
3. *That school is bad. ♦ Why? ♦ The students are not learning the Latin language, and the teachers do not teach the Latin language.*

4. *Publius, are you a teacher? ♦ Yes. I teach the Latin language daily. My students are learning the Latin language. ♦ I also am a teacher, but in my school we do not teach the Latin language. ♦ Why do y'all not teach the Latin language in y'all's school? ♦ My school is small.*
5. *Quintus, why are you not learning the Latin language? ♦ I don't have a book about the Latin language. ♦ I have many books about the Latin language. I can give a book to you. ♦ Thank you! I like the Latin language.*
6. *There is a book about the Latin language on the table. Who is learning the Latin language? ♦ I and my sisters are learning the Latin language.*
7. *Teacher, I can't learn the Latin language today. ♦ Why, student? ♦ I am tired.*
8. *Why is the king not leading the soldiers today? ♦ The king is sick today. He is staying in his bedroom today. ♦ Perhaps the king's wife can lead the soldiers. ♦ The king's wife is a strong queen! The queen can sit on her horse and can lead the soldiers.*
9. *Claudia, why do you always run with your dog? ♦ My cat can't run with me.*
10. *Hello, Helen. What's up? ♦ Today I am walking to the theater with my brothers.*

LESSON 146

1. *My daughters want a dog. ♦ Why? ♦ They love dogs. ♦ Perhaps they can have a cat.*
2. *Hello, friend. What's up? ♦ We want to walk to the temple of Minerva now.*
3. *That sailor wants our money! ♦ That sailor is a pirate! ♦ I never give money to pirates. I want to fight! ♦ I want to run!*
4. *I want a farm. ♦ Why? ♦ I want to plow the fields, and I want to take care of horses.*
5. *I want a new chair. ♦ Why? ♦ I don't like this chair.*
6. *Hello, king! ♦ Hello, farmer. ♦ King, I have a farm, but I don't have pigs. Perhaps you can give pigs to me. ♦ Yes. I can give pigs to you. ♦ Thank you, king. You are a good king.*
7. *Who wants a book? ♦ Librarian, I want a book. I am learning the Latin language, but I don't have a book about the Latin language. ♦ I can give a book about the Latin language to you. ♦ Thank you!*
8. *I don't like this castle. I want to build a new castle. ♦ King, your castle is large. Why do you want a new castle? ♦ This castle has small bathrooms. I don't like small bathrooms. ♦ But you have a large dining room.*
9. *Why are you reading a book about farms? ♦ I want to build a farm. ♦ Do you have a field? ♦ Yes. ♦ Do you have a horse? ♦ Yes. ♦ Do you have*

a pig? ♦ Not at all, but I want a pig.
10. *The soldiers are leading the horses into the stables.*

LESSON 147

1. *I don't want your money.*
2. *You don't want to run today. Why? ♦ I am tired.*
3. *That student does not want to read her book.*
4. *We don't want to clean our bathroom. ♦ Why? ♦ It is not dirty. ♦ Y'all's bathroom is dirty!*
5. *Why do y'all not want to learn the Latin language? ♦ We want to learn the Latin language, but we don't have a book about the Latin language. ♦ I have many books about the Latin language.*
6. *They don't want a dog. ♦ Why? ♦ They want a cat.*
7. *Father, we don't want to clean our bedrooms. ♦ Why? ♦ We want to read books.*
8. *Julia is leading the students out of the library to the school.*
9. *Do you like this restaurant? ♦ Yes. This food is good, and pirates are absent.*
10. *Hello, Rufus. What's up? ♦ I am running to our farm because my mother is sick. ♦ I can run with you! ♦ Thank you. You are a good friend.*

LESSON 149

1. *Hello, William. How are you? ♦ Well. How are you, Julia? ♦ I am doing well. ♦ Why are you coming to my market today? ♦ I am grocery shopping because today my husband is having dinner at home with his sisters and his brothers.*
2. *Friend, where are you? I am in front of the library. ♦ I am coming to the library now. ♦ Why are you absent? ♦ Forgive me. I am hurrying to the library!*
3. *Why do you never come to my city? ♦ I don't like the king of your city. ♦ Our king is bad, but this city is good. Our city has many trees, good restaurants, and a large market.*
4. *Hello, Cornelius. Is your sister at home? ♦ Tullia, why do you come to my house daily? ♦ Your sister is my friend.*
5. *Hello, Portia. How are you doing? ♦ I am doing well. ♦ I want to give a gift to you. ♦ What is the gift? I like gifts! ♦ It is a book. ♦ Thank you! I love books! I read books often. ♦ You're welcome. It is a book about pigs. ♦ I am not a farmer!*
6. *The farmer is leading the new horses to his farm.*
7. *Hello, Robert. What's up? ♦ I can't come to the seashore with you today. ♦ Why can't you come*

with me? ♦ I like the seashore, but today I am sick.

8. *I want to learn the Latin language. ♦ Why? ♦ I like the Latin language. ♦ Do you have a book about the Latin language? ♦ Not at all. ♦ Perhaps I can give a book to you. You can read my book. ♦ Thank you. ♦ You're welcome.*

9. *The king is leading his soldiers to the sea. ♦ Perhaps they want to sail to the island of the pirates! ♦ Perhaps. The soldiers have many boats. ♦ The king and the soldiers want to fight with the pirates!*

10. *Students, why are y'all running out of the school? ♦ We don't want to learn the Latin language today!*

LESSON 150

1. *I hear my dog. Do you hear my dog? ♦ Yes. He wants food!*

2. *King, can you hear the inhabitants of the city? ♦ They have food, right? ♦ Not at all. They are demanding food. ♦ Why are they demanding food? ♦ The wives of your soldiers are demanding food because you never give money to the women's husbands. ♦ My soldiers are bad. They never obey me.*

3. *I don't want to walk through the forest. ♦ Why? ♦ I hear the wolves in the forest.*

4. *My cat, how are you? ♦ I am doing poorly! I don't have food! I want food! ♦ I am giving food to you now. ♦ Thank you. I like this food. ♦ You're welcome.*

5. *Teacher, we don't want to read our books today. ♦ Bad students, why do y'all not want to read y'all's books today? ♦ We want to walk to the seashore. ♦ I also want to walk to the seashore.*

6. *This student never obeys the teacher. ♦ Perhaps that student can't hear the teacher.*

7. *Hello, my dog. How are you? ♦ I am doing poorly. ♦ Why, Fluffy? ♦ I am angry. I am a dog, but my name is "Fluffy." I want a new name. ♦ Perhaps I can give a new name to you. ♦ "Fidus" is a good name.*

8. *Hello, Tullia. What's up? ♦ I am walking to the city with my sister. ♦ Why are y'all walking to the city? ♦ We are walking to the library because we want new books. ♦ I am walking to the sea with my brothers. My brothers want to swim in the sea.*

9. *Girl, where are you learning the Latin language? ♦ We are learning the Latin language at my school.*

10. *We lead the girls to school daily.*

LESSON 151

1. *I'm going to the bathroom.*

2. *Sempronia, why are you going through the forest? There are many wolves in the forest. Can you hear the wolves? ♦ Yes. I hear the wolves, but I do not fear the wolves. ♦ I always go around the forest because I fear the wolves. ♦ I don't want to go around the forest. I want to go through the forest.*

3. *I never go to the market without money.*

4. *Father, I want to hear a story. ♦ I can tell a story about small pigs to you. Do you like that story? ♦ Thank you, Father. I like that story. ♦ You're welcome, my daughter.*

5. *Many cats are in the road. Why are cats running through our city? ♦ The cats are going to Robert's house. ♦ Why are they going to Robert's house? ♦ Robert gives food to the cats daily.*

6. *Hello, Aemilia. What's up? Why are you in the library? ♦ Sometimes I come to the library. ♦ I also. Often I sit in the library and I read books. Now I'm reading a book about the seas.*

7. *I want to learn the Latin language, but I can't. ♦ Why? ♦ In my school, the teachers don't teach the Latin language and the students don't learn the Latin language.*

8. *I always come to your cafe because you have good food.*

9. *King, your soldiers don't want to fight with the inhabitants of the town. ♦ Why? ♦ The inhabitants of the town are the soldiers' friends.*

10. *Hello, sailor. What is your name? ♦ My name is Cornelius. ♦ Why are many cats present in your boat? ♦ My cats always sail with me. They love the sea.*

LESSON 152

1. *Mother, give money to me!*

2. *Run to the city! ♦ Why? ♦ Pirates are coming now!*

3. *Give a new sword to me!*

4. *Learn the Latin language! ♦ I don't want to learn the Latin language. I want to go to the seashore.*

5. *There is water in our boat. ♦ Swim to the seashore!*

6. *Read your book.*

7. *Give your money to me! ♦ I never give money to pirates.*

8. *Student, sit in your chair!*

9. *Run out of the town!*

10. *Carry the wood!*

LESSON 153

1. *Carry water to the stables!*

2. *Boys, sit in your chairs!*

3. *Sons and daughters, clean y'all's bedrooms!*
4. *Girls, run into the house!*
5. *Soldiers, walk to the castle!*
6. *Boys, take care of the horses. Give water and food to the horses!*
7. *Soldiers, fight with the pirates!*
8. *Learn the Latin language!*
9. *Go into the city!*
10. *Hurry to the theater!*

LESSON 154

1. *Don't run through the school!*
2. *Don't have dinner in bad cafes with sailors!*
3. *Don't plow the fields. Go into the stable and take care of the horses.*
4. *Don't swim in the sea! Swim in the river!*
5. *Cat, don't sit on the table. ♦ But I always sit on the table. I like this table. ♦ Why do you never obey me? ♦ I'm not a dog. I'm a cat.*
6. *My brothers, don't fight. Obey our mother.*
7. *Don't lead the soldiers into the castle.*
8. *Don't sail to island of the pirates!*
9. *Don't build a boat. ♦ Why? ♦ We don't live near a river.*
10. *Don't go to the cafe without me.*

CLASSICAL
PRONUNCIATION GUIDE

This abbreviated guide to classical pronunciation will provide a few of the most important points to keep in mind when adopting a classical pronunciation of Latin.

CONSONANTS

c always sounds like the *c* in *cat*, never like the *c* in *ceiling*
g always sounds like the *g* in *garden*, never like the *g* in *gelatin*
s is always a hissing sound as in *pass*, never a *z* sound as in *is*
t always sounds like the *t* in *time*, never a *sh* sound like the *t* in *promotion*
v always sounds like the *w* in *wild*, never like the *v* in *violin*

In Latin, the letter *i* is used two ways. First, it is used as a vowel (see vowel chart below). Second, it is sometimes used as a consonant before a vowel. When you see the letter *i* before a vowel, it sounds like a *y*. For instance, the Latin word **iam** is pronounced *yahm*. In some Latin textbooks, the letter *i* is replaced with the letter *j* when used as a consonant. So, the word **iam** could be written **jam**, but is still pronounced the same way.

VOWELS

In Latin, there are short vowels and long vowels. Long vowels have a mark over them. This mark is called a *macron*. Short vowels do not have a mark.

LONG VOWELS

ā sounds like the *a* in *father*
ē sounds like the *a* in *play*
ī sounds like the *e* in *me*
ō sounds like the *o* in *comb*
ū sounds like the *u* in *tube*

SHORT VOWELS

a sounds like the *a* in *art*
e sounds like the *e* in *net*
i sounds like the *i* in *it*
o sounds like the *o* in *poke* (short duration)
u sounds like the *u* in *put*

DIPHTHONGS (COMBINATIONS OF VOWELS)

ae is pronounced like the word *eye*

au is pronounced like the *ou* in *mouse*

ECCLESIASTICAL PRONUNCIATION GUIDE

This abbreviated guide to ecclesiastical pronunciation will provide a few of the most important points to keep in mind when adopting an ecclesiastical pronunciation of Latin.

CONSONANTS

c always sounds like the *c* in *cat*, except when it comes before *e, i, y, ae,* or *oe*. In these cases, it sounds like the *ch* in *cheese*

g sounds like the *g* in *garden* when it comes before a consonant or before *a, o,* or *u*. When it comes before *e, i, y, ae* or *oe*, it sounds like the *g* in *gelatin*

g and **n** together sound like the *ny* in *canyon*

r is lightly rolled

v always sounds like the *v* in *violin*

VOWELS

The type of ecclesiastical pronunciation used in this book does not distinguish between long and short vowels with regard to quality of sound.

ā and **a** both sound like the *a* in *father*

ē and **e** both sound like the *e* in *bet*

ī and **i** both sound like the *e* in *me*

ō and **o** both sound like the *o* in *no*

ū and **u** both sound like the *u* in *tube*

DIPHTHONGS (COMBINATIONS OF VOWELS)

ae is pronounced like the *e* in *bet*

au is pronounced like the *ou* in *mouse*

GLOSSARY

ā, ab *from*

absum *I am absent*

acta *seashore*

ad *to, toward*

adsum *I am present*

aedificō *I build*

aeger *sick*

aegrōtō *I am sick*

ager *field*

agō *do*

agricola *farmer*

ambulō *I walk*

amīca *friend* (female)

amīcus *friend* (male)

amō *I love, I like*

angustus *narrow*

ante *in front of*

aqua *water*

arbor *tree*

argentāria *bank*

argentum *silver*

arō *I plow*

audiō *I hear*

aurum *gold*

balnea *bathroom*

bene *fine, well*

Bene mē habeō. *I'm doing well.*

bestia *beast*

bibliothēca *library*

bonus *good*

caelum *sky*

canis *dog*

casa *house*

castellum *castle*

cēnō *I have dinner*

certē *certainly*

cibus *food*

circum *around*

cotīdiē *daily*

cubiculum *bedroom*

culīna *kitchen*

cum *with*

cūr *why?*

cūrō *I take care of*

currō *I run*

dē *about*

dēleō *I destroy*

dēsīderō *I long for, I want*

discipulus *student*

discō *I learn*

dō *I give*

doceō *I teach*

domī *at home*

dōnum *gift*

dūcō *I lead*

ē, ex *out of*

ego *I*

eō *I go*

equus *horse*

es *you are*

est *he is, she is, it is, is, there is*

estis *y'all are*

et *and*

exedrium *living room*

fābula *story*

familia *family*

fēlēs *cat*

fēmina *woman*

fessus *tired*

fīlia *daughter*

fīlius *son*

flūmen *river*

fortasse *perhaps*

frāter *brother*

fundus *farm*

gladius *sword*

habeō *I have*

habitō *I live*

haec *this* (feminine)

hic *this* (masculine)

hoc *this* (neuter)

hodiē *today*

hortus *garden*

hypogaeum *basement*

Ignōsce mihi. *Forgive me.*

illa *that* (feminine)

ille *that* (masculine)

illud *that* (neuter)

in *in, on, into*

incola *inhabitant*

īnsula *island*

inter *between, among*

interdum *sometimes*

īrātus *angry*

ita *yes*

iter *journey, way, road*

labōrō *I work*

laetus *happy*

lātrīna *bathroom*

lātus *wide*

lēctus *bed*

legō *I read*

libenter *you're welcome*

liber *book*

lignum *wood*

longus *long*

lūna *moon*

lupus *wolf*

macellum *market*

magister *teacher*

magnus *great, large*

Male mē habeō. *I'm doing poorly.*

malus *bad*

maneō *I stay*

marītus *husband*

māter *mother*

mare *sea*

mēnsa *table*

mē *me*

Mē paenitet. *I'm sorry.*

meus *my*

mihi *to me, for me*

mīles *soldier*

minimē *not at all*

mōns *mountain*

multus *many, much*

mūrus *wall*

narrō *I tell*

natō *I swim*

nauta *sailor*

nāvigō *I sail*

nesciō *I don't know*

nōlō *I do not want*

nōmen *name*

nōn *not*

nōnne expects positive answer

noster *our*

novus *new*

num expects negative answer

numerō *I count*

numquam *never*

nunc *now*

obsecrō *please*

obsōnō *I grocery shop*

oppidum *town*

pāreō *I obey*

parvus *small*

pater *father*

patria *homeland*

pecūnia *money*

per *through*

pīrāta *pirate*

placent *they are pleasing*

placet *he, she, it is pleasing*

poēta *poet*

pōns *bridge*

popīna *restaurant*

porcus *pig*

porta *gate*

portō *I carry*

possum *I am able*

post *behind*

postulō *I demand*

prope *near*

properō *I hurry*

propter *on account of*

puella *girl*

puer *boy*

pugnō *I fight*

pūrgō *I clean up*

quaesō *please*

-que *and*

quid *what?*

quis *who?*

quod *because*

Quōmodo tē habēs? *How are you?*

quoque *also, too*

rēgīna *queen*

rēgnum *kingdom*

rēx *king*

saepe *often*

salvē *hello* (singular)

salvēte *hello* (plural)

saxum *rock*

scapha *boat*

schola *school*

scrībō *I write*

scūtum *shield*

sed *but*

sedeō *I sit*

sella *chair*

semper *always*

servō *I guard*

silva *forest*

sine *without*

soror *sister*

spectō *I watch*

stella *star*

sum *I am*

sumus *we are*

sunt *they are, are, there are*

superō *I conquer*

suus *his, her, its, their*

tablīnum *office*

tabula *writing tablet*

tē *you*

templum *temple*

terra *earth, land, soil*

theātrum *theater*

thermopōlium *cafe*

tibi *to you, for you*

timeō *I fear*

trāns *across, on the other side of*

trīclīnium *dining room*

tū *you*

tuus *your*

ubi *where*

urbs *city*

uxor *wife*

valē *goodbye* (singular)

valeō *I am well*

valēte *goodbye* (plural)

validus *strong*

veniō *I come*

vester *y'all's*

via *road*

vīcīnia *neighborhood*

videō *I see*

vir *man*

volō *I want*